Installing Automobility

Urban and Industrial Environments

Series editor: Robert Gottlieb, Henry R. Luce Professor of Urban and Environmental Policy, Occidental College

For a complete list of books published in this series, please see the back of the book.

Installing Automobility

Emerging Politics of Mobility and Streets in Indian Cities

Govind Gopakumar

The MIT Press
Cambridge, Massachusetts
London, England

© 2020 Massachusetts Institute of Technology

This work is subject to a Creative Commons CC-BY-NC-ND license.

Subject to such license, all rights are reserved.

The open access edition of this book was made possible by generous funding from Arcadia—a charitable fund of Lisbet Rausing and Peter Baldwin.

This book was set in Stone Serif and Stone Sans by Westchester Publishing Services.

Library of Congress Cataloging-in-Publication Data

Names: Gopakumar, Govind, author.
Title: Installing automobility : emerging politics of mobility and streets in Indian cities / Govind Gopakumar.
Description: Cambridge, Massachusetts : The MIT Press, [2020] | Series: Urban and industrial environments | Includes bibliographical references and index.
Identifiers: LCCN 2019036374 | ISBN 9780262538916 (paperback)
Subjects: LCSH: Transportation, Automotive—Social aspects—India—Bangalore. | Automobiles—Social aspects—India—Bangalore. | Traffic congestion—India—Bangalore—History. | Urban transportation policy—India—Bangalore. | City planning—India—Bangalore. | Sustainable urban development—India—Bangalore.
Classification: LCC HE5691.B3 G67 2020 | DDC 303.48/32095487—dc23
LC record available at https://lccn.loc.gov/2019036374

150377129

To Bengaluru for giving me so much
and
to Smitha, Tejas, and Saashwath—I would be lost without you all

Contents

Preface: Automobility as Anthropocenic Fluid   ix
Acknowledgments   xiii

1   **Installing Automobility in Bengaluru**   1

2   **Locating Congestion in Bengaluru**   25

3   **Regime of Congestion**   67

4   **Infrastructurescapes of Privilege**   99

5   **Automotive Citizenship**   137

6   **Shabby Automobility**   169

7   **Displacing Automobility**   205

Notes   221
References   247
Index   273

Preface: Automobility as Anthropocenic Fluid

I write this book for the Earthbound, and I locate this book within the incredibly thorny human-dominated period in planetary evolution—the Anthropocene (Lewis and Maslin 2015)—that an overwhelming scientific consensus appears to suggest we, the Earthbound, have entered.[1] A looming environmental disequilibrium at the planetary scale, which is now conclusively related to human activities, is a notable feature of the Anthropocene. Its thorniness is a product of several interlocked and coarticulated human-driven phenomena. Addressing one phenomenon in isolation is ineffectual and even counterproductive because of the existence of robust linkages with other phenomena that often have radically different pathways of expression. Such a situation poses an enormous existential challenge not just because of the frightening consequences for a humankind teetering on the threshold of environmental catastrophe but more so because our tried and tested mechanisms of intervening could prove to be less than effective in pulling us back from the tipping point.

Resolving such situations is inherently knotty because its complex intricacies span multiple boundaries. Such boundaries are particularly enduring because they spring forth from the modernist cosmological order humans have constructed. Thus, ontological, disciplinary, jurisdictional, and legal boundaries have proliferated from our intent to reduce complexities, and, with it, intensely intertwined problems appear particularly intractable in their scale. The profusion of such problems and their mutual imbrication has given rise to a widespread portent of a systemic, even terminal crisis. While some see in this crisis an opportunity to remake the planet afresh through more comprehensive road maps (Hawken 2017), others see hope to pull back in the gentle living that indigenous peoples practice (Raygorodetsky 2018). The notion of a crisis also indicates a point of inflection when humanity has the chance to look in the mirror and describe what the philosopher Isabelle Stengers (2015) refers to as "a second history" (25). Critical scholarship sees in the contemporary crisis a range of prognoses, both dire and hopeful—a future ordering that heralds a coming barbarism (Stengers 2015), new ways of thinking of the relations between society and nature that diminish the capital-centric mode of organizing (Moore 2016), and transcending the boundless modernist human experiment with the planet (Latour 2017). Across these writings, a common thread is deep dissatisfaction with the current modes of engaging with nature and humanity, which more than anything else have come to define the current anthropocenic moment. Indeed, for some, the Anthropocene falls short as a category to express the complex civilizational turning point (that spans nature, society, economy, and culture) humans face if we are to lead the planet in a different, more hopeful direction. From this standpoint, the Anthropocene is better understood as a period of transition rather than an epoch. Harking at a planet of thresholds and tipping points certainly connotes a period of change and transition; however, it does not say what should follow the Anthropocene. Haraway (2015) proposes the Anthropocene as a discontinuous boundary event that we the Earthbound should ford. She enjoins us to imagine the Chthulucene as a future epoch of refuges that shelter rich multispecies assemblages. According to Haraway, the Chthulucene would spell out planetary relations marked by attachments and limits.

Heeding these philosophers, if we, the Earthbound, are to fashion a less barbaric and more bounded arena for human activities, how can we use crisis as a trigger to spur our empirically grounded intellectual explorations to achieve a more hopeful future? Relevant to this book, Mimi Sheller has sought to situate mobility justice within planetary crisis. Basing her work on the relational ontology of the new mobilities paradigm, Sheller (2018) speaks of three interlinked crises manifesting in our contemporary world—climate crisis, urbanization crisis, and refugee crisis—that are fundamentally related to how we move ourselves and our commodities. She posits that in the current juncture, the triple crisis facing humanity revolves around the unequal power relations embedded within mobility (Sheller 2018, 1). For Sheller, combating the crisis of humanity requires articulating a multiscalar concept of mobility justice. Embedded within it is a multilayered politics of mobility, which includes dimensions ranging from the biopolitics of the body, transportation access, urban infrastructure struggles, transnational movement, and planetary ecologies.

Automobility is intensely entangled within Sheller's architecture of mobility politics. It is a machinic complex (Sheller and Urry 2000) that powerfully organizes transportation arrangements in the Western world.

At a spatial level, automobility manifests in its imprint on urban morphologies and their infrastructural patterns. Thus, cities designed with dense downtown cores and expansive suburbs radiating away are imaginable only through networks of access-controlled highways spreading out from downtowns that ferry cars back and forth for daily commutes. Such a spatial manifestation is underwritten by a resource-extractive political economic system. But automobility exerts its imprints on society too. It shapes the (im)mobilities that diverse peoples experience when they navigate their way around cities. In multiple ways, it encodes into regimes the mobility of the dominant urban, white, male, and elite segments while simultaneously marginalizing the mobility needs of the rest. Despite its extractive and exclusionary footprint, the persistence of automobility lies in the complex momentum forged between cultural norms; national, political, and economic imperatives; and industrial and resource-extractive engines.

Although locating automobility within a trans-scalar typology of mobility politics is useful, it does not fully recognize the enormous reach that it mobilizes across boundaries—not just political and jurisdictional but also the ontological between society and nature. I believe that automobility has emerged as a key system of relationalities that flows across boundaries and emerges in places around the world, gathering resources, technologies, norms and discourses, actors and organizations as it manifests. Urry (2005), in his disquisition of the global, categorized two main forms of systems of relationality that circulate: global networks and global fluids. The latter, according to Urry, includes examples such as automobility and is produced within particular contexts on the basis of local relationships that at the same time have an impact on distant places. Fluids pooling in particular contexts, according to Urry, also generate situations that perpetuate their presence. As a fluid, automobility, flows across locations on the planet, creating conditions for its action. In the Anthropocene, automobility is a keystone fluid that is driving human domination of the planet. Its pooling in particular locations is orchestrated with engines of resource extraction and economic and political regimes that perpetuate the conditions for their action. These patterns of pooling may differ from one region to another, but they broadly replicate a machinic complex that is consuming the planet.

Installing Automobility delineates the pooling of automobility in Indian metropolitan cities. It describes how the machinic complex of automobility has come to be organized and the particular technopolitical strategies through which it has put down roots within the metropolitan soil in India. In what follows, I emphasize that the entrenching of automobility in the

Indian urban terrain is accomplished through the assembly of a technopolitical constellation. Much of what readers will find in the rest of the book is a fine-grained analysis of the dynamics through which this constellation has become energized in the city of Bengaluru in south-central India. If at some point, the reader feels overwhelmed by the overdose of the fluid of automobility in Bengaluru, it bears keeping in mind the larger motive behind the book: we the Earthbound need to displace automobility and other anthropocenic fluids before we can realize a planet that is not just humane but also terrane.[2]

Acknowledgments

This book grew out of a long and fond association with the city of Bengaluru. In 2001, I started work as a researcher there. Since this was the first time that I was living in this city, I spent my free time on weekends and holidays exploring the city—its different roads, sights, and neighborhoods, as well as its food, festivals, and fairs. Traveling around the city with the fresh eyes of an outsider, I was struck by how the layers in the city's historical experience were stitched together like a patchwork quilt. The orientation of roads, architecture, and spatial organization of one neighborhood more often than not differed from its adjoining locality, thereby revealing their diverse historical provenances. Thus, a visit to any neighborhood was like visiting a different city in itself, and this was an incredibly intriguing experience and drove me to explore more of the city. That urge to explore remained with me even after I left the city to pursue graduate studies and even when I returned almost annually to pursue fieldwork for different research projects. It is this urge that bolstered my research inquiries. I therefore first acknowledge and thank the fullness of the city of Bengaluru: its residents (past and present) for their actions, its managed environments (shady but dwindling avenue trees, stray dogs, cool but particulate-laden breezes, manicured but cloistered gardens, gentle rain and occasional floods, and always malodorous rivers/drains/tanks) for their generosity, its temperamental infrastructures for their support, its automotive vehicles for their loud insistence, its coffee shops for lubricating so much of my writing, its delightful cuisine (especially benne masala dose, kesar bhath, and holige) for keeping me in good spirits, and its Gods (large and small) for their blessings. Without all of them, this research may not have been possible.

That being said, a few individuals and organizations in the city have been vitally important. Without their patience, encouragement, and help, this could not have been a satisfying endeavor. First on the list are the two Vinays of urban activism—Vinay K. Sreenivasa and Vinay Baindur. I consider it a great privilege to have benefited innumerable times from Vinay Sreenivasa's generosity and camaraderie. Vinay has unstintingly shared his astute but scholarly understanding of urban governance, his connections with the Bengaluru Bus Prayanikara Vedike, Hasiru Usiru, and several other community and progressive organizations in the city, and his contacts with officials, politicians, and scholars. Vinay Baindur is a walking archive on urban governance and administration in Bengaluru, which he generously shares with any visiting researcher. In addition to interviews, chats, and conversations, he shared multiple files, reports, plans, and maps without which this book could not have been as rigorous. I am deeply grateful to both Vinays for their consistent help.

Deepak Malghan's support on multiple occasions has been particularly vital by ensuring accommodation at the Indian Institute of Management (IIM) Bangalore for extended periods. The sylvan environment on the campus has been particularly conducive to writing. Thank you, Deepak, for your kind help. I also gratefully acknowledge the support and help from several individuals and groups in Bengaluru—Srikakulam Rajani for her ready research assistance, the Alternate Law Forum, Shaheen Shasa at Hasiru Usiru, Bindu Menon and Kiran Prakash at New Indian Express for help with permissions, K. Subramanya at Deccan Herald, Leo Saldanha at the Environment Support Group, the staff at Terrace Gardens and the Management Development Centre, IIM.[1] I thank Savitha, Chinmayi Arakali, B. Viswanath, Ashwin Mahesh, Ramdas Rao, Narendar Pani, Govindaraj, and many others for sharing their time generously to make this project successful.

This book in fact began to take shape in Montreal and Mumbai. In Montreal, I acknowledge Concordia University for its support in my scholarly endeavors and the Social Science and Humanities Research Council for the funding that supported the research underlying this book. At Concordia, I gratefully acknowledge my colleagues at the Centre for Engineering in Society, Amir Asif and other colleagues in the Gina Cody School for Engineering and Computer Science, and the staff at the Webster Library. David Sadoway, as a postdoctoral fellow, brought a cheery and insightful energy that made doing research in Bengaluru so much fun. Thank you! In addition, I acknowledge Craig Townsend, Kregg Hetherington, Owen Chapman, Peter Stoett, Rebecca Tittler, Raymond Paquin, and other researchers at the Loyola Sustainability Research Centre for their scholarship and ideas. I also thank Yogi Joseph, my PhD student, for his helpful comments and editing on certain chapters. I especially thank Madhav G. Badami at McGill University for being a friend and fellow traveler on this journey. We bonded during our contemporaneous stint at IIM Bangalore in July 2017 when we shared our exasperations at the automobilization of Bengaluru, our love for benne masala dose, and our hopes for a more sustainable and equitable Bengaluru. Our friendship has blossomed, and my family looks forward to the grand dinners that Madhav and his wife, Anita, host.

In Mumbai, I was fortunate to have written considerable portions of this book at the Indian Institute of Technology (IIT), Mumbai, between April and August 2016. There, I was hosted as visiting faculty at the Centre for Urban Science and Engineering. I especially acknowledge Krithi Ramamritham, Ronita Bardhan, Arnab Jana, and students and staff at the Centre for Urban Science and Engineering for their generous support and ready help, especially during a period of restricted mobility. I also thank the administration and library staff at the institute for their help during my stay there. I owe great thanks to my collaborator and friend N. C. Narayanan at Centre for Technology Alternatives for Rural Areas (C-TARA), IIT. I thankfully acknowledge NC and his wife Sindhu *chechi*'s tremendous hospitality with numerous invitations for meals, combined with interesting and wide-ranging conversations. I appreciate the help that many of NC's students provided, especially Neelam Rana, Gautam Ganapathy, Poonam Argade, and Chanakya. I acknowledge Uncle Sreekumar and Aunty Ambika for their concern and help during my stay there.

I feel great privilege from my association with a community of scholars around the world who have evinced interest in my work and on multiple occasions have gone out of their way to aid and further my research. I count David Hess and Langdon Winner among my foremost guides in navigating the academic enterprise. Others, such as Andrew Karvonen, Steve Graham, Mimi Sheller, Massimo Moraglio, Smriti Srinivas, Ole Jensen, Jochen Monstadt, Itty Abraham, Sulfikar Amir, and Rutul Joshi, have engaged, supported, and advanced my research irrespective of disciplinary affiliations or the lack thereof. I remain indebted to them.

I also acknowledge the help and prompt assistance of the editorial team at MIT Press's Urban and Industrial Environments series, especially Robert Gottlieb, Beth Clevenger, Anthony Zannino, and the three anonymous reviewers for their insightful comments. Beth and Anthony deserve high praise for maintaining high standards of academic publishing while also being kind and helpful at the same time. Their efforts have made finishing this book an exercise devoid of the thorns that usually accompany such an enterprise. I acknowledge with thanks Judith Feldmann and others on the production team at the Press for their support in making this work into a book.

Chapter 4 is an expanded and substantially rewritten version of an article that was published earlier in a peer-reviewed academic journal: G. Gopakumar,

"Who will Decongest Bengaluru? Politics, Infrastructures and Scapes," *Mobilities* 10, no. 2 (2015): 304–125, first published online on December 9, 2013, by Taylor & Francis Ltd. Reprinted by permission of the publisher (Taylor & Francis Ltd., http://www.tandfonline.com). Chapter 3 is an expanded and substantially rewritten version of an article that was published in a peer-reviewed academic journal: G. Gopakumar, "Regime of Congestion: Technopolitics of Mobility and Inequality in Bengaluru, India," *Science as Culture*, first published online by Taylor & Francis Ltd. Reprinted by permission of the publisher (Taylor & Francis Ltd., http://www.tandfonline.com).

A large group of friends and family have been a source of solid support in the research and writing phases of this book. I owe an enormous debt to all of them for enriching my life. Parag and Sanjana have been a wonderful set of friends. It has been such a pleasure to go with them on a Saturday evening to share a meal or see a film with them while taking a break from research in Bengaluru. I also gratefully acknowledge Parag's parents' ready welcome to host me on numerous occasions in their home. Raju and Nirmala welcomed me into their home during my annual trips to Bengaluru. I have especially enjoyed our Sunday morning culinary expeditions in search of unique Bengaluru dishes. I gratefully acknowledge the support provided by Aunty Brinda and Uncle Prasad during my stay in the city. My heartfelt thanks also go out to Bindu chechi and Narendran chettan for the warmth and welcome they have extended to me on numerous occasions. Ananth's ready wit and his infectious laugh have been a source of immense relief. I am thankful to Rajneesh and Pavithra for having taken the time to translate a key work from Kannada for my research, and in other small ways, they have shown their friendship to our family. As our closest friends, Hari, Pavan and Archana, and Tanay and Prerna have provided a net of support that has contributed to our family's well-being.

My immediate family has been the anchor around which my life has revolved. My *Ammumma* and Smitha's *Ammumma* leave an important imprint on our lives. My brother and sister-in-law (Chettan and Chechi) for their help, especially in the last few months. I am deeply thankful to Amma and Daddy and Mama and Papa for being there for all of us. Having you with us, especially during Smitha's hospital stay, on our weekend conversations and our annual trips, has grounded our lives. But it is to Smitha, my wife, partner, and companion, to whom I turn to with immense gratefulness. Your energy and fortitude in the face of all that I displace in life has been a source of constant amazement at my good fortune to have you with me. Finally, Tejas and Saashwath, our heartthrobs, Mamma and Dadda cannot thank you both enough for bringing so much joy and happiness into our lives.

1 Installing Automobility in Bengaluru

Dawn at K. R. Market

In July 2014, in partnership with the Bengaluru Bus Prayanikara Vedike (or the Bengaluru Bus Commuter Forum), I scripted, directed, and led the shooting of a documentary film, *Social Life of a Bus*.[1] The film relies on streetside ethnography and sociotechnical methods to demonstrate how context-specific factors, such as a changing urban political economy, shifting requirements with urban mobility, and the dynamics of social interaction in a city riven by fault lines of class, language, and gender intertwine with the materiality of the bus to shape public transit in the city (Gopakumar 2016). *Social Life of a Bus* was filmed over a week with a crew composed of a cinematographer, a sound recordist, a taxi driver, a camera assistant, and me. We started early in the morning each day and drove around to different locations in Bengaluru,[2] parked the car, and scouted around for interesting vantages for our shots. One shoot was particularly significant for thinking about the configuration of mobility in Bengaluru and other metropolitan cities in India. It reveals the bind that these cities are trapped within.

We set off especially early one morning. The city was quiet, and its usually traffic-clogged arteries were vacant. Speeding past shuttered shops and through deserted streets, we reached the Krishna Rajendra Market (K. R. Market), the sprawling and frenzied market in the center of the city (at the intersection of N. R. Road and Avenue Road located just south of the *peté*, or the precolonial market settlement—at least an hour before sunrise. However, even at this early hour, the market was a hive of activity and industry.[3] The market itself is located in a red-painted colonial building and a more recent brown concrete structure to its north. But the market has long spilled out of these confines and has located itself along Avenue Road and at the verge of the broad intersection adjacent to the market (see figure 1.1). Stilting across the intersection are the columns carrying the Mysore

Figure 1.1
A shot of K. R. Market from *Social Life of a Bus*.

Road flyover, one of the city's oldest flyovers and forerunner to many such structures that now stud the cityscape.

The intersection itself was a teeming mass of pedestrians; porters; shoppers; shopkeepers hurrying toward buses balancing huge bags of produce for their shops around the city; flower sellers selling fresh stalks of roses or large garlands of jasmine, chrysanthemums, and marigolds; vendors; and vehicles of all shapes, including autorickshaws looking for passengers, cars, mini-trucks, and motorcycles, all weaving around the buses that crawled out from the K. R. Market bus terminus. Filming from within the hustle and bustle of the market was an enormously insightful experience for me because it drove home in my mind the occupation of streets in urban India. One of my first sensory experiences in this road was the persistent honking. The insistent and often frustrated blaring of horns called attention to the challenges of motorized driving on the road where slowing, swerving, or stopping for someone who obstructed a driver's pathway was inevitable. Automobile users quickly realized that much of the carriageway was occupied by pedestrians, vendors, pushcarts, and other modes of movement. Vehicles inched through the intersection but always gave way to pedestrians and other road users who moved as they chose on the road. Emboldened by this setting, our team decided to take numerous shoots following individuals as they wove through the throng of vehicles and people, often evoking more blasts of horns.

Next, we decided to take some vantage shots of the market intersection from the flyover. Since there was no sidewalk on the flyover, our taxi driver advised us against walking there and suggested that we instead drive there. A very different streetscape awaited us when we drove onto the flyover. Clearly marked with traffic lanes and designed to carry two lanes of vehicles in either direction, at this early hour, vehicles flowed past at frightening speeds. Unlike in the intersection below, here on the flyover there were no humans, only vehicles on the carriageway. And the vehicles were different from the ones below; here, they were inanimate metal capsules hurtling to their destination without a thought for objects in their path. When we slowed to a stop on the flyover for our shoot, our taxi driver warned us that we could not stop here too long as it would hold up traffic and we should be careful about moving around on foot. Once we disembarked, we scurried to the front of the parked taxi and, protected by the car, took our shots. Although we were successful in capturing revealing shots of the tumultuous intersection below, we were repeatedly reminded of our intruding presence on the flyover by the screaming horns and the rush of the wind. Once done, we scurried back into the taxi and were glad to drive down from the flyover back into the more humane domain on the ground.

The starkly different experience in both locations—a frustrated motoring at road level in front of the market and easy travel above on the flyover—is thought provoking. The carriageway in front of the market and on the flyover reveals very different spatial and organizational dynamics. The road space in front of the market is remarkably inclusive and defies rigid spatial compartmentalization. Pedestrians, buses, vendors, shoppers, cars, motorcycles, and pushcarts all intermingle, interact, and negotiate their claims to road space in an ongoing and dynamic fashion. But for automobile users, this spatial and mobile fluidity appears as congestion and disorder and evokes frustration and irritation. On the flyover, road space is devoted entirely to motorized movement. The absence of a sidewalk or any other spatial partition (apart from the median divide) is a clear indicator. All available space is reserved for motor vehicles. Here, motorized vehicles encounter a design that allows them to move with minimal challenges to their claim on the road. Other forms of claims to space (such as when our film crew took our shots) are actively discouraged. What do these radically different wayside experiences playing out in such close proximity tell us about streets and mobility in India?

Two lines of reasoning follow from this situation. First, urban space often evokes contradictory feelings of familiarity and unease. Thus, even as the automobile user experiences discomfort with the overwhelming congestion and disorder in the market, a sentiment of ease and joy is produced at the same time in the face of fluid, almost clinical movement of vehicles on the flyover. Does this suggest that congestion in front of the market is an undesirable state from its pervasive disorder and that fluidity on the flyover is an especially desirable state? Such an emotion confirms that we have become habituated to consider the new and modern (the flyover in this instance) as desirable.[4] How could we explain such contradictions in such close proximity? To my mind, and this is the second line of thought that springs from the situation at K. R. Market, such contradictions indicate an underlying construct that adapts an automotive outlook (what some have called a windshield view) and casts congestion in the marketplace as a problem requiring rectification. The solution to the problem of congestion is the flyover that offers motorized vehicles the option to effortlessly bypass the market's congestion. But such a construct possesses enormous political consequences. The claims of automotive users to urban space are valorized through the exercise of power to allow them to bypass the process of negotiation and interaction with other constituents in society. How did such a state of affairs come to be? Such a state is particularly stark because it contrasts with the image of the archetypal Indian street.

In the next section, we investigate how the changing portrayal of congestion on roads in India points toward the installation of the construct of automobility on Indian roads. The section seeks to deploy, following Gordin, Tilley, and Prakash (2011), narratives as products of what these authors refer to as "historically-grounded analytical categories" (3) to fathom how dystopic sentiments surrounding on-street congestion have been mobilized to construct the edifice of automobility on Indian roads.

Portraying Congestion on Indian Roads

Portrayals of traffic on roads, both historically and now, have solidified a reputation of its dystopic propensity. Although traffic has been portrayed consistently as a problem, what is curious is how the narratives of traffic congestion have shifted considerably over time. While still enmeshed within the matrix of colonial power relations of the early to mid-twentieth century, congestion was commonly represented as a qualitative problem of the mind-set of the colonized peoples of India. The problem of congestion was conceived as the inability of Indians to inhabit roadways in a civilized manner and instead engage in competitive jostling for road space. Since the start of the twenty-first century, though, traffic and on-road congestion have been largely portrayed as a quantitative problem driven by the rising numbers of vehicles, which can perhaps be managed through advanced technologies and economic incentives, thus recalling Mumford's notion of a quantitative mind-set of improvement. The shift in the historical narrative of dystopia from a qualitative problem of the mind-set of subjugated peoples to a quantitative problem rising out of vehicle population is critical for grasping how roads and mobility have changed and how locations such as K. R. Market have become commonplace.

The manifestation of traffic congestion on the streets as a qualitative problem can be traced to the multiplicity of uses and users competing for road space in the absence of clear guidelines regarding how it should be apportioned. For a long time, roads in India have largely defied rigid spatial compartments that have become the norm in many other urban locations. In other places, zoning of city roads within largely inflexible modes have far greater public acceptance, and as a result, the partitioning of road space between competing uses appears far more defined. By this, I suggest that road space is either reserved exclusively for a primary use (and closely related secondary uses), or there is a clearly demarcated spatial partitioning of available road space for a few competing uses. Thus, in some cases, roads—their infrastructure and design and adjoining land uses—are unambiguously designated and demarcated for a primary use, such as uninterrupted automobile transit on expressways or the grid-like downtown streets dedicated to office buildings and peak-hour traffic. In other contexts, as in some Western European roads, there has been a pronounced thrust for formal spatial partitioning of roads whereby a few identified uses occupy clearly defined slices of road space (A. Jain and Moraglio 2014, 522).

In comparison, Indian streets appear (and certainly appeared in the past) to possess a far more fluid mode of sharing road space among different users and uses. Indeed, Jain and Moraglio go so far to propose that "the informal mode of (self-) governing street space gives a more dynamic picture and resembles the 'layers of uses' which can cope with the vast variety of users and uses much better" (2014, 523). They suggest that what one finds on Indian streets is a dynamic process of apportioning road space between different users such that the outcome is a complex, interleaved layer of uses on the road. They argue that this interleaving of multiple uses reflects the fragmentation of public space in India; although distinct social groups exist in public, they do not fashion a shared understanding of public space. Fragmenting of road space in the context of an absence of consensus between different social groups leads to a hierarchical system of apportioning road space. Dominant social groups on the road tend to acquire a lion's share, while others face a diminishing prospect, something that one now finds with the steady rise of vehicular population.

This level of qualitative nuance is more often than not absent in the colonial portrayal of the experience of traffic in India. Accounts of the heterogeneity of traffic on Indian roads point instead to a dismal melee-like atmosphere. One visiting British member of Parliament, writing in the early twentieth century in his observation, spoke of the kaleidoscopic panorama composed of

> heifers, goats, pariah dogs scavenging for their meals; the electric cars, the gharries and broughams [both horse-drawn carriages]...the slow-moving bullock carts, with their creaking lumbering solid wheels; the clanging of car and carriage bells, the constant shouting of drivers and others, the occasional glimpse of a carefully closed palanquin [a litter], swung from long bamboo poles...all these, together with the moving stream of people with their flowing white garments which crowded the dirty, ill-kept footpaths and streets. (Hardie 1909, 9)

First-time observers invariably commented on the sheer multiplicity of movement that intermingled on the streets. The braiding of these multiple streams of traffic engendered different sound and rhythmic patterns: the clanging of electric bells, the creaking of the cart, the grunt of the pack animal, and the incessant human yelling. The multiplicity of visual and aural stimuli on the streets by themselves quickly left observers overwhelmed.

With the rapid growth in motorization by the second decade of the twentieth century, motorcars contributed to qualitatively newer forms of congestion and danger in many Indian metropolises. Hazareesingh notes in his history of colonial Bombay that "the twelve thousand motor vehicles in circulation contributed substantially to increasing congestion, competing for street space with trams, ox carts, victorias, bicycles, and pedestrians...[exposing] pedestrians to risk on all major roads" (Hazareesingh 2007, 68). The rise of motorization further heightened the palpable sense of unease and horror that observers gave voice to in their writings about Indian cities. Words like *chaos*, *disorder*, and *mess* had been used for some decades prior to India's independence in the middle of the twentieth century as shorthand to denote an exotic but dismal state of affairs.

With the close of the colonial period, the unease of Western observers translated into a sense of disdain regarding the ability of Indians to run their affairs as a sovereign people. As Arnold (2012, 127) noted, Sir Francis Tuker, a senior British Indian army officer, in his memoirs of the last two years of British rule in India, observed Calcutta's dystopian traffic as a harbinger of the catastrophe that awaited the irresolute Indian once the order and the protection of the British Raj was withdrawn. In many colonial (and even neocolonial) accounts, the sad chaos on Indian streets was a signal of the fecklessness of all things Indian: their culture, modes of driving, traveling, and inhabiting the road, as well as systems of governance and education. Writing about the metropolis of Calcutta in 1971, more than a couple of decades after the eclipse of the British Empire, Geoffrey Moorhouse (1971) describes a narrative of imminent metropolitan collapse, a process that is irreversibly underway in the city's transport system with the incessant heaving and pushing of masses of pedestrians negotiating motor traffic and bullock carts, handcarts, tramcars, bicycles, ramshackle buses swaying side-to-side from extreme overcrowding, and poorly maintained trams nestled precariously on their tracks. Left to themselves, Indians will take this process of dissolution forward, Moorhouse concludes, to a truly dystopian self-destructive finale.

The solution in some of these narratives is for greater import of Western models of street life. Only by making Indian streets a copy of the Western street and by making the Indian behave in the way a Westerner would can dystopia on these streets be averted and Indians participate fully in the benefits of urban modernity. Arnold (2012) documents instances where the state of traffic in the late-colonial metropolis becomes the impetus for reforms to train Indian children in proper civic life:

> By the 1930s English-language papers were full of schemes to teach schoolchildren the "rules of the road." A playground game complete with miniature pedestrian crossings and road junctions, was created to improve how traffic worked.... In June 1938, 30,000 schoolchildren across the country were receiving road safety training. (Arnold 2012, 135)

Left to themselves, Indian children would be socialized to replicate the chaos on the streets. It is only through education that children can bring a change to this unsatisfactory situation.

But despite this early thrust toward disciplining and reorganizing, quantitative conceptions of controlling the explosive automotive growth have become dominant in recent times in policy and the popular discourse (even though international reporting still relies on occasion on colonial tropes of chaos in their contemporary narratives) surrounding the dismal state of congestion and road circulation. For instance, although the *New York Times* speaks of "'parking wars" in New Delhi's car-saturated terrain or the *Guardian* highlights New Delhi's "traffic chaos," there is a discernible suggestion that Indian cities need to do more to address the burgeoning vehicular population.[5] Thus, in a recent article on Mumbai's traffic situation titled "Why Mumbai Should Get Over Its Obsession with Cars," the *Guardian* states:

> Mumbai seems to be off the map in terms of implementing current innovations in urban transport policy making. Despite widespread aspirations of emulating other Asian cities such as Singapore and Shanghai, a number of transport interventions are surprisingly absent. This includes urban road pricing or congestion charging, first pioneered by Singapore in the 1970s.... Mumbai also lacks public bike-share schemes despite their rapid recent spread across the globe, and unlike an estimated 166 cities internationally, does not contain any Bus Rapid Transport Systems (BRTS).[6]

To draw another illustrative example, as part of a series, "Tomorrow's Cities," in March 2013, the British Broadcasting Corporation (BBC) focused on the near-impossible state of traffic in Mumbai. The main cause for this gloomy situation, according to the BBC, was the rapidly growing vehicular population in the city: "In a city of 18 million inhabitants there are 1.8 million motor vehicles. The number is growing every day as more drivers take to the roads and frankly, there isn't enough road to go around."[7] In what could only be considered a major shift in the diagnosis of traffic congestion, the accepted solution to the quantitative congestion caused by too many automobiles on the streets is for greater use of technologies that will better manage traffic circulation. The BBC article mentions that with support from the World Bank, the city has established a traffic control center that monitors and intervenes in traffic flows at key junctions around the city in real time through a network of sensors, cameras, and signals.

Since the early 2000s, the circulation (or not) of traffic has emerged as a key policy issue in metropolitan India with a host of projects, reports, and policy papers (see figure 1.2 for an example) attempting to define and address the issue of traffic and traffic congestion, such as the National Urban Transport Policy of 2006, draft of National Urban Transport Policy of 2014, Sustainable Urban Transport Project, India of 2009, Report of the High Powered Committee on Decongesting Traffic in Delhi of 2016, and the National Transit Oriented Development Policy of 2017. Common to these reports is the recognition that congestion in the circulation of traffic is predominantly a result of rapid growth in the motor vehicle population. For instance, an appraisal conducted by the World Bank of the Ministry of Urban Development's Sustainable Urban Transport Project notes that

> India's continuing urbanization and surging economic growth over the last decade has led to an inevitable rise in ownership and use of motorized vehicles

Figure 1.2
Cover of report on decongesting traffic in New Delhi (source: Ministry of Urban Development, Government of India).

> across cities and towns.... The average two wheeler and car ownership levels in metropolitan cities have more than doubled, and motorized per capita trip rate has also increased 60 percent.... Recent studies show that in many Indian cities where walking, cycling, and use of buses have traditionally dominated, the share of the use of two-wheelers, and, more recently, private cars, has been increasing dramatically. (World Bank 2009, 1)

Traffic congestion in this case is articulated as a quantitative measure: the number of vehicles on the road. The sheer rise in the number of motor vehicles running on the street has clogged road space, and their numbers have become the barrier for speedy and smooth movement. Congestion as an excessive accumulation of traffic (Stopher 2004) is considered a variable that indicates the technical capacity of infrastructures. The expansion of material infrastructure to increase system capacity is a commonly adopted technical solution to congestion. Thus, building more supply-oriented infrastructures—more roads, more expressways, more flyovers—is proposed as the solution to congestion. Quantitative measures of congestion also pave the way for deploying economic instruments such as congestion charges (Hensher and Puckett 2005; Eliasson 2008) to structure incentives in ways that can modify the infrastructure use to reduce congestion.

The reliance on technical solutions to ease congestion is a far departure from the earlier focus on modifying Indians' behavior and values. How does one reconcile the transition from one account of congestion to a radically altered one? How did the paradigm of congestion in Indian cities shift so markedly and quickly (over a few decades) from a predominantly qualitative assessment of congestion to a quantitative notion of congestion caused by excess automobiles on the road? The proximate explanation is that the notion of congestion has changed in response to the colossal growth in vehicular population in Indian cities. As the number of vehicles on the road increased, the conception of congestion accordingly shifted. While there is no denying the galloping growth in vehicular population (in 2005, there were 81 million vehicles on Indian roads; by 2015 this number had grown to 210 million), such a linear causal relation between vehicular growth and the experience of congestion is especially convenient from a public policy or law enforcement perspective. By equating the rise of vehicular population with the growing experience of congestion, political and bureaucratic elites have been able to cast congestion as an administrative problem that needs a solution. With the recent rise of quantitative conceptions of congestion within the popular consciousness, the administrative and enforcement apparatuses in cities have sought to manage congestion reactively and incrementally—widening a road here, building a flyover there, designing a signal-free arrangement on an arterial corridor, providing dynamic information boards, or reserving space for motorized traffic—all in the pursuit of a speedy and smooth drive for motor vehicles on the road.

Urban administrators in India, in a fashion similar to what Mumford had predicted, react to the growing vehicular population and address congestion incrementally. Their efforts to manage the problem of congestion appear to continually constrict the space available in metropolises for any purpose other than transportation. The simple linear sequence of cause and effect of motor vehicle growth, congestion, and decongestive efforts is as much an artifact of administrative optimism as it is a Mumfordian dystopic reading. However, neither administrative optimism nor Mumfordian pessimism does a good job in explaining the complex interrelated linkages that bind together historical roots with social, political, and material entities engaged in shaping street use. The web of linkages that has come to define the growing motorization is grounded within the contextual endowments of the Indian city. Instead of simple cause-and-effect relationships, motor vehicle growth, congestion, and efforts to ameliorate the congestion are interconnected with specific social and material entities to voice a political manifestation. The case of K. R. Market in the beginning of the chapter is insightful. The flyover bypassing the market was an exercise at privileging automobile users with a smooth, quick ride while at the same time neglecting the mobility needs of the nonautomobile users in the market.

Automobiles and Automobility

That automobiles are an inescapable presence in many societies around the world does not come as a surprise. Although exact figures are not available, with skyrocketing rates of vehicle sales, it is widely accepted that the global vehicular population (comprising all manner of motorized vehicles, including two- and four-wheeled motorized vehicles) has breached the 1 billion mark, and by 2020, it is expected to be nudging 1.5 billion (Sperling and Gordon 2009). Given these numbers, automobiles have indeed acquired a pervasive presence. This is particularly true of Western and industrialized countries that have been witness to an extended period of growth in automobile numbers and where the per capita penetration of automobiles has been consistently high. But despite its widespread presence, the imprint that automobiles make on societies around the world has not received sustained recognition. In fact, efforts to critically interrogate the position of the automobile in Western countries have gathered sustained scholarly attention only in the new millennium.[8]

The omnipresence of automobiles often leads to simple characterizations as exterior forces that bear on their host societies. Based on recent empirical research, however, the consensus appears to be that the role of automobiles in transforming lives is less than straightforward. Instead, automobiles are technologies that are now recognized to mediate and intersect with core elements of contemporary lives in Western societies in a complex and polyvalent manner. Fundamental Western values of individualism and liberalism, for instance, find exemplary expression through the individual autonomy that automobiles are said to extend to those who rely on them

(Chella Rajan 2006). At the same time, automobiles and autocentric developments simultaneously possess aspects that both enhance and reduce the public and private spheres. Thus, as Sheller and Urry (2003) have astutely observed, private drivers, franchised by driving licenses, forge a community united by a set of practices for mobility and navigation that have come to dominate the public sphere even as they exclude those who do not or cannot drive. However, cars, by providing enclosed spaces, offer motorists the possibility of retaining a quasi-privatized environment within the public realm. The imprint of the automobile thus has articulated new domains for expressing the public/private divide for city residents.

Automobiles exert an expanding footprint in diverse social and political domains too. Matters of politics and governance expressed, for example, in designing automotive safety (Beckmann 2004) or in governing the motorway driver (Merriman 2006) indicate the expanding scope of the automobile. Similarly, social and cultural associations with the automobile revealed through identities and logics of automotive consumerism (Gartman 2004) or the affective attachments that have displaced other forms of relationships (Latimer and Munro 2006) are further examples of its regnant footprint. Another manifestation of the intense entanglement of automobiles within contemporary Western existence is the constitution of a range of hybridized subjectivities imbricated with the automotive presence—car drivers, hotrod enthusiasts, automotive masculinity, and pedestrians on automotive roads (Dant 2004; H. F. Moorhouse 1991; Bonham 2006; S. Jain 2005). In all these cases, personhood is forged not just at the instance of but also inextricably through the automobile. Yet another manifestation of the automobile is in the configuration of the Western automotive city—an urban site for a breathtaking exercise of power that coerces, constrains, and limits in order to facilitate the movement of numerous quasi-private metal capsules. This power configures an arrangement of domination through which claims to public space are weighed and evaluated against the overarching privileging of automotive travel on the streets (Sheller and Urry 2000; Thrift 2004).[9]

How have arrangements of domination attendant on the presence of automobiles been understood? Urry, one of the premier scholars of auto and other mobilities, suggests that in order to begin understanding the political valence of the automobile, it is necessary to understand it as automobility—a complex that unites multiple social, technological, ideological, and cultural aspects with modes of consumption and resource use (Urry 2004). It is the combination or the interlocking of these specific aspects into a system that "generates and reproduces a 'specific character of domination'" (Urry 2004, 25).

What then is the specific character of domination that is manifested through automobility? A key feature of automotive domination is its extraordinary persistence across time and space. In its persistence, automobility reveals a regime quality that exercises explicit ideological, governmental, and political controls to powerfully shape society (Bohm et al. 2006). For scholars, an interlocking, power-filled, and persistent automotive regime is a particularly troubling prospect on at least two counts. First, as a regime with extraordinary stability, automobility has shown itself to be resistant to efforts to limit, manage, or otherwise reduce its environmental and social footprint. But despite its stability, many have argued that it would be possible to unlock the existing system during critical junctures or "tipping points" (Urry 2004, 36). Such junctures could be characterized as animating particular alignments between dominant macrolevel frames and microlevel niches of counterdiscourses, movements, and practices that generate transitions away from the existing automotive regime toward a more sustainable mobility regime (Sheller 2012; Geels et al. 2012). Second, the power embedded within regimes of automobility creates an uneven field of motility (Kaufmann 2002), with some benefiting from seamless and affirming experiences of travel even as they secede to suburbs and edge cities to avoid interacting with those perceived as threatening (Henderson 2006). For others, such as the gendered, the poor, and recent immigrants, a range of barriers and disenablements proliferate through automobility. But as Walks notes, these disenablements and associated "new forms of vulnerability, inequality, and politics" find articulation within the political economic structures of contemporary capitalism (Walks 2015, 5). The specific enunciation of an unequal automobility, it can be argued, is not just a product of the regime constitution but its intersection and inflection with newer norms and modes of neoliberalism underpinning policymaking. It is this intersection that has furthered the expression and reproduction of social inequalities. One particularly durable means through which social inequalities are expressed is the design of the streetscape in cities. According to Agyeman (2013), an autonormative streetscape design has become the norm in planning whereby "the road became synonymous with the car and other users were squeezed out" (111). A democratized streetscape design, Agyeman argues, has the potential to displace the autonormativity embedded within planning practice. He suggests that a complete streets policy—that includes a broader definition of road users, ensures connectivity to multiple transit modes, and incorporates input from the community of road users—could offer a means to democratize the form of city streets (Agyeman 2013, 124).[10]

The inquiry into the automobile in Western society contrasts notably with the recent and rather tentative scope of research on automobiles and automobility in India. Research has been tentative in the sense that in much of it, authors pay inordinate attention to unique situational traits and exceptional historical circumstances that have shaped automotive presence on Indian roads without offering insights into its linkages with wider systems of governance and politics that pervade urban society. Instead, dominant streams of research locate the automobile in India in recent times within three registers: the car as a vehicle for a contested modernity; automotive practices on the road, which constitute a shared sense of nationwide community; and automobiles as markers of consumption that realize middle-class aspirations for social status.[11] In the first register, automobiles become a means for understanding change in Indian society. For instance, Sardar's writing (2002) on the presence of the Ambassador car on Indian roads paints a picture of how an individual passenger is ferried by the car. For Sardar, multiple experiences of dwelling within the car, navigating chaotic traffic, and viewing the roadscape all offer a window into how India "runs" as a postcolonial country as it seeks to modernize. The picture Sardar sees through the windshield of the Ambassador car is not a pretty one, but it comes laden with allusions to the Indian experience of modernity in the late twentieth century, leading him to surmise that he "is borne along within the very essence of Indian modernity" (Sardar, 2002, 216).

The second register for locating the automobile in India arises from relating its everyday presence on the road with a common sense of national identity. Edensor (2004) proposes that iconic vehicles, roadscapes, and everyday practices of driving together forge a national identity in ways similar to that constructed by spectacular ceremonies or high cultures of nationhood. Thus, driving on Indian roads appears to happen in the context of minimal state regulation; nevertheless, there exist unwritten conventions and norms that govern automotive travel. These conventions include such facets as reliance on horns to loudly navigate traffic on the roads, the precedence given to larger vehicles, neglect of formal traffic signs, and drivers subverting material infrastructure such as road signs or speed breakers embedded with regulatory force (Edensor 2004; Guffin 2015). Such practices, Edensor, would argue, are constitutive of the cultural identity of being an Indian. A final register of research on the automobile in India centers on the vital role that automobiles (especially cars) play as important status symbols for the "new middle class" (Fernandes 2006). Despite internal contradictions, the new middle classes are united in their collective aspiration for a comfortable and good life defined by conspicuous consumption and expressed through multiple consumption choices. Cars occupy a critical position within this consumption landscape. Thus, according to Nielsen and Wilhite (2016), the spotty success of the Tata Nano car in the Indian market despite its greater affordability and novel design needs to be understood within the car's inability to be a vehicle for rising social mobility aspirations of the new middle classes.

These strains of research into automobiles on Indian streets, while no doubt perceptive, offer limited insights for understanding how Indian cities are being transformed as they increasingly play host to automobility—a system of domination that is abetted by automobiles but possesses social, technological, cultural, and ideological dimensions. Cars and automobiles in India do, no doubt, possess a lively social life. In addition, they have leveraged an active political presence in recent times. By focusing on the social constituents of automobiles, there has been a tendency to gloss over its political ramifications. This dearth in engaging centrally with the political constitution of automobility in India is all the more stark given the sustained attention that critical planners have directed recently to the question of urban mobility in India. Writing about urban transport policy in India, the urban planning scholar Madhav Badami notes that

> policymaking related to urban transport has focused predominantly on road infrastructure development and transport system management to accommodate and improve the traffic characteristics of motor vehicles...meanwhile, budgets for the provision of infrastructure and facilities for pedestrians and cyclists have been minuscule. (Badami 2009, 44)

Along the same lines, the urban transport planning scholar Rutul Joshi and others suggest that "the emerging automobile culture in Indian cities and how it impacts urban transport governance and decision-making is an important area that policymakers must address to ensure a successful transition to a low carbon future" (Joshi, Joseph, and Chandran 2016, 131). Given these cautionary remarks regarding the growing reach of an automobile culture in Indian cities, critical social analysis should follow suit and examine how automobility as a political entity has come to lodge itself in cities in India. Simply put, in the Indian (metropolitan) context, how can we understand the installation of automobility? What are its components that situate it within the unique historical, social, and political character of the city?

In this book, I identify automobility as a political constellation that has become lodged in Indian cities. In understanding automobility as a political constellation, I follow the lead of Matthew Gandy (2011) and Roger Keil (2013) in their use of the term *constellation* as a means to draw attention to the "details and textures of everyday life in the modern city" while informed by "context, historical specificity, and multidimensionality" (Gandy 2011, 5). Arrangements of infrastructure provisioning are particularly amenable to being characterized as constellations because they are constituted through relational webs that possess multiple social, institutional, and technological dimensions. Writing about plural arrangements of water and sanitation systems in the suburbs of cities in the global South, Monstadt and Schramm (2013) refer to the multiple sociotechnical arrangements as constellations rooted within varied spatial, socioeconomic, and technological morphologies. Automobility as a political constellation thus is understood in this book as embedded in the historical context of Indian cities, but at the same time, it is enmeshed within a complex sociotechnical matrix of institutions, landscapes, infrastructures, technologies, actors, plans, and manifestos that endow it with enormous valence to shape the experience of moving around in the city.

In the next section, I briefly outline the key objective of this book: *how automobility as a political constellation has come to be installed in the city of Bengaluru in India*. In doing so, I introduce readers to the metropolitan city of Bengaluru and indicate why studying it is appropriate to understanding how automobility has come to be a defining technopolitical project in Indian cities.

Installing Automobility in Bengaluru

Located on a high tableland in south-central India, Bengaluru is the political, administrative, economic, educational, and sociocultural capital of the Indian state of Karnataka (figure 1.3). After the 2011 census, Bengaluru city's population stood at 8.5 million and had a growth rate of 96 percent between 2001 and 2011 (Directorate of Census Operations Karnataka 2011), making it the third largest city in the country.[12] Given its large and growing population, as well as its status as the capital of the state, Bengaluru has exerted an enormous footprint on Karnataka state's social, political, and economic life. With it has come a commensurate degree of interest among political elites in Bengaluru's affairs. Historically, as a commercial entrepôt in precolonial times and the seat of the British colonial enterprise in the region, the city has attracted attention over an extended period. In the immediate postindependence period, Bengaluru's stature was considerably enhanced with the location of several large public sector enterprises and educational institutions. As we shall see in the next chapter, these developments have exerted an important influence on the city's response to a perception of congestion in the city. In recent times, at least

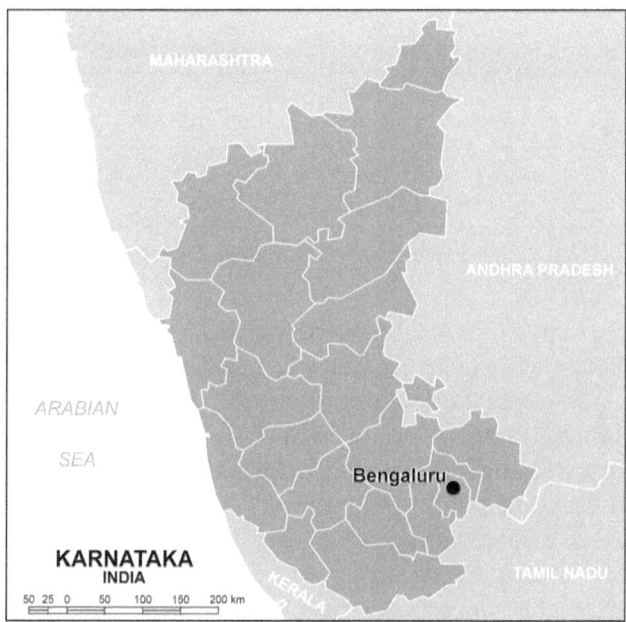

Figure 1.3
Map of the state of Karnataka with the location of Bengaluru.

since the 1990s, with the formation of a cluster of information technology and biotechnology industries and the thickening of the trope of Bengaluru as India's silicon city, the city finds itself embroiled in yet another cycle of heightened attention and awareness.

One manifestation of the heightened attention that Bengaluru receives revolves around what could be called a sustained automotive presence, which registers not only through the proliferation of automobiles circulating on city streets but also in newspapers, popular media, and daily discourse. From table 1.1, it is evident that sustained automotive presence is related to the enormous growth in automobiles on city roads that has even outpaced population growth. Thus, while in 2001 there were only 1.6 million vehicles, ten years later this number had more than doubled to 3.7 million vehicles and then more than tripled to 5.5 million vehicles over the fourteen years since 2001. With this rapid growth, Bengaluru has acquired the dubious distinction of possessing the second-highest number of vehicles and being the second-highest fuel consumer among Indian metropolises.[13] The surging growth in automobiles has been accompanied by almost continuous commentary regarding the (worrying) rise in automotive presence

Table 1.1
The Growth in Human and Vehicular Population in Bengaluru

Population (in millions)	2001	2005	2011	2015
Humans	5.1	6.0 (estimate)	8.49	9.7 (estimate)
Vehicles	1.6	2.5	3.7	5.5

Sources: RITES (2011); Directorate of Census Operations Karnataka (2011); KRTO (2015)

in local and national media.[14] In electronic social media, the discourse on automobiles in Bengaluru is certainly quite prevalent. On both Twitter and Facebook, there exist (at the time of writing this book) numerous traffic tags such as #BengaluruTraffic, where social media users post their observations, comments, and frustrations regarding traffic and roads. On Twitter handles, such as the Bangalore Traffic Jam Updates @BLRJams, users update each other on the emerging traffic situation in the city. In addition, with Google Maps and FM radio stations introducing live traffic updates in Bengaluru, relying on media and technology to navigate traffic is yet another means through which Bangaloreans have registered automotive presence in their lives (figure 1.4).[15]

Automobility is understood here as a political constellation that enrolls not just automobiles but a slew of other technological, material, social, and historical elements. It is through the interaction of these different elements that automobility as a political constellation comes to be installed in a city. While the sustained automotive presence in Bengaluru, when compared with other metropolitan cities in India, is the one very compelling reason for studying automobility in the city, it is not the only reason. Several social and historical reasons make Bengaluru, in comparison with other cities, an attractive site for the study of how automobility has come to be installed. One notable reason is the historical continuity in governments (in Karnataka) relying on technology for achieving social objectives. This technocratic constitution of governance originated in the colonial Mysore kingdom under a special historical situation (see chapter 2 for details) and has since acquired deep institutional roots in the everyday administration of provincial and urban affairs. Thus, continuing into the postindependence period, the administration of the government of Karnataka notably is a frontrunner in adopting new technologies and techniques to achieve governance objectives—so much so that the willingness to experiment with technologies to achieve contemporary governance objectives has played a significant role in according Karnataka the status of a frontrunner state in implementing economic reforms.

Figure 1.4
Advertisement of live traffic updates on Google Maps on a bus shelter.

A second compelling reason is the opportunities extended to men from privileged social backgrounds (more often than not, upper-class, technically educated Brahmin men)[16] to forge an agenda of change in state and urban affairs. In this case too, there is a strong historical precedent in the predominantly Brahmin *dewans* (chief ministers) of the Mysore kingdom (see figure 2.1 for the location of the kingdom within India). M. Visveshvaraiah, the engineer-turned-statesman/*dewan* who pioneered several technological, educational, and industrial advances in the Mysore kingdom in the early twentieth century, was a particularly notable example. In current times, Bengaluru remains porous to the interventions of men of privilege. For example, Nandan Nilekani, Ramesh Ramanathan, and Ashwin Mahesh, all from privileged backgrounds, have been successful in participating and shaping urban affairs in the city. In fact, Mahesh has candidly described the openness extended to privileged nongovernmental people to intervene in public problem solving as follows:

> Privilege in urban India is going from a structure of caste to a structure of caste and class together.... Bangalore is cosmopolitan but it retains its privilege structure.... [In order to make a difference], you have to know what are the contours of your ecosystem [of privilege]. The essence of the ecosystem [in Bangalore] is social networks of people of privilege from diverse backgrounds, and this is true among the educated elite and also among the political elite. (Interview with Ashwin Mahesh, May 24, 2011)

The long tradition of openness to (and visibility of) networks of privilege in shaping urban outcomes in the city makes Bengaluru, more than any other Indian city, a particularly revealing case of how automobility is being established in India.

The final reason for locating this study in Bengaluru is its long history of visibility in India. Since colonial times when the Mysore kingdom was depicted by the British as a model for the rest of colonial India, Bengaluru/Karnataka has been the model for the rest of the country. One consequence of this historical trajectory has been a greater willingness on the part of the state's political and administrative elite to experiment with reforms. For administrators around the country, Karnataka's pioneering experience in decentralization in the 1980s served as a model for devolving planning to the grassroots (Aziz 1993; Crook and Manor 1998). In current times too, Bengaluru's experiments with urban service delivery, government–civil society partnerships (Bangalore Agenda Task Force and the Agenda for Bengaluru Infrastructure Development are recent examples examined in detail in subsequent chapters), and early adoption of technologies and institutional models have all been a source of attention for urban administrators around the country. Partly as a result, Bengaluru and Karnataka state have been widely acknowledged as leaders in reform (Kirk 2005; Manor 2007). Through a combination of sustained automotive presence and unique social and historical processes, a study of automobility's inception in Bengaluru promises to have wider resonance in the Indian and global Southern context.

The rest of this book explores how automobility as a political constellation has come to be installed in the city of Bengaluru. It describes constituents of Bengaluru's automobility constellation, each of which brings a dimension that has deep contextual roots in the city: its history, society, politics, and infrastructures. This contextual presence is not a static background effect but a dynamic and processual influence that shapes how automobility has become lodged in Bengaluru. It manifests in both macrolevel urban governance processes and microlevel everyday practices. Institutional arrangements of the state and municipal governments, arrangements of infrastructure development, as well as practices of driving, and social media use, contribute to installing and interiorizing automobility within the city landscape. Through this dynamic influence, automobiles and associated modes of mobility in the city acquire enormous stability. As we shall see, the stability does not insulate it from contestations and negotiations that often exert considerable wear and tear on the constellation of automobility in the city. The grinding down may not unseat the constellation, but it wears down the edges of the system, giving it a decidedly shabby look. Bengaluru's automobility may not be a spit-and-polish affair; however, that does not mean it can be wished away. It has sunk deep roots in the city, and transitioning to a low-carbon and equitable constellation of mobility is not going to be easy.

Chapter 2 presents a historical look, spanning two hundred years, at congestion in Bengaluru. Connecting with the overriding instrumentality in controlling vehicular traffic, which one encounters in the histories of Western cities at the dawn of the automotive age, this periodization serves two purposes. First, it decenters the predominance that rising vehicular numbers have acquired in the constitution of the contemporary narrative of congestion in Bengaluru, thereby opening the possibility of looking for other historically rooted sociopolitical actions that continue to shape the experience of congestion and automobility. Second, I posit that congestion in Bengaluru is not a new phenomenon and that there have been many efforts to address congestions of different kinds in Bengaluru's history over the past two hundred years. These different efforts have left behind material, institutional, and sociopolitical residues that continue to shape the experience of traffic congestion in Bengaluru to this day. But more important, common to the different efforts is the exclusive reliance on instrumental technocratic interventions to manage congestion.

Chapter 3 explores the discursive paradigm that characterizes mobility, problematizes congestion, and generates solutions for it in the particular context of Bengaluru. I propose that since the late 1990s, the paradigm that structures urban mobility and infrastructure in the city can be characterized as a regime of congestion. Building on the work of scholars in science and technology studies, I understand the regime of congestion as a technopolitical regime. Through this theoretical framing, I argue that the regime of congestion is reconstituting the nature of streets in Bengaluru with the intent of privileging the physical and discursive occupation of street space by private automobiles. Such occupation has far-reaching political consequences for the quality of mobility in Bengaluru. I show that Bengaluru's regime of congestion is marginalizing the mobility needs of the poorer residents of the city while privileging the mobility needs of the motorized.

In chapter 4, I explore the constitution of an infrastructure landscape of automobility. I define the term *infrastructurescape* as an approach that locates infrastructures as vital elements within an active urban landscape, embedded with the power to shape the experience of the urban resident in the city. The chapter traces how the particular embedding of infrastructures of mobility in Bengaluru's landscape has ingrained elite privilege deeply into the landscape, thereby reducing the possibility for more inclusive mobility and inhabitation in the city.

Chapter 5 demonstrates the constitution of a collective identity of automotive citizenship. I show that the identity of this citizenship is not a transient phenomenon that emerges only when one is ensconced in a vehicle but is made durable through the assembly of a range of social, artifactual, and technological materials, such as drivers and their practices of driving, redesigned street-side artifacts, social media platforms, and traffic management policies. In doing so, I draw on recent STS research in material participation and the constitution of material publics to articulate automotive citizenship as a mobile belonging on the road that reifies social inequalities. A direct outcome of the crafting of automotive citizenship is privileging automotive travel by seeking to minimize automobile congestion while at the same time proliferating congestions and imposing immobilities on (and thereby actively disenfranchising) the nonmotorized.

In the penultimate chapter, I examine the process that attends the installation of infrastructures of automobility in Bengaluru. I argue that automobility has a contested, and therefore a challenged, presence in the city. The challenge arises from diverse sources, including powerful institutional actors, rivers, waste, places of worship, and political ideologies, all playing a part in contesting the presence of automobility. In describing the dynamic of the challenge, I rely on a combination of Lefebvrian rhythmanalysis and the posthumanist performative turn in social sciences to locate how the deployment of infrastructure triggers particular displacements in society and thereby engenders challenges. I characterize the interactive dance between the thrust to deploy infrastructures and the challenges arising from displacement as an ongoing interaction between *affordances* and *congestions*. Such interactions, I contend, gnaw at the achievement of a smooth, seamless vision for motorization, thereby instating what I refer to as a shabby version of automobility.

I conclude the book by addressing three aspects. First, I synthesize the empirical material presented in earlier chapters to summarize how automobility as a political constellation has come to be established in Bengaluru. Second, I address the contribution this book makes to scholarship in urban mobility and in sustainable and equitable urban environmental change. Finally, building on the book's empirical content, if automobility is a political constellation that has engendered new manifestations of dystopic congestion in Bengaluru and other cities of India and the global South, then this chapter proposes a call for displacing automobility and establishing an alternate low-carbon and equitable paradigm of mobility. Elaborating on the empirical chapters, I make three suggestions for displacing automobility: unlocking the regime of congestion, mobilizing pro-poor and nonmotorized infrastructurescapes, and performing acts of taking back the streets, thereby franchising pedestrians, vendors, and bicyclists.

Conclusion

At the beginning of this chapter, I suggested that the situational contradictions at K. R. Market were the outcome of an underlying political construct. This construct, I claim, is the constellation of automobility. I made the argument that the dramatic shift in the portrayal of dystopia on city streets in India is a result not just of the enormous growth in numbers of private automobiles on Indian roads, but of the installation of automobility as a powerful technopolitical constellation. The rest of the book explores how automobility has come to take root in Bengaluru. In the next chapter, I describe the historical constitution of congestion in Bengaluru with an eye to explaining its solidification in the contemporary narrative of congestion in the city and the associated predominance that instrumental explanations have acquired in addressing change in the city.

2 Locating Congestion in Bengaluru

Narrative of a "Congested Bengaluru"

Talk of traffic congestion in the contemporary city of Bengaluru, arguably more than any other city in India, is omnipresent in public discourse and popular culture. What is particularly notable is that this talk is anything but homogeneous. Multiple threads interweave and enrich the narrative of congestion in the city. The heterogeneity of congestion is due not only to multiple forums and venues where a range of people have voiced their interpretation, opinion, expertise and even exasperation regarding the pervasive presence of congestion in Bengaluru city but also to the plurality in the narrative of traffic congestion with its multiple generative bases. By far the dominant base for the narrative of a congested Bengaluru is the enormous growth in automobiles in the city. Other sources, such as lack of interagency coordination, flooding, worker unrest, and the morphological structure of the city, have all contributed to the constitution of the narrative of a congested Bengaluru.

One recent contributor to the automotive population growth thread of the "congested Bengaluru" narrative is IBM, the multinational corporation that most people still associate with personal computers and business automation. IBM seeks to transform itself as a major player that provides management solutions at a planetary scale to governments, cities, and communities. A significant thrust in its corporate strategy has been to employ predictive analytics, collected from a plethora of sensors, to design management solutions for creating what it calls smarter cities. Designing a smarter transportation management network is one key sector for IBM to intervene in order to transform the organization of urban infrastructures of service provision. The exponential growth of vehicular traffic on city roads, IBM suggests, is the pivotal reason behind traffic congestion.[1]

In 2011, IBM conducted the Global Commuter Pain Survey with the aim of advancing its agenda of smart transportation. The study surveyed 8,042 commuters from twenty cities across six continents to gauge their subjective perception of the "emotional and economic toll" of daily travel to work (IBM Corporation 2011).[2] A key finding of the survey was that Bengaluru had the sixth worst commuter pain index among the twenty surveyed cities with an index score of 76. This score compared positively with respect to cities like Mexico City (108) and Beijing (95) but was noticeably inferior to the corresponding indexes for Los Angeles (34), New York (28), and London (23). This particular finding received some attention in local, national, and international news media, with articles confidently stating that residents of Bengaluru, as a result of its explosive and largely unplanned, growth, now suffered the sixth worst commute in the world.[3] The fact that only twenty cities around the world were surveyed and that the survey was subjective in scope was all too often overlooked in the rush to frame a newsworthy story. Thus, *Times of India*'s Bengaluru edition titled the story, "Bangalore Is the 6th Worst City in the World for Commuting."[4] The story interviewed a few car commuters who corroborated the storyline: all roads are packed with cars and there is limited space for parking all these cars in the central business district.

IBM's answer to traffic congestion through a technologically intensive system of traffic management that brings together demand-responsive protocols with interconnected devices finds some resonance in the popular narrative of a congested Bengaluru burgeoning with automobiles. The *Times of India* commissioned the market research agency Synovate to conduct a survey of commuters to inquire about the reason behind traffic congestion, and a quarter of the survey participants saw the need for improved systems of traffic management.[5] The reliance on new technological devices, such as surveillance cameras and intelligent software protocols, as tools to boost the effectiveness of monitoring and decongesting city streets in real time is a recent consideration.[6] These devices for managing traffic congestion were integrated with the involvement of Bengaluru's major software companies into a comprehensive plan (Bangalore Traffic Improvement Project [B-TRAC] 2010) to modernize traffic management in Bengaluru and "to address the issues of traffic congestion caused by spiraling vehicular growth in the city" (Ramanayya and Anantharamaiah 2008).[7] Launched with the objective of reducing traffic congestion in the city by 30 percent, more than half of B-TRAC 2010's budget was earmarked for implementing an intelligent transportation system, including surveillance and enforcement cameras, as well as interconnected traffic signals.

Occasionally other threads, intertwined within the popular discourse of a congested Bengaluru, become visible in the public limelight. One significant strand of the narrative is a reliance on piecemeal solutions to manage congestion. These may be proposed by any of the multiple state-level bureaucracies that control different aspects of infrastructure development, land use and planning, traffic movement, public transport, and road maintenance. For example, Bangalore Development Authority (BDA), as the local planning and development authority, is tasked with enforcing the city's master plan and with developing housing and infrastructure that conforms to prevailing planning norms. Of late, organizations such as the Directorate of Urban Land Transport and the Karnataka Urban Infrastructure Development and Finance Corporation (KUIDFC) have been tasked with conceiving and implementing infrastructure-based solutions to the problem of traffic congestion. These different actors bring with them a range of preferred solutions: infrastructures such as flyovers and signal-free corridors, incentive schemes such as congestion tax, dedicated lanes for buses or cycles, or policy innovations such as a parking policy. The presence of multiple institutional actors with their varied, often mutually incompatible solutions is yet another facet of the narrative of traffic congestion in contemporary Bengaluru.[8] A related facet of the problem of congestion is the absence of a comprehensive integrated strategy to address the rising tide of traffic blockages.[9] Instead, a piecemeal approach is prevalent, with each actor proposing an innovative solution that addresses the problem as they see it. It is another matter that many of these innovations either remain on the drawing board because they are impractical (conceived with limited citizen input or are not applicable in the local context), or because Bengaluru's civic agencies do not have the funding to implement them. In other situations, innovations are introduced on a limited basis with much popular fanfare but then are rarely scaled up to make any significant impact. A good example was the introduction of bicycle lanes in some residential areas of the city.[10] Despite an enthusiastic start, they ceased to function according to plan for several reasons, such as encroachment by motor vehicles, poor police enforcement, and the absence of coordination among different agencies.[11]

In comparison with these systemic strands in the congested Bengaluru narrative, an episodic aspect is often seen in the city's congestion narrative. Traffic disruptions, often extensive in scope, are triggered by a particular alignment of events: heavy rains, sporadic instances of worker agitation, or the arrival of an extended holiday weekend, for example. Bengaluru's landscape was once studded with man-made lakes (referred to locally as tanks) that were interconnected by water channels. This system of tanks and channels served an important purpose of regulating stormwater flows. With largely unregulated urbanization, many of these tanks and their interconnecting channels have been encroached on or built over, thereby disrupting routine hydrological flows. As a result, heavy monsoon rains invariably spark flooding, making several city roads impassable by cars. Flooding is thus one periodic factor behind instances of congestion and disruption in the city.[12] Similarly, mass rallies, strikes, and protest marches have also had the effect of sabotaging fluid flows of traffic, often drawing the ire of middle-class urban residents whose daily commuting routines face disruption.[13] One example was the result of a protest organized by nonunionized garment workers that blocked traffic movement on several arterial roads.[14] Another feature peculiar to Bengaluru is the incidence of enormous traffic blockages coinciding with the onset of an extended holiday weekend. Such weekends provide opportunities for recent migrants to the city to return to their extended families living in other parts of the state or in adjoining states. The result is that the regions surrounding the city railway station and the intercity bus terminus (popularly referred to as Majestic) are overwhelmed by vehicles ferrying travelers. These periodic events of traffic congestion are in many ways related to unique urban attributes of Bengaluru—its structure where the predominant mobility hubs for intercity rail and road travel are concentrated close to the historical center of the city and to the administrative and political establishments of Karnataka state.

How do we make sense of the multiple threads woven within the narrative of a congested Bengaluru? What can we understand from a narrative of congestion that is as varied and differentiated as to encompass the call for smart transportation systems that will flexibly and in real time reduce traffic congestion and at the same time include traffic blockages caused by the episodic flooding of city streets, a result of the widespread illegality in land use regulation? Historicizing congestion and its many manifestations in Bengaluru is one way to understand its contemporary significance for the installation of automobility in the city. Such an inquiry requires us to broaden the scope of examining congestion purely in instrumental terms as a response to the ever-increasing (human and vehicular) population in the city. But this is a challenging venture because historicizing congestion in ways that unravel its complex sociopolitical genealogy is particularly difficult given the predominance of linear, technologically determinist, and internalist accounts of congestion in several fields, such as economics, engineering, and public policy. Such linear accounts are promising for these fields because they justify their methods to intervene in cities to rescue them from the crisis of vehicular congestion. Prior to locating congestion and Bengaluru in a historical context, therefore, I make a detour into the history of congestion in Western cities in order to identify the particular moment when dehistoricization and instrumentalization became the norm in the efforts to address congestion.

Instrumentalization of Traffic and Congestion

Traffic congestion has become commonplace in cities around the world. But historians have confirmed that urban congestion, and specifically traffic congestion, has a long recorded history going back all the way to the ancient city of Rome in the last century before the Common Era.[15] A far more intense curiosity regarding traffic and congestion is visible among historians of industrializing Western cities between the mid-nineteenth and mid-twentieth centuries, arising largely from the need to explain the extraordinary automobile centricity of contemporary urbanism in these contexts. For most of the nineteenth century, congestion in Western city centers was characterized primarily by a range of nonmotorized vehicles, such as carriages, wagons, horse-drawn omnibuses, and rail-bound horsecars, competing for road space with pedestrians (McShane and Tarr 1997). Despite scientific managerial efforts to transform the urban horse into a living machine (McShane and Tarr 2007), horrific instances of human and animal casualties, not to mention logjam congestion in cities, contributed to a widespread desire to replace the horse as the prime mover of urban mobility. By the first decade of the twentieth century in the United States, internal combustion engine–powered automobiles were fast taking over as the preferred mode for urban travel.[16]

The arrival of the automobile age in the United States and Western Europe, accompanied by the occupation of city streets by cars, historians have noted, was a particular historical achievement made possible in part by powerful social and economic arguments (McShane 1994; C. W. Wells 2012).[17] Despite this, traffic congestion was eventually recast as the excessive concentration of personal automobiles on city streets. Such a characterization was especially convenient for the development and professionalization of measures to control automotive traffic and congestion. Thus:

> The growth of motorization in the 1920s often preceded effective traffic control and management. This led to both chaotic confusion and congestion in many business centers.... These conditions led many cities to (1) establish traffic regulations and controls, (2) remove produce markets from central cities, and (3) increase the width of streets. Chicago, for example, relocated the South Water Market, built two-level Michigan Avenue and Wacker Drive, (4) banned left turns in the "Loop," and

(5) signalized downtown intersections. Other cities also began to manage their traffic, and the field of Traffic Engineering emerged. (Falcocchio and Levinson 2015, 20)

What is apparent from this quotation is the causal emergence of measures to tackle the rise in traffic congestion in American streets and, with it, the creation and spread of the field of traffic engineering. It would appear that as the number of cars increased on the roads, decision makers, engineers, and city managers acted in a concerted fashion, aided by a compliant public, in refashioning roads and cities to the imprint of the automobile. Peter Norton's 2008 work, *Fighting Traffic: The Dawn of the Motor Age in the American City*, is particularly illuminating because he spotlights the struggles associated with refashioning the city. He demonstrates how this process of the takeover of city streets in the United States by the automobile was a contingent achievement marked by fiercely fought disputes that sought to alternatively discipline the pedestrian and the driver. The linear, unproblematic emergence of the field of traffic engineering in response to the growing chaos and congestion of automotive traffic is thus an outcome of the dehistoricization of a complex political achievement. By dehistoricizing the contingent achievement of reserving and reforming road space for the exclusive use of automobiles, the marks of struggle and opposition have been elided. In its place, instrumental pathways for managing congestion that were originally outcomes of struggle have become the norm.[18]

The period immediately after World War II witnessed the consolidation of automobility in European and American cities. New methods of transportation engineering, such as road traffic capacity studies, road design, and urban planning initiatives such as inner-city freeways, parkways, grade separators, and underpasses emerged to tackle the headlong growth in automobiles in Western cities.

> Traffic engineering control methods alone could not keep up with the growing traffic demands. Congested conditions in cities were eventually alleviated by the freeway construction associated with the Interstate Highway system. Many cities built radial freeways with central area freeway loops that diverted through traffic from city streets. (Falcocchio and Levinson 2015, 24)

Faced with clogging cities, decision makers in many Western cities were hard-pressed to adopt comprehensive policy prescriptions for ameliorating the congestion or deconcentrating it. Thus, planners in many cities in the West, especially in United States, responded by proposing a grid of intracity urban freeways that diverted traffic away from the congestion in the inner-city core (contributing in a real way to their postindustrial disemboweling). New York City, according to Maxwell Lay (2011), demonstrated this shift to the fullest through the efforts of Roberts Moses, the city's "master builder." In an effort to stay ahead of traffic congestion, Lay notes, "From 1934 to 1968, Moses presided dictatorially over infrastructure construction in New York and built 16 motorways, seven major bridges, and 416 miles (670 km) of parkway" (Lay 2011, 39).[19]

In comparable fashion in the UK, the *Traffic in Towns* report (also known as the Buchanan report), submitted in 1963 to the Ministry of Transport, exemplifies the burgeoning interest in remaking cities in the imprint of the automobile through a hierarchy of distributor roads and highways. But at the same time, the Buchanan report articulated a new dimension in the response to traffic and congestion: restricting automobile use in the interest of safeguarding what it referred to as "environmental capacity." In achieving this goal, the report called for prioritizing collective movement through public transport over those undertaken privately (Ministry of Transport 1964; see also Buchanan 1983). Despite its stated mission to conserve cities in the face of the onslaught of automotive traffic, others have proposed that an overarching imperative of the Buchanan report was to provide for cars, thereby installing driving as a privileged mode of urban mobility (Hillman 1983).[20]

The past hundred years of automobile presence on city streets have been witness to the rise of the fields of transport engineering, traffic studies, and urban transport planning that seek to tackle the presence of congestion on city roads. What is extraordinarily significant about the rise of these fields of traffic management is the subtle erasure of specific social, political, cultural, and spatial acts that together facilitated their growth and establishment. Thus, I argue that the sole identification of the automobile with the experience of traffic congestion is a product of dehistoricizing a specific period of urban change in Western cities.[21] It is this process of dehistoricizing that not only allowed the development of the fields of transport engineering and road design (themselves a product of erasure) but also promoted policy interventions (such as those advocated in the Buchanan report) that paradoxically attempted to untie the bonds that tie together congestion and automobile growth.

In the face of the pervasive dehistoricizing of traffic congestion from spiraling automotive growth, a historically rooted understanding of congestion as a sociopolitical process is very much necessary. Single-dimensional, and often linear, narratives of congestion as automobile growth have translated into a picture of cities being overwhelmed by their vehicular population. These then become the basis for multiple instrumental modalities of intervention into the problem of congestion. In unraveling the evolution of the narrative of congestion in Bengaluru, we adopt a historically embedded framing of congestion as a complex sociospatial process that possesses different aspects in different time periods. The existence of these aspects has contributed to the constitution of the complex narrative of congestion in contemporary Bengaluru.

Layers of Congestion in Bengaluru

Most historical accounts of Bengaluru begin from the mid-sixteenth century when the city was raised as a fortified market town at the intersection of prominent trade routes in the southern part of the Deccan Plateau (an elevated table land occupying much of peninsular India). Emerging as a stronghold of Kempegowda (1510–1570), a regional chieftain (*palegar*), the city was founded in 1537 by a grant from Achyuta Raya, a king of the Vijayanagara Empire (Hasan 1970, 1; Stein 1987, 83).[22] The settlement of Bengaluru at that time was composed of a fortified stronghold with a cluster of settlements that took root just north of the fort. The fort and settlement together formed the nucleus for the city. Reflecting the variability of the political climate in medieval South India, the settlement (referred to as *peté* or market), similar to the fort, was enclosed within mud walls and surrounded by a thorn-filled moat.

In the past five centuries, Bengaluru has grown from that medieval nucleus into the sprawling metropolis with a vehicular population of more than 7 million. How does one relate the history of five centuries with its specific sociocultural and political economic shifts to the particularly vexatious situation many find themselves in today vis-à-vis congestion? How does one explain the intertwining of different strands in the narrative of congestion in Bengaluru, be it vehicular growth, multiple bureaucratic interventions, flooding, worker unrest, or morphological structure of the city? The means to answer this question is to rely on history as a resource. Colin Divall, a historian of transport and mobility, has enjoined us to create a "usable past" (Divall 2010, 939). History in this understanding (especially its record of generations of social, political, and economic choices) is a context that exerts a powerful shaping influence on restricting how we view contemporary issues, as well as the range of choices available in addressing them.[23] History then becomes an important tool to not only understand how the present (of a congested city) came to be but also reveals how we perceive congestion in a particular way while disregarding other aspects of congestion in plain sight.[24]

Accordingly, I present a layered periodization of the history of congestion in Bengaluru over the past two centuries. But despite this expansive focus, much of the period of interest is on the twentieth century.[25] Table 2.1 presents the periodization of the evolution of congestion in Bengaluru.

Locating Congestion

This schema recalls similar yet different periodizations of urban change in the city. Pani (2009) presents stages in Bengaluru's emergence as a resource city in different historical phases of globalization: a colonial stage, a garment stage, and an information technology stage. While Pani adopts a predominantly macropolitical economic reading of urban change, Nair's (2013) nuanced understanding of urban change, fostered through the complex interaction of power, spatial intervention, and urban organization, presents a periodization that centers on stages of urban modernization. Thus, Bengaluru's existence as a modern city is constituted through sequential phases of indigenous modern, colonial modern, national modern, and global modern—each with its characteristic urban form and particular techniques of exerting institutional power to make spatial organization.

In table 2.1, I set out four phases of congestion spanning a period of more than two hundred years to historically locate the experience of congestion in Bengaluru. I record four phases of congestion in four sequential periods—native congestion (1799–1881), bacteriological congestion (1881–1949), unplanned congestion (1949–1991), and flow congestion (since 1991). I assess each phase of congestion along four axes: key actors, diagnosis of congestion, spatial intervention, and residues. The first axis lists the actors who in each period have been confronted and provoked by what

Table 2.1
Periodization of Congestion in Bengaluru

Phase of Congestion	Key Actor(s)	Diagnosis of Congestion	Instrumental Intervention	Residues
Disorderly congestion (1799–1881)	Colonial government	Native disorder	Parallel city, "British" municipalization	Colonial enclaves, materialized offices
Unhealthy congestion (1881–1949)	Mysore government	Unhealthy overcrowding	Planned layouts, technological instruments	Sanitary water drains, sociospatial segregation
Unplanned congestion (1949–1991)	Planning bureaucracy and parastatals	Unplanned growth and population increase	Master planning, green belt, satellite townships, industrial dispersion	Pervasive illegalities Parastatal organizations
Blocked congestion (1991-present)	Public private partnership, Special Purpose Vehicles (SPV)	Blockage of flows	Infrastructure—flyovers, expressways	Middle-class aesthetics and land speculation

they see as a debilitating malaise at play in the city. I depict this malaise as a form of congestion, a justifiable leap given the multiple connotations associated with the word "congestion."[26] I rely on the plurality of meanings associated with the term to periodize and diagnose congestion in each phase, even when actors in these phases might not consciously self-identify the malaise as congestion. The perception of this malaise changes in each phase, and I employ the next axis, diagnosis of congestion, to assess how actors have problematized the malaise pervading Bengaluru. A diagnosis of congestion in the city becomes the impetus for the key actors of that phase to intervene in reordering urban space. The next axis catalogs the spatial interventions that have been authored in Bengaluru to address the diagnosis of congestion. The final axis describes the residues or outcomes that have manifested in the long run from the spatial interventions in the city. Spatial interventions to decongest the city often possess consequences that are not immediately evident but instead manifest themselves over time as residues on the social, political, and spatial fabric of Bengaluru. These residues then induce particular manifestations of urban morphology, land use, and infrastructures, which in turn shape the experience of congestion in the city.

Disorderly Congestion (1799–1881)

Soon after its founding in 1530, Bengaluru remained predominantly a regional military and administrative center with the adjoining *peté* housing service castes—weavers, potters, and small merchants—who catered predominantly to the fort and the needs of the immediate region. The region surrounding the inchoate urban cluster was composed of dispersed villages, whose economies were predominantly dependent on small-scale agriculture supplemented by market gardens and orchards. The system of agriculture in the Deccan Plateau (whose antiquity, according to historian Burton Stein, reached back to the first millennium in the present era) hinged on irrigation provided through interconnected networks of tanks (rain-fed storage reservoirs).[27] Indeed, over the next six centuries from the turn of the first millennium, there is almost an unbroken record of tank construction, and related maintenance and irrigation works from the southern Karnataka region surrounding Bengaluru (Dikshit, Kuppuswamy, and Mohan 1993). During that period, this region came to be ruled by several kingdoms: the Cholas, the Hoysalas, and, by the fifteenth century, the Vijayanagara empire.

Bengaluru's founding as a strategic capital for a regional chief in the early sixteenth century was conditioned by a unique pattern of distributed sovereignty in the Vijayanagara kingdom.[28] Bengaluru, founded by the chieftain Kempegowda, initially as a military encampment (*palayam*), transformed over time into an urban place (Gupta 1991, 129). The weakening and imminent collapse of the Vijayanagara kingdom in the mid-seventeenth century propelled some sweeping economic shifts in peninsular India. First, after the decisive defeat of the Vijayanagara kingdom in 1565 and the sack of the capital at Hampi to the north, interpeninsular trade routes shifted southward, thereby favoring Bengaluru with a locational advantage (Heitzman 2004, 26). Second, the faltering of the empire freed the chieftains of Bengaluru to play a stronger entrepreneurial role in developing their capital as a center of production by developing the *peté*. This they did by inviting weavers and artisans to their town and facilitating conditions for mercantile exchange (Stein 1987, 129).

By the late eighteenth century, the *peté* was a thriving center of economic production, with its success arising primarily from textile manufacture. Textile production in the city was specialized into three streams of manufacturing—export-oriented products such as silk, fine products to meet the demand of local elites, and coarse weaves for the poor (Pani, Anand, and Vyasulu 1985, 5). The demise of the Vijayanagara empire and the resulting economic changes thus created an opportunity for Bengaluru to transform from a predominantly strategic military encampment into a vital node in economic production and emporia trade (Nair 2005, 28; Gupta 1991, 125). During this period, Bengaluru *peté* retained its medieval form as a teardrop-shaped walled settlement perforated by four portals in the cardinal directions. A dense hive of streets, lanes, and tracks branched off into the quadrants formed by two intersecting avenues (one north-south and other east-west) that connected opposing sets of gates. Following a native idiom of land configuration, different quarters were allotted to different caste communities. This allocation is reflected in the *peté* by identifying localities with particular commodities or particular castes.[29] This occupational and caste-based allocation of urban space infused communities with the autonomy to organize and put their shares to use for productive, communal, ritual, or residential purposes in relative independence. The intermingling and juxtaposition of multiple everyday activities, each in intimate proximity of the other, spoke of the prevalence of a particular urban form and planning. Nair describes the early *peté* thus:

> The roads were largely meant for pedestrian traffic.... It was more likely that the street was what was left after the houses had been built.... Indeed the street was an extension of the home, with jagalis (raised platforms) flanking the entrance to the home where women often sat and worked or rested.... Other homes opened

into small private courtyards, a space for domestic chores, or sometimes places where skeins of silk were dyed in vats of colour. (Nair 2005, 46)

By the beginning of the nineteenth century, at the conclusion of the protracted Anglo-Mysore Wars, the Mysore kingdom and Bengaluru (which by that time was a part of the kingdom) had come under British colonial rule (figure 2.1 is a map of Mysore within peninsular India before the last Anglo-Mysore War of 1799).

In a move that had profound significance for the future of the city, the British in 1807 decided that they would permanently station their occupying forces in Bengaluru. British troops (including their native complement) came to be located about two miles northeast of the Bengaluru *peté*, separated from it by a broad swath of parkland and dense stands of trees. Here, British military planners had the opportunity to design a settlement (the Bangalore cantonment) distinct from the native idiom of land configuration in the *peté*. Nair (2005, 46) notes that British colonizers had very little patience for the spatial organization of the *peté* and purposely designed the cantonment to serve the needs of an administrative and military colonial elite. The physical separation between the *peté* and the cantonment was deliberate: to develop the cantonment as an alternate urban nucleus separate from the *peté* and distinct enough to prevent the gradual seeping of native ideas in use of space into the fabric of the cantonment (Pani 2010, 61). This move was reinforced by a native population (predominantly Tamils from Madras, the major English colonial outpost in South India) that was ethnically and linguistically different from the Kannada-speaking population in the *peté*.[30] Anthony King has described the urban settlement of the cantonment (like similar counterparts around India) as inscribed with specific functional, symbolic, and pedagogical motivations that reinforced the power structure of the colonial order (King 1980, 1990). At a functional level, the cantonment housed the upper echelons of the military and administrative apparatus of the British colonizers. The symbolic and pedagogical aspect of the British settlement more often than not reinforced the cantonment's functional role. Particular ideas of spatial morphology prevalent in the metropolitan society were imported and implanted in the cantonment to afford both colonizers and natives with an urban landscape and a visual experience that heightened the dominance of the colonials.

Designed primarily to service its English residents and the needs of the military personnel stationed there, the economy of the cantonment was overwhelmingly dominated by service-oriented activities, with very little productive capacity in the form of factories or artisan manufacturing.

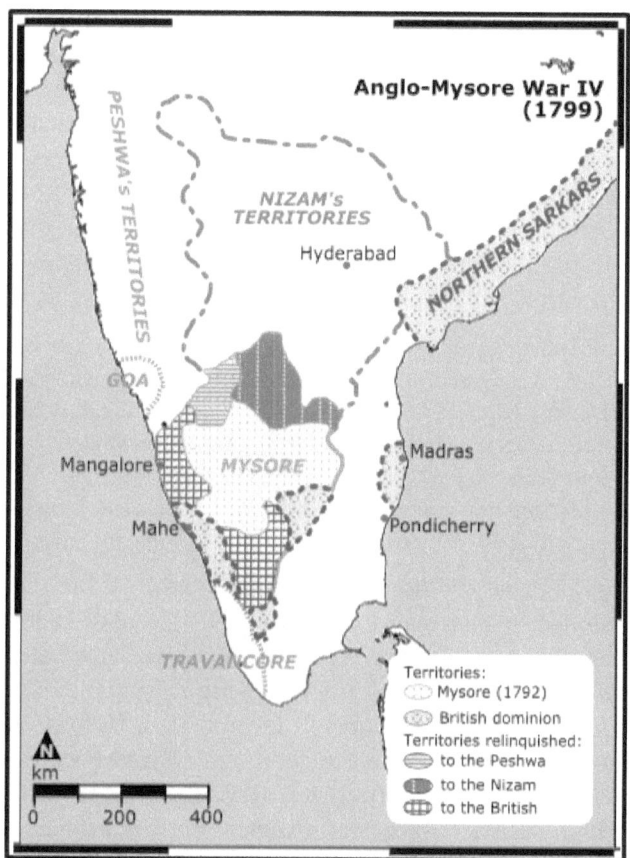

Figure 2.1
Map of Mysore in 1799 (source: Wikimedia commons).

Economic activities were confided to strictly zoned commercial and market spaces, such as Commercial Street and the General Bazaar. European homes, largely bungalows set within well-tended gardens and enclosed compounds, were similarly restricted to residential "towns," such as Cleveland Town, Pottery Town, and Langford Town.[31] In contrast, native inhabitants of the cantonment, many of whom provided domestic labor or household services, lived in densely packed settlements, often in the vicinity of European areas. At the heart of the cantonment were the barracks, administrative offices, churches, and parade grounds for English and native troops, all strung together by broad and straight tree-lined avenues built for wheeled carriages and processional marches.

For much of the nineteenth century, the key actor in the making of Bengaluru was the colonial government.[32] Starting with the establishment of the cantonment in 1807 and then continuing more directly after 1831, when the British assumed direct control over the administration of the kingdom of Mysore, the colonial government sought to intervene in urban development by introducing a radically different vocabulary and organization.[33] In Bengaluru, their effort was motivated in part by what they perceived as the disorder of the native city. A Wesleyan priest in 1840 recorded the contrast eloquently:

> Within the gate [of the peté] a scene opens, strongly contrasting with the broad avenues, the military groups, the intermingling of lawns, gardens, and villas, which grace the adjoining cantonment....You see a long, moderately narrow street, with houses of one low story, flat-roofed, whitewashed, and windowless....On turning into the bazaar...your disappointment will be woeful. Instead of grand buildings and glittering display...there is the same long narrow, low street. (Williams 2010, 85)

These scenes of perceived disorder were the ammunition the colonial government needed to intervene in the city. Between 1834 and 1870, two British commissioners, Sir Mark Cubbon and Lewin Bowring, played an indelible role in intervening in the disorderly congestion of the native city. They did so through attempts to incorporate a "British order" into the administration, which, some suggest, "transformed Bangalore from a medieval township to a modern city" (Hasan 1970, 138). The achievement of administrative reforms was manifested through the development of an impersonalized system of administration and the related location of the administrative apparatus within a centralized office housed in public administrative buildings. Administration under the commissioners was marked by the decisive shift away from the segmented system of caste leaders acting as judicio-political authorities for their respective castes toward an impersonal and unified system based on universalist principles articulated by a bureaucrat. Pani and others note some novel means adopted by the administration, ranging from caste rotation, community representation, and candidate selection, to consciously delink selection of administrators from endogamous caste monopoly. For instance, "the British adopted a policy of rotation of castes for important administrative positions in the Bangalore Cussbah [the *peté* and adjoining areas]" (Pani et al. 1985, 18).

Yet another shift was from the spatially distributed decision making within the various occupational and caste pockets in the *peté* toward its materialization within specific spaces. These spaces materialized as *cutcheries*, where the reformed administration was carried out and natives selected on the basis of social representation were invited to decide on the public affairs of the *peté* and the province at large:

> Instead, an organised Panchayat system was established throughout Mysore, and Bangalore was made the highest centre of judicial authority. This helped to establish Bangalore's supremacy as the judicial centre and therefore the inhabitants of the petteh (had to go) to various cutcheries to act as Panchayatdars there. (Pani et al. 1985, 17)

With the British assuming control over the administration of Mysore in 1831, Bengaluru became the heart of their administration. One of the first tasks to occupy their energies was to locate office spaces suitable for lodging their administration. The only buildings they identified were those located inside the fort—the palace and administrative buildings of Bengaluru's erstwhile ruler, Tipu Sultan.[34] Until 1865 at least, these offices were located in the public administrative buildings in the fort. With the resulting growth in administrative offices, the fort proved inadequate and so the Attara Katcheri (also referred to as the Old Public Office building (1867) and the new public administration buildings (1865–1866) were constructed on the parkland that separated the *peté* and the cantonment. The familiar cycle of growth in administrative capacity, resulting insufficiency in existing office space, followed by the search for newer office accommodation, and then subsequent construction of newer buildings in the urban space, has its origins in this period and was, I might add, a precursor of the congestion in the administrative center in the city.[35] During this period, the reform of native disorder in Bengaluru achieved through the process of office materialization and impersonalized administration culminated in the municipalization of the *peté* and the cantonment.[36] In 1862, the *peté* as a precolonial urban settlement with its caste-segregated warrens was transformed into a legible entity governed henceforth by an impersonal administrative apparatus as the Bangalore City Municipal Board and subsequently as the Bangalore City Municipality. The city's municipal office was located in the fort and then later shifted to the district office in the emerging administrative quarter of the city. This move marked a radical break from a native organization composed of caste-specific modes of urban governance and place-making to an impersonal and universalistic municipal organization. A majority of these administrative offices came to be located in the neutral zone separating the *peté* and the cantonment.

The disordered congestion phase, initiated within the confines of colonial contact, was predicated on a diagnosis of "native disorder." The *peté*, forged in the political economic turmoil of the late Vijayanagara period, with its spatially segmented and organizationally involuted structure was, in the minds of ruling colonials, symptomatic of congested disorder. Their solution paradoxically was marked by both disengagement and intervention. In the cantonment, they created a rival pole to the *peté* where they demonstrated an alternative vocabulary to organizing and restructuring land and social relations. Not satisfied with their urban withdrawal, in the period following 1831, the colonials intervened in the municipalization of the *peté*. This colonial strategy of decongesting Bengaluru signals the launch of instrumental approaches to managing congestion in the city. With each phase, newer instrumental approaches are inaugurated. The municipalization of Bengaluru's *peté* and cantonment with its impersonalized administrative bureaucracy and materialized offices is a legacy of decongestion from this period.

Unhealthy Congestion (1881–1949)

In 1881, the British formally transferred administrative authority to the kingdom of Mysore and its new monarch, Chamarajendra Wodeyar X, with an appointed *dewan* (prime minister) heading the kingdom's administrative machinery. Although this was a hard-fought victory for the royal family, the terms of the transfer evoked a continuing sense of anxiety (prevalent for most of this period) in the minds of the ruling elite with regard to the longevity of the kingdom. Given that the kingdom's political autonomy was entirely a British construction, which could be revoked by the colonial overlords at the slightest provocation, the ruling elite's anxiety was quite legitimate.[37] This ongoing insecurity combined with the burden of the subsidy payment to the colonial government of India generated a strategy of state-led transformation that had important consequences for the shaping of urban space. The most critical aspect was to visibly maintain continuity with the judicial, revenue, and public management systems of British administration instituted during the previous fifty years of British commissioner rule (1831–1881) in the province. This continuity was so vital to the maintenance of political autonomy that it became a constitution of sorts for a program of state action that emphasized governance while marginalizing politics or power sharing (Manor 1977; Nair 2011).[38] A second aspect of the process of state-led transformation was the fabrication of a discourse of development that undergirded the state's actions. This paradigm of development, Gowda has lucidly demonstrated, was constructed to "include the certitudes of mercantilism, social evolutionism, and orientalism" (C. Gowda

2010, 90) as conceptual bases. According to Gowda (2010), this particular construction of development was based on two contradistinctive notions. First, the Indian is, for a variety of cultural and religious reasons, backward when compared with the industrious European. The ruling elite in the kingdom operated on the assumption that it governed a people who were victims of a cultural malaise—the absence of industriousness and initiative. Thus, while addressing engineers in Mysore in 1910, engineer-turned-statesman M. Visvesvaraya (1860–1962), then *dewan* of Mysore, notes:

> There is a similar disproportion in the working and earning capacity of the two races [Indian and European] in every grade of life and in every sphere of activity.... An Englishmen, unless asleep, feels an invisible compulsion to be doing something, to consider time of some importance. With us [Indians], according to custom and tradition, the charm of life consists in ease—ease from the absence of compulsion to do anything.... Slackness is the worst curse of the country. (Visvesaraya 1917, 11)

The characterization of the Indian as slack and indolent in contrast with the industrious European is a trope that was widely shared (and rued) by the ruling elite of the kingdom. Such a bleak characterization of the Indian could not have been productive if it was not accompanied by a strategy to redress this unsatisfactory situation. The Mysore elite proposed a second notion to redress the cultural disadvantage of the indolent Indian. According to them, this disadvantage could be corrected by charting a course of state interventions. In their understanding, the development of modern scientific and technological capacity, harnessed in the service of industrial capital and more generally toward socioeconomic progress, becomes the means for realizing the transition in the archetypal Indian. Thus, addressing graduates at a university convocation in 1919, Krishnaraja Wadiyar, the maharaja of Mysore, observed that

> the modern age is characterised by knowledge and cultivation of the physical sciences and by their increasing application to the methods of economic life. Scientific knowledge and economic progress go hand in hand and form the very foundations of national life, and unless we achieve both, we are bound to fall behind in the march of progress. (Wadiyar Bahadur 1921, 250–251)

Born from its founding angst to maintain political autonomy in a colonial context, this particular discourse of development in the colonial Mysore state had a profound influence on the elaboration of processes of deliberate change constituted as a "development regime" (Ludden 2005). A development regime comes to include, as articulated by Ludden, "institutions of education, research, media, technology, science, and intellectual influence," which wield power and authority in society far in excess of the government alone because it resides also within "physical instruments of power over nature" and "cultural instruments of authority over people's minds and morality" (Ludden 2005, 4043). By incorporating and embedding science and technology within statecraft, development regimes indicate their predilection for furthering particular political projects. This was particularly true of the British colonial regime in India. As historians of science and technology have conclusively shown, for the British in India, science and technology were pliable instruments of power in the construction and maintenance of the colonial enterprise and in reinforcing the civilizing mission of the late colonial state in India (see Adas 1990; Arnold 2000). Struggling with the exigencies of conserving a modicum of autonomy in the context of indirect colonial rule, the state of Mysore sought to employ science and technology to further colonial recognition, which, governing elites reasoned, was the strongest insurance against political takeover of the kingdom.

Bengaluru, as the largest city[39] as well as the administrative and commercial center of Mysore, emerged as a crucial site for this development regime for gaining colonial recognition. Over seventy years (1881–1949), one sees the steady accretion of a backbone of scientific and technological capacity, which arose from the synergies of locating producers and consumers of institutionalized science and technology in close proximity within the city. Thus, public institutions of higher education in science and engineering, research institutes, and administrative offices jostled with a growing cluster of modern industrial enterprises. Producers and consumers of science and technology, the kingdom's elites were convinced, would collectively engender an orientation toward a scientized process of social and economic change. Textile mills were frontrunners in this process in Bengaluru. Early landmarks included the opening of the Maharaja of Mysore Spinning and Manufacturing Mills in 1884, followed by the Bangalore Woolen, Cotton, and Silk (known later as Binny) Mills in 1887 (Singh 1964, 51). The pace of industrialization accelerated with the inauguration of the Kaveri Electric Power Scheme in 1900 and the subsequent expansion in electricity generation and distribution.[40] Private entrepreneurs launched new mills in 1919, 1922, and 1925. In the absence of wider private investment, the Mysore government pioneered industrialization in the interwar period by nurturing both government-owned industries, such as the Government Soap Factory in 1917, Government Porcelain Factory in 1930, and Government Electric Factory in 1935, as well as state-supported private enterprises, such as Mysore Lamp Works in 1937, Mysore Chrome Tanning Company in 1935, and Mysore Stoneware Pipes and Potteries in 1937.[41]

In the meantime, the thickening of Bengaluru as a node for technoscientific education, research, and for its utilization in statecraft was well underway. This was realized through the founding of educational and research institutions, the presence of a critical mass of government administrative establishments, and the existence of networks for the circulation of ideas between educational enterprises and administrative decision makers. The ruling elites surmised that through such actions, it would be possible to raise a citizenry that was not just engaged with Mysore's developmental project but also possessed a rational and scientific temper to intervene effectively in reshaping Bengaluru and, ultimately, the Mysore kingdom. In this administrative enterprise, the Mysore monarch was aided by *dewans* who embodied a rational outlook to the fullest. Imbued with enormous utilitarian zeal, Visvesvaraya an engineer who served as *dewan* of Mysore from 1912 to 1917, epitomized this perspective. In a speech to Central College in 1912, he clarifies that education divorced of the objective of urban social reform is not a goal worth aspiring for:

> It is not in the glory of Bangalore as a seat of learning that we are interested. What intimately concerns us is the equipment of the city for developing the intellectual ability and executive power of our citizens and for the training it should afford to prepare future manufacturers, merchants, business men, economists, lawyers, sanitarians, engineers, statesmen, etc. (Visvesvaraya, 1917, 27)

This strong reform-inflected vision for the goal of learning, analyzing, and intervening, underlies many of the Mysore regime's showpieces—its newly established colleges, technical schools, and research laboratories. This is exemplified in the founding of the Indian Institute of Research, an institute for research and learning in both theoretical and applied technology and sciences. The foundation of this institute was laid in 1911 by the maharaja with the express purpose of contributing to an industrial renaissance and to "develop the Arts and Industries on scientific lines" (Wadiyar Bahadur 1921, 124). Yet another step in the direction of technological literacy was met with the establishment of an engineering college in 1917. The college, a constituent of the University of Mysore, granted its students degrees in civil or mechanical engineering. Wider technical literacy at the operational level was provided through industrial schools such as the Mechanical Engineering School in 1913, the Government Weaving Institute in 1912, and the Krishnarajendra Silver Jubilee Technological Institute in 1938.[42]

Both the ideas and trained persons produced by Bengaluru's educational establishments of science found a ready home within the growing administrative apparatus of the kingdom housed in the city and centered around the Attara Katcheri. In addition to other administrative departments, this is where the *dewan*'s office was located (Hasan 1972, 143). With the Attara Katcheri as hub, the expansion of administrative capacity was marked by a creeping occupation of the parkland (the contemporary Cubbon Park) that formed the axis linking the city and the Civil and Municipal Station (Nair 2002, 1205). Numerous offices of the Mysore government, district and subdivisional offices, the police headquarters, city magistrate courts, the revenue office, the Bangalore jail, and the British Residency radiated out from the Attara Katcheri.[43]

The concentration of the administrative apparatus in the heart of the city made a vital contribution to the circulation of a rational discourse in the city. In addition to injecting ideas of rationality and development into public discourse, the government played an equally important role as a consumer of products, processes, and systems of technoscience. Thus, the Government Central Industrial Workshop was developed in 1897 for "manufacturing general engineering equipment such as trusses, tanks, and castings…, undertaking repairs, and supplying spare parts to [different government departments] such as PWD [public works department], and Sanitary and Electrical departments" (Government of Karnataka 1990, 269). Similarly, the Mysore Industrial and Testing Laboratory was established in 1931 to test products or processes to be purchased by the government. Such entities realized the role of incorporating technoscience within the daily job of running the administration.

Multiple quasi-governmental and private networks arose at this time to facilitate the circulation and maintenance of a rational discourse that advanced socioeconomic development and scientific advances as critical to comprehensive social transformation. Mysore's pioneering deliberative bodies, the Representative Assembly (established in 1881) and the Legislative Council (established in 1907), performed a salutary role in enjoining citizens to engage with the government-modulated development discourse.[44] The Mysore Economic Conference, founded in 1911 as a specialized deliberative body, which by providing an ongoing interface for the official bureaucracy with "men of enlightenment, public-spirited citizens, prominent agriculturists, merchants etc." (C. H. Rao 1929a, 1), extended an additional avenue for mobilizing a rational developmental discourse.[45]

Within Bengaluru itself, the construction and circulation of this powerful discourse of improvement aided by a technoscientific backbone of industries and educational institutions had the effect of categorizing the city as congested and in need of urban reform. Congestion in Bengaluru during this period was predicated on a complex absence of well-being. This lack was understood in a manner that surfaced interconnected spatial, social, biomedical, and technical aspects. The remedies proposed to counter this debilitating condition accordingly manifested spatial, social, biomedical, and technical features. I refer to the recognition of complex impairment in Bengaluru's condition during this period as an unhealthy congestion. In doing so, I am echoing Ranganathan's observation that "colonial administrators [in Bengaluru] felt compelled to create a modern bacteriological city cleansed of social and physical ills, an adjunct to capitalist urbanization, by laying a sewerage network for the city" (Ranganathan 2015, 1309).[46] Bengaluru, as host to an unhealthy congestion, was the arena for a range of interventions that resulted in a dramatic shift in its spatial, technological, and social constitution. The government of Mysore, with its strongly interventionist discourse and technological instruments, was the key actor in addressing the unhealthy congestion.

As early as 1894, Bengaluru, especially the environs of the city (previously called the *peté*) and the native bazaar in the civil and military station, were being referred to as overcrowded and congested areas where houses were constructed in close proximity with inadequate light and ventilation and roads were too narrow. Rice in the *Mysore Gazetteer* notes,

> Owing to the circumstances of its origin, the rapid growth of the town and the various hands through which it has passed, the streets in the old parts are often narrow and mostly irregular in appearance....Bangalore, however, presents the lively aspect of a Hindu town, the main streets being generally crowded, with pedestrians, among whom vehicles of all kinds, from the carriage or brougham of the high official to the rude jatka of the merchant trader and the slow and heavy-laden bullock cart, thread their difficult way through dint of vociferous shout....The peculiar odours of the eastern bazaar pervade the streets...and the universal babel gives evidence of the out-door life of the people. (Rice 1897, 44–45)

While Rice was content referring to the "peculiar odours" encountered, the famous writer R. K. Narayan was more direct. For him, the old part of the city was not only congested in appearance but was a cesspool that breeds vermin and was therefore ripe for reordering:

> And here we have closely packed houses, abutting shop fronts, narrow winding roads, and a perfect jam of pedestrians and vehicles; and behind all this is a dizzying network of lanes and by-lanes. The Municipality has a great deal to do here. It should be an up-hill task to...straighten the roads...and clear away, choking, vermin-breeding buildings. (Narayan 1944, 70)

These impressionistic views of congestion and overcrowding noted by visitors to the city were often corroborated in official reports that located the old city or the native settlements in the civil and military station as primary loci for epidemic outbreaks.[47] Compounding the congestion on the streets, the arrangements for proper flows of human waste emissions from within the domestic confines to the exurb were subject to frequent disruption, which resulted in their mixing with and overwhelming other flows that coursed through Bengaluru. Prior to 1896, when the city started receiving piped water supply, most residents were dependent on water from the Dharmambudhi and the Sampangi tanks for their daily needs. The water from these tanks was distributed around the city through open-air supply channels to a system of troughs (or *karanjis*) from where inhabitants could draw water (Srinivas 2013a, 11).

This system of water conveyance was particularly susceptible to fouling on account of several factors. First, wastewater exiting households followed open-air drains that during periods of excess flow (such as during rains) intermingled with water flows in the supply channels. Second, during summer, when the Dharmambudhi tank was dry, it was not unusual for the dry tank bed and supply channels to find alternate use as a latrine. Srinivas notes that "as a result when the rains came all the filth was deposited into the tank and it emitted an offensive smell" (Srinivas 2013a, 11). Finally, prior to 1882, most people in the city relied on cesspit latrines, which deposited human excrement within pits that required periodic emptying by the municipal "scavenger." Given the cheek-by-jowl nature of dwellings in the city, there was usually no alternative access (by means of, say, a conservancy lane) for the scavenger to evacuate the latrine other than entering the resident's home. But the act of entering the home was considered a major transgression within the caste-segregated arrangements of dwelling prevalent in the city at the time. Thus, in many cases, latrines were evacuated only every two or three years. Extended periods for discharge of latrine pits made them particularly vulnerable to overflow onto streets and drains, contributing further to the unsanitary constitution of the city.[48]

The multiple mingling of metabolic flows in the streets of the old city and native bazaar was particularly problematic for a new breed of sanitary engineers and public health inspectors who made their entry in Bengaluru from the 1880s.[49] From 1892 on, Mysore organized a separate sanitary department as part of the government's public works department with the express purpose of designing and executing water supply, drainage, and conservancy works throughout the kingdom (C. H. Rao 1929b, 358). A sanitary engineer headed this department. At the municipal level, sanitation emerged as a priority in both the city and the civil and military station by 1862 when a conservancy tax (*kachara terige*), related to the size of the dwelling, was levied on residents (Government of Karnataka 1990, 650). In 1882, the Bangalore city municipality decreed a municipal bylaw requiring daily evacuation of latrines by municipal workers.[50] That sanitation occupied considerable energy in the municipality is evident in the size of municipal expenditures devoted to conservancy work. Conservancy accounted for 18,035 rupees out of a net municipal expenditure of 157,207 rupees in 1893–1894 (Rice 1897, 50), which then rose to 35,000 rupees from a net municipal expenditure of 250,000 rupees in 1903–1904 (Meyer et al. 1908, 368).

The declining reliance on tanks for providing water supply and on open air water supply channels and stormwater channels to ferry water to residents and then to downstream tanks precipitated a shift in the alignment of the social, spatial, and technological facets of the city's hydrological infrastructure. Malini Ranganathan documents "the recasting of 'stormwater drains' as 'sanitary water drains' was set in motion by the colonial project of improvement" (Ranganathan 2015, 1309). She patches together a story of multiple coincidences. First, changing technological paradigms of municipalization happening elsewhere in the world, in the context of the politics of colonial recognition in Mysore, led to the installation of piped and treated water supplies in the late nineteenth century in Bengaluru. This prompted the progressive disuse of tanks and open-air water channels as sources of water. Second, the characterization of native modes of inhabiting the city as environmentally unsanitary and morally inferior prompted a process of overhauling the waste management regime in the city. Stormwater channels for discharging urban wastes earlier, maintained through community efforts, became locations for an incipient sewer network. The shift in the physical reality of these channels was accompanied by a terminological shift with these channels being recast as receptacles for the filth and refuse of urbanization. The residues(!) of this shift, as Ranganathan points out, exist to the present day, with channels that at one time conveyed water now carrying a potent sludge of sewer pipes, untreated sewage, industrial wastes, and solid wastes, thereby elevating the risk of flooding in the city.[51]

Although a major spatial intervention, the reconstitution of stormwater channels wasn't the only intrusion on urban space in the city. This period also bore witness to the initiation, tentatively at first and then with deliberate energy, of planned residential divisions that incorporated new norms of modern hygiene and sanitation, while at the same time explicitly retaining primeval social norms of caste and hierarchy. Between 1898 and 1899, Bangalore's predominantly native residents—in both the city and the civil and military station—struggled with an epidemic of the bubonic plague.[52] Even as the disease wrought havoc on residents, with about ten thousand deaths reported in Bengaluru and the surrounding district alone (Heitzman 2004, 33), a quarter of the residents deserted the city, precipitating the collapse of city commerce. The outbreak of the disease proved to be a watershed for efforts to sanitize and decongest the city. In addition to some near-term measures directed at decontaminating the city,[53] several longer-term actions sought to employ epidemic prevention as a motivation to dramatically alter the sociospatial organization in the city and, more important, rejig the relation between residents and urban space. One of the first actions undertaken by the Mysore government was to employ the plague as a pretext to decongest the old quarter of the city. Hundreds of houses, deserted on account of death or infection, were demolished. A joint executive committee formed by the city as well as the civil and military station gave special attention to standards of sanitation, building occupation, and provision of light and ventilation. And as drains in the city were repaired and cleaned, houses were regularly inspected to assess their standards of sanitation. About 651 houses were considered unfit for occupation and were demolished. With a view to easing overcrowding, the extremely congested old Tharagupet locality was partially demolished and a new Tharagupet developed to accommodate the spillover. A further 893 houses were "marked under the Land Acquisition Act for opening new roads and lanes in the congested part of the city" (Government of Karnataka 1990, 90).[54]

Plague infestation in Bengaluru evoked a more systemic response beyond these reactionary instances of dealing with congestion. Both municipalities, the city as well as the civil and military station, undertook to plan, with some urgency, the expansion of the city and the provision of well-spaced and well-drained housing sites.[55] These planned extensions to both municipalities were conceived of by special town improvement committees, which the Mysore government constituted periodically. According to town and country planning norms, extensions were "laid out in gridiron or chess-board plan. [These extensions] were rectangular with boundary roads running north and south and east and west" (C. H. Rao 1929b, 113). Two extensions to the city in 1898 can be traced to the immediate postplague urban scenario. Malleshwaram (291 acres) and Basavangudi (404 acres) were laid out in the north and south of the city as model suburbs that offered an alternative hygienic lifestyle to the crowded and congested old quarter.[56] Both extensions set new standards of sanitation. Conservancy lanes, dedicated to channeling waste flows through underground sewers and open drains, ran behind houses in these extensions. The hermetic separation of metabolic flows promised by the extensions offered such elevated levels of sanitation that planners spoke of these extensions as "plague-proof towns" that were not just improved ways of living but were also pedagogical in the sense that there can "be no going back to the Indian method of constructing abutting buildings with no voids between them" (Stephens 1922, 238).[57]

The Bangalore Town Improvement Committee was reconstituted multiple times (in 1908, 1913, and 1922) after the plague to plan and organize new extensions to the city that gave concrete form to decongesting and sanitizing the city. The city and civil and military station together assembled nearly thirty extensions during this period. However, even as they operated with sanitary zeal, planners and engineers took scrupulous care to ensure that these planned layouts conformed closely to the implicit caste-based segregated hierarchy. Brahmins overwhelmingly monopolized multiple fields of Bengaluru's social, economic, and political action during this period. Until 1920 at least, Brahmin men dominated almost the entire senior administration of Mysore's government. Even while acquiring modernist aspirations, nascent news and media organizations, leading lights of the modernist *Navya* literary movement in Kannada, as well as budding theater, music, and film societies, were nevertheless managed almost entirely by Brahmins. In a society where Brahmins almost exclusively dictated social order, spatial order in the new extensions could not but have been reflective of it. Nair is incisive in her comments:

> Within these layouts, hierarchies revolved around caste...so that the largest and best-placed sites were for the Brahmin community...[and] the five principal divisions for the different castes were limited by cross roads....Physical distance between homes thus considerably diminished the possibility of undesirable social contact....Malleshwaram similarly had eight blocks, one for each "particular section of the people." (Nair 2005, 51)

Addressing unhealthy congestion in Bengaluru was aided by the simultaneous circulation and accretion of multiple facets—a discourse of improvement born out of a foundational anxiety among Mysore's governing elites; reliance on a technoscientific logic for articulating the developmental discourse; a zeal for sanitizing the city from pathogens and cultural ways of inhabiting; and a scrupulous attention to maintaining the hierarchical social order. This particular patterning of unhealthy congestion in Bengaluru cast some long-lasting residues within the urban fabric. A technoscientific logic to development, the recasting of waterways as waste channels, the characterization of native modes of urban living as unhygienic, and caste-based spatial orders have been manifestations of decongestive efforts since this time.

Unplanned Congestion (1949–1991)

A defining start to this period occurred in 1949 with the union of the municipalities of Bangalore City and the Bangalore civil and military station into the Bangalore City Corporation (known in Kannada as the Bengaluru Mahanagara Palike, or BMP; Heitzman 2004, 41). The amalgamation of the two municipal entities into the BMP, happening as it did in the first years after India's independence in August 1947, was an occasion for the inauguration of a dramatically altered apparatus for governing processes of spatial planning, land acquisition, and infrastructure planning. This apparatus was at least explicitly motivated by an imaginary of congestion in cities. Congestion is imagined in this phase as the result of two moments: the increase in an urban population classed primarily as workers employed in industrial establishments and the unplanned expansion of the city to meet the needs of this inflow.

The footing for this apparatus of urban planning has roots within the broader national Nehruvian discourse on socialist-style planning of the economy and society in independent India, which heavily prioritized a scientific approach to state-led intervention (B. Chakrabarty 1992).[58] The insertion of this interventionist discourse of development onto processes of spatial reordering in Bengaluru was aided by the parallel presence of strong impulses for improving urban space in postcolonial Mysore.[59] We saw in the previous section that Bangalore town improvement committees were periodically constituted to plan and develop residential extensions. By 1945, this process had congealed into permanence with the passage of the Bangalore City Improvement Act of 1945, which brought into being the Bangalore City Improvement Trust (BCIT) as a permanent body. The BCIT was tasked with "(i) Extensions of residential areas to relieve the congestion in the city; (ii) Construction of houses for middle and lower middle class people; (iii) Location of industrial suburbs for large and small industries; (iv) Laying out of industrial housing areas" (Singh 1964, 110). The notable difference between its objectives and its earlier manifestation as the town improvement committee was in the priority given to industrial planning. This priority was a reflection of the emergence of Bengaluru by the early 1950s as a growing nucleus for massive public sector enterprises that provided employment to thousands of workers.[60] Rapid industrialization and related housing and servicing needs over the next decades only escalated the strident demand for planning instruments to manage this process.

With independent India's swing toward import substitution policies that privileged the development of indigenous manufacturing capacity sheltered within state-owned enterprises, publicly owned industries emerged as favored pathways for industrialization. In Bengaluru, four large public sector units (PSU)—Hindustan Aircraft Ltd., Indian Telephone Industries, Bharat Electronics Ltd., and Hindustan Machine Tools—were established on the western and northern outskirts of Bengaluru.[61] These units became important anchors for an industrial ecosystem composed of ancillary small and medium industries and informal repair and tooling workshops that sprang up and depended on these larger units for subcontracting opportunities (Heitzman 1999, PE-3).[62] With employment in these units ranging between five thousand and fifty thousand, these units collectively accounted for more than eighty thousand jobs in the city even as late as 1991, when the era of public sector enterprises was in irrevocable decline. Many thousands more depended on these units indirectly for their employment. Both Nair and Heitzman in their histories of the city document the role of these public sector units as a powerful engine not only for demographic growth but also for the urban economy. Heitzman, specifically notes:

> The addition of 30,000 public sector manufacturing jobs on the outskirts of the city within a period of less than twenty years helped drive the metropolitan population to 1,207,000 in 1961 and significantly increased the pressure on infrastructure. It also irrevocably shifted the economic balance of the area around the city. In 1951, 71 percent of the workers in Bangalore District still worked in agriculture; by 1961, this had declined to 50 per cent, and by 1971, to 40 per cent. (Heitzman 2004, 45)

The combined economic and demographic shift, orchestrated by Bengaluru's PSUs, were significant drivers in the reordering of the city.[63] Starting in 1961 with the passage of the Mysore (now Karnataka) Town and Country Planning Act (KTCP), the state of Karnataka inaugurated "a process architecture that embeds not only the rationality to plan a 'good' urban form but also possesses technologies of control (backed by the full force of law) to prescribe, govern, and proscribe certain kinds of urban land-use" (Sundaresan, 2013, 120–122).[64] The KTCP legislated into reality the Bangalore Local Planning Area, the territory over which the Bangalore Local Planning Authority (constituted in August 1967) had exclusive jurisdiction to ordain the mosaic of land use in the city (Ravindra 1996, 92).[65] The instrument for achieving this goal was the development plan or the master plan. Development plans for Bengaluru, legitimized by formal legislative authority, begin with the interim Outline Development Plan (ODP) of 1972 followed by the Comprehensive Development Plan (CDP) of 1984.[66] Given its legal base in the KTCP, the planning authority for the city as the executor of the CDP commands absolute authority over land use and the process of land use change in the city. Land use change that does not conform to the proposals for land categorization and zoning contained in the CDP stand in violation of its KTCP mandate and is illegal and therefore penalizable by law.

The creation of a planning apparatus in Bengaluru was paralleled by a momentous shift toward professionalizing Karnataka's public administration. Up to the 1960s, line departments of the state governments, staffed by full-time generalist bureaucrats, conducted much of the administration in Mysore state. By the 1960s, several new demands for growth and development created new imperatives for bureaucratic capacity. For one, advancing private industrial growth could no longer be limited to providing a favorable policy environment; instead, governments were increasingly required to nurture the industrial sector by ordering advantageous factors of production, such as land, capital, and training. This form of intensive state involvement called for agencies that accomplished specialized tasks. Furthermore, rapid population growth in cities like Bengaluru became the prompt for an enhanced capacity to deliver essential services like water supply and sewerage, transport, and electricity.

This capacity was especially required to execute more sophisticated technical projects, for example, to pipe water from distant sources. In Bengaluru's case, by the 1960s, it was evident to the Mysore government that the city's need for water could not be met by local sources like the CRS waterworks at Tippagondanahalli. Instead, water would have to be pumped uphill over 100 kilometers from the Cauvery River. Executing the project with its numerous technical, administrative, and jurisdictional challenges was far beyond the capacity of the city government.[67] Spearheading social and economic development in the 1960s therefore prefigured a new architecture of public management that not only possessed specialized technical and administrative capacity but also entailed the political space within which to operate unhindered. Statutory entities (also referred to as parastatal bodies), constituted through an act of the state legislature, arose as a vehicle of choice to achieve these objectives.[68] Since then, the state has extensively used the possibility of constituting parastatal bodies for achieving particular tasks. A commentator on the state's administration suggests that these organizations contribute to the systemic undermining of local democracy:

> Karnataka has a large number of parastatal bodies.... Boards and corporations are parastatal bodies. They are single-purpose organizations which, while being part of the government enjoy a certain amount of autonomy, as they are incorporated bodies. As such they are independent from normal government functioning regarding such matters as appointments, raising of loans from banks, expenditure etc. And yet, the state government often stands guarantee for loans taken by them. (Chandrashekhar 2011, 68–69)

In response to the specter of population and economic growth and associated social, economic, and technical challenges looming over Bengaluru, the state instituted numerous single-purpose parastatal bodies centered on the city. The task of purveying urban infrastructure, given its technical challenges, was readily parceled out to the Karnataka State Road Transport Corporation (constituted in 1961 with the Bangalore Transport Service as a division to service intracity travel) and Bangalore Water Supply and Sewerage Board in 1964. Constructing affordable housing for low-income groups, especially those living in informal settlements, was assigned to the Karnataka Housing Board (established in 1962) and the Karnataka Slum Clearance Board (in 1973). The financing of industrial development was farmed out to the Karnataka Industrial Investment and Development Corporation (in 1964), while the Karnataka Industrial Area Development Board (in 1966) assumed the contentious role of land acquisition agent for individual industrial ventures and industrial enclaves.

Karnataka government's preference for professionalizing public administration had its ripples in Bengaluru's planning apparatus. Up to the mid-1970s, the Bangalore Local Planning Authority developed proposals for land use planning, while the City Improvement Trust developed residential layouts and sites to house the city's growing population. The presence of these two agencies operating under dissimilar legal frameworks and the resulting absence of coordination between the planning and development aspects of land use in the city became the pretext for establishing a single entity that would integrate and professionally manage Bengaluru's land control. In 1976, the state government established the BDA as a statutory parastatal body to incorporate, within one organization, both planning and development functions. The BDA is vested with enormous planning and executive powers to accomplish its legislative mandate. In exerting its mandate, BDA is also armed with powers to penalize inappropriate land development in the city, regulate construction activity, and acquire private land to develop housing and commercial complexes in the public interest.

This institutional structure of planning and development for Bengaluru is undergirded by two intentions. First, planning is a practice of state intervention, which rectifies the congestion caused by unplanned growth by promoting a dispersed and therefore healthier urban settlement. The objectives of the KTCP Act of 1964 clarify this purpose by proposing "(i) to create conditions favorable for planning... with a view to providing full civic and social amenities for people in the state... (iv) to direct the future growth of populated areas in the state with a view to ensuring desirable standards of health and hygiene" (Government of Karnataka 1963, 65). From the act's objectives, it is clear that the planned growth of cities will contribute to relieving the ill effects of congestion. Second, professional public management of the planning process is essential to fully realize the social benefits of rectifying unplanned urban growth. The BDA Act of 1976 that brought the BDA into being specifies that "haphazard and irregular growth would continue unless checked by the Development Authority and it may not be possible to rectify or correct mistakes in the future" (Government of Karnataka 1976, 103). Born from this surety of purpose, the planning apparatus deploys some specific techniques, mechanisms, and measures to ensure a planned and otherwise dispersed settlement pattern.

One planning technique for gauging and shaping urban settlements is by relying on the categorization of land use into parcels identified as, for example, residential, commercial, open spaces, transportation, or agricultural. This technique forms the basis for most forms of planning instruments. Land use classification paves the way for at least two pathways to dictate the spread and dispersal of settlement patterns in the city and thereby alter patterns of congestion. First, at an aggregate urban level, land use categorization is a means of conceiving the desirable city that has the optimum amount of land dedicated to particular kinds of permitted uses. Ravindra suggests that Bengaluru's CDP of 1985 was influenced by the norms for optimum land use ratios in a city laid down by the national Town and Country Planning Organisation (TCPO; Ravindra 1996, 100). The TCPO suggests that good land use patterns required metropolitan cities to aspire toward reserving 35 to 40 percent of their land to residential use, 12 to 14 percent for industrial use, and 4 to 5 percent for commercial use (Ministry of Urban Affairs and Employment 1996, 147). Such a normative pattern of land use is ultimately derived from the requirement to ensure that population densities in large and metropolitan cities in the country remain within one hundred to two hundred persons per hectare (146). The subtext being that the denser cities are, the more congested, unhealthy, and unproductive they become. The desirable pattern of land use also forms the basis for a normative structure for processes of urbanization at work in the city. This structure needs to reconcile concentrative and deconcentrative thrusts of urban growth. Thus, mechanisms are introduced within the planning framework to nudge processes of urbanization toward desirable ends. For example, mechanisms such as growth boundaries or green belts are fundamentally concentrative by preventing expansion beyond a limit, while satellite townships and growth poles attempt to siphon growth away from centers of concentration by dispersing growth. The planning processes in Bengaluru, be it BDA's CDP of 1985 or the metropolitan region's structure plan of 1995 incorporated both these mechanisms.[69]

Second, categorization prescribes or proscribes particular forms of land use within broad classifications. Thus, the planning instrument permits only a narrowly specified list of uses within each category, be they residential, commercial, industrial, or something else. For example, BDA's zoning regulation C1 within the commercial category permits, among other things, minor shops or milk booths, and tutorial centers not exceeding fifty square meters. Regulation I1 within the industrial category permits such uses as the manufacture of aerated water and food beverages, bedding material, printing, and publishing, while T1 in the transport category allows multilevel car parking, bus shelters, or gas stations (BDA 2007, 12–15). The mix of commercial (C1, C2, C3, C4, or C5), industrial (I1, I2, I3, I4, or I5), transportation (T1, T2, T3, T4), and urban amenities (U1, U2, U3 or U4) categories that are permissible within the confines of a particular locality is strictly limited and controlled by the zoning regulations.

A development technique that seeks to deconcentrate the built-up area is through building bylaws that intervene at the level of individual structures and plots. These bylaws specify the relation between a building and the plot of land on which it is constructed. In this way, new construction is adequately spaced and ventilated, and the densities of inhabitation are reduced. Bengaluru's building laws specify four measures to control the concentration of inhabitation: maximum plot coverage (as a percent of plot area), floor-area ratio (FAR), setbacks, and maximum height (Ravindra 1996, 109). By varying the allowable limits of these measures across the city, planners exert a clear preference for the nature of the built environment in the city. The 1984 CDP demarcates the city into three zones: A—intensely populated areas, B—the central administrative area and its surroundings, and C—all other areas within the conurbation (Ravindra 1996). Within each of these zones, the permissible magnitude of each measure is altered to reflect the plan's preference for spacing and separation.

The institutionalization of this elaborate apparatus for land control, despite its grounding within an extensive legal framework composed of laws, rules, measures, and enforcement mechanisms, has engendered pervasive illegality by the state and citizens in the use of land and the construction of buildings. Based on anecdotal evidence, Sundaresan records that 50 to 75 percent of the buildings in Bengaluru are constructed in violation of planning norms (Sundaresan 2013, 19). These violations in planning guidelines are not quite this easily categorizable, however. The imprint of violations includes multiple social groups and locations. A diversity of structures such as private apartment complexes, upper-middle-class bungalows, lower-middle-class revenue layouts (privately designed housing subdivisions), and urban poor settlements are implicated in a vast network of illegal transactions involving the use of land. Illegality is produced not only through covert actions undertaken under the cover of darkness or through stealth, as when a home owner violates zoning laws to rent a portion of his or her home to a commercial enterprise, but also through overt and everyday actions. Thus, the affluent homeowner who occupies the sidewalk in front of his house to construct a private garden or the local community that builds a shrine on the sidewalk are both in contravention of the law. State actors are equally implicated in using land in contravention of their own laws. Thus, bus termini, stadiums, or public office buildings have been built either by encroaching on tanks or in violation of zoning laws such as the green belt (Nair 2005; Sundaresan 2013). Not all of this illegality has attracted similar levels of scrutiny or concern, which leads Rosario and Liang (2006, 20) to conclude that land use possesses differential degrees of illegality. Often illegality by the state or by propertied middle classes is easily regularized by newer redefinitions of public purpose or by new iterations of the law.[70] Land uses by the urban poor through arrangements of squatting, for example, are more often than not perceived by the state as threatening and therefore become targets of evictions, bulldozing, and other forms of forced displacement.

The institutionalization of a sophisticated apparatus of master planning in this period was founded on a diagnosis of congestion in the modernizing Bengaluru. This diagnosis characterized population growth without planning as the problem. Master planning by specialized instruments, such as zoning laws and building bylaws could curb congestion in the rapidly expanding city. But the reliance on instruments of master planning to order the city has spawned multiple illegal transactions in how land is used. The pervasive illegality of master planning highlights the partialness of the decongestive thrust of this period.

Flow Congestion (1991–Present)

A watershed year in the constitution of the most recent phase of urban change and congestion in Bengaluru was 1991.[71] Riding on the national wave of economic liberalization, the year marks a decisive break in the understanding (among decision makers, middle classes, and elite corporate groups) of the role of the city. The planned city and its spatial interventions were inspired by the desire to minimize the congestion brought on by unplanned growth. In the period following 1991, although these motivations persisted, they were eclipsed by interventions rooted within a new construction of congestion understood as the blockage of metabolic flows coursing through the "body politic" (Harvey 2003) of the city.

The intense association that developed between the city and the imaginary of "Bengaluru as India's Silicon Valley" was the impetus for the constitution of this new understanding of congestion. "Bengaluru as India's Silicon Valley" was itself triggered by a diverse and rapidly expanding cluster of information and communication technology (ICT) enterprises in the city (Manimala 2008, 117), itself the product of an evolving policy, institutional, and industry landscape from the mid-1980s to the mid-1990s. Presaging the shift toward greater liberalization in 1991, the policy and institutional environment extended by the national government for the growth of ICT shifted with the predominantly restrictive "demiurge and custodial" interventions prior to the mid-1980s giving way to "midwifery and husbandry" modes of state action that encouraged private entrepreneurialism (Evans 1995, 210). Instances of liberal policies—for example, the Computer Import Policy of 1984 and the Software Export, Development and Training Policy of 1986—provided the foundation for the nascent software industry in India.[72] While the early growth of the industry on account of the supportive policy setting in the 1980s was largely driven by the overseas placement of 'bodyshopped' professionals within client organizations, growth by the early 1990s was largely being fueled by offshore turnkey contracts that overwhelmingly came to be located in Bengaluru (Parthasarathy 2004, 672; 2010; Saxenian 2002). This shift toward clustering and then the agglomeration of the IT industry in Bengaluru was a key turning point that subsequently resulted in the acquisition of the "Silicon Valley of India" designation. It was fueled by such factors as the location of the country's first software technology park, with its provision of dedicated infrastructure and communication facilities for tech entrepreneurs, and the critical presence of a technically qualified labor force in public sector units and numerous engineering colleges in the vicinity (Parthasarathy 2004; Heitzman 2001; Thatchenkery, Kash, and Stough 2004).[73]

Bengaluru's emergence as a node for IT enterprises and becoming the Silicon Valley of India was the outcome of a deliberate strategy of casting the IT industry (and allied knowledge-based productive enterprises) as a key vehicle for ushering prosperity into the country. Thus, the success of the IT industry, as indicated by its explosive growth in terms of the number of enterprises, the number of people employed, and the revenue generated, became the symbol for market-led growth within the post-1991 liberalized economic setting, which not only provided for Indians but also raised their economic status (Upadhya 2009). This industry thereby became a public justification for the national economic strategy. Champions of the IT industry with their ethical and responsible business practices and their educated middle-class roots were portrayed as icons of reform (Upadhya 2004). Corporate leaders such as N. R. Narayana Murthy and Nandan Nilekani of Infosys and Azim Premji of Wipro were contemporary India's pedagogues who could teach other Indians how best to achieve a successful presence in the globalizing world. Their insight into the contemporary global economy contained lessons for multiple social, cultural, and political arenas. Riding on this construction of a pedagogical role for the software industry starting in the 1990s, the footprint of the industry expanded across a range of urban domains, from corporate work and workplace organization and middle-class lifestyles and aesthetics, to the built environment, and, most notable, urban governance.[74]

Innovations in workplace culture and organization were a response to the high volatility in the labor market for IT professionals. They were manifested in the pervasive flexibilization of labor expressed through a range of flexible working arrangements, work timings, contracts, and locations, complemented by technological flexibility in the ability of employees to work on multiple software platforms, work routines, and technologies (Upadhya 2010). The imprint of the software industry and its personnel has been particularly foundational in the articulation of new forms of middle-class lifestyles and aesthetics.[75] As a key locus for the industry, Bengaluru has been a favored site for the expression of a middle-class public discourse. This discourse, visible in mainstream media, advertisements, and street-side billboards, constructs a desired landscape composed of malls, shopping complexes, and gated housing developments that integrate residential, commercial, leisure, and service activities with high-rise apartment complexes, all strung together seamlessly by urban infrastructures geared toward establishing and maintaining global consumerist lifestyles. This discursive landscape in the city is presented as an aspirational goal for the new middle classes to consume in their pursuit of a lifestyle indistinguishable from other global nodes.[76] A key element of this discourse is embodied within an aesthetic of the urban built environment marked by gleaming glass and steel facades, granite foyers, and manicured lawns. Stallmeyer documents how corporate ICT and real estate developers in Bengaluru profoundly impelled the emerging configurations of spatial and built form in the city toward a recognizably global or international image (though informed by local interpretations) marked most notably by what he calls "software glass":

The role of architects in the CBD, Electronics City and the future IT Corridor is, or will be, dictated in large part by the demands of ICT corporates and real-estate developers. The demands of ICT corporates and real-estate developers dictate the need for flexible interior spaces that can house the maximum number of worker cubicles, and the need for recognizably "global" and "international" imagery. (Stallmeyer 2006, 327)

Possibly the most intrusive pedagogical role adopted by the IT industry was to insert their corporate and techno-managerial acumen within urban governance in Bengaluru. Often proposed as experiments to increase the intelligence of urban management, a range of ventures led by what Solomon Benjamin calls "corporate-outsourced NGOs (CONGOs)" (Benjamin 2010, 104) came to mediate the state-citizen interface starting from 2000. These ventures ranged from formal (and more enduring) public-private platforms and planning task forces to (often sporadic) private interest groups, unofficial panels, and private consultative entities. Although distinct in their internal dynamics, two themes resonated across the new civil society organizations assembled in the city since about 2000. First, the existing infrastructure base was not only inadequate to service Bengaluru's rapid population expansion but was of inferior quality to fulfill its global ambitions. Second, there existed across the multiple participants (both public and private) in these ventures a growing sense of exasperation with the status quo on infrastructure development and services in the city. The underlying argument was that if Bengaluru's decision makers were serious about making the city a global hub, they would have to radically alter how infrastructures are conceived, executed, and used. The presence of new civil society organizations, combined with their targeted interventions in Bengaluru's infrastructure governance, are constitutive of an "elite policy circuit" in the city (Benjamin and Bhuvaneshwari 2006). This circuit, comprising a diversity of individuals, was drawn from the state's political and administrative elite, as well as chief executives of Bengaluru's infrastructure utilities and corporate leaders from the IT and allied industries.

The Bangalore Agenda Task Force (BATF), founded in 2000, was a pioneering and, in many ways, most intrusive new civil society organization.[77] It had ten members, half drawn from the corporate sector. Established with official sanction through a government order (G.O. UDD/400/MNY/99), the BATF envisioned a collaborative platform for corporate citizens to work with the city's civic stakeholders: city government (BMP), Bangalore Development Authority (BDA), police, and major utilities, such as water, electricity, and public transport. The objective was "to enable [civic] stakeholders to upgrade standards through focused capacity building" in order to "recommend appropriate technology and measures of service levels; adopt best-in-class practices; identify internal champions per project; [and implement] strategic financial interventions" (BATF 2000, 3). Despite its very broad objectives, the BATF operated within a relatively circumscribed domain of intervention, limited to physical infrastructures, especially those that had a visible presence on the urban landscape and therefore contributed directly to the image of the city:[78]

> The language, activities, and partner service providers of the BATF alongside the initiatives of the Krishna-led government promoted an overall urban development agenda centred on the provision and management of physical infrastructure without comparable emphasis on social and economic requirements of the city. (Ghosh 2005, 4916)

Interventions were directed toward infrastructures such as public toilets, road design, bus shelters, traffic signage, and street furniture (see Gopakumar 2009 for details about BATF's Nirmala Bangalore toilets). In each of these cases, BATF designed and piloted models that were to be exemplars of design processes, type of materials, and execution processes, which civic stakeholders could then replicate in the city. In 2004, Krishna was voted out of power for his aggressive Bangalore-centric policies, and the new government, nervous about voter disapproval, did not renew (something no successive government has attempted to do) the mandate of the BATF (Gopakumar 2009).

The dissolution of the BATF became the occasion for the IT industry to bring considerable pressure to bear on the government to demonstrate its seriousness in resolving infrastructure problems in Bengaluru. Prominent IT leaders such as Murthy and Premji spoke publicly against the sorry state of infrastructure in the city and how it was hindering corporate performance. Matters came to a head when the IT industry decided to boycott the state government's annual fair for the industry: BangaloreIT.com.[79] While the boycott was later reconsidered, tensions over infrastructure in the city between the government and the IT industry have been long-standing and have drawn responses from both sides. In 2008, the government of chief minister B. S. Yediyurappa created yet another infrastructure task force: the Agenda for Bengaluru Infrastructure and Development (ABIDe). Unwilling to replicate BATF's executive authority in infrastructure, ABIDe was constituted as a planning initiative that would provide a report for several civic domains, such as water supply, transportation, and governance. In January 2010, the task force produced the Plan Bengaluru 2020 report that, while focusing on infrastructure, also included allied sectors, such as heritage, the urban poor, public health, and education. In the meantime, the Bangalore City Connect Foundation (BCCF) was launched in 2007 as a private consultative body comprising industry volunteers who offered their technical and managerial expertise to support infrastructure managers. BCCF was cosponsored by the Confederation of Indian Industry (an industry lobbying group) and the Janaagraha Centre for Citizenship and Democracy.[80] Two initiatives that arose from the partnership between BCCF and government agencies were the Bangalore Traffic and Transport Initiative and Tender SURE, the latter an especially controversial effort offered a design manual to guide the process of constructing roads in the city.[81] In addition to these collaborative ventures, independent initiatives of the IT industry in association with industry associations and media have articulated urban visions, such as the Agenda for Bangalore proposed by the Bangalore Political Action Committee (BPAC) or the Bangalore–High Point in a Flat World proposed by the Bangalore Chamber of Industry and Commerce–Economic Times panel discussion.

The IT industry, with its acquisition of the Silicon Valley of India image and its resulting escalating interest in remaking the city (especially into one that prioritizes the easing of blocks to attaining world-class-city status), although a powerful influence, is not the sole performer. Public spending on infrastructure, undertaken as a means to make the city world class, routed through a parade of targeted nationally funded programs and administered by specialized infrastructure authorities in the state, reinforced this characterization of the period.

The inauguration of the process of economic liberalization in 1991 was followed by a gradual shift at the national level toward incorporating a reform agenda within public spending for urban development. Since 1991, the agenda for spending by the national government in urban development has been dominated by reforming how state and city governments directed and used funding to develop their cities. This period saw a succession of programs starting from the Mega Cities scheme and including massive programs such as the Jawaharlal Nehru National Urban Renewal Mission (JNNURM). In common across these disparate programs was a thrust toward infrastructure development and, more significant, financial sustainability. Accounting for cost recovery in infrastructure development involved instituting complex arrangements for managing infrastructure projects. State governments responded to these shifts by establishing dedicated managers. Karnataka founded the Karnataka Urban Infrastructure Development and Finance Corporation (KUIDFC) in 1993 as the nodal agency for planning, financing, and executing infrastructure projects. Since its founding, KUIDFC has become the managing agency for implementing programs of the union and state governments, as well as several projects sponsored by international funding agencies such as the World Bank and Asian Development Bank.

One of the first infrastructure programs that KUIDFC managed was the megacities scheme, initiated in 1993–1994 "to develop city-wide infrastructure in mega cities by adopting cost recovery measures to build a 'Revolving Fund' for undertaking infrastructure projects on a self-sustained basis" (KUIDFC 2006, 3-1). Under the program, various civic agencies in Bengaluru (such as BDA or BMP) executed infrastructure projects.[82] However, in the absence of a coherent plan that tied the different projects together, a key shortcoming was the inability of the projects to realize benefits at the city level (KUIDFC 2006, 3–15). In 2006, funding under this program (and other nationally sponsored urban reform programs such as City Challenge Fund and Urban Reform Incentive Fund) were subsumed within the flagship JNNURM program (2006–2015), which attempted to address the shortcoming by establishing a mandatory strategic framework for project proposals.[83] Bengaluru's city development plan's initial vision statement identifies infrastructure as the primary descriptor of a world-class city: "To transform Bangalore as world-class metropolis providing its citizens a high-quality of life in a sustainable environment, with *state-of-the-art infrastructure*, service delivery, and connectivity" (iDeCK 2006, 65; emphasis added). It then goes on to propose that one of the main reasons the city is "under stress" is the congestion in the road and transport system. The plan proposes a comprehensive mobility plan to "resolve issues pertaining to congestion in traffic and lack of transport infrastructure in the city" (iDECK 2006, 108) by nurturing public transportation and nonmotorized forms of transport, along with active discouragement of private modes. Despite this progressive strategy, a majority of the twenty projects (including twelve grade separators and underpasses) that received funding from JNNURM were designed to ease the movement of automotive (predominantly privately owned) traffic at key intersections in the city. Fed by national funding priorities, state decision makers and project managers have arrived at infrastructure as the predominant pathway to shape a world-class Bengaluru by eliminating flow congestion in the city.

One key shift in national priorities toward infrastructure in the postliberalization phase has been toward commercialization (Ministry of Finance 1996).[84] Karnataka's powerful bureaucracy has been a "thought leader" that facilitates the development of commercialized infrastructure consistent with the latest trends proposed by international agencies or the national government. One example of such leadership has been the swing away from government as an infrastructure provider toward government as a participant within a policy ecosystem composed of parastatal entities, private firms, and consultants. In 2000, the government launched the Infrastructure Development Corporation of Karnataka (iDeCK) with the purpose of establishing an institutional mechanism to leverage private investment in infrastructure. Unlike its predecessor, KUIDFC, an infrastructure project manager for the government, iDeCK positions itself as an infrastructure consultant that simultaneously engages private firms and government agencies in order to successfully propel partnership ventures. As such, KUIDFC and iDeCK have assumed a significant role in the emerging infrastructure scenario following JNNURM's thrust toward greater private participation. While KUIDFC was the nodal state agency that evaluated infrastructure projects, iDeCK authored key strategic plans such as the city development plan for Bengaluru, as well as project reports for solid waste management and transit centers in the city. Together, these entities have introduced a new architecture for infrastructure projects in the city. Whereas in the past, infrastructure planners or utilities conceived, designed, and executed infrastructures in their entirety, the heightened scrutiny of infrastructure by the IT industry in this period coincided with the entry of new entities that seek to insert private energy in terms of capacity and finances into the process. These new entities have shoehorned new architectures of the public-private partnership, such as special-purpose vehicles and infrastructure consortia, into Bengaluru.[85]

Assembling infrastructure corridors is yet another recent mechanism for public-private partnerships in infrastructure for Bengaluru. Infrastructure corridors, usually anchored on a single large-scale infrastructure, attempt to spearhead a wider socioeconomic transition within the globalized setting. Such efforts have been principally occupied with the identification, assembly, and repurposing of large parcels of land. The Bangalore International Airport (28 square kilometers), Bangalore-Mysore Infrastructure Corridor (117 square kilometers), and the IT Corridor (113 square kilometers), for example, have acquired a significant footprint on the urban periphery.[86] However, the process of repurposing land has been far from transparent or even democratically legitimate. In fact, the process has been largely opaque in part because of technocratic oversight (exerted by parastatal bodies) and the near-complete absence of any consultative or democratic thrust. The opacity of the process has played a role in making land use planning inaccessible to the majority of the population (Ghosh 2006, 691). The assembling of large parcels of land through a process with limited local political legitimacy into corridors far in excess of the immediate needs of the project has raised the speculative intent underlying these actions (Goldman 2011) whereby the land development machinery of the government appears to be requisitioned to further private projects. Since the government of Karnataka is empowered by legal instruments to acquire private land to further public purposes, the extensive routing of land for these privately executed infrastructure projects has posed questions regarding the underlying public intent. Indeed, Nair suggests that

> now the growing clamour for "infrastructure" reflects and serves the speculative intent, where highways and corridors are intended to engender urban growth rather than service them.... As a consequence, these new modes of production "bypass" the city as we know it. (Nair 2015, 56)

Against this backdrop, the city has emerged since 1991 as an arena for the prioritization and reinterpretation of infrastructures to minimize flow blockages in the circulation of not only traffic but also global capital, world-class city norms, and elite and middle-class discourses on lifestyle and modernity. Bengaluru's emerging identity as India's Silicon Valley or a putative world-class city has contributed to the redefinition of infrastructure as a means to support and further economic, informational, and human flows. In this context of heightened attention to infrastructure, congestion is blockage that could potentially disrupt these vital economic flows. Thus, road and traffic congestion, pervasive on Bengaluru's roads, is perceived against a matrix of decisions and processes that frames infrastructure in particular ways and proposes solutions to problems affecting them.

Conclusion

With more than 7 million vehicles crawling on its streets, congestion on Bengaluru's roads is very real. At first glance, the popular narrative of Bengaluru as a congested city (that one finds circulating in the popular media or in polite conversation) appears to be overwhelmingly dominated by the explosive growth in vehicles. But digging a little deeper into the narrative of a congested Bengaluru, one finds some discordant threads that point to congestion from a variety of reasons, as disparate as street flooding from an evening downpour, lack of administrative coordination, protests by workers, or even the start of a long weekend. How do we reconcile the presence of these multiple strands in the narrative of congestion in Bengaluru? Are these strands minor distractions in the context of the predominant story of automobile growth?

Examining the historical record in Western cities is instructive, given that the experience of congestion in the context of spiraling automobile growth was experienced as early as the middle of the twentieth century in these settings. The danger of interpreting congestion solely in terms of rising vehicular population leads to an instrumental reading of congestion that in Western cities has led to advances in traffic engineering, economics, and management. But these advances, riding on a thoroughgoing dehistoricization of congestion, have had consequences for their cities that are only now trying desperately to climb out of the hole that the deep embedding of autocentricity has rendered to their urban fabric. Arguing for locating congestion within a historical evolution, I propose a periodization of how, from the nineteenth century to the present time, questions of congestion in Bengaluru have been framed in particular ways and have evoked particular instrumental responses. These actions were motivated by specific political agendas and compulsions, and they have left spatial residues that now collectively shape the experience of congestion in the city.

Acknowledging the historic location of the experience of congestion is an effort to realize the limitations of an instrumental reading of congestion in Bengaluru. The problem of congestion on the roads is far more multidimensional than we choose to recognize. Instead, an instrumental assessment of automobile growth has become the predominant motivation behind interventions in urban space to address the issue of congestion on Bengaluru's roads. As we shall see in subsequent chapters, such an instrumental intervention has intertwined with particular political interests, social agendas, and technological pathways to generate and locate the constellation of automobility on Bengaluru's roads. In the next chapter, we consider the assembly of a technopolitical regime that governs the reordering of streets in the city to facilitate the greater circulation of automobiles.

3 Regime of Congestion

In September 2016, the cabinet of the government of Karnataka approved the construction of a 7-kilometer flyover (which came to be referred to in the media as the "steel flyover") to reduce congestion for those traveling from the city center to the airport and northern suburbs. As we shall see in the next chapter, the road from the city center to the airport had been the target of an earlier intervention to construct a signal-free corridor. As a result, this stretch of roadway is encrusted with multiple segmented arch flyovers and underpasses. The decision by the state's cabinet to approve this project became the spark for a period of sustained mobilization against the project. By October 2016, efforts to question the project had coalesced into the Citizens against Steel Flyover movement (Nagarajan 2017). Although there were multiple participants in the movement, public protests were led by Citizens for Bengaluru (CfB), a civic group that refers to itself as a "voluntary movement of, by, and, for the people of Bengaluru. The movement is focused on improving the quality of life, for all, in the city" (Citizens for Bengaluru 2018).[1] A range of demonstrations, including a human chain of five thousand people, public lectures, awareness campaigns on social media, and flash mobs were organized against the project during the next few months.[2] These protests revolved around an imperative slogan—"steel flyover *Beda!*" (Do Not Want the steel flyover!). This slogan became a rallying cry for not just street-side protests but also for a call for community building on social media with #steelflyoverbeda, on Twitter and Facebook, becoming spaces for commentary, photographs, videos, and announcements directed at an audience convinced that the city did not need yet another flyover, let alone a steel one.

A vital thrust associated with this protest was the pioneering critique that this imperative slogan engendered. It called out the urban development and planning paradigm dominant in the city, which relies on mega-infrastructure projects to facilitate the movement of people. This chapter seeks to understand this discursive paradigm that orders congestion by characterizing mobility in Bengaluru, problematizing congestion, and generating solutions for it in the particular context of the city. I propose that since the late 1990s, the paradigm that orders urban mobility and infrastructure in the city can be characterized as a regime of congestion. The work of Winner (1980) and Hecht (2009) from the field of science and technology studies (STS) is foundational for understanding the regime of congestion as a technopolitical regime—a structure of decision making that embeds the technological in order to enact goals possessing enormous political ramifications. I argue that the regime of congestion is reconstituting the nature of streets in Bengaluru with the intent of privileging the physical and discursive occupation of street space by private automobiles. In doing so, I show that the regime's politics are unambiguous: marginalizing the mobility needs of poorer inhabitants of the city.[3]

In the next section, I unravel the technopolitics of congestion in the city of Bengaluru by first offering a conceptual framing for technopolitical regimes in India's postcolonial urban context. In doing so, I acknowledge the need to inflect the concept of technopolitical regimes (conceptualized predominantly within a Western Euro-American context) by the unique political locus afforded by contemporary Indian cities. Although ensconced within the messy and contested, but ultimately more inclusive, history of postcolonial urbanism (which in itself is distinct from the Western experience), the thrust of metropolitan urban governance in India since 2000 is inclined toward "worlding" the city (Roy and Ong 2011). "Worlding" implies the discursive and physical transformation of city infrastructures, public spaces, and landscapes with the intent of incorporating a world-class aesthetic into their constitution.

The following section briefly illustrates the amorphous yet contested occupation of road space in urban India. Since the late nineteenth century, road space has been occupied and apportioned quite differently from late-twentieth-century roads in Western cities. Briefly presenting this historical context locates the sweeping nature of transformation attempted on Bengaluru's roads. The penultimate section presents the core empirical material by describing the particular constitution of the regime of congestion in Bengaluru. The footprint of this regime, I will show, privileges mega-infrastructure investments geared toward facilitating smooth automotive flows, while at the same time options are diminished for safe and affordable commutes for poor and nonmotorized residents of the city. Furthermore, I suggest that the regime of congestion contains at its core a self-perpetuating cycle that ensures that the operation of the regime reinstates itself, thereby locking Bengaluru's mobility onto an unsustainable and inequitable pathway.

Building Contemporary Indian Cities

The colonial period was transformative to the construction of Indian cities. As we saw in chapter 2 in the case of Bengaluru, Indian cities in the colonial encounter emerged as sites of experimentation, as noted by Anthony King (1976), where imported ideas of Western land management were not only implemented but tried out with specific political intents. More often than not, Western urban ideals were tested for the sole benefit of colonial elites even as natives were excluded from their purported benefits.[4] Emerging norms of how cities should be planned and infrastructures should be provisioned in pursuance of livability were advanced in colonial neighborhoods such as the cantonment or the civil lines (residential quarters of the military and administrative British elites, respectively), while native dwelling spaces were condemned as inferior and unlivable. Organizational patterns prevalent in indigenous urban habitations (as noted in chapter 2) were withering away, hastened by the systematic introduction of an impersonal municipalization. Over time, though, with the greater diffusion of modern planning norms, more native settlements followed the example set by elite colonial settlements. Independence saw the total adoption of modern planning within the aegis of the Nehruvian national project of planning and rooted ultimately within the agency of modern technoscientific development (Arnold 2013).

Within Nehru's vision, cities were represented as steps in the direction of modernization (even as villages were problematized as stagnant dens of tradition that required targeted attention by the modernizing developmental state). Cities thus became the natural site for locating modern technoscientific industries, education, and a workforce that would usher in the fundamental transformation of Indian society. Being aspects of modernization, cities, according to Nehru, were low-hanging fruit in the national journey toward socioeconomic development. In his mind, it was not in the cities but in India's remote rural areas that the real challenge of transforming India existed. A widely held belief in the initial years of independence was that the full force of planning directed at Indian cities would quickly resolve any residual problems in the city, thereby placing them securely on the path to modernization. Once that could be accomplished, the developmental energy of the new nation could then be redirected almost exclusively at villages. Accordingly, from the mid-1950s starting in Delhi, development and planning authorities produced master plans as an instrument to rationally build and plan Indian cities and their infrastructures. The apparatus of modern city planning was instituted in Bengaluru shortly after this in 1961 with the passage of the Mysore (now Karnataka) Town and Country Planning Act. The act provided the statutory framework that not only enshrined the normative rationality to plan cities but also incorporated mechanisms that both prescribe and proscribe land use (Sundaresan 2013).

Political Society and Dual Infrastructure Modes

Despite this planning apparatus, the transition to modern norms and standards underpinning Indian urbanization remained a distant dream in the burgeoning cities of the 1970s and 1980s. Historian Gyan Prakash notes, "The state has produced a powerful discourse that acts upon the urban space and population, but its historicism fails to grapple with the challenge that cities pose" (Prakash 2002, 5). One key fault line in urban intervention was the rise of informal settlements, or what Nandy calls the "unintended city—the city that was never a part of the formal master plan but was always implicit in it" (Nandy 1998, 2). In the meantime, the failure of state-led land redistribution efforts, combined with the absence of robust agricultural production in rural areas, contributed to a rising tide of rural migrants flooding large metropolitan areas seeking livelihood in industrial clusters or the service economy. The rising in-migration during this period swelled the numbers of the laboring poor, who settled without legal title on the margins of city sidewalks, adjacent to railway tracks, or unused public land.

This large influx, combined with the logic of electoral mobilization and welfare distribution, pressured infrastructure agencies in cities to provision essential services (for example, water, sanitation). Chatterjee (2004) proposes "political society" as a category to explain the extralegal relations the state entered into with the urban poor in this period:

> Governmental administration of welfare for the urban poor necessarily had to follow a different logic from that of the normal relations of the state with citizens organized in civil society. The city poor frequently lived as squatters on public land, travelled on public transport without paying, stole water and electricity, encroached on streets and parks.... The various urban development projects of the 1970s and 1980s took it for granted that large sections of the poor would have to live in the city without legitimate title to their places of habitation. The authorities nevertheless provided slums with water and sanitation, schools and health centres. Electricity companies negotiated collective rates with entire squatter settlements in order to cut down the losses from pilferage. (Chatterjee 2004, 135)

The presence of large masses of people squatting in the city became a major challenge for urban administrators. These administrators were legally constrained from providing infrastructure services to the squatters because of the lack of titles. Nevertheless, norms of welfare demanded some accommodation to meet the essential needs of the poor.

Since the 1970s, the efforts of governments to reconcile the demands of the titleless urban poor for services with the rights of legally titled citizens have resulted in the prevalence of a bimodal system of service provision in Indian cities. Thomas Hughes's understanding of large technical systems, initially proposed in *Networks of Power* as "interacting components of different kinds such as technical and institutional" (T. P. Hughes 1983, 6) and then later specified as messy, complex interconnections between physical and nonphysical or social artifacts, including organizational, scientific, and legislative artifacts (T. Hughes 1987), is particularly relevant for understanding the systems of service infrastructure. Central to this systemic logic of infrastructure is the idea that the technical and social components come together to forge a seamless web, whereby the system cannot be understood separate from its technical and nontechnical organizational parts.

The prevalence of a bimodal system was substantiated on the urban Indian landscape through the creation of technologies and organizational components associated with each system of infrastructure provision. For instance, in Indian cities, one finds broad, tree-lined avenues in affluent and planned neighborhoods existing in close proximity to narrow dirt tracks that serve as streets in informal settlements. In a similar fashion, street-side water taps and community toilets are the norm in slums, while the wealthy possess individual water and sewer connections. The plurality of infrastructure associated with this bimodal system can be characterized by two relatively distinct sociotechnical footprints: the archipelago (Bakker 2003) and the tendril (Gopakumar 2014). The archipelago refers to islands of standardized infrastructure provision, and the tendril indicates mass service mechanisms that address (through a range of legal, semilegal, and illegal means) the needs of the political society. As I have written in the context of water supply systems:

> Within the fragmented urban waterscape, at least two interspersed spatial and technical footprints of infrastructure provision serve the urban population: archipelagos of networked supply and tendrils of informal supply.... Thus, an archipelago is composed of its technical artifacts of infrastructure provision but also its line engineers, valve-men, meter readers, metered users and government regulators.... Outside the archipelagos of networked supply, the socio-spatial and socio-technical plurality of infrastructure arrangements in the South becomes

> evident. This urban landscape does not possess standardized "black-boxed" connections to the water-supply networks that are common within the archipelago. (Gopakumar 2014, 397–398)

The coexistence of these dual modes of infrastructure provision was premised on very different kinds of legitimacy. Standardized means of provision were backed by the moral legitimacy of a law-abiding citizenship. Mass provision, meanwhile, was backed by the popular legitimacy of politically mobilized populations claiming a right to the city and exerted through a combination of neighborhood groups, political fixers, ward-level politicians, and political parties. Governmental actors negotiated the provision of services between these two systemic modes. This field of negotiation guided the politics of service provision—when and where taps ran dry, or roads were resurfaced, or the price for bus fares.

Making the "World-Class" City
From the 1990s, and certainly with redoubled force from the early 2000s, this field of negotiation among the civil society (composed of entitled citizens), local infrastructure agencies, and the political society has transformed considerably. The impetus for change, Chatterjee notes, is the result of two simultaneous shifts: the priorities of government agencies with regard to service provision and in the conceptions of the city among the civil society. As a result, while civil society is increasingly impatient about claiming the city exclusively for themselves on the basis of their moral standing as taxpaying citizens, the outlook of public agencies governing cities has transformed into that of providers of infrastructure that will catalyze economic growth. In other words:

> On the one hand [is] greater assertion by organizations of middle-class citizens of their right to unhindered access to public spaces and thoroughfares and to a clean and healthy urban environment. On the other hand, government policy has rapidly turned away from the idea of helping the poor to subsist within the city and is instead paying the greatest attention to improving infrastructure in order to create conditions for the import of high technology and the new service industries. (Chatterjee 2004, 144)

These shifts have irrevocably changed from what used to be a more open field of negotiation that hospitably offered some modicum of service for the poor migrant into a polarized field of power that unfairly sets up the disenfranchised poor in political society against the wealthy civil society and uncaring public actors guided by neoliberal considerations of profit and loss. Although some have observed that this field of contestation is not quite so monolithic, riven as it is by internal differentiation (Kamath and

Vijayabaskar 2009), the creation of an urban politics of space and service that is tangibly hostile to the poor has been corroborated by many scholars (Baviskar 2008; Coelho and Raman 2010; Ghertner 2015). One reason for the emergence of this politics has been an alignment of interests between city/state governments and the globalized middle classes. This alignment is the result of the common interests in reimagining Indian cities as "world class."[5] Partnering with organizations dominated by the globalized middle classes offers a tangible pathway to intervene in urban space and services to transform them into sites of value in the global economy. In the Indian context, Bengaluru has a particularly long history as a test bed for a range of partnering enterprises that intervened in infrastructure services (Kamath 2013; Sadoway and Gopakumar 2017).

Technopolitical Regimes
The part played by technology in the constitution of this emerging and polarized field of power in Indian cities has been largely unstated and has received inadequate attention from scholars concerned with the vector of change in urban governance. In many studies of service provision in Indian cities, technological infrastructures, if they make an appearance, do so as an inanimate stage prop against which human contestations over access and rights play out. Of late, though, some India-focused scholars have begun attending to the materiality of technologies of infrastructure and examining how they are deeply implicated in the composition of a variety of urban contestations (McFarlane and Rutherford 2008; Anand 2011; Wissink 2013; Harris 2013). In so doing, these scholars have called attention to what STS scholars have long maintained: the design and construction of technologies embody them with valences that further particular political projects (Feenberg 1999; W. E. Bijker 2007). These scholars have argued that the focus of scholarship on the contestations surrounding technology is symptomatic of the widespread unraveling (from the mid-twentieth century) of the narrative of technology as progress. Indeed, Jasanoff proposes that these contestations connote the emergence of "technology as a site and object of politics" (Jasanoff 2006, 759), with contestations over technology expressed as politics of risk, standardization, and, notably, design. The variegated expression of technological politics leads some scholars to suggest that not paying attention to technology runs the risk of disregarding important aspects of politics in the contemporary world (W. E. Bijker 2006).

But how our contemporary lives are ordered by technological arrangements cannot be explained entirely by paying attention to the technopolitics of individual artifacts alone. Instead, following Langdon Winner

(1977) allows us to discern how technical devices and systems structure our lives in a fashion similar to legislated acts:

> Technology in a true sense is legislation. It recognizes that technical forms do, to a large extent shape the basic patterns and content of human activity in our time....A crucial turning point comes when one is able to acknowledge that modern technics, much more than politics as conventionally understood, now legislates the conditions of human existence. New technologies are institutional structures within an evolving constitution that gives shape to a new polity, the technopolis in which we do increasingly live. (Winner 1977, 323–324)

As technological development proceeds, Winner notes, new technologies are added in a piecemeal fashion to the existing technological structure. It is this accretion of technologies that has far-reaching political ramifications for society. First, piecemeal addition of technologies ultimately reinforces the existing constitution of the technopolis, thereby giving more concrete shape to a particular political dispensation. Second, the incremental addition of technologies into a structure effectively camouflages the larger picture of political phenomena being assembled in society. Thus, public awareness or scrutiny of these changes is effectively muted, and somnambulism toward technology appears to be a dominant motif in society.

At the same time, however, the design of technical systems contains multiple different possibilities for ordering our lives. Design choice, then, recognizing the many possibilities that exist, is a political decision that needs to be carefully considered because it has outcomes that can affect who wins and who loses. Along these lines, Winner notes that: "societies choose structures for technologies that influence how people are going to work, travel and communicate and so forth over a very long time. In the processes by which structuring decisions are made, different people are differently situated and possess unequal degrees of power" (Winner 1986, 127). Taking this argument forward to its logical conclusion, when a particular design is chosen, such a decision quite often carries the intent of achieving specific social outcomes. Changing design outcomes are thus power-laden decisions that can affect the lives of those they target. Such design choices—whether they are the irrigation system in independent Sri Lanka (Pfaffenberger 1992) or the low overpasses on Wantagh Parkway in New York—become the stuff of politics that serves to embed inequity and bias. For instance, Winner showed that Robert Moses, New York city's mid-twentieth-century master builder of monumental public works such as highways and bridges, designed parkways such as the Wantagh Parkway on Long Island with unusually low overpasses. The low clearance height on the overpass prevented buses from traveling on the parkway, thereby reserving these roads almost exclusively for automobiles. Such design endeavors, Winner points out, were testimony to Moses's racial and class biases. Since most African Americans and poor whites were dependent on buses, Moses sought to limit access for these groups to privileged neighborhoods on Long Island through the design of low-clearance parkways. Thus, while affluent whites from these suburbs could easily drive home, the less privileged were effectively barred from living in these neighborhoods.[6]

Technological orders, as demonstrated by the Long Island parkways, are extraordinarily durable and thus continue to shape and modulate the choices that societies make with regard to a range of infrastructure services.[7] We can conceptualize these persistent technological orders by contrasting two methods that have been proposed: sociotechnical ensembles (W. E. Bijker 2010) and technopolitical regimes (Hecht 2009). Sociotechnical ensemble is a concept for understanding how contemporary social orders are built. The focus of this concept is to determine how a combination of technical and institutional arrangements acts together to give stability to a social order. The key point that requires an explanation is the nature of interlinkages that exist among the various elements that together constitute the ensemble. The term *ensemble* suggests that the elements act in unison, but it does not specify the kind of political intent that is assembled through the ensemble. It is here that Hecht's concept of technopolitical regime proposes a different pathway to grasp the particular political ordering that is mobilized through social and technical components. The term *regime* is widely used in several fields of social science to indicate a power-laden entity that accomplishes a mode of rule. Hecht's notion of the technopolitical regime builds on this understanding by explicitly incorporating a material and discursive aspect into the concept. For Hecht, technopolitical regimes indicate "the tight relationship among institutions, the people who run them, their guiding myths and ideologies, the artifacts they produce, and the technopolitics they pursue" (Hecht 2009, 17).

What makes Hecht's notion of technopolitical regimes more suitable than sociotechnical ensembles for framing congestion are two factors: the attention to the political discourses that underlie the construction of the regime and the diffused agency of the regime given the tight relationship between the different components of it: artifacts, institutions, actors, and discourses. Managing congestion does not happen merely through linkages between social and technical elements but is embedded with discursive aspects. Discourses, as we shall see, are powerful organizing devices that pull the different elements together into a singular entity. This one factor leads Hecht's conceptualization of technopolitical regime to appear appropriate. A second factor is that the diffused agency of the regime arising from the tight interlinkages between regime components distributes the power to reshape society, thus obscuring the ability to assign causality to any one component. No one regime component—artifact, institution, discourses, or actors—is solely responsible for its effect. Agency is a product of the skein of relationships that underlie the regime. Because of its ability to obfuscate agency and rely on discourses to gather together different components, the technopolitical regime emerges as a powerful force that orders its host society while achieving particular political goals.

Urban Technopolitical Regimes

Hecht's concept of technopolitical regimes as vehicles for the expression of politics has been relatively underexplored in the urban context. The application of the regime concept in urban areas was initially focused on public-private coalitions—informal partnerships between local politicians and local business elites—and how these effected the governance objectives of cities (Stone 1989). Of late, scholarship has shifted away from a focus solely on political coalitions to understanding how morphologies and materialities of infrastructure provisioning in close coordination with political and territorial networks make regime operation real. In this direction, Gullberg and Kaijser (2004) propose city-building regimes as an approach to understanding how particular groupings of actors and their coordinating mechanisms produce particular patterns of changes in the urban landscape. Hodson and Marvin (2010) also suggest that constructing purposive urban transitions in the face of contemporary pressures of the macrolevel socio-environmental landscape of cities requires an understanding of the degree of alignment between urban political networks and sociotechnical regimes. Along similar lines, Gopakumar (2012) suggests that urban sociotechnical regimes, with their technological imperatives and political constraints, administer the provision of infrastructure services. Jochen Monstadt (2009) attempts to integrate this shift by proposing that attending to the constitution of "urban infrastructure regimes" requires an integrated analysis of several dimensions: sociotechnical, political ecology, and sociospatial. He suggests that conducting a regime analysis of urban infrastructure requires "consideration of the interplay of urban, sociotechnical, and socioecological factors" (Monstadt 2009, 1937). However, much of this literature on urban infrastructure regimes has not yet attended to the deeply political imprints that such orders impose on cities. The opportunity here is to examine how urban regimes become sites where material entities further political projects.

Applying the concept to the Indian context, I propose that urban technopolitical regimes are powerfully reordering the field of negotiation between civil society, governmental agencies, and political society in Indian cities, thereby diminishing the rights of the poor and the marginalized in the city they live in. In the process, Indian cities appear poised to make the transition away from a more inclusive politics that granted the urban poor some measure of occupancy rights. Instead, a hostile politics marked by crafting exclusionary spaces, where the poor are actively marginalized, to service world-class city aesthetics is increasingly becoming the norm. The diffused agency of urban technopolitical regimes prevents an easy assignment of causality. No one actor can be pinpointed as steering the transformation of Indian cities. In the next section, I briefly present how urban studies scholars have characterized street space and associated contests in India.

Streets in Indian Cities

Indian streets have a persistent image problem. For many years, starting from colonial times, observers of its thoroughfares have been appalled and overwhelmed by the sights (not to mention sounds and smells) that have assailed them through their travels (see Doron and Raja 2015). Colonialists (be they administrator, hygienist, or missionary) from the early eighteenth century have acerbically commented on the incorrigibility of Indians to show restraint when inhabiting their streets. Nationalists from the early twentieth century and sundry administrators, citizens, and individuals in the postindependence period took up the charge of exhorting their fellow citizens to reform their street persona and curb their wild roadside excesses. Seen from a modernist lens (something that many of these observers carried as a badge of honor), there is much to criticize in Indian streets—the juxtaposition of multiple flows of human consumption (eating, drinking) and waste emission (spitting, vomiting, urinating, and defecating); the ceaseless jostling by humans compounded by the sensorial experience of sweaty and odorous bodies in a hot and humid environment; the scant concealment of municipal waste flows on the street with their pervasive visibility (and smell); and the diversity of human activities on the street blurring the boundary between public and private. Inquiring into the absence of immaculate order in Indian street habitations, ethno historians Dipesh Chakrabarty (1992) and Sudipta Kaviraj (1997) have both argued for an ethnohistorical understanding of the evolution of the public sphere and the position of dirt and garbage in Indian cities.

Kaviraj suggests that within the sociocultural logic of Indian settlements, the public or "outside" occupies a paradoxical position. It is a space that in contradistinction to the privileged inside of communal domesticity possesses little or no ritual value. At the same time, the outside is also a contested space where the plebian aesthetics of the lower classes challenge middle-class versions of a sanitized urban modernity. This paradox has come to define how scholars have paid attention to and understood the rhythms of Indian streets.

The low ritual value of the street in comparison to the pristine interiors of the household has allowed the street to be host to a range of activities that could not be performed indoors.[8] Thus, in addition to "normal public" activities on the street, Indian streets are also locations of activities often classed as private. This ethno-historical context has endowed Indian streets with some unique performative characteristics. The diversity on Indian streets in terms of the plethora of human activities encountered is one unique characteristic. The surfeit of human activities, Appadurai (1987) notes, constructs diverse street cultures that blur the line between public and private life. Appadurai adds that

> for all this variation—which makes it essential to think of street cultures in the plural—there is something shared, which justifies the use of the singular. The two most important features of what is shared are the great range of activities that occur on Indian streets and give them their ambience and the way in which street culture blurs the line between private and public life. (Appadurai 1987, 17)

According to Edensor (1998), the sheer diversity of social practices one encounters on the typical Indian street relates to several unique situations. First, functional uses arising from the intent to pursue a livelihood or meet household needs are themselves complex due to the dense diversity of spaces along the street. Second, social transactions of leisure, worship, companionship, or even just gazing are often staged on the street. Third, for some, the pavement on the margins of the street is home, and, for them, chores of domestic reproduction or body regulation have perforce to be conducted in full view (Edensor 1998). Such diversity of exchange, Edensor argues, hinges on an arrangement of distributed regulation, at once contextual and contingent, but far less surveilled than on contemporary Western streets. The diversity of social spaces and exchanges has led others to suggest that Indian roads (unlike those in Western societies) make legible an underlying ecology composed of "complex webs of interconnected activities and phenomena" (Mehta 2015, 97).

In addition to diversity yet another defining attribute of Indian streets is conflict. Underlying the almost unregulated commotion of human activities on the surface of the street are forms of control and contestation that have shaped the experiences, routines, and activities of different groups on the street. At one level, control and contestation play out at the physical plane in the ever-present jostling that pervades navigating movement in Indian cities. No one is exempt from the equalizing thrust of this jostling—including planners who see their best-laid plans subverted by the spatial claims of others on the street. In his exceptional ethnography of streets in Delhi's Old City, one of Ajay Gandhi's reflective informants said as much—"*sabko adjust karna padta hain*"—"they all have to adjust" (Gandhi 2015, 273). But on another level, forms of control and contestation are so elusive and situated that it takes ethnographic following to reveal the labyrinthine workings of control on the street. Gandhi observed how subtle the workings of watchfulness were when he discovered that two roadside tea sellers he frequented were police informers who, even as they doled out tea, kept a watch on the nearby goings-on (2015, 271). Such inconspicuous measures of control were countered, according to Gandhi, by an equally dispersed obduracy to reform that exposed and eroded projects of officiousness.

This narrative of a timeless street that grinds down and outlasts all efforts to straighten it is evocative of the power of the little man on the street. But it does not quite capture the real toll that the operation of state power effects on the denizens of these chaotic streets.[9] Neither does it reveal the total power brought to bear by the state through specific regimes of street reordering in order to push through larger projects of city building. That these regimes have not been entirely unsuccessful in transforming Indian urban streets and neighborhoods is evident from the degree of change wrought in the last 150 years of modernist intervention. Despite these modernist interventions, Anjaria (2012) proposes that

> today's Indian streetscapes are an accumulation of a century and a half of municipal, police and elite residents' efforts to transform them. This does not mean the street has been subsumed into a logic of architectural modernism; but equally, nor does the street represent a complete inversion of it.

Thus, the picture that emerges is of Indian streets being targets of a relentless onslaught of modernist regimes of intervention. But on the streets, these regimes do not remain untouched. Over time, according to Partha Chatterjee, imposed regimes and models of city building "turn into an impure, inefficient, but ultimately, less malevolent hybrid" (2004, 145).

Rise of Automobilization

One such intervention is automobilization, understood here as a regime of domination composed of multiple social, cultural, technical, and ideological components interconnected with relations of power (Urry 2004; Bohm et al. 2006). Recent scholarship points to the growing footprint of automobilization on the street space of Indian cities. Several factors signal its rise. One ready indicator is the enormous growth in vehicles. As seen in table 3.1, the motor vehicle population in India has skyrocketed, especially since 2010, reaching over 210 million vehicles in 2015. This increase is particularly stark when we consider the rate of motorization (expressed in the number of vehicles per 1,000 people). Between 2005 and 2010, the rate increased from 74 vehicles to 109 vehicles per 1,000 people (an increase of 35 vehicles), but in the next five years, the increase was almost twice as much (58 vehicles per 1,000 people). With the galloping growth in automobiles, the presence of the motor vehicle on urban streets is inescapable.

The growing presence of automobiles on the streets is assisted by the intersection of popular discourse, policy frameworks, and institutional mechanisms that facilitate automobilization. Joshi, Joseph, and Chandran (2016) indicate the creation of a culture of automobility rooted in industrial incentives, corporate advertisement strategies, popular aspirations, and easy financing. At the same time, the uncritical import of planning frameworks such as transit-oriented development (TOD) into conventional transport planning procedures in India, given the high densities in cities, contributes instead to the gentrification of neighborhoods and mass transit (Mohan 2013). Examining public transportation systems, especially bus transit, in Indian cities, Kharola (2013) argues that policy and institutional

Table 3.1
Motor Vehicle Population in India and the Rate of Motorization

Year	Motor Vehicle Population (in millions)	Rate of Motorization (in vehicles/1,000 people)
2005	81.50	74
2010	127.75	109
2011	141.87	119
2012	159.50	132
2013	176.04	144
2014	190.70	154
2015	210.02	167

Source: Government of India (2017).

interventions such as taxation and government duties have consistently impeded the financial sustainability of these entities, thereby indirectly prioritizing personal transport. Yet another contributing factor in the rise of automobilization on Indian streets is visible in the occupation of streets by the private automobile. Joshi and Joseph (2015) examine the conundrum that despite the large proportion of poor daily cyclists on Indian streets, they are a rapidly receding presence on major thoroughfares. These authors suggest that their vanishing presence reflects their continuing invisibility in planning and policy discourse as reflected in the lack of street-level infrastructure that promotes secure cycling.[10] Along similar lines, Badami (2009) argues that pedestrian accessibility manifested in improved facilities for nonmotorized road users has not been a priority in transport planning in the country. He suggests planners and decision makers possess a "car windshield view" (48) of mobility on the streets, which precludes the voices and views of the pedestrian and nonmotorized. These recent instances of road transformation indicate that despite cultural resources that emphasize the diversity of street spaces, powerful forces have sought to reorder the streets in the country in the pursuit of a greater imprint of automobility. In Bengaluru, I contend, the rise of automobilization is being ordered by establishing the regime of congestion.

Bengaluru's Regime of Congestion

The basis for Bengaluru's regime of congestion arises from the dominance that the imaginary of Bengaluru as India's Silicon Valley has acquired in policy and popular discourses. As we saw in chapter 2, despite the differences in the evolution of Bengaluru and of Silicon Valley, the imaginary of Bengaluru as India's Silicon Valley initially arose from the rapid clustering and subsequent agglomeration of information technology (IT) enterprises in the city. Over time, this became the prod for the gradual dominance of the imaginary in domains outside industrial and corporate policy. In addition, the success of IT enterprises allowed leaders in the sector to adopt a wider role in society. Their success became a lesson for how the city ought to reshape its built environment and its infrastructure footprint to realize a successful presence in a globalized world.

Based on this imaginary, the operation of the regime has played out in the city in two sequential phases.[11] The earlier phase, prevalent between the late 1990s and about 2010, portrayed mobility infrastructures in the city as inadequate for the enormous growth spurt experienced. Thus, infrastructures in the city were inadequate to keep up with the demands of a rapidly growing vehicular population. In the second phase, prevalent since 2010, the growing vehicular population in the city has, paradoxically, become the primary problem plaguing the city. This phase has inaugurated a new round of infrastructure development that seeks to control the growth in vehicular numbers by building newer infrastructures that target the more affluent vehicle-owning population. In the process, the regime has locked the city into a carbon-intensive and inequitable trajectory of moving around the city.

Despite the discursive differences of these sequential phases, a common thread across them is their almost exclusive reliance on megaprojects, understood here in the Flyvbjergian (2014) sense as complex achievements that possess long gestation periods in planning and implementation. Phase 1 sought to strengthen road infrastructures by relying on a range of technological infrastructures, such as flyovers, underpasses, overhead highways, and junction-free corridors, that elevated the seamless movement of automobiles in the cityscape (the next chapter elaborates on this) into an end goal. In phase 2, the alarming growth in vehicles prompted a new legion of megaprojects, such as rapid mass transit, multistoried park-and-ride facilities (referred to locally as traffic and transit management centers, TTMC), and air-conditioned low-floor buses. The overt aim of this round of construction was to signal alarm at the galloping growth in vehicles while also offering a means to persuade affluent vehicle owners to rely on an urbane and comfortable public transit. As we shall see, associated with the infrastructure arrangements in each phase are specific actor groupings and political and administrative processes that together animate a discourse of mobility and infrastructure in the city. In this section, we examine each of these phases.

Phase 1: Addressing Infrastructure Inadequacy

Since the late 1990s, the regime has constituted a discourse of infrastructure that embeds a specific understanding of infrastructure and its deficiencies. A common thread visible in the official and popular discourse is the representation of infrastructure in general, but mobility infrastructure in particular as largely inadequate for Bengaluru's growing needs, especially if the city continues to be represented as India's Silicon Valley. In official documents, infrastructure inadequacy formed the basis for several initiatives to reshape the city and its governance framework. Thus, reports (such as the Karnataka state's Urban Development Policy of 2009) that deal with urban infrastructure questions were unambiguous about the inadequate transportation in the city. According to the policy, city roads were said to "suffer from serious deficiencies—inadequate road capacity…which hinder the free movement of vehicles" (Urban Development Department 2009, 13). Inadequate roads were also identified as a key constraint in Bengaluru's City Development Plan (proposed by BBMP) to meet the growing vehicular demand. It noted that:

> the road network...is underdeveloped in terms of size, structure, continuity and connectivity....Thus most of the roads have inadequate carriageway widths to cater to growing traffic at an acceptable level of service. (iDeCK 2006, 32)

This diagnosis of infrastructure inadequacy is powerfully echoed in the Strategic Operations Plan of the Bangalore Traffic Improvement Program 2010, which notes:

> Bangalore City has witnessed a phenomenal growth in vehicle population without a commensurate increase in either road space or in the number of traffic police. As a result, many arterial roads and intersections are operating much beyond their capacity. (Ramanayya and Anantharamaiah 2008, ii)

Common to these official pronouncements was the inadequacy of road infrastructures to support the needs for smooth and unhindered vehicle movement. The solution was to increase the development of road infrastructures that promote the free movement of vehicles.

At the same time, the discourse in popular news media reinforced the inadequacies of roads to meet the needs of road users. But this discursive construction possessed some notable features. First, it was vehicle owners who were cast as the designated users of the road. Second, roads were classified as conduits that exist for the unfettered circulation of vehicles. A final feature of the media construction was that hindrances to vehicle movement on the road were considered a crisis that required public intervention. During the 2000s, news articles consistently noted the "woes" that commuters and Bangaloreans faced while moving around the city. For instance, in 2008 in a survey of (automotive) commuters conducted by the *Times of India*, more than 50 percent of the respondents blamed poor or inadequate road infrastructure as the primary reason for vehicular congestion.[12] But it is the travails that the IT industry faced in navigating the "infrastructure bottlenecks" in the city that attracted much media attention. The diagnosis of the problem lay in the inability of road infrastructures to cater to the changed needs of the population. Despite the growing population, a thriving IT industry, and a mobile population, road infrastructure was predominantly marked by "narrow roads and bylanes, not to mention potholes [that] make it difficult for...registered vehicles to ply on the road."[13] The sheer lack of quality infrastructure in the city imposed costs on all vehicle users, but especially the IT industry, which is exceptionally sensitive to the lifestyle needs of its youthful and mobile tech set. Poor infrastructure was presented as dramatically reducing the desirability of tech companies to locate and operate in Bengaluru. If this problem were not addressed, the city's inadequate infrastructure could precipitate a mass exodus of the industry.

The watershed year of 1999 marked the launch of Bengaluru's regime of congestion on both political and technological fronts—the election of S. M. Krishna as chief minister of the state of Karnataka and the inauguration of the city's first megaproject (the 2.65 kilometer flyover on Mysore Road sponsored by the national government's Mega City Scheme) were foundational to the city's regime. On assuming office, Krishna proceeded to actualize a vision that sought to make Bengaluru into a global city that would be an attractive investment destination and support the lifestyles of its globally mobile residents. The Bangalore Agenda Task Force (BATF), comprising corporate and managerial elites and appointed in 1999 by the state government to advise the chief minister on urban affairs, was a key element in the incipient regime. BATF's imprint on the city was wielded through several technological and administrative ventures. One key mechanism was the Bangalore Summit, a biannual extravagant public gathering organized for the consumption of the media or a largely middle-class audience. These gatherings allowed the task force to publicly monitor the actions of the city's "civic stakeholders"—for example, agencies that oversaw planning, water supply, public transportation, and municipal government (BATF 2001):

> [BATF] was supposed to plan for Bangalore, you know, give ideas and targets to all...seven service agencies of Bangalore and hold them accountable at six-monthly summits....So the service agencies were responding to the BATF and so the councilors [elected representatives to the city council] were getting bypassed. Because these people [BATF] are setting the agenda and asking them [service agencies] to be accountable to them. (Interview with K. Chamaraj, CIVIC-Bangalore, May 7, 2011)

But it was not just the everyday business of infrastructure making that BATF was supervising through these summits: its goal was to use such interventions to script an agenda "devoted to marketing a 'brand' of the city and to create a discourse of becoming 'world-class'" (Kamath 2013, 279), which reinforced the prevailing popular discourse on infrastructure. It was against this agenda of change that infrastructure interventions proposed by different civic stakeholders were measured. Civic agencies accordingly modulated their responses by spotlighting major works that addressed this agenda of change. Big, splashy megaprojects that conformed to the popular aspirations for seamless vehicular movement were particularly attractive to this form of public accounting. For instance, BDA's status report at the second Bangalore Summit gave great prominence to four mega-infrastructure works, including the development of two grade separators on the orbital outer ring road (BATF 2001).

Meanwhile, new programs in urban development from the national government, such as the Mega City Scheme, provided the impetus for conceiving mega-infrastructure projects. The inauguration of the Mysore Road flyover in 1999 initiated the ongoing reliance on megaprojects to enhance road infrastructures. Since 1999, both the BBMP and BDA have together constructed more than fifty mega-infrastructures (such as flyovers or underpasses) in the city with the aim of streamlining vehicular movement by eliminating intersections and the associated delay from traffic signals. The construction of these structures requires extensive redesign of street intersections. After the project has been approved, one of the first changes is to widen the intersection to accommodate the new structure and the access roads around it. In densely populated Indian cities, widening the intersection does more than alter the physical morphology of the street and the adjoining properties: it also changes the cultural rhythms of intersections:

> What happens when you have signal-free corridors?... You cut down a lot of street trees. There are very few vendors.... The street is meant for a variety of purposes. The street is meant for travel either by vehicle or by walk. It is meant for street trees to be there.... It is meant for street vendors, not just for their livelihoods but also to give low-cost access to goods and services to people. It is a place for people to meet and socialize in a variety of ways. But now streets are being remodeled so that it serves...a certain kind of transport. (Interview with V. Srinivasa, Bengaluru Bus Commuter Forum, July 28, 2014)

Establishing these mega-infrastructures is a demanding process that requires extensive overhaul of administrative processes associated with the construction of public works. This is because the scale of investment needed to finance the construction of such structures usually far exceeds the capacities of public monies. Instead, infrastructure managers have to rely on private and institutional financing to accomplish the goal. However, in order to receive the injection of such funds, administrative processes have to assess and control for a range of risks that can affect the balance of financial inflows, costs, and the project work schedule. Such factors are rarely a concern when projects are funded solely by public funds, but when they are receiving financing from other sources, assessing risks that can affect the returns on the investment is inescapable.[14] A key requirement was an infrastructure finance manager who would ensure that public implementation agencies followed these emerging project management considerations. As noted in chapter 2, the Karnataka Urban Infrastructure Development and Financing Corporation (KUIDFC) was created in 1993 as a public limited company owned solely by the government of Karnataka in order to "prepare, formulate and implement projects, schemes, and programmes relating to infrastructure development in the urban areas of the state" (KUIDFC 2017). With its creation, KUIDFC became the main agency in the state for implementing a range of urban infrastructure projects in the state funded by the government of India, the World Bank, the Asian Development Bank, and other financial institutions. In Bengaluru, KUIDFC was the infrastructure manager for several infrastructure projects, starting in 1996 with the national government's Mega City Scheme.

The creation of the KUIDFC was a major turning point. It allowed the state to acquire the professional capacity needed for executing mega-infrastructure projects financed by international, institutional, and private sources. The reliance on professionally managed mega-infrastructure projects was incumbent on the creation of two innovations: the introduction of "super-bureaucrats" (Urs and Whittell 2009) and the development of infrastructure investment plans. Each of these means ultimately reinforced the city's dependence on megaprojects for addressing the discourse of infrastructure inadequacy

The complexity of managing infrastructure projects financed by nonpublic sources has placed a great premium on administrators who can spearhead the project of managing infrastructures within traditional bureaucracies. Since the early 2000s, the favored response of Karnataka's chief ministers has been to appoint super-bureaucrats to lead the charge of reforming project management in key infrastructure agencies in Bengaluru:

> Super bureaucrats are hand picked, trained, and placed in crucial positions and kept there long enough to institutionalize reforms, while [most] other bureaucrats are shifted every six months. (Interview with K. Urs, Action Aid, May 2011)

The state of Karnataka has a long history of relying on able administrators and nurturing administrative capacity. Placing super-bureaucrats in key positions is a recent response adopted by the state administration to gather the capacity needed to reform the city bureaucracy and remake the city. Super-bureaucrats, who have come to lead Bengaluru's public infrastructure entities such as the BDA, BMTC, BWSSB, and the BBMP, enjoyed several benefits. They were not only retained in these public infrastructure entities for extended periods of time; they often revolved between these different entities or were appointed for a second term. Furthermore, they were often given preferential administrative training by international agencies such as at the World Bank or Harvard University's Kennedy School of Government. The time they spent at these organizations allowed them to be plugged into the transnational circulations of "mobile policies" (McCann and Ward 2011, xxii), giving them an opportunity to participate in the global shuttling of policies, techniques, and innovations and the revolving door of policy actors—consultants, bureaucrats, academics, and policy analysts. This exposure allowed them to tap into these transnational policy conduits to source their wish list of policies, administrative innovations, consultants, and experts, even after their return from their overseas training.

Yet another innovation that emerged in response to the possibility of seeking nonpublic sources of financing for infrastructure projects were the multiple infrastructure investment plans to justify the funding. Each of these plans sought to create a wish list of all possible projects that could address the city's perceived infrastructure inadequacy. One example of this future-oriented strategy was the proposed capital investment plan for Bengaluru city created by BBMP. The central premise underlying this plan was that the inadequacies in the city's mobility infrastructure affected the seamless movement of vehicles in the city. The proposed redress to this situation was massive investments in mega-infrastructure projects. The plan proposes three elevated road corridors, twelve signal-free corridors, and 500 kilometers of road-widening efforts as signature projects that the city government would like to develop at a cost of ₹22,000 crore (about $3.3 billion in 2018 rates) (BBMP 2009, 8).[15] The city development plan, produced by KUIDFC for the national government's JNNURM program, similarly proposes a humongous investment of more than ₹50,000 crore (about $7.7 billion in 2018 rates). This plan proposes megatransportation and road infrastructures, such as the Metro, airport high-speed rail link, and grade separators (iDECK 2009, 145):

> They [the government] have drawn up a traffic and transportation plan for the city for 40,000 crore rupees [about $6 billion]. It is being developed by KUIDFC. . . . The investment that is being contemplated for Bangalore, that too only for road infrastructure in terms of expressways, underpasses, flyovers, one high-speed rail-link to the airport. All kinds of infrastructure only to go to the airport. That too when only 30,000 people travel to the airport every day. . . . The high-speed rail-link itself is 3000 crores. In addition, all the road widening, and a highway on stilts to go to the airport. (Interview with K. Chamaraj, May 11, 2011)

The expectation is that infrastructure plans bridge a gap in the existing level. By proposing large infusions of capital for infrastructure development, it is possible to rectify the shortcomings in the city's infrastructure, thereby allaying congestion.

This technopolitical constitution of infrastructures through megaprojects, investment plans, corporate task forces, and super-bureaucrats, is often noted in the media discourse surrounding congestion. In May 2006, soon after Shankarlinge Gowda became commissioner of the Bangalore Development Authority (BDA), he reassured city residents, especially the IT industry, in an interview with the *New Indian Express*, that his highest priority as one of the city's most influential super-bureaucrats would be to "focus on infrastructure." He added that "work on flyovers and underpasses have been dragging on for long.... Everyone uses a flyover or a road. BDA's aim will be to make Bangalore livable for everybody."[16] The conflation of flyovers with the public good and the interests of the IT industry with the common interest are consistently reinforced in the media discourse. Government media advertisements and publicity materials are yet other means through which this discourse of infrastructure inadequacy is produced. A government of Karnataka advertisement in September 2007 showcased an aerial view of the spaghetti flyover at Hebbal as a prominent example of "multi-dimensional development for Brand Bengaluru" (figure 3.1). The advertisement seems to suggest that the ability of the flyover to provide fluid movement of vehicles exemplifies multidimensional development for Brand Bengaluru, which, as we shall see in the next chapter, embodies a particular cityscape that reifies the demands of the globally mobile middle classes for a world-class city.

Figure 3.1
Advertisement of a flyover in Bengaluru (source: New Indian Express).

Phase 2: Controlling the Automobile Population

The year 2010 was significant because it marked a shift in the popular discourse underlying mobility in Bengaluru. The rapidly growing vehicular population and the growing congestion that automotive commuters experience in traveling around the city precipitated a shift in the discourse away from one centered on addressing inadequate infrastructures to one focused on controlling automobiles.[17] In the media discourse, this shift became visible with coverage that highlighted the problems arising from the growth in motor vehicles.[18] For instance, the *Hindu* reported on an initiative launched by the city's police to curb vehicles on the road:

> To tackle the infamous tag of a traffic-choked city, the Bangalore Traffic Police are all set to kick off a carpooling drive.... While buying vehicles is a fundamental right of the people, we need to reduce the number of vehicles on the road. (*Hindu*, February 24, 2013)

Senior bureaucrats echoed a similar notion of crisis arising from the steep growth in vehicles is echoed by:

> I think the most important characteristic of transport scenario in Bengaluru is the phenomenal rise in the number of automobiles...so naturally there is the resultant traffic congestion. (Interview with Advisor on urban affairs, May 18, 2011)

It is noteworthy that despite the shift in discourse toward controlling automobiles, the road space itself still remains the domain of automobiles. All other modes and forms of occupation of road space are secondary to vehicular use.

Accompanying the discursive shift in mobility in the city is a different constellation of elements. Thus, new corporate task forces, infrastructures, super-bureaucrats, and investment plans came to take the place of the earlier cast of regime components and through their interlinkages give voice to the changed discursive construction. Reprising the role of the BATF in the second phase was a new task force, ABIDe (Agenda for Bengaluru Infrastructure Development). Given BATF's controversial history, ABIDe was structured not so much as an interventionist actor but as a planning advisory body. It released its Plan Bengaluru 2020 in January 2010 to outline sectoral strategies that city infrastructure agencies could adopt and implement in their respective domains in the quest for a livable world-class city. The plan devoted considerable attention to reforming traffic and transport management in the city. In line with the discourse at that time, the plan sought to identify congestion in the relentless growth in vehicles in the city (ABIDe 2010, 34). However, in order to address this situation, the plan sought to propose a technomanagerial orientation to guide urban mobility in the city. Thus, the plan suggested an architecture of mobility infrastructures, such as improved connectivity to the airport, signal-free interchanges between ring roads and key radial roads, better linkage between the Metro and other mobility modes through park-and-ride facilities, feeder bus networks, and pedestrian access (ABIDe 2010, 52, 54), to prioritize high-mobility radial and ring corridors in the city.

In addition to flyovers, a new collection of megaprojects animated the regime of congestion in the city after 2010. The infrastructures proposed as a solution to the wide prevalence of vehicular gridlock present in Bengaluru were the Metro, the monorail, and a peripheral ring road.[19] Investment plans produced in this phase reflect the shift to this new cast of infrastructures. The comprehensive traffic and transportation plan proposed for the city of Bengaluru, for instance, set out the Metro, high-speed rail link, and bus rapid-transit corridors, all to the tune of more than ₹50,000 *crore* (about $8 billion) as capital investments designed to curb the spiraling growth in traffic congestion (RITES 2011, 9–13).

The Bengaluru Metro is a recent example of a megaproject that seeks to streamline mass transit in the city with the aim of reducing the presence of private motor vehicles on the road. The Metro is constructed and managed by the Bangalore Metro Rail Corporation Limited (BMRCL), a joint venture owned by the governments of India and Karnataka. BMRCL began construction in 2006, and eleven years later, in 2017, phase 1 of the Metro, comprising 42 kilometers of track in two intersecting lines, was completed at a cost of more than ₹14,000 *crore* (about $2 billion). Of this amount, the government of Karnataka's contribution amounted to more than ₹5,000 *crore* ($0.75 billion). A further 76 kilometers of lines to be constructed as part of phase 2 of the Metro is expected to cost more than ₹27,000 *crore*, or nearly $4 billion (BMRCL 2016). The government of Karnataka's contribution to phase 2 is expected to be on the order of ₹9,000 *crore* (or about $1.25 billion).

For some, this level of financial commitment on the part of the state government is worrisome. First, despite the Metro's enormous financial footprint, it is designed to carry far fewer commuters than the bus transport system. While intracity buses currently carry more than 5 million people daily, the maximum daily ridership on the Metro (including phase 2) is projected to be about 2 million (in 2021), or about 40 percent of what the bus service (Bangalore Metropolitan Transport Corporation, BMTC) carries currently. Second, the large financial support for the Metro exists in stark contrast to the shrinking state support for the bus transit system in the city. Indeed, in 2017, credit rating agencies that monitor the ability of agencies to borrow funds downgraded BMTC's credit rating on the basis of the declining financial support it received from the state government for operational expenses (ICRA 2017).

> When you are spending 38,000 crores [both phases 1 and 2 of the Metro] to solve one part of one problem of one city and then you [the state government] are saying that there is no money for public health, education or transportation. BMTC hiked its fares and asked the government to reimburse taxes to the tune of 200 crores. But the government said there is no money. Is this justified?...The state does not find it a problem to support the Metro though, which is only going to serve one fourth of the numbers BMTC serves. (Interview with V. Sreenivasa, Bengaluru Bus Commuter Forum, July 28, 2014)

This form of lopsided spending and prioritizing of transportation infrastructures has come to characterize the phase of controlling vehicle population. The state government appears willing to subsidize a very capital-intensive mode of transport like the Metro while at the same time giving short shrift to people-intensive options such as the intracity bus system.

Such infrastructure solutions have not been without consequences for urban society. Driven by the dominant discourse, the public purse is largely directed at infrastructures such as the Metro that, by assuring a comfortable ride around town, could potentially reduce the dependence of commuters on private vehicles. Although this may very well be the case, such single-mindedness of purpose has privileged the mobility of those who can afford vehicles. Those whose mobilities involve different modalities—such as walking, cycling, or pushing carts—are quickly excluded from such a calculus. Recent efforts, such as introducing air-conditioned low-floor buses and transforming different bus terminals into glass-faced park-and-ride facilities integrated with high-end commercial establishments (referred to locally as traffic and transit management centers; see figure 3.2) are stark examples of an inequitable imprint. The introduction of numerous air-conditioned, low-floor buses (referred to locally as Volvo buses after their manufacturer) in the city's intracity, public transit fleet since 2006 is a particularly revealing case of how a dynamic of inequity is imprinted onto the intervention (figure 3.3). The logic behind these buses is clearly with a view to providing comfortable transit options for more affluent commuters. The reasoning is that if this group finds their commutes to be comfortable, the city's public transit provider, BMTC, can wean them off their reliance on private automobiles. In comparison with non-air-conditioned buses (the so-called ordinary buses), air-conditioned buses provide a more comfortable environment that insulates riders from the dust, the heat, and the sounds of a congested city. They charge a significantly higher fare over the base fare that BMTC charges citizens. The BMTC currently operates about ninety routes with air-conditioned buses, which far exceed the ten routes of subsidized bus services it runs for the urban poor.[20] On some routes, there is a

Figure 3.2
Supermarket integrated within a traffic and transit management center.

preponderance of air-conditioned buses in comparison to ordinary non-air-conditioned buses (figure 3.3 displays an example):

> On several routes, for example the 335E which serves the ITPL [International Tech Park Limited] area, the number of [air-conditioned] Volvo buses are huge...There are more than thirty Volvo buses on that route but there are only eight ordinary buses. (Interview with V. Sreenivasa, July 28, 2014)

Such an uneven distribution of buses in the city has exacerbated the mobility of several groups of individuals in the city. One casualty of such a distribution has arisen from disadvantaging those who cannot afford to travel by these buses. Given the declining state support extended to BMTC to meet its operational expenses, the company has had to rationalize its bus services on the basis of their profitability. Thus, the priority for air-conditioned buses has come at the cost of a range of services such as minibuses or buses with cheaper fares that could potentially make life easier for the urban poor in the city.

> There are currently no bus services inside slums [informal settlements] in the city. Slum dwellers have to get down 1 to 2 kilometers away and walk to reach their homes. Before, they [BMTC] used to run minibuses within slums and smaller

Figure 3.3
Low-floor, air-conditioned Volvo bus on the 335E route.

neighborhood roads, they now have cancelled these routes. Now, only larger buses are run and these cannot enter such areas. (Interview with Savitha, Bengaluru Slum People's Association, July 23, 2014)

The loss of minibuses and the absence of bus services close to home have had an enormous impact on the mobility needs of the city's poorer residents, especially women.

In the absence of modes of personal mobility, city residents rely on bus services to ferry them from their homes to schools, colleges, and places of work, often many kilometers away. When bus services are not present in the near proximity of their homes, individuals even have to walk a few kilometers to access bus service. In an expanding city like Bengaluru, such commutes in many cases mean leaving home very early and returning late at night on poorly lit or deserted streets. The time involved and the perceived lack of personal safety in making these commutes often force women and young girls to modify their educational and career choices, which affects their prospects for social mobility. Recent episodes of informal settlements being relocated from the center of the city to the far peripheries have exacerbated the economic precariousness that the urban poor, especially women, endure.

> Two months ago, around 800 families living in a slum...in the heart of the city were evicted. They have been moved near a village called Kudlu, 15 kilometers away. Near their relocation site there are only two bus services in the morning—one at 5:30 a.m. and one at 8:30 a.m. Five-thirty is too early to catch to work, and 8:30 is too late. So if you don't want these services, you have to walk a good 2 kilometers. While coming back in the evening, there is only one bus that comes back near their relocation site. Otherwise, you have to walk back a fair distance that is not well lit and is unsafe. (Interview with V. Sreenivasa, July 28, 2014)

Poor women and girls are doubly vulnerable. Moving to the peripheries has reduced the opportunities available for job advancement. At the same time, poor transit service at the peripheries, partly the result of BMTC's overarching prioritization of high-end services, has compounded their economic and social vulnerability.

In addition, given the unaffordability of fares on air-conditioned buses, ordinary buses are subjected to severe overcrowding with "passengers packed like cattle with even women passengers forced to stand on the footplate of the bus" (interview with Savitha, July 23, 2014). One outcome of the severe overcrowding has been greater instances of physical harassment of women conductors (ticket collectors) and commuters on the bus. Although intracity buses in Bengaluru have demarcated zones for women and men, extreme overcrowding often overwhelms such separation and creates opportunities for potential harassers to act with impunity. In response, several citizen groups have requested BMTC to ameliorate crowding on buses by purchasing many more ordinary buses:

> One easy way for BMTC to solve this [harassment] problem is to put more buses in the peak hours. This is what we have been telling them but they have been refusing.... But the technocratic policymaking comes here and they put in CCTV cameras on the buses. You have 6,600 buses, how many cameras are you going to put? One camera is not enough. You have to put two or three.... And who is going to monitor 12,000 to 18,000 18000 cameras? (Interview with V. Sreenivasa, July 28, 2014)

The inability of BMTC to address the availability of ordinary buses, the intense crowding on ordinary buses, and the needs of women and poor commuters all point to a shift in the vision for public transport services in the city.

> What you see is that Bangalore seeks to be gentrified, where all the services are geared toward satisfying the needs of the middle-class population, which has a growing clout in policymaking.... The urban poor are slowly losing their right to the city. (Interview with Ramdas Rao, People's Union of Civil Liberties, July 23, 2014)

This shift makes visible two classes of public transport services in Bengaluru: comfortable, air-conditioned buses to lure the middle classes away from their vehicles and overcrowded, ordinary buses that transport the poor and voiceless majority. This shift is animated in the context of the city's regime of congestion and its powerful underlying discourse of controlling automobile growth. The determination of the regime to control vehicular population in the city has led to several initiatives. The growing inequality in transport services in the city, riding on the overt preference for busing that caters to the affluent, is a noteworthy realization of regime operation.

In addition, the widespread experience of overcrowding, unaffordability, and harassment on ordinary buses has established an atmosphere that is uninviting to commuters. Abandoning buses in favor of personal vehicles is a choice that stems from the undesirable environment that many find within buses. For those with the means to purchase a light motorcycle or a second-hand car, the crushing experience of commuting by bus often tips the balance in favor of driving. Abandoning buses for private automobiles then directly feeds vehicular congestion, provoking newer interventions through the regime of congestion. This dynamic points to the self-perpetuating cycle that exists at the core of the regime of congestion. As vehicular congestion manifests itself on city streets, efforts to prioritize public transit to lure the motorized away from their vehicles result in commuters abandoning overcrowded and unsafe ordinary buses in favor of private automobiles, which contributes further to vehicular congestion.

Conclusion

The regime of congestion in Bengaluru, constituted as a technopolitical regime, is power laden and shapes decision making in urban mobility. At the same time, the self-perpetuating cycle within the regime of congestion locks Bengaluru into a mode that is at once unsustainable, carbon intensive, and inequitable. On the one hand, operationalizing the paradox of more anticongestion measures leads more people to choose driving, which exacerbates vehicular congestion on the streets, thereby requiring more action from the regime. On the other hand, the operation of the regime also reveals its politics. The growing inequality in public transport, manifested in the overcrowding, unaffordability, and harassment experienced during bus commutes, arising from the urgency to address vehicular congestion in Bengaluru, is a political consequence of the city's regime of congestion.

Three corollaries that demand elaboration follow from the chapter's central argument that Bengaluru's regime of congestion is a technopolitical choice that is provoking an unsustainable and inequitable trajectory of change in the city. First, although much of the literature on technopolitical regimes has been conceptualized within Western contexts, I rely on the concept to explicate its operation in the contemporary context of non-Western cities. Technopolitical regimes as hybrid sociotechnical orders are a very apposite framing to describe the recent shift in Indian cities as they pivot away from their postindependence history of bimodal infrastructure provision that granted a modicum of occupancy rights to the titleless urban poor in the city toward the increasing capture of urban governance and service provision by exclusionary discourses of the world-class city. By invoking Chatterjee's concept of political society and the scholarship on urban change in contemporary India, I employ a deliberate means to relocate the concept of technopolitical regime within the theater of struggle on Indian roads.

Second, the utility of the concept of the technopolitical regime in the context of Bengaluru's roads rests on its authorlessness. Roads in Bengaluru are increasingly being redefined through technopolitical strategies into spaces reserved for a burgeoning automobility. At the same time, we have shown that poorer bus users and pedestrians are progressively excluded from roads and their mobility needs deterred, nudging them toward motorization. Capturing this shift within the technopolitical regime concept emphasizes the authorlessness of changes wrought on Bengaluru's streets. Bengaluru's regime of congestion is established through the networking of diverse elements, such as a discourse of congestion, superbureaucrats, mega-infrastructure projects, and investment plans. The presence of these multiple elements diffuses the agency of the regime, thereby preventing any one actor or entity from being held responsible. This is particularly significant because it has far-reaching implications for the question of political accountability associated with the congestion in the city. If the agency for authoring changes is diffused across multiple elements, no single organization or political actor can be held responsible for vehicular congestion even as the situation progressively evolves in an unsustainable and inequitable direction.

Finally, we have seen that the operation of the regime of congestion unleashes a cyclical dynamic that perpetuates an unsustainable and inequitable operation. The presence of this dynamic at the core of the regime is a leading cause for its stability. How does one displace a regime that contains within its operation the seed for perpetuating its existence? Given the interlinkages of the different entities that diffuse the agency of the regime, addressing the one source that can unlock regime operation is not productive. What is required is a multipronged venture that addresses regime operation on multiple organizational, infrastructural, and discursive dimensions.

In the next chapter, I demonstrate how multiple competing sociotechnical landscapes (or infrastructurescapes) of decongestion have proliferated in the city, partly in response to automotive growth. Endowed with power and purpose, these infrastructurescapes intervene and shape the mobile behavior of the residents of the city in ways that for the most part prioritize a mode of motorization sprouting from the calculus of political elites and the world-class city desires of social elites.

4   Infrastructurescapes of Privilege

In May 2016, the Kannada film *U-Turn* was released in theaters across Bengaluru and Karnataka. The film tells a unique tale of the protagonist—a young intern working for the *New Indian Express*—who investigates several incidents concerning an illegal traffic maneuver (the eponymous U-turn) made by motorcyclists on the so-called Double Road flyover in Bengaluru. The flyover is one among the older flyovers operational in Bengaluru. It was constructed along with the Mysore Road flyover in 1999 with funding from the national government's Mega City Scheme. The then newly created Karnataka Urban Infrastructure Development Finance Corporation (KUIDFC) oversaw project construction. The heroine of the film discovers that in the course of each day, several motorcyclists set aside the loose stone blocks that divide opposing traffic streams on the flyover before they perform a U-turn. With a sudden rush of adrenalin, viewers discover that all those who performed this move on the flyover met with an unnatural end. The rest of the movie unravels this mystery. What is particularly notable about the film is that the script is at once taut with the tension of a whodunit yet speaks of the frailties of the human condition in a landscape writ large by concrete infrastructures, such as flyovers, underpasses, and grade separators (figure 4.1).

The film, written, produced, and directed by Pawan Kumar, went on to become an enormously popular film with a significant message.[1] Following a recent trend, the movie was largely crowd-funded by several individuals who had confidence in Pawan's ability to narrate a convincing tale. But it was not the film's mode of production, novel though it was, or the heart-throbbing mystery at its core, that gave *U-Turn* a special appeal for a host of common Bangaloreans who flocked to theaters to see the film. Instead, the film's appeal, to my mind, stemmed from the implicit elevation of the Double Road flyover to the status of an important character in the narrative. The choice of the Double Road flyover is apt because few other pieces of infrastructure embody the frenetic but discordant pace of mobility in the

Figure 4.1
The "25th day" poster of *U-Turn* plastered, ironically, on the barrier of a flyover under construction.

city as it does. For those who visit the city occasionally, the flyover is just one more structure in a city teeming with flyovers. But for resident motorists, this flyover is much more than a structure of concrete and steel. It possesses a character that is a product of a history of shifting (and therefore perplexing) directional arrangements of roads in central Bengaluru since 2000. In response, the flyover has witnessed various combinations of one-way, cross-flow, and bidirectional traffic at different points since its completion, with even a notable instance of a traffic signal being installed on the flyover to regulate traffic.[2] Motorists have learned that while they are navigating this flyover, the direction of movement, the width of the traffic lane, the amount of traffic, the speed of movement, and even the nature of the median divider can all change from time to time, and motorists need to recalibrate their tacit knowledge of the road to the changed circumstance.

The flyover's agential status in *U-Turn* is a public acknowledgment of the deep salience that mobility infrastructures have acquired in the context of a rapidly automobilizing city. But how does one excavate the salience of infrastructures in this city? I propose *infrastructurescape* as an approach that locates infrastructures as vital elements within an active urban landscape, embedded with the power to shape how the urban commuter comes to grips with mobility in the city (Gopakumar 2015b). The construction of infrastructures such as flyovers, road redesign efforts, and bus stations is often justified as a means to reduce traffic congestion on city roads. However, the enduring presence of these infrastructures on the city's landscape more often than not helps to shape the experience of the city. In so doing, they reinforce particular practices of motorization activated by privileged networks of actors—or what Benjamin and Bhuvaneshwari (2006) have referred to as an "upper policy circuit" composed of high political, bureaucratic, social, and corporate elites—and by, more important, reinforcing particular technopolitical sensibilities of movement. For example, flyovers, grade separators, and underpasses are designed to allow automotive movement to bypass intersecting streams of traffic. But a reliance on such infrastructures constructs a landscape that embodies the prioritization of a motorization designed by the privileged to the exclusion of other modes of (nonmotorized or collective) movement.

Ascendance of Decongesting Bengaluru

The salience of infrastructures in Bengaluru has been on the ascendance since the city entered the current phase of flow blockages in the early 1990s. As noted, this phase coincided with the prioritization and reinterpretation of infrastructure on a massive scale. It is during this ongoing phase that congestion has come to be understood as blockages that could potentially disrupt vital economic flows in an interconnected world. Thus, the decongesting of infrastructures—actions seen to promote and prioritize infrastructures to enhance particular kinds of mobilities—has become quite widespread since the 1990s. However, the period since 2006 is particularly noteworthy for the systematic attention being lavished on infrastructures. This period is of interest because of the concurrent operation of several social, political, and administrative processes in Bengaluru, which have contributed to an abnormally heightened salience of infrastructure and congestion in the city.

Infrastructure Development
One particularly influential process at play was the Jawaharlal Nehru National Urban Renewal Mission (JNNURM). Inaugurated by the national government in 2006 with a budget of ₹50,000 crores (about $10 billion) and implemented in sixty-five influential cities in India (including Bengaluru), JNNURM sought to systematically reform the technological and the

governance aspects of infrastructure development between 2006 and 2014, and in so doing, it would "revision Indian cities" (Sivaramakrishnan 2011).[3] This was said to be a necessary step because "the development and expansion of physical infrastructure enhances the ability of cities to be 'engines of economic growth,' thereby sustaining social and economic progress" (Government of India 2005).

JNNURM set out to achieve this manifesto of infrastructure development through two broad thrusts: first, employing reform conditions to alter how infrastructure is developed in Indian cities, and second, relying on large capital-intensive infrastructure projects. Its key aim was described as "enhancing urban service delivery and civic infrastructure through improvements in urban management, land management, financial management, and stakeholder participation" (Ramachandran 2009, 28). The mission realized these proposed urban improvements through a portfolio of reforms, operationalized through a highly regulated, top-down managerial process with specific criteria, strategies, and tools that required specialized skills often unavailable to municipal governments (see also Gopakumar 2015a). The top-down nature of its reform orientation, specific strategies and criteria for projects, and operational hierarchy have facilitated the entry of specialized technical consultants into municipal infrastructure development.[4] Framed as projects, the building of infrastructures has become an exercise that requires consultants to guide the project from initiation and approval to execution.

JNNURM's second major thrust that had enormous consequences for the salience of infrastructures in Bengaluru was its reliance on large capital-intensive projects arising from the availability of enormous funding for citywide infrastructure development. City and state governments saw in this program an opportunity to tap into large flows of capital. But in order to access this capital, a primary condition was for city governments to create a city development plan (CDP) with components such as mobility plans, an urban poverty plan, and others. The CDP would articulate a vision for the city and how infrastructures would contribute to realizing that vision. The reasoning was that, for example, transportation infrastructures are key vectors that shape how the mobility of the city is planned, but the choice of infrastructures must necessarily be shaped by overarching value commitments embedded within the vision articulated by the CDP. However, given the easy availability of funds through JNNURM, accessing funds became a major driver behind the design of CDPs (Mahadevia 2011). In the rush to maximize fund transfers, CDPs were tailored to incorporate massive capital-intensive infrastructure projects. For example, when Bengaluru's CDP made a total plan for ₹22,500 crores (about $ 4.5 billion) (iDeCK 2009), about half of this budget was earmarked for road and road infrastructures. Much of this investment was directed toward capital-intensive projects, such as an elevated inner ring road and peripheral ring road, road overpasses, air-conditioned intracity transport buses, and a high-speed rail link to the airport. Figure 4.2 is an example of an underpass in Bengaluru constructed with JNNURM funds (note the JNNURM logo painted on the central span of the structure).

JNNURM, as Sadoway et al. (2018) show, is not an isolated national government project. Its legacy, manifested through key signatures, such as "flexible networks of key policy actors and advisors; mobile policy ideas, best practices and norms, which got translated into the JNNURM's operational mechanics and its 'reform-oriented' funding conditionalities; and the pervasive role of consultancies in all aspects of the program" (78), endures to varying degrees in more recent national urban transformation projects. Despite its formal closure in 2014, capital-intensive national programs, such as the Smart Cities Mission or the Atal Mission for Rejuvenation and Urban Transformation, have incorporated JNNURM's signatures to a varying degree. Thus, the footprint of capital-intensive infrastructure

Figure 4.2
Underpass in Bengaluru constructed with JNNURM funds (photo: David Sadoway).

projects, limited public involvement, and reliance on technical consultants continue to shape the urban landscape.

Bengaluru's Municipal Vacuum

Toward the end of November 2006, the state government of Karnataka decreed that the jurisdiction of the city of Bengaluru would expand more than three times from 226 square kilometers to 800 square kilometers by annexing and incorporating seven towns and municipalities that adjoin the city. This decision was followed by the equally unexpected decision to dissolve local democratic institutions including the city council of Bengaluru in this expanded region.[5] The reasoning behind this move was that democratic processes underpinning municipal governance would have to wait for the administrative processes of municipal reorganization to be completed before taking root once again. Based on a variety of administrative pretexts, the period of waiting for municipal elections stretched from November 2006 to March 2010. During this time, an administrator appointed by the government of Karnataka oversaw municipal functions conducted by a largely unaccountable bureaucracy.

This period, I believe, offers for two important reasons an intriguing window into, as Star suggests, how "infrastructure is sunk into and inside other structures, social arrangements, and technologies" (Star 1999, 381). First, with the distraction of council hall politics put temporarily on hold, administrator rule would arguably expand rational bureaucratic action and consequently pave the way for quick decisions on critical infrastructural priorities in the city, such as road-widening works, infrastructural projects like automated and multilevel car parking lots, and inner and outer ring roads. The second, and perhaps subtler, reason is that it makes manifest the growing irrelevance of political decision making at the municipal level in the governance and management of urban infrastructure in the city. Benjamin and Bhuvaneshwari (2006) have argued how the increasing authority of technocratic parastatal organizations over infrastructure management in Bengaluru is increasingly delinking decision making into two parallel but aloof "policy circuits." One circuit is composed of parastatal organizations, high bureaucrats in state and municipal administration, and elected elite in the state government, namely, the chief minister of Karnataka state and ministers "in charge of Bengaluru," while the other more plebian circuit corresponds to the dense mesh of patronage and mutual exchange chains that tie elected councilors with "political society" (Chatterjee 2004): grassroots political and governmental functionaries, and marginalized, subaltern urban populations. Seen in this light, the dissolution of the city council marks the overt interruption of the lower policy circuit and its ability to shape the outcomes of municipal governance. It also provides an unfettered opportunity for the upper policy circuit to take sole control over infrastructure development in the city.

Urban Activism by Bengaluru's New Middle Classes

Bengaluru's transition to India's Silicon City was accompanied by a rapid expansion in the scale of urbanization. A key feature that marks urban change in contemporary Bengaluru is the relentless search for successful technical solutions to infrastructure congestion. Problem solving with new technologies, techniques, and methods (often pioneered for the first time in India) has become an established idiom of urban management in the city. Although infrastructure deficits are commonplace in other cities in India, a factor that distinguishes Bengaluru is the significant voice the "new middle classes" (Fernandes 2006) have acquired in advocating the reshaping of urban space and infrastructures in order to redress the infrastructure condition in the city. These "newly-renovated citizens" (Nair 2005, 347) and the managerial elite, with their technocratic visions of urban change, are bolstered by the unprecedented successes they have experienced in a globalizing economy. These interventions, often accomplished in partnership with the state government or technocratic parastatal organizations, seek to inscribe infrastructures as conduits that increasingly facilitate transnational flows of capital, information, goods, and services. Instituted in 1999 as an experimental venture, the Bangalore Agenda Task Force (BATF) was a pioneering example of a partnership mobilized by a cluster of influential new economy industrialists and middle-class activists such as Ramesh Ramanathan (cofounder of Janaagraha[6]) with the express intention of modernizing the city's infrastructure and urban services. The five years that BATF was active were witness to three assertions by the middle classes with regard to infrastructure development. First, the design and development of urban infrastructures needed to conform to global standards and imaginaries. Second, sophisticated technical and managerial knowledge was crucial to achieve these high standards. Finally, the requisite expertise resided with highly qualified, globally educated new middle classes in the city. Through these assertions, the new middle classes have succeeded in establishing a presence in infrastructure development that has largely endured even after BATF was disbanded in 2004.

The truncation of the lower policy circuit with the dissolution of the city council in 2006 is particularly significant because it also marks a period of renewed vigor and action in the claims made by this influential group of urban residents on the imaginaries and imaginations of Bengaluru. One notable development is the role that many members of the BATF played in the institutionalization of JNNURM as a national program of urban change. In a recent paper, other researchers and I have described how JNNURM arose through the interactions between political leaders and high bureaucrats in the national government and key members of the BATF (Sadoway et al. 2018). BATF members like Ramesh Ramanathan were placed in key positions as chair of the National Technical Advisory Group (NTAG) in JNNURM and as members of the government of India's High Power Expert Committee on Infrastructure and Financing that reviewed JNNURM's performance. Such roles have served to boost the visibility and reach of new middle-class groups in Bengaluru's urban governance. A second notable development was the launch of numerous types of partnership ventures that act as Trojan horses (recalling the characterization of Solomon Benjamin, 2010) to attract attention to Bengaluru's infrastructure needs while also enhancing the involvement of new middle-class actors in urban governance. At least three types of such organizations are visible.

One type of new middle-class organization is a high-level infrastructure task force exemplified by ABIDe or the recently constituted Bengaluru Blueprint Action Group (BBAG). Such task forces typically generate plans of action. They create opportunities for new middle-class actors to establish bonds with senior bureaucrats and state political leaders, who also tend to participate in these ventures. Such bonds open the way for greater involvement in official efforts (such as participation in the 2013 committee to restructure Bengaluru's municipal government) or facilitating other new middle-class actions. A second type is a citizen platform where the city's civic issues are discussed and proposals for change are produced. An example is the Agenda for Bangalore (AfB) produced by the Bangalore Political Action Committee. Launched in 2013 by Narayana Murthy, executive chairman of Infosys (a leading software firm based in Bengaluru), AfB proposed several measures, including the development of strong infrastructure, promotion of citizen inclusion in governance and the improvement of governance structure to improve the quality of life of all citizens in the city (BPAC 2013). A final type of organization is an urban stakeholder partnership initiative such as the Bangalore City Connect Foundation (BCCF). As a partnership between Janaagraha and the Bangalore Chamber of Commerce and Industry, BCCF sought to develop long-range technical expertise in local government. It proposed several showpiece transport and road infrastructure initiatives, such as the Tender Specifications for Urban Road Execution (Tender SURE) and Bangalore Traffic and Transport Initiative.

Seen against this background, the period beginning in 2006 was marked by the interplay of three factors: enhanced capture of infrastructure development within the upper echelons of government, the strengthened claims of Bengaluru's new middle classes for enhanced infrastructure, and the presence of large reform-driven schemes of infrastructure development. As a result, this period offers a "truth spot" (Gieryn 2006), or an experimental occasion when the embedding of infrastructures is made intelligible. Riding this urban experimental moment (Karvonen and van Heur 2014), deliberate instances of the unclogging of congested urban infrastructures, such as widening roads, constructing underpasses, and other transport infrastructures, are visible everywhere in Bengaluru's infrastructure landscape and are of particular interest to this inquiry. While the literature on recent processes of change in Bengaluru has highlighted its underlying politics (Benjamin 2010; Nair 2005), there has been limited appreciation for the ways in which both technological and social strategies have come together to shape the city and its mobilities. The experimental moment after 2006 provides an opportunity to comprehend how infrastructures are being assembled in Bengaluru, thereby shaping the perception of mobility in the city. The next section suggests infrastructurescapes as a perspectival approach to identify the landscapes that are being assembled to decongest mobility.

Mobilizing Infrastructurescapes

The concept of infrastructurescape builds on the growing recognition that a perspectival approach to the "world out there" is invaluable as a methodology for glimpsing phenomena constituted through the complex intermingling of people, particular interests, and artifacts. A perspectival approach is useful to examine a landscape in order to unravel the particularities of its constitution—which artifacts dominate the landscape, which social groups have contributed, and what interests lie behind their constitution. A perspectival approach can direct readers' attention in two directions that are integral to research since the mobilities' turn. The foremost rationale for a perspectival approach is to highlight the subjective dimension of the researcher who is actively and consciously engaging urban India from his particular angle of vision as a Western-trained academic of Indian origin. But such a perspective is partial if is not accompanied with a reading of how power resides within fluidities and immobilities. Heeding Anne Jensen's recent proposal of "seeing mobility" (A. Jensen 2011), a perspectival point of view allows us to see how "(im)mobile people or policymakers act on mobility" (Jensen 2011, 255). Visibility is a particular concern given that decongestive work is often rendered invisible due to its routine nature. A perspectival approach can disinter and make visible its hidden constructions. Second, I seek to turn our attention away from the host of sedentary methods of classical social science toward mobile methods (Buscher, Urry, and Witchger 2011) arising from a postnational, mobile sociology (Urry 2000). The interest here is to use methodological insights of studying mobility to secure and capture insights about mobile phenomena like (de)congestion: "Methodological and conceptual innovations...brought about by outside perspectives...is a necessary step in engendering new languages and insights that facilitate the understanding of emerging aspects of the (im)mobile world: (D'Andrea, Ciolfi, and Gray 2011, 155). The key insight produced by infrastructurescape as a methodological or conceptual innovation is to make visible how structure and power are assembled through infrastructure decongestion.

By framing the concept of infrastructurescape as a perspectival construct, I seek to relate it to terms such as *scapes* and *landscapes* common within scholarship in landscape studies, anthropology of global cultural flows, and mobility studies. For most of us, landscapes can be understood as representations of land and space outside the narrow confines of our individual selves. Understood in this fashion, landscapes are always visualized from the perspective of the viewer.[7] Despite this perspectival subjectivity, the sociomateriality of landscapes constrains the scope of interpretation that the viewer engages in. In other words, socially and materially co-constructed objects and arrangements, such as buildings, trees, rivers, and roads that exist in any vision of landscape, "[talk] back...[and set] up resistances...[that] [make] it not possible to do or to think, or to experience certain things" (Bender 2006). By influencing the viewer's visions, thoughts, and actions in subtle ways, landscapes come to be imbued with power. In this way, they are political devices that influence people who enter the landscape to become conscious of a particular message. This message could either reinforce particular relations of inequality or remind people of the underlying ideology that normalizes such relations (see Jones, Jones, and Wood 2004).

Interventions in landscapes are thus a favored means for scripting specific responses from viewers. In parallel, scapes have emerged as framing concepts in the anthropology of global cultural flows and mobility studies. Although they share the perspectival nature of seeing and glimpsing with landscape, scapes diverge from landscapes in their attention to sociomaterialities of flow and movement that penetrate and pervade the contemporary world out there. The anthropologist Arjun Appadurai, a proponent of the concept of describing global cultural flows, directs us to scapes because they grasp the fluid yet irregular shapes that global flows have acquired as they blanket and suffuse sociocultural relations (Appadurai 1996). Taking a different but related view, John Urry, the advocate of the "mobilities turn" in social studies, suggests that scapes as component aspects of global sociomaterial networks and fluids provide an ontology for how sedentary places are constructed. Scapes, according to Urry, "are the networks of machines, technologies, organizations, texts, and actors" (Urry 2000) that reconstitute configurations of space and time and thereby create novel connections and disjunctures. In this sense of the term, scapes of mobility and flow within a critical relational geography are not just constitutive of particular places but also reveal contestations and politics (O. B. Jensen 2009).

Building on these theoretical strands, infrastructurescapes are understood as sociotechnical webs that enroll material elements of infrastructure, people, texts, advertisements, manifestos, protest rallies, and advocacy meetings into heterogeneous assemblages.[8] The heterogeneity of the scape is a product of the variety of materials that together constitute it. This articulation of infrastructurescape is inspired by Matthew Gandy's (2014) recent work, where he understands the intersection of landscape and infrastructure by attending to how water mediates the visible and invisible domains of urban space. These intersections acquire a heightened salience in the cities of the global South where "the relative absence of water infrastructure is paradoxically reflected in a jumbled landscape of pipes, open sewers, tankers (often controlled by organized crime to extract rent from the poor), water vendors (selling sachets of 'pure water'), and buckets (to store available water)" (Gandy 2014, 7). An infrastructurescape therefore not only enrolls particular material infrastructures that stand out in the urban landscape but reaches back into the sociopolitical landscape of the city to tie together the infrastructure with specific institutional or corporate or activist groups that were involved in their development and associated manifestos, advertisements, campaigns, or meetings organized to further these infrastructural associations.

Two attributes that specify an infrastructurescape are its technological sensibility and its organization. The technological sensibility of a scape is inextricably linked to its materiality as manifested in infrastructure projects, artifacts, exemplars, and models that make specific flow pathways. By "sensibility," I refer to a kind of sentiment or response that is evoked in the viewer (and user) of infrastructures. The choice of particular infrastructures in a scape thus pronounces specific sentiments. But the nature of the technological sensibility also suggests a means to incorporate technological artifacts within a worldview of the city. Infrastructurescape architects thus attempt to employ key infrastructural investments to animate particular kinds of imaginaries of what the city should be and the kinds of mobilities that need to be prioritized. The organization of the scape reveals specific social intentions achieved through patterns of linkages that connect social and technological entities. Specific value commitments regarding gains from deploying particular infrastructures accompany these social intentions. Thus, while the technological sensibility of the scape pronounces the sentiment of an urban worldview, its organization displays an underlying value commitment. Together, these qualities of technological sensibility and organization further the particular mobilization of the scape in the city. The work of mobilizing the scape is analogous to sociotechnical imaginaries that, according to Jasanoff and Kim (2009), operate "in the understudied regions between imagination and action, between discourse and decision, and between inchoate public opinion and instrumental state policy" (123). As entities that bridge the difference between imagination and policy action, infrastructurescapes can be compellingly mobilized to shape and direct infrastructure decision making.

How can we, by relying on infrastructurescape as an analytical frame, understand some Bengaluru projects that address congestion of movement in the city? Are there scapes that bind together deliberate technological projects as they seek to refashion the city? I next identify the scapes and imaginaries mobilized using a diversity of social and material construction supplies to decongest Bengaluru city.

Infrastructurescapes of Decongestion in Bengaluru

Three infrastructurescapes prevalent in Bengaluru inform and guide how infrastructure congestion has been tackled in the city: Sarkarada Bengaluru (SB), Brand Bangalore (BB), and Namma Bengaluru (NB).[9] Each of these scapes manifests a vision of what Bengaluru should look like in the future. These visions of the city are often not articulated in a grand, all-encompassing fashion but are instead issue-focused, fragmented visions. Decongesting infrastructure is a recurring thread in the imaginary of each scape. Each of these imaginaries arose through conscious strategies to build a heterogeneous assembly of people, institutions, media summits, and manifestos with infrastructure artifacts, such as underpasses and traffic management systems. These scapes do not exist in isolation but often possess shared nodes (organizations or infrastructure initiatives) that span scape boundaries.

Sarkarada Bengaluru

The SB infrastructurescape assembles a perspective to decongest infrastructure that links together the Sarkar (government of the state of Karnataka), especially its top political leadership (chief minister or minister in charge of Bengaluru),[10] and technocratic parastatal organizations that develop and manage infrastructure in the city of Bengaluru[11] with exemplary infrastructure technologies. Several infrastructure technologies commonly associated with this scape, include "magic-box" underpasses (figure 4.3), transit management centers, elevated roads, orbital ring roads, and grade separators (which allow traffic at an intersection to travel unhindered). Sponsored advertisements and newspaper articles that publicize the inauguration of specific infrastructure technologies, along with policy manifestos of urban development that regularly appear in the media, are vital ingredients that cement together the SB infrastructurescape.

Figure 4.3
Magic-box underpass at the Cauvery Circle intersection.

The assembly of these heterogeneous entities mobilizes a particular perspectival strategy to decongest infrastructures in Bengaluru. I illustrate this with one brief example: the development of a signal-free corridor from central Bengaluru to the new Bengaluru International Airport on the northern periphery of the city. With the inauguration of Bengaluru's new airport in May 2008, state decision makers began considering multiple options to provide a seamless connection between the city and the airport. Although they considered several alternatives, such as a high-speed rail connection and a dedicated monorail to the airport, time and economic considerations contributed to selecting the solution of providing a signal-free path for vehicular traffic on Bellary Road. The solution required a series of grade separators to allow traffic to move unhindered in the north-south direction on Bellary Road. Three infrastructural solutions were proposed to achieve this seamless movement: magic-box underpasses (figure 4.3), segmented arch flyovers (figure 4.4), and a 22-kilometer tolled and elevated expressway north of the city's outer ring road. The first two solutions were engineering innovations that employed the "segmented element technology," a technology that could (on paper at least) realize projects speedily. In this technology,

Figure 4.4
Segmented arch flyover on Bellary Road.

concrete boxes cast according to design specifications, in a remote location, could be brought to the construction site and quickly assembled in the shape needed to form the underpass or flyover. The innovative dimension arose from the fact that these precast concrete boxes eliminated the need for in situ construction techniques that often were time-consuming and labor and capital intensive. In fact, BBMP was so confident the magic box technology would be a game changer in infrastructure construction that it announced that using this technology, the seven underpasses proposed along Bellary Road could be constructed in three days flat![12]

The tolled expressway north of the outer ring road provides a dedicated 22 kilometer elevated corridor for vehicular traffic (primarily private cars or taxis) heading to the airport and beyond, and it was completed in January 2014 at the cost of ₹680 crores (about $110 million).[13] The expressway is built on stilts over the widened Bellary Road. Development of the airport expressway as a solution to the problem of congestion is not an isolated example. Two other intracity expressways, the 20 kilometer Nelamangala tollway and the 10 kilometer Bangalore Electronic City Tollway were inaugurated in 2010 (figure 4.5). Each of these expressways was developed through a model of infrastructure finance whereby the private company that constructed the expressways would recoup their expenses by levying a toll for a specified duration. Following this period, the infrastructure would revert to the public. In addition to these expressways, the recently built Nandi Infrastructure Corridor Enterprise's (NICE) peripheral ring road is yet another controversial tolled expressway.[14]

The array of infrastructure artifacts—not only elevated expressways, underpasses, and grade separators but also traffic and transit management centers and orbital ring roads—mobilized as part of a strategy to decongest, is indicative of the infrastructurescape's technological sensibility. This sensibility could be characterized as a predicament marked by grand solutions and megaprojects that are compatible with existing ways of doing things. Indeed, Vinay Sreenivasa of the Bengaluru Bus Commuter Forum observed that

> several of the changes that we are seeing in Bengaluru today are because of these big ticket projects, you know, megaprojects. One is the Metro; then there is a push for signal-free corridors. Why do you have a signal-free corridor? Because the cars can travel faster, they don't have to stop. And they [infrastructure managers] say that signal-free corridors are being done to prevent traffic jams. But what caused the traffic jams in the first place? The cars. What are you doing now? You are making it easier for the cars. (Interview with Vinay Sreenivasa, July 29, 2014)

The scape's technological sensibility for megaprojects is matched by an organization that brings together an exclusive grouping of actors with

Figure 4.5
Bangalore Electronic City Expressway threading over the NICE peripheral ring road.

political-administrative power and technical expertise. SB infrastructurescape actors, include political leaders, senior bureaucrats (referred to in chapter 3 as superbureaucrats), parastatal bodies, industry and commerce associations, large construction firms, and infrastructure consultants and engineers. This organizational preference shapes in particular ways the nature of problem framing, solving, and executing solutions to address congestion of transport infrastructure. At one level, this manifests as administrative rationality. For instance, the magic box underpass was an indigenously developed solution proposed by a construction firm and adopted by a task force for improving airport connectivity.[15] A range of administrative considerations—substantially reduced costs, ease of assembly, and minimal disruption of commuters during the construction phase—motivated the adoption of this technology. Although these considerations are necessary for effective project implementation, administrative intelligence alone is usually insufficient for charting and shaping trajectories of mobility patterns required to meet particular social and political objectives. This is the domain of leadership, and it manifests a notable aspect of the scape's organization.

Infrastructurescapes of Privilege

Leadership in the SB infrastructurescape rests on the elected political leaders of Karnataka state. Since the early 2000s, the leadership role has been provided by the chief minister of the state of Karnataka, usually assisted by a minister in charge of Bengaluru. In 2010, the scape leaders were the chief minister of the state of Karnataka, B. S. Yediyurappa, and the minister for Bengaluru, R. Ashok (figure 4.6), as well as a senior bureaucrat, such as the adviser on urban affairs. From 2013 to 2018, S. Siddharamaiah as chief minister and K. J. George as minister for Bengaluru provided leadership on the city's infrastructure development. Leadership of the infrastructurescape is demonstrated through a strategy I describe as stewardship. The overarching thrust in the SB infrastructurescape is to portray the political leadership as stewards actively engaged with the congestion problems in the city, but at the same time, they remain largely unaccountable to urban residents. Their portrayal as stewards is crucial since it suggests limited ownership and a limited role in conceptualizing solutions; stewards also do not author proposals or propose particular development trajectories informed by a vision; instead, they maintain a hands-off approach, thereby giving technocrats free rein. As stewards, both the chief minister and the minister in charge may provide a nudge here and a push there to infrastructure efforts but the actual work of planning, designing, and implementing are understood to be technical exercises best left to large technocratic parastatal bodies (figure 4.7).

Their stewardship role is visible in instances when bureaucrats provide on-site updates to political leaders on the progress in construction. Stewards limit themselves to making largely obvious comments, such as about

Figure 4.6
Yediyurappa and Ashok, seen inaugurating a flyover (left) and the Sanjaynagar grade separator on the way to the airport (right) (source: *New Indian Express*).

Figure 4.7
Yediyurappa (in white) and Ashok give a nudge to Bengaluru's infrastructure (source: *New Indian Express*).

the pace of the construction, how soon the project will be completed, or whether the project needs to be speeded up to ensure quicker completion. But it is when an infrastructure is inaugurated (or when a foundation stone is laid) that stewards make their finest appearance. Such instances are invariably accompanied by government-sponsored, full-page newspaper advertisements or multipage information supplements (figure 4.8). Advertisements are sponsored by the implementing agency, usually Bengaluru's city government (BBMP) or a major parastatal organization (BMTC or BDA). The chief minister usually occupies a larger-than-life image in these promotional materials. The steward's image is accompanied by an appealing slogan like, "Bangalore city on the move," or, "Assuring a smooth drive." In addition, advertisements usually connect the inauguration with the realization of the chief minister's dream. For example, figure 4.8 portrays how BBMP helps realize the chief minister's dream of "developing infrastructure to transform Bengaluru into a global hub."

Although the SB scape appears to envision a pathway toward infrastructure decongestion that is packaged as global in its ambitions, there is a significant difference between SB and Brand Bangalore, the other scape that has overtly global ambitions for the city. One reason is how infrastructures fit within the calculus that the chief ministers have constructed

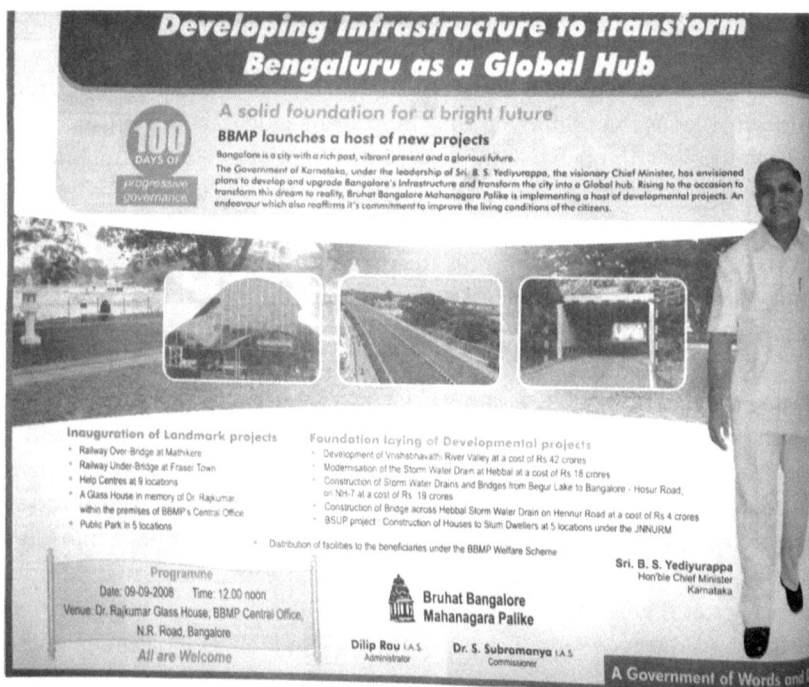

Figure 4.8
BBMP's infrastructure advertisement heralded by Yediyurappa (source: *New Indian Express*).

for advancing their political interests. By identifying themselves through media publicity as stewards of the city's infrastructures, political leaders are depicted as offering infrastructure for residents. Infrastructures, however, are proposed not as functional elements in a well-defined plan but as a material legacy of the leader's "visionary leadership." In the years to come, the massive flyovers, underpasses, and expressways become markers of the contribution a leader made. This is significant because it suggests that it is the materiality of the infrastructure—embodied in its dimensions, its longevity, and its massiveness but not its functionality—that contributes to its legacy. In other words, the bigger the infrastructure, the greater the demonstrable legacy it grants its benefactor. As Leo Fernandes of the Environment Support Group notes, "All these [mega] projects are essentially…to leave a legacy, not to make cities functional" (interview with Leo Fernandes, July 29, 2014). The desire to leave a visible legacy is a powerful motivator of political action. Thus, solutions for resolving infrastructure congestion are proposed and implemented by the state government. The practices of assembling this scape reinvent and reify the privileged position of the state's political elites, and the government with its established ways of building infrastructure emerges as the primary interlocutor of the global in Bengaluru. Thus, despite the overtly global ambitions of the scape, the work of mobilizing the SB infrastructurescape is a provincial process with solution proposals, design, and implementation being accomplished by parastatal organizations, such as BDA or BMTC, with the involvement of local technical firms and contractors. Political leaders are content with performing a benevolent stewarding role.

Brand Bangalore
With the phenomenal rise of the new economy industries in Bengaluru, the new middle classes have benefited the most from the wealth of global intellectual, informational, and economic capital that now is routed through their city. The maintenance of Bangalore as a global knowledge hub with standards of infrastructure comparable to those of other international cities lies at the heart of the vision proposed by the Brand Bangalore (BB) infrastructurescape. Ramesh Ramanathan, cofounder of Janaagraha and a key participant in this scape, asked, while reflecting on the planning and design of cities, "Why don't we plan out our cities better? Why don't we think through these problems a little more coherently because building a metro is not like buying vegetables?," suggesting that the current ways of doing things are inappropriate for a globalizing city.[16]

The recent prominence of this imaginary is reflected in the dense and heterogeneous associations it has acquired. BB is organized around an ecosystem of actors, such as industry associations (Bangalore Chamber of Commerce and Industry), multiscale advocacy groups such as Janaagraha, urban stakeholder partnership initiatives such as Bangalore City Connect Foundation (BCCF),[17] task forces such as ABIDe (and earlier by BATF),[18] policy entrepreneurs (such as Ramesh Ramanathan and Ashwin Mahesh, founder of Mapunity, a social technology platform), and charitable foundations. Staffed by highly competent technical professionals who bring skills in engineering, planning, and project management, these social actors actively engage the government and the general public at multiple levels and through multiple arenas. Mediating the relations between scape actors is an array of material entities: plans and technical documents, such as ABIDe's Plan Bengaluru 2020; the redesigned Vittal Mallya Road (a model road that integrates modern road design principles with the latest in street furniture, pavement surfacing, and shaping); and the Big10 direction-oriented bus services launched by BMTC (figure 4.9). Other entities associated with the scape are the India Urban Conferences convened by Janaagraha (in collaboration with Yale University and the national Ministry of Urban Development), and media summits, such as *Economic Times*'s "Bangalore: High Point of the Flat World," that brought together representatives from BB, including the cofounder of Janaagraha with senior state-level technocrats and the adviser on urban affairs to the chief minister. Tangible partnerships like the Bangalore Traffic and Transport Initiative (BTTI) represent yet another scape venture. BTTI was founded as a joint effort between the industry-supported BCCF and the Bangalore Metropolitan Land Transport Authority to create a nodal platform for addressing traffic and transport issues in an integrated manner.

In order to understand the specific technological and organizational strategies marshaled by the BB infrastructurescape, we examine briefly some efforts undertaken. In August 2007, the Bangalore City Connect Foundation (BCCF) was established as a registered trust with both Janaagraha and the CII as founding members (Baindur 2017, 125). BCCF launched several initiatives that focused on traffic and transport in the city, specifically on urban

Figure 4.9
Big10 bus service in Bengaluru.

design, transport planning, and traffic engineering. These efforts included the design and development of a model road (Vittal Mallya Road), the institutionalization of the BTTI, and the planning of a feeder network of buses that connect with the Metro network (BCCF n.d.). The redesign of Vittal Mallya (VM) Road is particularly significant because, as Sadoway and Gopakumar (2017) note, the road came to serve as a test bed for the formulation of Tender SURE (Specifications for Urban Road Execution), a guide for road design specifications and a manual for road execution, including work specification, tendering, and contracting. Tender SURE was jointly authored by BCCF and India Urban Space Foundation (now Jana Urban Space Foundation or JUSP),[19] which was then adopted by the government of Karnataka as a guide for roadwork execution in seventeen selected arterial roads in Bengaluru's central business district.[20] The redesign of VM Road was initiated solely by private financing (the UB group and Prestige Construction group) whose real estate interests abut both sides of the road. With its inauguration in June 2010, VM Road presented a roadscape that was considerably different from the one most Bangaloreans see (figure 4.10). Among the design innovations are infrastructure ducts and stormwater drains concealed from plain sight, below the pedestrian walkway; a road surface of uniform width and level; and a pedestrian walkway clearly demarcated from the road space through linked bollards and uniform pavement heights. Many of these design features have been imported into Tender SURE.

Another example of the BB scape is visible in the steering role played by the ABIDe task force in articulating a direction-oriented traffic management system.[21] This system would decongest traffic movement along the Big 10 arterial roads in the city.[22] Plan Bengaluru 2020, produced by ABIDe, proposes "an aggressive strategy of junction elimination...formulated to reduce travel time on Big10 arterial roads to ORR [outer ring road] and beyond" (ABIDe 2010, 46). One visible manifestation of this intent was the introduction of Big10 intracity bus services. Introduced in February 2009, Big10 buses, with their distinctive green and black livery and bilingually readable logo (figure 4.9), ply dedicatedly on the Big10 arterial roads. Prior to 2009, intracity bus services in Bengaluru ran exclusively to a destination orientation with buses radiating out from three major bus terminals (Majestic, Market, and Shivajinagar) to different points in the city. Such a system, ABIDe argued, contributed not only to increased congestion on city streets (from running numerous buses with overlapping routes on arterial routes) but also to extended wait times for commuters (R. Gowda, Mahesh, and Pabbisetty 2014).[23] Their recommendation, conceived and implemented by ABIDe's core member Ashwin Mahesh, was to introduce direction-oriented

Figure 4.10
A view of the renovated VM Road.

bus services in the city that would travel back and forth along the city's radial routes. Mahesh's innovation lay in conceiving an entire intracity bus system with numerous directional and cyclical bus routes (figure 4.11).

While these diverse social and material interactions at multiple levels emphasize a sensibility that values technological sophistication, they also call attention to partnership as a strategic imperative that mobilizes the scape. The dynamic of partnership underlies several social and material enterprises initiated by the scape. The ABIDe Task Force, BTTI, the redesign of Vittal Mallya Road, and Big10 buses create platforms for explicitly forging partnerships with a range of actors both within and across scapes. Working through these platforms, scape actors have successfully established cross-organizational partnerships that seek to pull in actors from the other scapes, especially the governmental scape. For example, Tender SURE road execution proceeds in partnership with the BBMP, and the Big10 buses were launched in partnership with the Bangalore Metropolitan Transportation

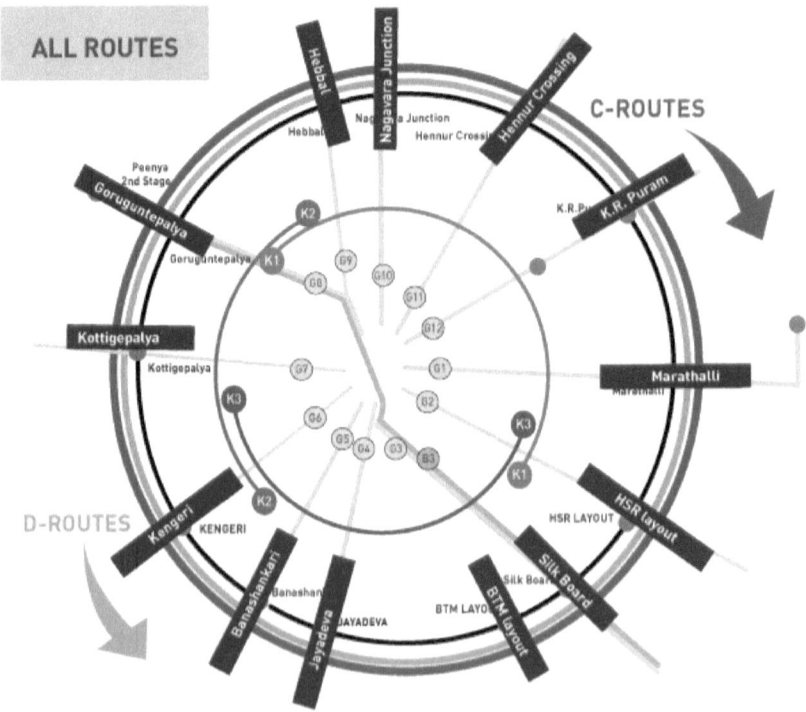

Figure 4.11
Schematic of the direction-oriented bus system in Bengaluru (source: Mapunity).

Corporation (BMTC). It is possible for these diverse enterprises to take root in the city because Bengaluru extends the possibility for different stakeholders to participate in the governance of the city. At least two factors shape the nature of this participation. The first arises from the fragmentation of infrastructure planning and governance arrangements in the city. The presence of dedicated parastatal bodies like the BMTC or the BWSSB, which exist independent of the city government to manage city infrastructures, has not only weakened the ability of the city government to speak for the city as a whole but has, in addition, promoted a segmented approach to infrastructure management. In an interview in May 2011, Ashwin Mahesh, a core member of ABIDe, proposed that

> [since] there is no integrated planning authority, everybody does their own plans, so anybody who begins to integrate anything is powerful.... If you are BMTC managing director or the head of any other parastatal, you don't have the data or tools to visualize multiple aspects of the city on a technology platform the way I can...so anyone who can do things like that will have some knowledge advantage over the formal system. (Interview with Ashwin Mahesh, May 24, 2011)

A fragmented urban administration has extended opportunities for partnerships to intervene and redress resulting technological and managerial deficiencies. More often than not, partnerships offer integrative solutions that are beyond the scope of what can be accomplished from within rigid bureaucratic silos. They offer unconventional pathways such as the Big10 direction-oriented bus system or Tender SURE road design process that work with existing bureaucratic structures but at the same time channel new ideas and techniques of urban design that circulate globally.

Second, any such partnership has tended to reinforce existing structures of privilege in the city, with particular social groups being predominantly represented. Thus, any external partnerships on infrastructure and planning are exemplified by "the social networks of privileged people from diverse backgrounds...finding common cause in issues of the city" (interview with Mahesh, May 24, 2011). For instance, core members of partnerships, such as BATF or ABIDe, were overwhelmingly staffed by highly educated Brahmin men who have ethnic roots outside Bengaluru. But it is not only ethnic or sociocultural roots that have contributed to the structures of privilege underlying partnerships. Yet another compelling factor has been transnational networks of corporate wealth and influence. Connections with corporate wealth are not difficult to discern in most instances of partnerships. BCCF, for instance, was supported by the Confederation of Indian Industry (CII), a lobbying group for business groups. In other instances, such as ABIDe or BATF, corporate members from high-tech sectors are overwhelmingly represented at the table. For Vinay Baindur, these partnership platforms provide a venue to "identify and set a vision for the city by corporates such as those from IT/BT sectors, real estate developers, and transport and infrastructure contractors" (Baindur 2017, 127). Providing a concrete example, he mentions that it was as a result of corporate lobbying exercised by CII and the information technology and biotechnology firms that JUSP was asked by the government of Karnataka to "design and prepare the detailed project report for the implementation of the Tender SURE project on Bengaluru's roads" (128). Even as the faith in the ability of the privileged outsider to fashion visionary urban change in the city has seemingly become commonplace in Bengaluru, it has reinforced disparities by attending almost exclusively to zones of privilege and commerce, while disregarding peripheral regions that are overwhelmingly populated by the socially and economically disadvantaged. The next scape seeks to address this perceived bias and reclaim Bengaluru for this disenfranchised majority.

Namma Bengaluru
Namma Bengaluru (NB) is an infrastructurescape mobilized by an assortment of progressive and nativist organizations with strong affiliations to "political society" (Chatterjee 2004). It has recently begun articulating a more strident but often also more diffused position on infrastructure congestion. Organizations that populate this scape include the Bengaluru People's Forum (a collective of progressive environmental, social, and policy advocacy organizations) that includes organizations such as the Environment Support Group; CIVIC Bangalore; networks and platforms such as Hasiru Usiru and Bengaluru Bus Prayanikara Vedike (BBPV);[24] the more chauvinistic Bengaluru for Kannada and Kannadiga groups, such as Karanataka Rakshana Vedike (KRV) and Kannada Sene; residents' welfare associations; community-based organizations; and the subaltern "new trade unions" (RoyChowdhury 2003).[25] A facet that unites these disparate groups is an explicit agenda of reclaiming and reterritorializing Bengaluru in the interest of the majority, less privileged, less mobile, or otherwise excluded inhabitants of the city. For such groups, infrastructure congestion and existing decongestive efforts are a symptom of skewed policy priorities that by favoring the interests of the (global) elite contribute to furthering the marginalization of the urban poor, gendered, and differently abled in urban space and infrastructure. The diversity of grassroots urban actors with their agenda of extending access to clogged infrastructures to the underserved is a key organizing principle of this scape.

Unlike the previous two scapes, the diversity of actors with their differing motives and interests ranging from the progressive to the techno-optimist to the chauvinistic, confer the NB infrastructurescape with a relatively diffused constitution that nudges the scape in often contradictory directions. For example, contemporary Kannada linguistic parties like KRV, motivated by a chauvinistic agenda of safeguarding the Kannada language and cultural practices, have increasingly resorted to intolerant, and even violent, measures directed occasionally at destroying public and personal property. Such actions have militated against the possibility of such groups' building interorganizational coalitions with more progressive organizations committed to reterritorializing the city.[26] Interorganizational civic forums and networks have, however, proliferated recently by tapping into a diverse substrate of grassroots community organizations, networks, residents' associations, professionals, researchers, activists, and motivated individuals. Interorganizational forums, such as the Bengaluru Bus Prayanikara Vedike (or the Bengaluru Bus Commuter Forum, BBPV), Bengaluru Janara Vedike (or the Bengaluru People's Forum), Bengaluru Road Widening and Transport Projects Impacted Communities (BATPIC), coexist and intermesh with civic citizen networks, such as Hasiru Usiru (or Green Life) and Praja (or Citizens).

These multiple groups bring differing agendas, organizational strategies, and interventions to bear on the question of mobility in Bengaluru. The Bengaluru Janara Vedike, for instance, came together in March 2010 as a platform for several progressive voluntary organizations (such as ActionAid, Alternate Law Forum, Slum Jagattu, Garment and Textile Workers Union, and Hasiru Usiru) to monitor the governance of the city (Environment Support Group 2010). The release of the Janara Pranalike (or People's Manifesto) marked the inauguration of the Bengaluru Janara Vedike (figure 4.12). The manifesto outlines "progressive policies and measures that we feel, the people of Bengaluru deserve" (Bengaluru Janara Vedike 2010, 3) in several areas, including public transport and mobility. The mobility measures outlined in the manifesto range from outright demands, such as "signal-free corridors must be scrapped forthwith," to practical suggestions such as "[arterial roads must be decongested by disallowing parking" (6). Since the launch of the manifesto, though, the activities of the Bengaluru Janara Vedike have been quite circumscribed and largely limited to an online forum for sharing information and coordination.[27] The relative dormancy of the organization is also seen in the BATPIC—an interorganizational network that coalesced in July 2012 to "work as a network of solidarity amongst impacted communities to resist illegal displacement and unsustainable and wrong projects" (Environment Support Group 2012).

Janara Pranalike
People's Manifesto

for the consideration of voters and candidates
participating in elections to the
Bruhat Bengaluru Mahanagara Palike, March 2010

evolved by
Bengaluru Janara Vedike / Bangalore People's Forum

A Forum of various progressive organisations including:

Urban Research Centre, The Avenue Road Traders Associations, Slum Jagattu, Sangama, Samarthanam Trust for the Disabled, Parishkaran, Nightingales Medical Trust, Maraa, Kilikili, Janasahayog, Jana Arogya Andolana Karnataka, Hasiru Usiru
, Garment and Textile Workers Union, Environment Support Group (Environment, Social Justice and Governance Initiatives) , Concerned for Working Children, Community Health Cell, Centre for Education and Documentation
, Bengaluru Slum Janara Kriya Vedike, Aneka, Alternate Law Forum, ActionAid

Figure 4.12
Janara Pranalike, or People's Manifesto (source: Bengaluru *Janara Vedike*).

The dormancy in the BATPIC forum could be related to its incapacity to translate the localized impacts of transportation displacements into a citywide mobilization for urban transformation that will change how the city builds transportation infrastructure. This despite the network being supported by established voluntary organizations, such as the Environment Support Group and Alternate Law Forum, and linked to the active Hasiru Usiru network; residential associations, such as the Bangalore South Residential Welfare Association; and place-based community groups, such as Citizen Support Group Rajajinagara, Koramangala Initiative, and We Care for Malleshwaram.

In contrast, Hasiru Usiru (HU) and Bengaluru Bus Prayanikara Vedike (BBPV) have been relatively active agents of the NB infrastructurescape, and they have been more successful in reshaping (in a nominal fashion, at least) the city's dominant infrastructurescapes. HU began its existence in 2003 as an informal group of citizens concerned about the rampant felling of trees along avenues in the name of road widening. It is now predominantly an Internet-based network (with a listing of over eight hundred members in its Yahoo group), which also includes a much smaller core group (ranging from eight to twenty-five members) who meet face-to-face to initiate and coordinate major HU action events.[28] Since its inception, the seven-year period up to about 2010 could be characterized as a phase of expansion as HU grew not only in terms of membership (partly due to its increased visibility from greater campaign activities in the city scape) but also in spheres of emphasis. During this phase, HU expanded its emphasis from an initial largely reactive (protest-oriented) effort to save trees along avenues in the city to a more proactive (awareness and educational) approach to "reclaiming Bengaluru's commons" in the face of what the group believed was a systematic onslaught on the city's livability (figure 4.13).[29] Despite these shifts in emphasis, this period served HU to realize a watchdog role that not only monitored Bengaluru's urban environment but also safeguarded its marginalized inhabitants (Enqvist, Tengo, and Orjan 2014). Since 2010, however, HU has sought to complement its watchdog role through a constructive approach that offers practical guidelines, suggestions, and measures for public agencies in Bengaluru.[30] BBPV is yet another active interorganizational platform that exists within the NB infrastructurescape, but it occupies a different organizational footprint from HU. Whereas HU is a network of individuals, BBPV is a composite "collective of various organisations and commuters" (Bengaluru Bus Prayaanikara Vedike 2013), including HU; the Alternate Law Forum; voluntary organizations such as the Garment and Textile Workers Union; Vimochana (a women's rights group);

Figure 4.13
Poster of the Reclaim Bangalore's Commons Campaign (source: *Hasiru Usiru*).

and progressive political parties, such as the New Socialist Alternative and Praja Rajakiya Vedike. Capitalizing on the shifts in HU's campaign portfolio (with whose core organizational actors, there is considerable overlap), BBPV has assembled a far more diverse repertoire of campaigns (such as the "50 *paise* campaign" for affordable bus fares), festivals (Janasnehi Busigagi or For People-Friendly Buses), public hearings (Makkala Adalat or children's court), and measures and recommendations such as the Bengaluru Bus Manifesto.

In contrast, with the dominant organizational strategies of stewardship and partnership in the other infrastructurescapes, the key organizing principle of scape actors has been citizenship. Efforts to construct NB are mobilized around the strategy of extending citizenship to less mobile and less privileged residents of the city. The imaginaries of decongesting infrastructures provide an opportunity to reconstitute infrastructures to allow greater voice for the marginalized in making decisions. Pursuing inclusive forms of citizenship, mobilization of the scape is often marked by protests directed at interventions made by actors through other infrastructurescapes in the city. But in developing citizenship as a key organizing principle, key NB scape actors have had to reflexively confront questions of maintaining popular legitimacy, sustaining volunteer participation, and reducing elite bias while simultaneously being aware of their roles in perpetuating these biases. This stems from an intense awareness of the unconscious biases that could potentially be inserted into the NB infrastructurescape because of the predominantly privileged educational and social backgrounds that key mobilizers in the scape possess. In seeking to counter these innate biases and still mobilize a citizen orientation, core scape actors relied on what Rao (2014, 141) refers to as an "ideological connect [that] contributed to the development of a shared worldview." This shared political viewpoint, motivated broadly by social justice or counterhegemonic liberation ethics, seeks to develop a praxis that first generates critical awareness of the existing situation in the city among the masses of the excluded; spurs collective mobilization directed against specific interventions in the urban commons; and suggests specific measures (through alternative manifestos) that can direct governments to more inclusive and equitable outcomes. This praxis, scape mobilizers believe, can lead the NB infrastructurescape to operationalize a just and inclusive citizenship in Bengaluru. Although this praxis is the source of the infrastructurescapes' greatest strength in mobilizing actors for a common cause, it also poses limitations for the kinds of interventions that are considered appropriate to the scape. For example, core members of the Hasiru Usiru network view the group Praja, which also considers itself a citizen network, with distrust.[31] A key reason is due to the collaborative partnerships that exist between Praja and state agencies. Instances of such collaboration exist in the case of the Mobilicity Unconference (with the directorate of urban land transport) and the Bus Day event (with the BMTC). Such efforts signal their lack of political consciousness, which allows Praja to participate in the status quo without attempting to change it in favor of those who are currently excluded.

The predominantly counterhegemonic praxis that underlies the constitution of the NB infrastructurescape has shaped its technological sensibility. The dominant technological sensibility one associates with the scape is ideational. Being products of ideation, technologies associated with the scape exist in a prescriptive future commonly articulated within manifestos, reports, and pamphlets. The launch in 2010 of a Janara Pranalike, or People's Manifesto, that outlines a position on mobility and decongestion, which is much more inclusive (figure 4.12), is an effort to ideate a coherent technological sensibility of infrastructure change that is aligned with organizational principles of citizenship. Thus, a key thrust of the People's Manifesto is that "all spaces of mobility must preserve and protect the right of way of pedestrians and cyclists" (Bengaluru Janara Vedike 2010, 5). The manifesto articulates an alternate vision of streetscape and associated road infrastructures. For example, it calls for secure and interconnected cycling lanes that allow anyone to travel anywhere in the city and for prioritizing cheap and affordable public transport on the roads. At the same time, the manifesto is strident in its disapproval of megatransportation projects, flyovers, and underpasses. Despite this vocal call for an alternate technological sensibility of mobility in the city, there are surprisingly few instances of artifacts that seek to reclaim roads for pedestrians and cyclists. An exception is when residents in a neighborhood block a road in an effort to prevent their neighborhood roads from becoming a crowded thoroughfare (figure 4.14). Stone bollards are erected often by residents (with the support of the local councilor or the local police station) in the road to create a material barrier that prevents motor vehicles from using the stretch. Doing so allows residents to protect their streets from becoming yet another conduit for intracity circulation of traffic. Apart from such stray instances, the absence of more ubiquitous and more momentous artifacts for reclaiming streets and streetscapes for the marginalized has accorded the scape a predominantly ideational technological sensibility.

Comparing Infrastructurescapes of Bengaluru

In this chapter, we have encountered three infrastructurescapes of decongestion that have become prevalent in Bengaluru in the second decade of the twenty-first century—Sarkarada Bengaluru (SB), Brand Bangalore (BB), and Namma Benguluru (NB). Figure 4.15 outlines some key nodes and links that constitute the sociotechnical network underlying each infrastructurescape. Given its heterogeneous character, nodes in each infrastructurescape can be social or organizational or artifactual. Building on the brief narratives of each scape, I propose three empirical dimensions to compare them: key organizational principle, technological sensibility, and value commitment. Table 4.1 depicts the comparison of the three infrastructurescapes across these dimensions. Each infrastructurescape is organized through a unique pattern of actors that foreground, through their actions, a key principle that animates the effort. This organizing principle informs the reasoning that underlies the strategies of scape building. The SB scape is organized around the notion of stewardship with regard to infrastructure development. Stewardship suggests facilitation of an ongoing process determined not by some future aim or goal but by historical constraints and short-term benefits to state political and administrative elites. The BB and NB scapes are motivated by a future-oriented vision of change. Whereas BB is motivated to realize a world-class future for the city, it does so through

Infrastructurescapes of Privilege

Figure 4.14
A connecting street blocked at both ends by hand-cut stone bollards.

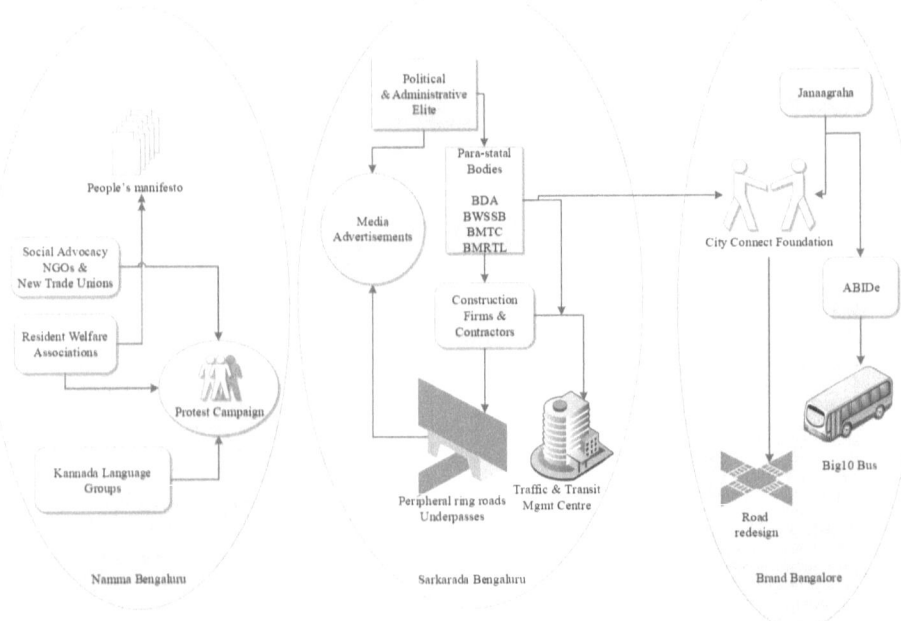

Figure 4.15
Sociotechnical networks of Bengaluru's infrastructurescapes.

the organizing principle of solidifying partnerships with a wide array of urban actors—both governmental and nongovernmental. NB seeks to further a socially just future that addresses the needs of the marginalized by organizing around the conception that mobility and street use represent an integral element of the experience and exercise of citizenship.

In addition, each scape's organizing principle finds concrete expression through its associated technological sensibilities. The nature of the material fabric of the infrastructurescape, as expressed through the diverse array of technologies and artifacts, offers deep insight into its constitution. But sensibility also suggests decentering our gaze away from technological attributes alone toward processes through which artifacts relate to scape actors and their projects. Thus, in understanding the technological sensibility of SB, the reliance on mega-infrastructure projects, such as magic box underpasses and segmented arch flyovers, needs to be appreciated within the political calculus of constructing infrastructure in the city. The prevalence of massive infrastructure projects closely tied to leaving legacies rather than serving a functional aim allows the technological sensibility of the SB scape

Table 4.1
The Characteristics of Bengaluru's Infrastructurescapes

	Sarkarada Bengaluru	Brand Bangalore	Namma Bengaluru
Technological sensibility	Legacy infrastructures	Global exemplars	Ideational futures
Organizing principle	Stewardship	Partnership	Citizenship
Normative orientation	Political spectacle	Proselytization	Inclusivity

to be characterized as legacy infrastructures. Thus, in doing so SB reinforces existing political and institutional interests without proposing a transformative process of change. BB's change orientation is facilitated through the development of a host of exemplars, including road redesign efforts, alternate bus routes such as the Big10, and bus transportation studies, which introduce new ways of building infrastructure in conformity with international technical and aesthetic standards. Although NB possesses an alternate vision of socially progressive change (as articulated in the People's Manifesto), its technological sensibility is considerably more ideational in the absence of existing artifactual exemplars that embody this vision. The example of hand-cut stone bollards used to restrict the flow of automobiles in neighborhoods is an isolated but graphic example of efforts to create scapes that embody a human-scale relation between infrastructures and people.

The intersection of specific organizational principles and technological sensibilities embeds each infrastructurescape with unique normative commitments through which scape members attempt to further particular political orientations or purposes that they subscribe to. The expectation is that these normative commitments elicit particular forms of behavioral reactions among the traveling public that beholds or uses these road infrastructures. On the basis of the mammoth technological sensibilities that pervade its infrastructurescape, SB assembles a scape where the spectacle of grand technological solutions is a key value commitment. In the minds of the main actors, the spectacle of infrastructure will evoke feelings of awe and even reverence for political leaders in users and beholders. Such feelings of respect and appreciation would bolster their image as decisive and capable leaders of the state, thereby contributing to their popularity. The focus on the value of spectacle downplays the functional aspects, thereby reinforcing the status quo of contemporary forms of movement and circulation in the city. Similarly, a combination of the motivation on the part of corporate and technical elites to partner with state actors and the ability to construct tangible exemplars embeds BB with an orientation that seeks to proselytize and convert state infrastructure elites and the general public to new modes of infrastructure conception, planning, and execution with new forms of inhabiting and moving on city streets.

The implicit agenda of BB promoters is that current modes of infrastructure development in the city are not in keeping with international trends, and this reflects poorly on the image of Bengaluru in a globally connected world. What is particularly noticeable is that it is the calculations of elites that dominate the normative orientations of both the SB and BB scapes. In this, the NB differs markedly from the other two scapes. By focusing on the interests of subaltern communities, the normative orientation of the NB infrastructurescape attempts to instill values of social justice and inclusivity into infrastructure development. Promoters of NB veer away from the objectives of SB and BB, which they associate with the ongoing exclusion of marginal groups in the city's landscape, and look to infrastructures that will enhance the capacity of the marginalized to assert their rights to coexist and flourish while reclaiming roads and other mobile commons for themselves.

Conclusion

Bengaluru serves as an intriguing illustration of the specific processes unleashed by perceived exigencies of automobile growth-driven congestion in the city. The empirical dimensions of infrastructurescapes delineated in this chapter are inextricably related to specific historical, political, and social factors at work in the city. For instance, the proselytizing appeal of the new middle classes in Bengaluru is as much a product of a recent history of a depoliticized society with subdued grassroots mobilization as it is of a state apparatus that is porous to privileged outsiders shaping policy priorities.

This story of change in the city offers three lessons for understanding how automobile congestion contributes to urban change. First, this chapter proposes infrastructurescape as an interpretative framework that allows researchers to understand decongestive work as political practice that assembles together a social, technical, and material landscape of automobility. Grounded within landscape and mobility studies, infrastructurescapes facilitate the visualization of the mechanics of power and influence within the context of urban infrastructure change. Three dimensions characterize the mechanics of infrastructurescape: a dominant principle that organizes the scape, the technological sensibility underlying it, and the nature of value commitments that emerge through its assembly. Second, the speedy pace of urbanization in Bengaluru, combined with technocratic public providers of infrastructure who are amenable to the technical sophistication of a self-obsessed and influential new middle class, have catalyzed the dominance of infrastructurescapes of privilege. Employing a sociotechnical framing, we are able to appreciate how the calculus of privileged sectors—political and administrative elites on the one hand and social and corporate elites on the other—has come to dominate infrastructure development in the city. In the face of legacy-oriented sensibilities of government leadership and the proselytizing appeal of global values and exemplars touted by the new middle classes, the cityscape available for the marginalized subalterns has dramatically shrunk. Apart from isolated examples of bollards driven into streets to shelter neighborhoods, infrastructurescapes in the city have been largely dominated by privilege. Finally, Bengaluru's landscapes of (de)congestion indicate how these are deliberate efforts that are laden with power and purpose. The assembly of social actors, organizations, interorganizational coalitions with artifacts, technologies, and plans into landscapes endow them with power. Accompanying this power is the intention to intervene to address congestion in the city. This intention to decongest Bengaluru resides not only in the minds of key promoters of scapes but is also captured within reports, plans, campaigns, and media advertisements. The combination of power and purpose embedded within the infrastructurescape grants it the agency to intervene in the mobility behaviors of urban residents of Bengaluru. Thus, given the technological sensibility of the three scapes in the city, the possibility for alternate paradigms of mobility appears quite remote.

In the next chapter, I discuss the constitution of a durable identity of automotive citizenship. I argue that this citizenship is expressed through a range of social, artifactual, and technological materials. The constitution of automotive citizenship privileges the belonging of automotive users on Bengaluru's roads while simultaneously disenfranchising a range of nonautomotive publics.

5   Automotive Citizenship

Experiencing Traffic in Bengaluru

Traffic congestion is a familiar occurrence in Bengaluru. It is encountered daily as one navigates the city's roads, its (dwindling) shady avenues, and even its massive flyovers and underpasses. During peak commute times in the morning and evening, the city's streets are choked with motorcycles, private cars, buses, and miscellaneous commercial or private vehicles ferrying people and goods to different parts of the city. The sheer volume of vehicular traffic on the city's road, at such times is a daily prompt that implants congestion deep within the lived experience of residents. At all times, the unceasing procession of automobile traffic, which begins early in the day and continues until late, contributes to the pervasive familiarity that Bengaluru's residents have of congestion. The familiarity with traffic congestion is reinforced with the widespread circulation of the narrative of "congested Bengaluru." As we saw in chapter 3, one of the pathways through which the "congested Bengaluru" narrative has acquired coherence has been from the explosive growth in private automobiles in the city. Since 2000, the number of motor vehicles registered in Bengaluru rose from 1.4 million to 5.95 million in 2015 (RITES 2011; KRTO 2015). This 325 percent rise in automobile population within just fifteen years has been a major driver behind the thickening of this narrative into one that exclusively tracks the swells and dips in the passage of automobilization in the city.

A short vignette can reveal much about how automobile congestion is received and responded to in the city. In this case, social media messages on Twitter from selected traffic police stations in Bengaluru (RT Nagar, Jayanagar, and Madiwala Traffic Police Stations) are particularly insightful. As of March 2017, each of these traffic police stations, which go by the Twitter handles @RTnagartr, @JnagarTr, and @MadiwalaTraffic, has a moderate social media profile with an average of five hundred to fifteen hundred tweets and is followed by about a thousand people each. Most of their posts concern routine policing efforts (photos of vehicles that have been towed for being parked illegally) or community outreach action (visits to schools to inform children of road safety and photos and videos warning against driving while intoxicated). However, occasionally, each police station posts messages on ongoing disruptions to on-road mobility. These messages are particularly informative because even when the target audience is unspecified in the message, the accompanying photos often reveal which section of road users the message is meant for. For instance, on October 10, 2016, @JnagarTR posted a message that warned of ongoing Tender SURE work (an effort to make city streets world class, which I described in some detail in chapter 4) on two roads within the jurisdiction of the police station. The photo (figure 5.1) shows a man walking on the street because the sidewalk was completely excavated. The message nevertheless ends with the directive to motorists to "Drive Safe and Cautiously." From this photograph, it is clear that the road users who are urged to make a change in their travel orientations are automobile users.

The responses to the narrative of congested Bengaluru seem to have come to be constituted in a narrow manner and are exclusively centered on automotive congestion. In other words, congestion in Bengaluru is defined solely through the interests, intents, and experiences of what I refer to here as an auto-mobile public. This public identifies predominantly with

Figure 5.1
Tweet by Jayanagar Traffic Police Station (source: @JnagarTr, Twitter).

navigating the city from within an automobile (a motorcycle or car). The defining of an auto-mobile public has privileged automotive congestion experienced by automobile users while discounting other forms of congestions such as missing or dug-up sidewalks (experienced by other publics) that are widespread in the city. However, it would be misleading to consider an auto-mobile public solely as an urban social group similar to, say, pavement dwellers, vendors, or real estate agents. Focusing solely on their social constituents, we would be missing a large part of the relationships that give this category their durability in urban space. Instead, I propose that underlying the constitution of the auto-motive public is the assembly of a collective identity that I refer to as automotive citizenship.

In this chapter, I demonstrate that automotive citizenship is not a transient collective experience that emerges every time a person sits on a motorcycle and kicks it loose from its support, only to subside when the person shuts off the automobile. Instead, automotive citizenship is a durable phenomenon constituted through the daily performance of navigating and traversing urban space in the city. I posit that automotive citizenship is an ensemble that ties several social, artifactual, and technological materials together into a performance whereby drivers, redesigned street-side artifacts, social media platforms, and traffic management policies play a part in the relentless social privileging of automobile travel in the city, even as it disenfranchises other publics. The resulting sociotechnical ensemble has together crafted a powerful presence in Bengaluru that seeks to minimize automobile congestion while at the same time proliferating congestions and immobilities for other urban publics (pushcart vendors, pedestrians, and public bus users, for example) endowed with less privileged sociotechnical ensembles.

Mobilizing Citizenship

Citizenship, commonly understood as a category of full membership within an ascribed sociospatial entity (usually the nation-state), is the product of a particular historical epoch marked by the entrenchment and internationalization of the Western European nation-state system (Held 1995). Within this understanding, the social attributes of citizenship arise from participation within a political community, while its spatial attributes point to the presence of boundaries—porous to the citizen-member but impervious to the foreigner. This static notion of citizenship, though still prevalent in legal and international geopolitical circles, is increasingly contested.[1] The locus for these contestations has centered on citizenship's central premise of a static and full membership in a political community. Contestations over injustices as diverse as livelihood, identity expression, access to natural and social resources, and exposure to environmental harms have spotlighted structural inequalities pervasive in many national societies but also questioned the notion that citizenship as full membership in a political community implies equivalent rights across all citizens. By exposing as fiction the official discourse of a homogeneous political community with the same rights, these contestations and their claims have been particularly successful in contesting citizenship and provoking the articulation of a "new vocabulary of citizenship" (Isin 2009, 367). According to Isin, due to the resultant flux in citizenship,

> It is no longer adequate (if it ever was), to think of states as "containers" of citizens as its members. New actors articulate new claims for justice through new sites that involve multiple and overlapping scales of rights and obligations.... This changes our conception of the political as well as of citizenship. (Isin 2009, 367)

The new vocabulary expressed through new actors within these new sites of contestations has shifted the conception of citizenship away from absolute and static categories, enshrined within legal, constitutional, or policy documents marked by either absence or presence toward fluid processual interpretations characterized by specific claims and actions of actors made in particular situations, to how these enact particular constructions of citizenship. Citizenship is made rather than given, wrested rather than granted. The combination of acts and performances of citizenship exercised by new actors within new sites has considerably expanded how political response and participation are marshaled. The performance of citizenship (as opposed to a disposition toward an outcome-oriented status) redirects the attention of the observer in a processual direction. In other words, we become concerned with how citizenship (as attempts to participate and belong in political processes) is constructed. However, such a process of citizenship enactment is a complex process that enrolls new subjects, sites, and scales (Isin 2008). What makes the process particularly involuted is the recursive role that acts and practices of individuals who are engaged in citizenly political participation acquire. Even as individuals deploy particular acts to engage in political participation, these very same acts construct the citizen-subject in their own image. It is this mutually co-constitutive dimension of citizenship performances—political actors deploying particular acts of citizenship, which then result in the portrayal of these very same actors as the embodiment of the citizen-subject.

The processual nature of constituting citizenship and the citizen-subject leads us to the question of how, where, and by whom these processes of citizenship are assembled. While the process orientation of how citizenship is assembled spotlights the acts, sites, and actors embroiled in its performance, it also brings center stage the relational quality of citizenship. The relational quality brings to the fore how citizenship is an (always provisional) achievement that is assembled with the aid of a diverse range of construction materials, each connected with other entities into a network. It is the viability of the network with its interconnected entities that allows citizenship to emerge as a network property. Actor-Network Theory (ANT) provides an analytical strategy for describing social worlds in terms of network relationships. Social worlds, ANT proposes, are a "continuously generated effect of the web of relations... materially and discursively heterogeneous relations that produce and reshuffle all kinds of actors, including objects, subjects, human beings, machines, animals" (Law 2009, 141).[2] Thus, it suggests that while objects are nodes in networks, these objects themselves exist as networks in their own right. The world or, more accurately, its ontology is only composed of networks all the way down.

Such an ontological standpoint has an important consequence for the agency to make change (social and otherwise). If everything including humans (thus far, considered by social science as prime architects of change in society) is a network, then how is agency exerted? ANT suggests that agency too is a relational effect that is exerted by "limited forms of ordering" (Law 2009, 146) achieved in cobbling the network together. Latour presents the example of the automatic door closer as a nonhuman artifact that has been delegated the task of closing doors after innately unreliable humans pass through without shutting the door behind them. Through this delegation, the automatic door closer becomes a moral actor "who" exerts agency in the closing of doors (Latour 1992). In this sense, ANT argues that within the network, agency to bring about a social phenomenon is exerted in a limited and distributed fashion by a combination of human, nonhuman, and technical entities.

But political participation and citizenship are hallowed activities that symbolize modern human existence and, as a result, have been long understood as exclusive arenas for the play of human exceptionalism. Political participation by the citizen is exclusively the domain of human agency with legal systems granting rights in political community almost exclusively to humans.[3] As Braun and Whatmore (2010) note, "The polis may well be understood [in political theory] as a place of lively public debate and its future understood as radically open to the play of political forces, but it consists solely of humans" (2010, xiv). The view that social collectivism and politics were the original human endeavors conducted in the nude (so to speak) unaided by material presence is challenged by technogenesis—that humans from the beginning of their history have been tool-using creatures whose condition was inescapably co-constituted by material devices. Of late, several scholars have sought to resuscitate the "technogenetic" view of human existence by acknowledging the role that technoscience and the material play in recent acts of politics and citizenly behavior. Heeding these efforts, it is becoming abundantly clear to researchers that technology and artifacts are inextricable to understanding contemporary politics. Arising from research into the performative participation of publics on the stage of governing science and technology (Michael 2009; Felt and Fochler 2010), researchers have recently sought to surface material participation as a "specific mode of engagement" (Marres 2016, 2) that incorporates the technological and the material in the enunciation of social and political affairs. Focusing on particular strategies and actions of everyday living, such as environmentally conscious product label reading, purchasing energy-efficient light bulbs, switching to green energy suppliers, a variety of entities—devices, settings, technologies and objects—are centrally implicated in the politics of participating in contemporary technoscientific life (Michael 2006).[4]

The imprint of material participation is particularly evident in the flows and mobilities that pervade our intensely interconnected socioeconomic and political reality. Indeed, social scientists who advocated "a mobilities turn" to counter the prevalence of sedentarist modes of social analysis associated the turn with the inclusion of materiality (Sheller and Urry 2006b; Hannam, Sheller, and Urry 2006). The mobilities turn suggests that densely interconnected flows and fluidities have come to define every aspect of our lives—to the extent that contemporary sociomaterial mobilities are said to accomplish the folding and imbricating of long-held modernist distinctions between public and private or citizenship and private life (Sheller and Urry 2003). In other words, mobile practices of private living are no longer just that, more often than not, they incorporate performances that embody engagement with the public sphere and the arena of politics. Thus, traversing a city on material artifacts such as a bicycle or a wheelchair is at once a means of private travel but also an embodied construction of citizenship (Aldred 2010; Gaete-Reyes 2015). In this context, the cycle (or wheelchair) as material object and associated road infrastructures of the curb, traffic lights, or sidewalks become settings or material devices that are enrolled in specific ways to further a public exercise of (or nonexercise of) citizenship. What is key is that the exercise of citizenship is intimately tied to the process of mobilizing spatial mobility and movement. It is specific acts and performances of movement undertaken by private individuals in public space that exercises citizenship or political participation.

As demarcations between the sphere of public practices and private actions often meld into seamless flows, mobilities in "liquid modernity" (Bauman 2000) have been particularly generative of new forms of articulations of citizenship (Desforges, Jones, and Woods 2005; Cresswell 2013). For instance, the mobility of specific groups may mobilize experiences of belonging or alienation, ordering or resistance. Such experiences are complex achievements realized through particular performative strategies of enrollment. As Spinney, Aldred, and Brown (2015) have noted, "Particular groups mobilise representations, artefacts, and technologies to conduct mobility and define the extent of citizenship" (326). Recalling recent thrusts in the scholarship on citizenship and material participation, what is particularly striking are the parallels between the performance of mobile citizenship and the enrollment of a range of settings, devices, and actors in the construction of a material engagement with the political. Such an understanding suggests that a range of entities, such as mobile citizens, technologies, material artifacts, government entities, and infrastructures, together fashion a script that enunciates a distinct citizenship. Attendant with this assembled citizenship are claims, experiences, interactions, and barriers that construct specific dimensions of citizenship. It is through such strategies of citizenship that particular groups feel franchised, while others endure immobilization. One group experiences the positive reinforcement of citizenship while simultaneously producing noncitizenship for others (see Gaete-Reyes 2015; Aldred 2010). Mobile citizenship thus becomes a pathway for the insertion and reification of wider social inequities: "Social inequalities relating to citizenship and mobility are materialized through interaction between personal, intersubjective, socio-technical, institutional, and environmental factors" (Gaete-Reyes 2015, 360).

The entrenching of motorization, accomplished on the back of a growing reliance on personal automobility, has exerted a definitive footprint on the configuration of political norms around the world. Its influence on citizenship and political participation has been particularly significant. The proliferation of car-driver hybrids has, Sheller and Urry (2006a) note, played a profound role in transforming the notion of public space populated by civil society. According to them, public space, understood in earlier periods as spaces for individuals to interact and deliberate and collectively render visible the civil society, have been reinscribed as public roads populated by the car-driver hybrids that transact their private business cocooned within their metal pods. As a result, the collective voices of these car-driver hybrids reflect the aspirations and the priorities of the "auto mobile." A civil society of automobility is the outcome. In yet another fashion too, automobility has mutually constituted the reigning "liberal disposition" of citizenship (Chella Rajan 2006). The autonomy of the individual, so prized within liberal political norms, is realized in practice by the automobile. The automobile, it is widely accepted, grants individuals the freedom to pursue their private interests unimpeded by state or collective interests. A protected space for the pursuit of private interests, such as the highway, exemplifies liberal political norms. Individuals who participate in automobility thus realize the promise of liberal citizenship—autonomous individuals who value and exercise the freedom to operate independent of state interference. In practice though, automobility exists as an exclusionary project that prevents those without a vehicle or without a driver's license, from participating in the ordinary business of living in automobile-sized cities, and, more important, from engaging with contemporary citizenly norms.

Mobilizing mobile citizenship, as I have attempted to do in this section, draws attention to the particular performances staged in the process of traversing space and how these materialize citizenship and political engagement. Recent scholarship in fields as diverse as citizenship studies, science and technology studies, and mobility studies permits us to locate how an incipient automotive citizenship in contemporary India could be imagined.

Construction of Technological Citizenship in Contemporary India

The wide prevalence of technoscientific advances in a range of fields, such as biotechnology, energy development, health care, and pharmaceuticals, has been particularly fertile for the proliferation of controversies regarding associated risks, especially within Western societies. Such instances of technoscientific controversies, often denoted as a crisis of confidence in science, have become the spur for calls made by governments to reframe the nature of engagement between legitimate experts and a range of concerned publics (Irwin 1995).[5] Experiments in refashioning a new dialogue between experts and publics have seen lay knowledge claims contesting official discourses and claims founded on legitimate expert knowledge (Irwin and Michael 2003). In response, emerging forms of lay-expert engagements, according to some scholars, appear to herald new configurations of scientific citizenship (Irwin 2001; Elam and Bertilsson 2003).

Technoscientific referents for the constitution of citizenship have a distinctive salience given India's postcolonial anxieties of simultaneously balancing development, nation building, and exercising sovereign authority.[6] In the initial postcolonial years, for national leaders tasked with transforming a predominantly agrarian economy through technoscience, a progressive farmer who uses the products of technoscience—irrigation, improved seeds, and fertilizers—was the archetypal Indian citizen. It was on the citizenship of hard-working Indian farmers that the modern Indian state was to be raised. Abraham and Rajadhyaksha (2015), however, posit that the early postcolonial Indian state's demands of exercising sovereign and disciplinary power in the context of structural inequality had considerably attenuated the possibilities of founding a technological citizenship with all citizens participating equally in the establishment of a technoscientific society. Indeed, these attenuated circumstances in the formation of the citizen-participant have continued over time. Thus, the post-1991 liberalization of the Indian economy and, subsequently, the enhanced participation in global economic flows have been instrumental in formulating new conceptions of transnational movement, success, and belonging, resulting in the emergence of a new archetype of the citizen-subject—the information technology (IT) entrepreneur. The celebration in the media of a breed of transnationally successful Indian IT entrepreneurs is, according to Chakravartty (2001), an outcome of how "new flexible strategies of accumulation [have] allowed for new modes of valorized subjectivity" (2001, 80). The proximal cause for the popular triumphalism regarding the global successes of the Indian digital entrepreneur arises from the enormous contrast s between flexible cyber-entrepreneurial dealings and the messy and ponderous procedures that supposedly cage the country's public management and governance systems. It is the figure of the successful IT entrepreneur that offers what Chatterjee (2004) refers to as "a pedagogical role" for the vast majority of unconnected masses in the country. At the core of this role is the valorizing of not only particular modes of lifestyle, education, and consumption but, more crucial, the leadership it provides to public matters and the moral authority it acquires to speak to those with political power on how best to address the nation's problems (Upadhya 2009).

Despite the hype, the citizenship of IT entrepreneurs in new India, as many have argued, remains fettered with multiple moorings in the layered social contexts from where it arose. Indeed, old patterns of social differences—class, caste, gender, and language—are not disjointed or vestigial to contemporary technological citizenship but are instead incredibly constitutive of its experience (Philip 2016). The reserves of moral authority of digital entrepreneurs in contemporary India, for example, point to the curious enrolling of entrepreneurial capacity and free-market liberalism with male, middle class, Brahmin privilege (Upadhya 2009). Similarly, emerging technological subjectivities of digital governance, for example, have spurred new forms of neoliberal biopolitics, characterized by furthering private gain and power in the name of directing public resources to the needy (Abraham and Rajadhyaksha 2015, 82). The archetypal Indian citizen may be socially anchored, but with the widespread circulation of images and narratives of technological citizenship in the media, several locations have emerged in popular consciousness as candidate sites for rehearsing the incipient subjectivities of a flexible, entrepreneurial citizenship. The hackathon is one particularly effervescent site where the dynamics of an emergent citizenship intersect with a manufactured urgency to make change that rivals statist notions of development, as well as with a middle-class politics to bypass messy democratic procedures (Irani 2015). Hackathons, according to Irani, are

> not just a place where technology gets made.... The hackathon celebrates the entrepreneurial actor who experiments in a world characterized by complexity and drives past contestation toward demos that mark experiments in progress. Such optimistic, high-velocity practice aligns, in India, with middle-class politics that favor quick and forceful action with socially similar collaborators over the contestations of mass democracy. (Irani 2015, 801)

Following Irani's lead, I note that candidate sites for the exercise of an incipient technological citizenship in India offer an alternate route that can potentially bypass the messiness of democracy. Associated with these alternate routes are new modes of claim making, channels of interaction, infrastructures, and material artifacts that together assemble a durable citizenship.

In this chapter, we see automobility as an apposite candidate site for the practice of technological citizenship in contemporary India. As with other forms of citizenship, I present automotive citizenship as a performative exercise moored within particular social and political contexts. These moorings underscore two mutually constitutive vital dimensions: they articulate a performance of disparity that privileges some groups disproportionately while others are disenfranchised and the architecture of the moorings spotlights the infrastructural, sociotechnical, and institutional practices, which in turn materializes automotive citizenship as a performance of disparity. The combination of materiality of citizenship and the performance of disparity place differential claims on road space. These claims on road space actively resignify what roads are meant for even as they redefine who can lay claims and how these claims come to be solidified. The next section identifies key material and performative elements of claim making on road space that denote the construction of automotive citizenship in Bengaluru.

Performance of Automotive Citizenship in Bengaluru

Multiple elements participate in the performance of automotive citizenship in Bengaluru. These could be the warm bodies of police officials and middle-class automobile-owning residents, the ruptured and broken sidewalks, the hard concrete pillars of the Metro erected on these pavements, the fleeting links on social media, the durable metallic bodies of cars and motorcycles, public plans and policies for managing traffic congestion, or road-side fences that cloister pedestrians within the sidewalk. Taken together, these and other elements and associated practices constitute a performance of claim making that collectively stage automotive citizenship in the city. By employing a street-side ethnographic lens, I identify three claims on road space that stage automotive citizenship—roads as unidimensional infrastructure, roads connoted for uncongested auto-mobility,[7] and road space reserved for practices of auto-mobility. These claims not only embody the formation of the ideal citizen-subject; they also privilege the circulation of automobility on Bengaluru's roads.

Roads as Unidimensional Infrastructure

In May 2016, to commemorate four years in office as chief minister of Karnataka, S. Siddaramaiah unveiled an advertising campaign that highlighted some of his government's salient achievements. The campaign was displayed prominently on several billboards and bus shelters throughout the city. In Bengaluru, the campaign centered almost exclusively on efforts undertaken by his government to enhance infrastructure in the city. On the overhang above one bus stop beside Cubbon Park in central Bengaluru, Mr. Siddaramaiah is shown announcing "Comfortable Commuting on Bengaluru Roads" accompanied by two images of roads that focus on the smooth asphalted surface that at the time of the shoot were relatively free of vehicles (figure 5.2). The subtitle beside the photographs clarifies what commuting comfort denotes with the statement: "Signal-free travel is necessary for commuting comfort."[8] To elaborate on what the government seeks to do to accomplish the slogan of comfortable commuting, the advertisement uses the back rest of the seats inside the bus shelter to list three efforts the government proposes. First, the government proposes to make important roads signal-free at the cost of ₹434.33 *crore* ($0.7 billion in 2018 rates). Second, in important locations in the city, road development has been proposed through the construction of overpasses, underpasses, grade separators, and eight elevated corridors, all at a cost of ₹665.50 *crore* (about $1 billion). Finally, at a cost of ₹560 *crore* ($0.85 billion), the government

Figure 5.2
Advertisement of road development in Bengaluru.

has decided to strengthen and develop 245 roads in the city. Such efforts will, the advertisement would have the reader believe, lead to a comfortable commuting experience for Bangaloreans. It is another matter that signal-free roads, elevated corridors, and grade separators are mega-infrastructure projects, which, as we saw in chapter 3, have been products of a techno-political regime of congestion that seeks to reorder roads as conduits for automobility. What is particularly intriguing is how the road space where these projects are to be inserted is too often perceived as *unidimensional*—a space that is signified solely as a conduit of automobiles, all other forms of mobility through that space being considered incidental or secondary and these make do with any residual attention scattered by the project.

One locale where the claims of signal-free automobile infrastructure on road space are starkly prominent is the junction of Mysore Road and the outer ring road—the so-called Nayandahalli interchange—in southwestern Bengaluru.[9] This intersection best exemplifies the metaphor of a concrete jungle, forested as it is by soaring concrete pillars that support the Metro, the Mysore Road Metro station, and the main carriageway of the criss-crossing Mysore Road and the inner ring roads. Vehicular traffic continuing

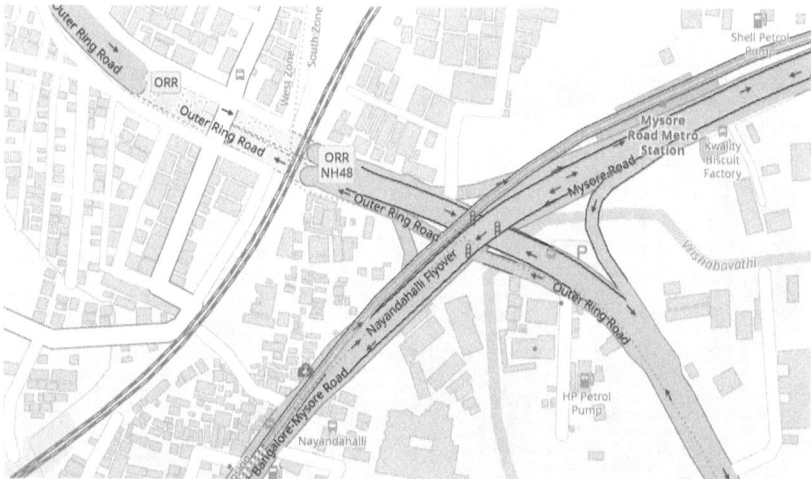

Figure 5.3
Map of the Nayandahalli interchange (© OpenStreetMap contributors, https://www.openstreetmap.org/copyright).

on these arterial roads speeds unhindered on elevated roads propped up by pillars inserted onto the road space of this intersection. Figure 5.3 indicates the spatial layout of the intersection. The southern border of the intersection is formed by the Vrishabhavathi River. North of the intersection adjacent to the Metro station is a large, open space for commuters to park their vehicles before riding the Metro. Low-density automotive and mechanical workshops or commercial warehouses occupy the remaining land adjoining the intersection.[10]

On the ground, we come by a grainier view of the Nayandahalli interchange. The relatively low density of built-up area adjoining the intersection accounts for its feeling of spaciousness. However, despite its airiness, a notable feature of the intersection is its clutter of concrete piers. The pervasiveness of columns is especially real in one's field of vision as a pedestrian standing and observing the intersection (figure 5.4). The regularity in the placement of these pillars as they span the crossroads points at the predominance of structural considerations of bearing the weight of the elevated road and Metro line more than any aesthetic or other pragmatic motivations. Apart from the pillars, the other feature is the unregulated nature of traffic flow in the intersection. Since the through traffic zips past overhead, the intersection at the ground level is predominantly used by public transit buses, vehicles turning from one road to another, or those

Figure 5.4
Ground view of the Nayandahalli interchange.

picking up or dropping off passengers at the adjoining Metro station. In the absence of a traffic light at grade, vehicles weave around pillars and other oncoming vehicles as they move in their desired directions. A final feature of the intersection is the lack of clear differentiation of road space clearly into pedestrian or nonautomobile zones. Thus, it is not clear how pedestrians, cyclists, and pushcart vendors are expected to navigate the intersection around the columns, between turning vehicles, and speeding buses. Pedestrian sidewalks exist in most margins of the intersection, but their design displays the signature of an incidental approach in their construction. Sidewalks are either discontinuous, unpaved, serve as covers for stormwater drains, or are appropriated to park vehicles.

In June 2016, I spent one afternoon walking around this intersection to observe and experience what it means to traverse this intersection when not ensconced within an automobile. Despite the interchange having been opened a year earlier, it was quite evident at the ground level that a disproportionate share of the project's attention had been lavished on the mobility needs of those in their automobiles overhead. Central features of the intersection are two towering lines of pillars—gray rectangular columns that fan out to support the elevated roadway and the cream-colored pillars carrying the Metro line. It is around these two arrays of columns that all manner of traffic movement in this intersection happens—vehicles turn around these columns as they flow from one road to the other; and pedestrians and other nonmotorized movers stop by the pillars before they scurry across the intersection. It is immediately clear that the columns have been shaped to facilitate vehicular movement. The Metro pillar possesses a rounded curb that hugs the base of the column to maximize the space for vehicles while also facilitating a smooth turn. Similarly, a yellow chevron turn sign affixed to the gray pillar warns drivers on Mysore Road that they should turn in front of the pillar to move toward the outer ring road (figure 5.4). Pedestrians have very few directions or affordances to facilitate navigation of the intersection. The curb surrounding the pillars does not offer any separation from the road space (figure 5.5a). Pedestrians have to continue walking on the road surface at the pillar while keeping an eye on vehicles turning ahead of or behind them.

While traversing the south side of the intersection, I noticed the sidewalk was being constructed along the verge of the road, directly over the stormwater drain (see figure 5.4). Such a construction strategy that provides physical cover for drainage channels while providing spaces for pedestrians is quite common in other parts of Bengaluru. What is particularly noteworthy in this intersection is that the pedestrian sidewalk coincides entirely with the cover for the stormwater drains. Purposing the pavement from drain covers has consequences for how this space is used and the amenities it supports (figure 5.5b of the pavement diagonally across the intersection exemplifies the consequences of this orientation). For one, since the pavement is located over the empty space of the drain, it is not possible to plant trees that can allow the hot cart pushers or cyclists to rest under the shade. Furthermore, after routine maintenance to de silt and clear blocks in the drains, crews are often unable to replace the cover flush in the gap, thus displacing the drain cover. Over time, these displaced covers not only create an uneven pavement surface, but also potentially leave dangerous gaping holes on the pavement surface. These are especially unsafe for children and the elderly who use the pavement. As seen in figure 5.5b, I encountered a

Figure 5.5
Photographs of the Nayandahalli interchange.

woman forced to walk with her two children on the road surface, on the north side of the intersection, because the gaps and unevenness on the pavement surface made it dangerous for her children.

As I walked farther along the pavement toward the Metro station, a new series of challenges arose beside the roadway. At this point, the course of the Vrishabhavathi River swings close to the road, constricting the road space. In an effort to reserve more space for the roadway, the builders had terminated the central median of the road and located the columns supporting the overhead roadway and the Metro line directly onto the sidewalks on either side of the road (figure 5.5c). The presence of columns on the sidewalk poses a challenge for pedestrians. As a result, on one side of the road, there is very little space on the pavement for any pedestrian mobility, forcing pedestrians onto the roadway; on the other side adjoining the river, the surface of the sidewalk is uneven, and the fencing that separates the road from the river is only partial (figure 5.5d). With a combination of the lack of sidewalk width on one side and a dangerous pavement on the other side, pedestrians are forced onto the roadway to negotiate their safety directly with vehicular traffic. Farther up the road and closer to the Metro station, pedestrians face a new set of challenges. The vehicles parked by Metro riders had spilled over from the adjoining Metro parking lot and stationed themselves on the sidewalk, thereby once again forcing pedestrians and other nonmotorized road users onto the roadway (figure 5.6). On the obverse side, the uneven sidewalk comes to an abrupt end against the retaining wall of the turn lane that directs traffic across the river (figure 5.5d). On that side, pedestrians have to edge forward on the roadway while hugging the concrete wall (with a growing sense of unease) until they find themselves plumb in the center of the road with oncoming traffic hurtling toward them. At that point, pedestrians have the choice of either scampering over to the central median of the road or crossing the turn lane on their right to regain the pavement.

The Nayandahalli infrastructure project makes clear the unidimensional nature of the claim on road space exerted by mega-infrastructure projects. The overarching thrust of the project design is solely concerned with the seamless movement of motorized vehicles on the overhead roadways (figure 5.5c). Their fluid movement, it would appear, is the sole priority of the designer/builder. All nonmotorized forms of movements are incidental and secondary to the design of the project, and all the other road users merit little consideration in project design. Thus, in the Nayandahalli intersection, scarcely any attention is paid to the needs of pedestrians or cyclists for continuous and safe pathways for travel.

Figure 5.6
Vehicles of Metro riders parked on the sidewalk.

Roads Connoted as a Zone for Uncongested Auto-Mobility

Exchanges on online social media, especially Twitter and Facebook, reveal new modes through which claims on road space are articulated. One claim that is particularly widespread on social media is that road space is connoted as a zone of uncongested auto-mobility. In these settings, a combination of a privileged English education, middle-class desires for urban order, and opportunities for social mobility through an online presence have meant that Facebook posts and Twitter handles on social media have consolidated an automobile-centric view of traffic congestion. In articulating the singular connotation of road space as corridors dedicated to automobile movement, social media users have found allies in official enforcers of traffic rules in the city—the Bangalore Traffic Police. Motivated by a desire to present a forward-oriented face, Bengaluru's traffic police force sees social media as key to its efforts to not only deploy technology to provide intelligent and real-time monitoring of traffic in the city but also as part of a push to portray itself as an enforcement agency that is consultative and citizen-oriented. This thrust is a product of the transformation of traffic management and enforcement in the city away from a traditional manual policing role to a technology-driven enterprise (National Police Mission 2016). We thus consider two aspects of recent social media activity on congestion in the city: efforts to use several creative means of infusing commentary on the traffic situation in Bengaluru and official efforts to control and manage congestion on city roads. Through these efforts, the claim that road space exists as a zone solely for uncongested automobile movement has solidified in the minds of social, governmental, and political elites in the city.

Social media commentary on congestion in Bengaluru is quite extensive and happens through multiple means. Hashtags such as #BangaloreTraffic on Facebook and Twitter are particularly popular for users to link their experiences on the road with others. In the Twitter hashtag #BangaloreTraffic, users share their diverse experiences of immobility in road traffic as they (and their vehicles) navigate city roads. What is particularly noteworthy is that users (predominantly male), although representing different communal, religious, and age groups, first and foremost relate to traffic as automobile users. Thus, it is common for users to observe on their particular predicaments as drivers: "It's 7:15 in the morning and I'm stuck at tin factory signal for the last half hour. #BangaloreTraffic," or "Happily parked in the middle of the road at Jeevanbima nagar 6th cross #BangaloreTraffic," or "#BangaloreTraffic—the only place where people turn right from the extreme left lane and left from the extreme right lane" (#bangaloretraffic 2019). Such commentary often elicits sympathetic responses or helpful suggestions from other social media users who empathize with the predicament of these users.

In many cases, users do more than provide commentary; they also propose measures to rectify congestion—"Political rally stopping traffic for what!!! Is the road the right place to protest #bangaloretraffic we are #secondclasscitizens," or "Hosur road has new U turns, but buses should not be allowed to take U turns. They take lot of space and cause traffic jam," or "Wud like to know logic of opening this eight feet cut [in the traffic median] on Marathalli ORR? It is causing mess. Both sides affected" (#bangaloretraffic 2019). Facebook groups such as Bangalore Citizen Traffic Control, Lets change Bangalore's Roads, and Traffic or Traffic Updates, each with a few hundred members, attempt to forge a community of people who more often than not seek to advance commentary to instigate campaigns to effect change. For example, the group Bangalore Citizen Traffic Control positions itself as a forum of citizen drivers who will record instances of traffic violations:

> This is a page dedicated to bring Bangalore Traffic to more normal standards; fight for rights; volunteer a bit; and take our quality of life to the next level. This page is dedicated to all you members who can record any traffic violation in Bangalore and post the video. (Facebook 2019)

Dedicated Twitter handles, such as @080traffic, @BangalorTraffic, @blrtraffic, and @BangaloreTraffic or dedicated Facebook pages, such as Bangalore City Traffic and Bangalore Traffic Jam Updates, also offer social commentary on traffic congestion. Another recent venture has been to develop Twitter handles for several neighborhoods and congested intersections in the city.[11] These dedicated efforts attempt to accomplish several objectives through online social media—first, to provide (often witty and satirical) commentary regarding the traffic predicament (from the perspective of automobile users) in the city; second, to provide information by users on emerging road situations to others; and to transform a frustrating travel experience faced by immobilized commuters into a platform for exerting citizen voices.

The final objective is especially significant because it renders online social media into a political tool for informing and influencing official efforts. Active social media sites like #BangaloreTraffic have been particularly attractive locations for established media outlets to reach out to an engaged audience and tap into ideas and opinions that are informed by everyday experiences of commuting over city streets. Thus, in July 2016, Mirror Now, an English language news channel (part of the Times Now media empire), advertised a program on Bangalore's traffic problem on #BangaloreTraffic, and it asked people to call in and share their views on the issues (automobile) commuters face while traveling in the city (figure 5.7). The program, titled "Bengalorean's Long Road Home," brought together an expert, an activist, a citizen, and a local political actor to discuss how the traffic situation in the city could be addressed. A key take away of the program was a call for citizens to participate more actively in governing the traffic situation in the city. News media presence on social media is a mutually beneficial situation that reinforces the potential for the message of traffic congestion to attract a wider audience, which then benefits the standing of media outlets.

In addition to news media outreach, a far more frequent mode for intervening in decision making is available through social media. Twitter, for instance, offers the ability for the social media–savvy individuals to engage with decision makers and officials by commenting directly on their official Twitter handles. Such modes of social media engagement permit individuals

Figure 5.7
Mirror Now's program on traffic in Bengaluru (source: @MirrorNow, Twitter).

to quickly and easily transmit their voices (of approbation and support) or opinions directly to high officials and political leaders. Furthermore, social media have vastly enhanced the reach that individuals have to a range of important people. Given their heavily publicized social media profiles, with a few taps of their smart phones, individuals can share their observations on traffic and congestion in Bengaluru with not just the city traffic police or city administrators but the chief minister of Karnataka or, if they choose, even the prime minister of India. As we shall see, given the push to use technology to boost citizen engagement in traffic enforcement and in urban administration, in general, social media users have noticed a greater receptiveness on the part of the official machinery to acknowledge or, at the very least, create space on their social media profiles for citizen input.

The possibility of citizens to engage in discourse with officials on social media appears to be important for both parties. For the automotive public, it creates the potential for their voice to be considered and their concerns redressed within the establishment, while for officials, it not only increases the number of citizen followers on their accounts but also creates opportunities for officials to be recognized for efforts made to smoothen congested roads in the city.[12] For example, when the traffic police sealed the traffic median on the Marathahalli bridge across the outer ring road in eastern Bengaluru, it was a cause for much celebration and approbation from motorists who saw the crisscross flows at this intersection (U turns, and right turns) as a major irritant for smooth commutes (see the tweet in figure 5.8 for an example of the appreciative feelings of relief and happiness experienced).

The ability to leverage social media to consolidate road space for unhindered automobility is perhaps most evident when one considers how official efforts to tackle congestion in Bengaluru are presented on a variety of social media platforms. This is partly due to the well-established footprint that official efforts have acquired to tackle day-to-day congestion on social media. Thus, official social media profiles of the Bengaluru Traffic Police (BTP) on Facebook and Twitter are complemented by official Twitter handles for all forty-two traffic police stations in the city, the three senior traffic police officials in the city (additional commissioner traffic and deputy commissioners of traffic, east and west), and popular but private Twitter handles of senior traffic police officials. The significance of social media for official efforts is reflective of the high degree of concern that the government accords to its online presence as part of a strategy to cultivate an image of greater citizen accessibility.[13]

Examining the Twitter profiles of senior traffic police officers, one finds numerous instances of citizen engagement: calls for opinions of motorists regarding traffic initiatives, prompt responses to traffic grievances with

Automotive Citizenship

Figure 5.8
Tweets on the median closure at Marathahalli (source: @HALAirportTr, Twitter.com).

directives to police officers to examine and report on the case, promises to consider the suggestions proposed by motorists to improve traffic flow, advice on emerging traffic situations, road safety campaigns, and suggestions for pedestrian and automotive safety. For example, the deputy commissioner of traffic ran a poll on Twitter requesting commuters to provide their opinion if their commute had improved after the median was closed on Marathahalli Bridge. An overwhelming 75 percent of the received responses affirmed that this initiative had "reduced [traffic] jam." In another instance, when a driver pointed out a defective traffic light on the street, the same officer directed his juniors to attend to the issue and report back. Similarly, because they got stuck at all three lights consecutively, a request from yet another driver to synchronize the three traffic signals in the heart of the city received an immediate response, with the officer tagging his juniors and directing them to look into the matter. For officials, such modes of citizen engagement offer a preview of an incredibly technologized future of urban governance envisioned in the smart city discourse (for example, see Kitchin, Lauriault, and McArdle 2015). Twitter dashboards portend the future of citizen-oriented governance, where citizens will voice their concerns on social media and technocratic officials will quickly attend to them. However, in all these cases, citizen engagement has articulated the view from behind the steering wheel (or the handlebar) and transmitted it through a mobile app, and as a result, it is these interests that receive official help. Voices from beyond the automobile or disengaged from social media rarely acquire the same levels of traction.

Even recent citywide campaigns (such as BTP Info/Public Eye and #selfieonskywalk) promoted by the traffic police force as a whole have more often than not catered to the needs of an English-educated, auto-mobile, middle-class citizenry. Public Eye was a freely downloadable smart phone app that is promoted by the traffic police in collaboration with Janaagraha's (the middle-class citizen group) "I Change My City" initiative.[14] Public Eye transforms any Bengaluru resident into a traffic vigilante who polices and monitors various kinds of traffic violations: riding without a helmet, driving without a seatbelt, using a mobile phone while driving, violating parking restrictions, and even driving on the sidewalk. Residents can use the app to take a photo or video of the violation and record the license plate of the vehicle. These incidents are then logged, investigated, and possibly ticketed by the traffic police. Public Eye has now been incorporated as a feature into a freely downloadable app—BTP Bangalore Traffic Info—that brands itself as an "Android app for Bangalore Road users in association with Bangalore Traffic Police" (Google 2019). In addition to the Public Eye feature, the BTP app provides a range of other features that include using live traffic maps, checking vehicle fines, and reporting traffic problems. Although presented as designed for all road users, features are obviously targeted toward the auto-mobile.

The recent #selfieonskywalk was a campaign promoted by Bengaluru Traffic Police to encourage pedestrians to use skywalks—elevated pedestrian crossings recently constructed over key intersections in the city, thereby keeping road space clear for automobiles. The campaign required individuals to take a selfie while using a skywalk. It then awarded five winners based on how effective they were in sharing their selfie within their social media networks and in persuading their social media acquaintances to take and submit selfies of their own. The expectation is that such a campaign structure could potentially snowball skywalk use, thereby justifying their construction. Despite these innovations, few of these structures are intensively used by pedestrians, even though they promise a safe transit across busy and chaotic intersections.[15] Indeed, these structures have more often than not enhanced barriers for pedestrian movement on the sidewalk.[16]

The push for increased citizen engagement in the Bengaluru Traffic Police can be traced to a marked shift in the policy landscape associated with traffic enforcement in the city. A key instigator for this shift was the Bangalore Traffic Improvement Project (B-TRAC), implemented in six phases between 2006 and 2011. B-TRAC outlined an ambitious plan to tackle traffic congestion brought about by a rising vehicular population through a multipronged strategy of technologically intensive and automated traffic management and enforcement system, a revenue model based on traffic fines, capacity enhancement of traffic personnel to enforce rules through technology, and flexible options for paying fines. The thrust has been to develop traffic enforcement mechanisms that rely on technology (remote enforcement cameras, centralized enforcement tracking, and ticket generation) to ensure transparency and user friendliness. A measure of this shift in temperament of traffic enforcement in the city is the exponential increase in instances of both violations and the quantum of fines assessed. Between 2007 and 2015, instances of violations increased more than five times, from 1.4 million to 7.6 million, with a corresponding increase in the fines assessed (National Police Mission 2016). Reimagining traffic enforcement within a revenue-driven strategy has had a vital effect on how citizens are perceived by traffic enforcers. By centralizing the mechanism of enforcement and ticketing within a remote database, traffic constables and citizens on the road have little room for negotiating the extenuating circumstances of the violation. Moreover, such negotiations are counterproductive for targets derived from a revenue-driven strategy. Citizen vigilante measures such as Public Eye that urge faceless citizens to report violations of others not only contribute to the remote centralization of enforcement mechanisms but also create innovative revenue streams for the police force. Given the overarching revenue-driven motivations of these measures, the traffic police force has attempted to reduce the grip that citizen veniality (in the form of bribes) and context particularity (in the form of circumstances) previously placed on the city's traffic enforcement. The unwritten rule of the new policy landscape in traffic enforcement is that the citizen, especially the auto-mobile citizen, is a potential paying customer who uses the road and, in return, should be provided uncongested service of automobility. In return, auto-mobile citizens abide by the increased pressures of traffic enforcement and revenue generation. By prioritizing revenue generation and transparency, the terms of the new social contract of traffic enforcement have aided the claim that road space is reserved for uncongested automobility.

Practices of Auto-Mobility

Everyday practices of managing, using, and segregating road space reveal how claims of automobility on Bengaluru's roads are maintained and reinforced. Walking the city streets, I observe a range of entities engaged in supporting and bolstering the claims of the auto-mobile on road space: drivers, vehicles (both motorcycles and cars), pavement railings, central medians, pavement tiles, driveways, and concrete.

Street-side fencing is quite widespread on Bengaluru's roads and is commonly employed to demarcate and segregate vehicular from nonvehicular space on the road. Most instances of fencing rely on metal railings, solidly embedded into the curb, to separate the roadway from the sidewalk (figure 5.9a). Given the crush of vendors, beggars, and pedestrians on busy sidewalks, some walkers might be tempted to step onto the roadway to reach their destinations in a speedy fashion. On other roads, an open sidewalk would be an invitation for push-cart vendors to park alongside the curb to sell their goods. Street-side fencing seeks to arrest the possibilities for these pedestrian transgressions onto the roadway (figure 5.9b). Instead, by clearly segregating one space from the other, designers seek to eliminate the fluid relation between nonvehicular sidewalks and the carriageway on the road. In an analogous fashion, street-side fencing is also employed to channel pedestrian and other nonmotorized flows to cross intersections only at designated zones. To achieve this, selected intersections along high-traffic corridors are often fenced off with metal railings all the way around. The reasoning is that it is safer and faster for all concerned to separate vehicular and pedestrian traffic at busy intersections. By restricting where pedestrians can step off the curb into the intersection, road designers believe that vehicles can complete their turn unhindered. Thus, practices of fencing (figure 5.9b) usually serve to interrupt pedestrians in the hope that the physical barriers will compel them to conform to the road engineer's objectives. But as seen in, fenced intersections sometimes provoke pedestrians onto the roadway, leaving the pavement space underused (figure 5.9d), thereby opening the way for alternative uses (as shown in figure 15.10a, colonized by two-wheeled vehicles as parking space). Despite their unintended uses, more extreme fencing arrangements have only increased in popularity on the roadscape. Fencing on some roads such as Hosur Road can run for many kilometers together in multiple rows without a gap on either side of the road (figure 5.9b). On other roads, human-size concrete barriers serve as impenetrable medians that not only divide opposing streams of traffic but, more important, disallow humans from contemplating crossing the road at grade (figure 5.9c). Such arrangements rely on the power of metal and concrete to create impervious barriers that discipline and engender particular forms of behavior among the non auto-mobile residents of Bengaluru.

Given its explosive growth, parking of vehicles is a particularly problematic issue in the city. The clamor for an effective solution to parking woes is frequently voiced in the media.[17] Much of the popular discourse is dominated by the absence of adequate spaces to park their vehicles. This is in spite of the fact that parking a vehicle (when a space is to be had) in the core of the city is quite an inexpensive affair and in the face of resistance from commercial and real estate interests, the city government has been

Figure 5.9
An array of fencing arrangements.

markedly reluctant to frame a parking policy that will make users pay for leaving their vehicles on the road.[18] Parking of vehicles is all too often dictated by the physical restrictions of space rather than any legal or ethical guides. While much of the popular attention on parking is seen in high-value areas in the core of the city and or near exclusive commercial zones, parking is a pervasive problem in several mixed-use neighborhoods where residential, commercial, office, and service uses exist side-by-side. In these locations, it is quite common to see vehicles occupying any available road space (figure 5.10) throughout the day. This is particularly true of high-density traffic corridors such as the outer ring road that thrust their way through residential neighborhoods in the inner periphery of the city. Walking along the outer ring road where it bifurcates the residential neighborhood of JP Nagar, one uncovers numerous forms of appropriations of road space nominally

Figure 5.10
Different forms of vehicular appropriations.

reserved for nonmotorized use. The presence of numerous residences along the outer ring road presents a physical advantage for parking vehicles. Homes with their flared and leveled openings that connect their driveways with the road are particularly convenient ramps for accessing the adjoining sidewalk (figure 5.10b). Vehicles desiring a parking space on the sidewalk drive onto the flared opening and instead of entering the private driveway, they maneuver to station themselves on the pavement. In the photo, four parked cars have overrun a substantial fraction of pedestrian space.

Another means of occupation is visible in front of commercial establishments (figure 5.10c). Given the challenge of finding convenient parking, shops and restaurants often redesign the sidewalk space abutting their establishments to make it convenient for their customers to park their vehicles. Instances of redesign quite often clearly demarcate the privatized space by using colored or patterned floor tiles. The difference in floor tiles on the sidewalk conveys a subtle message of ownership and control over what is nominally a public space. It tells the pedestrian or vendor that someone regulates who can use the space and for what purpose. It tells potential customers that parking is available on the sidewalk if the parking slots in front of the shop are taken. At the same time, it indicates to others that this is space reserved for customers only. Given that the space is leveled for the convenience of vehicular access, pedestrians and other nonmotorized users often face concrete barriers or steps due to the height difference (figure 5.10c) or uneven surface on the pavement (figure 5.10d). Figure 5.10a reveals yet another manifestation of sidewalk appropriation: fencing at intersections. Since these junction railings usually obstruct the improvised traverses that pedestrians choose to follow, many exit the pavement prior to the fenced region and continue across the intersection on the roadway. Such a decision fashions an underused space in the pavement that in the Bengaluru context usually prompts other road users to occupy the space. Motorcycle and scooter riders are quick to colonize such spaces for parking. This usually sets in motion a self-fulfilling cycle. The more vehicles pedestrians see in this zone, the less likely they are to walk through it, thereby fulfilling the informal reappropriation of this space for parking.

Possibly the more brazen practices of claiming road space for automobility happen through everyday acts of driving and riding. During times of congestion on the roads (especially at morning and evening peak hours), enterprising riders of motorcycles climb the sidewalk and ride their vehicles on the sidewalk, thereby bypassing the congestion on the road. Through these practices, riders usurp and expand the road space available for automobility even as they displace or even immobilize pedestrians (figure 5.11a). This occupation of the sidewalk is orchestrated through certain specific component acts. When the traffic movement on the road becomes sluggish, two-wheelers filter out of the mass of vehicles and become concentrated on the left curb of the road next to the sidewalk. When the main mass of vehicles come to a stop on account of a traffic light up the road, the two-wheelers begin clumping together at breaks in the curb of the sidewalk (figure 5.11b). These breaks in the pavement are usually the result of an entryway joining up with the road. Sloped breaks in the sidewalk are critical for vehicles to safely and comfortably mount the pavement. As more motorcycles clump together at a driveway, they climb up high enough to be able to enter the sidewalk. When one of them begins riding on the sidewalk, others in that clump usually follow. This acquisition of critical mass through clumping is crucial because pedestrians and other users are more likely to get out of the

Figure 5.11
Riding on the sidewalk.

way if they see a group of motorcycles charging down the sidewalk. Riding the sidewalk usually happens from one break to another. At the next break, the riders assess the possibility of riding farther on the sidewalk before deciding whether to continue on it or merge back into the main stream of traffic. Such acts of sidewalk riding emphasize the derivative and therefore subsidiary nature of the pedestrian space with respect to the main roadway. The sole purpose of the roadway is to convey automobiles; therefore pedestrian space exists at the pleasure of motorized vehicle users. If the motorized choose to drive on the sidewalk, it is a legitimate claim of citizenship that pedestrians and the nonmotorized need to accommodate.

In this section, I have put forward three claims that stage the performance of automotive citizenship in Bengaluru: the unidimensionality of road infrastructure, the connotation of roads for uncongested automobility, and the practices of expanding auto-mobility on road space. The performance of these claims seek to not only resignify road space into a space that is predominantly reserved for the procession of smooth and uncongested auto-mobility, but more important, they signal the constitution of the automotive citizen-subject in a dominant role on Bengaluru's streets.

Conclusion

In July 2011, the citizen environmental group Hasiru Usiru launched Come, Cross the Road (CCTR), a series of events with the objective of "gathering concrete and definite data on the specific issue of crossing roads and also to encourage a city-wide debate on the issue of making Bangalore a more pedestrian-friendly city" (Hasiru Usiru 2013, 2). Compiled in September 2013, the report on CCTR events, *Pedestrians in Bangalore—Walking a Tightrope: A report on Pedestrian Issues from a Rights Perspective,"* documents and catalogs the different dimensions of woes encountered by pedestrians crossing Bengaluru roads, the nature of pedestrian infrastructure available on the road, and the experiences of individuals ranging from street vendors to the aged and disabled (Hasiru Usiru 2013). After cataloging these issues, the report suggests that the situation on the ground presents a barrier that thwarts and hinders many from exercising the right to free movement and the right to livelihood, both rights that have been recognized by India's Supreme Court as following directly from (and therefore justiciable along the same lines as) the right to life, a fundamental human right guaranteed by Article 21 of the Indian Constitution.[19] The report proposes that this expanded rights framework available in the Indian judicial system signals the real possibility to affirm the *right to walk* as a justiciable right accorded to all humans. Failing to do so would stand counter to deep-seated values of equity and democracy enshrined within India's constitutional contract:

> As a democratic society striving for equality, being able to provide the right to walk to all residents is absolutely essential. Not being able to walk freely, safely, and securely will actually curb the freedom of people to enjoy their other rights. (Hasiru Usiru 2013, 37)

The clarion call for a legally enforceable right to walk that expands the constitutional obligations of the state in response to vulnerable pedestrians who face daily challenges on Bengaluru's roads to the skewed technological infrastructures of (auto-)mobility reminds us what Langdon Winner articulated many years ago: "Technology in a true sense is legislation...technologies are institutional structures within an evolving constitution that gives shape to a new polity" (Winner 1977, 324). The CCTR report clearly recognizes that the forging of the citizenship of automobility on the city streets is a worrisome trend pointing toward the constitution of a new polity with acts that implicitly legislate possibilities of movement and political engagement available to pedestrians. Expanding formal justiciable rights in the legal domain is thus a means to counter the creeping legislation of automobility on the streets.

Citizenship is a vital element of our contemporary lives. In common parlance, citizenship is the status of full membership within a representative political community. But understanding citizenship solely as status alone disregards the operation of citizenship as a political act. The installation of automobility in Bengaluru is such a political act that has enfranchised an auto-mobile public while at the same time excluding the nomotorized in society. The act of enfranchising, building up on recent advances in citizenship studies and science and technology studies, is constituted through an assemblage of actors, devices, practices, and settings. The infrastructures, practices, and practitioners of auto-mobility and their claims on road space collectively constitute an automotive citizenship in Bengaluru. Those who do not participate within this enterprise of claim making find themselves excluded at multiple levels and in multiple ways.

In the next chapter, we examine how specific interventions motivated to facilitate automobility came to be situated in Bengaluru. Despite the remarkable power that is marshaled through the regime, landscape, and citizenship of automobility in the city, the process of situating interventions, we shall see, is a remarkably contingent venture that exposes these interventions to numerous twists and turns that challenge and even alter their design and execution. The outcome, I suggest, is shabby automobility.

6   Shabby Automobility

I begin this chapter with two vignettes. First, St. Marks Road is a key traffic corridor in Bengaluru's central business district. The road intersects several important traffic corridors, such as Cubbon Road, MG Road, and Residency Road in the heart of the city and is referred to in the project report as a local collector road (Indian Urban Space Foundation 2012). Several important establishments, such as St. Mark's Cathedral, the Bowring Institute, several reputable schools, and high-value commercial properties find a home along this road.

St. Marks Road was one of the first roads in central Bengaluru to have been selected for redesigning as a Tender SURE road.[1] Tender SURE (as described in chapter 4) was proposed as a model for road redesign and execution that sought to, among other things, bury road infrastructures (such as water, sewage, electricity, and storm water drainage) within dedicated underground conduits below the pedestrian sidewalk, to make the road and pedestrian surface even and smooth, and to emphasize through design features the separation between different road uses. In January 2013, the city government (Bruhath Bengaluru Mahanagara Palike, BBMP) announced the call for proposals to redesign selected roads based on the Tender SURE model.[2] Construction began in September 2014, and the redesigned roads were inaugurated in June 2015 (figure 6.1). Although the cost per kilometer for redesigning roads according to Confederation of Indian Industry (CII) was almost five times the cost of resurfacing roads using conventional means, BBMP defended the redesign on the basis that these roads would be immune from the periodic utility work and the associated wear and tear of road infrastructures common on other roads. These roads were said to be immune from these deleterious effects for at least twenty years because all utility infrastructures are ducted and accessible below the sidewalk in special-purpose chambers. Nevertheless, since the redesigned St. Marks Road was inaugurated in 2015, the water board and the electricity company

Figure 6.1
St. Marks Road after numerous instances of digging.

have dug up the road on multiple occasions to service their infrastructure.[3] After each instance, the road had to be resurfaced, with expenditure of time and energy, to bring it back to the same exacting Tender SURE standards.

The second vignette is from southwestern Bengaluru. Close to the T-junction with Hosur Road, on Madivala Road, is one of Bengaluru's vibrant neighborhood markets. Locally referred to as the Madivala *santhe*, the market is over a hundred years old, and its location, in what used to be until a couple of decades ago the southwestern periphery of the city, is where producers and vendors gained quick access to bring their vegetable and fruit produce from the hinterland.[4] The market used to occupy the broad sidewalk on one side of the road adjoining the wall enclosing the staff residents of the national government in Bengaluru. But now, many of the market stalls have spread onto the raised central median of the Madivala Road. While the stalls on the sidewalk are semipermanent independent structures with sturdy metal roofs, supported by metal posts lowered into a tamped-down ground, the stalls on the median are improvised temporary structures with blue tarpaulin sheets thrown over to provide some weatherproofing. The tarpaulin sheets are tied to tree limbs, streetlight posts, and traffic signposts on the median. On closer inspection, I discovered one of the supporting posts to be a faded direction signboard (figure 6.2).

The signboard, now leaning to one side, consists of two metal posts with several horizontal metal plates that are arranged parallel to each other and spanning the posts. The faces of the plates were used to inform the road users. A part of the signage on the board was shrouded by the tarpaulin sheet, but it was evident that the signs were to direct road users in two directions. Turning to the left at the T-junction, traffic could go to Hosur (a nearby town in the neighboring state of Tamil Nadu), while turning right would lead traffic deeper into the city all the way to MG Road, the heart of Bengaluru's central business district. The designers had helpfully provided the same information in Kannada too. What was most striking about the sign was the broad plate at the top of the signboard. Originally painted in white, this plate was now a dirty yellow but the sign was legible. It said "b | a | t | f"—the stylized abbreviation of the Bangalore Agenda Task Force (BATF). Above the abbreviation was the task force's logo: a white paint–streaked arrow curving to the top right corner of a green square. The task force was instituted in 1999 with the express intention to give a bit of corporate spit and polish to Bengaluru's shabby streets. Before it folded in 2004, the BATF had launched numerous initiatives, including enhancing the visual appeal of the streetscape with trendy roadside furniture, signage (such as this one), and bus shelters. This signpost was a fading relic of BATF's efforts.

Both of these vignettes point to the abrasive effect that automobility as a political constellation endures in Bengaluru. The grinding down is evident especially in the case of infrastructures that face physical deterioration and displacement just by existing in the city. This process of whittling away of infrastructures is present regardless of which agency establishes the infrastructure or how expensive or impressive infrastructures are. The case of St. Marks Road reveals one aspect of the abrasive effect: the glaring absence of interinstitutional coordination between different utilities and the BBMP. In spite of the deep wells of support from the state's chief minister, its home minister, and senior bureaucrats in the state administration, the Tender SURE project was unable to marshal the support needed to conserve the integrity of its project. Instead, it had to retroactively resurface these cracks that emerged so soon after the road was opened to traffic.

The BATF, when it was active between 1999 and 2004, was an exceptionally influential actor whose efforts had the wholehearted support of the then chief minister of the state, S. M. Krishna. During its heyday, BATF's power allowed its interventions to keep the abrasive effects at bay. With the sun setting on BATF, its infrastructural interventions have been less than

Figure 6.2
BATF signboard in Madivala.

successful in keeping the forces of entropy at bay. Many of these interventions have now disappeared from public space. It would appear that this signboard on Madivala Road has survived partly because it has been repurposed to support market stalls, even as it leans precariously backward. In both of these cases, the dissolution of infrastructural efforts is particularly problematic because it calls into question the legacy that the constellation of automobility leaves in Bengaluru.

These vignettes point to the presence of a wider phenomenon that attends the installation of automobility. The political phenomenon of automobility in Bengaluru does not possess an absolute juggernaut-like footprint that shapes the city indomitably and obdurately. Instead, these vignettes point toward a contested presence of the constellation of automobility. Its enterprise on the city's streets faces a continuous, ongoing, and dynamic challenge that attempts to gnaw away at its achievements. These challenges can be posed at numerous stages of constituting the automobile city—conception, design, execution, and after implementation.

The sources of these challenges are diverse. As we saw in the vignettes, challenges to the stability of the enterprise of automobility can be directed by powerful institutional actors on account of the technical and economic constraints they operate within or by the passage of time and the actions of the "common" person on the street. The residues of past efforts to decongest and reorder the city (as we saw in chapter 2) often spark these contestations. Thus, as the case study of the elevated road demonstrates, challenges are sparked by the presence of a multiplicity of infrastructural authorities and the reclassification of drainage channels as repositories for all manner of urban waste and refuse. The alignment of these two residues initiated a sequence of events that enrolled a temple, popular religiosity, and sundry politicians to threaten the enterprise. We surmise that diverse actors prick at the enterprise of automobility in the city—misshaping a venture here, closing off a pathway there, and in most cases generally slowing the march of the juggernaut.

In this chapter, we examine the curious case of an elevated road constructed by the BBMP (with funding from the national government's JNNURM project) over the Vrishabhavathi River. The project was initiated in 2006 and nominally completed in 2017. The delay in the project, subsequent design modifications, and its partial success point to the contingent process of accomplishing the flyover's design mission of seamless automobile circulation at an important traffic intersection.

Before we study the nature and degree of success of this plan to improve automobile circulation, I employ (and advance) Pfaffenberger's (1992) notion of "technological dramas" to understand the nature of contestations that play out in the context of infrastructure building. Advancing Pfaffenberger, I suggest that it is necessary to examine the temporal and rhythmic (especially in the context of Lefebvre's notion of urban rhythms) dimensions to understand how "statements" of what a technology should do (in this case, what a flyover infrastructure should do) are challenged by counterstatements that operate along different temporal rhythms from the proponents of the technology. The conflation of these rhythms introduces complications that then result in the readjustment to the artifact and the project of automobility it serves.

Technological Deployment and Rhythms

Theater and drama commonly come to mind when we encounter the word *performance*. Lately, however, with the shift away from representational idioms in scholarship (Pickering 1995; Barad 2003), performance has acquired considerable traction in a range of academic fields, including feminist and queer studies, as well as science and technology studies that view actions as performances staged by actors within particular microscale settings. In doing so, it has allowed researchers to focus their attention on how practices are constituted through particular contexts and are, as a result, imbued with social and cultural significance. Pfaffenberger's (1992) notion of technological dramas is a prescient step in this direction.[5] Pfaffenberger reads the technological design and production process as a statement put forth by its design constituency with the explicit political aim of "altering the power, prestige, or wealth in a social formation" (1992, 285). But this statement of "regularization," as he calls it, does not go unchallenged and is often tracked by counterstatements, mobilized by social constituents who stand to lose from regularization, with a view to adjusting or reconstituting technological development. Performance in Pfaffenberger's view is marked by a strong interplay of intentionality on both sides of the performance—those crafting the statement and those responding with a counterstatement, each motivated by a clear sense of purpose of how their interests are (or are not) served through the technological intervention. Such opposing intentionality makes its appearance in controversial episodes of technological development marked by visible protest and upheaval. In more everyday and mundane forms of technological design and production not marked by explicit protest, what is the nature of the interplay of intentionality accompanying the performance of the technological drama?

The posthumanist move of taking material agency seriously offers new avenues for advancing Pfaffenberger's performative idiom. This move suggests that human agency in the world is always exerted in a material-filled field. Materials do not remain passive recipients of human action but instead react and respond in ways that in turn shape the actions of humans. While most would agree that human action happens in a material-rich field, the sticking point is whether nonhuman and inanimate materials, artifacts, and technologies can be understood to have agency in a manner equivalent to the actions that sentient humans routinely indulge in. The question of equivalence between human and material agency has exercised both proponents and critics alike. Indeed, proponents like those from the Actor-Network Theory (ANT) school insist on material-human equivalence as a matter of principle—the generalizable principle of human-nonhuman symmetry. Thus, for ANT's task of ontological description, it is obligatory to see human and material/nonhuman objects as ontologically equivalent and, indeed, interchangeable (Law 2009). In other words, when analyzing and describing the world out there, a collective of relations could be considered a human at times, while at other times, an overlapping set of relations could be considered a material. For critics, the question of equivalence between humans and materials is problematic on both political and moral fronts. At a political level, the project of material-human equivalence could potentially trivialize the hard-won gains of sociologists seeking to cut science and scientists down to size (Collins and Yearley 1992). More important, equating the human with the material on moral grounds is analytically indefensible, and even irresponsible, given that human intentionality and goal-driven behavior form the basis for legal and ethical guides in society.

Pickering's performative posthumanist turn identifies a way around this morass of human-material equivalence.[6] Pickering's (1995) resolution is to propose that material agency emerges in real time and only through practice. This quality of real-time emergence suggests that the nature and the response of material agency are unknowable in advance of the practice and can instead be experienced only through the process of practice. But it is not just material agency that is unknowable; human agency and its intentionality emerge through practice in response to how the material reacts to human interventions. In other words, material performativity and human agency are constitutively intertwined and stabilized in real time through practice (see Orlikowski 2007). This elaborate play between the human and the material is what Pickering refers to as the "dance of agency" (Pickering 1995, 21). The attention to the interactively stabilized everyday technoscientific practice marks a departure from Pfaffenberger's statement and counterstatement of technological dramas. Although performative, by focusing on episodic instances of human configuration and the adjustment of technology, such dramas are not attuned to the everyday forms of sociomaterial contestations and adjustments that proliferate in technological practice.[7]

Adopting a notably performative strategy, Akrich (1992) speaks of designers (or promoters) proposing a script for technologies, which arises from their vision of the world, but in deploying these technologies, actants in society respond with antiprograms that arise from the displacement of the technical interventions in the world. The dance between the program and the antiprogram corresponds to Pfaffenberger's statement and counterstatement, but at the same time, it signals a break by incorporating the sociomaterial nature of design and deployment of technologies. Incorporating sociomateriality in technological deployment, according to Akrich and Latour (1992), requires a new vocabulary, including *in-scription* (proposed by the engineer or designer), *subscription* or *de-inscription* (reaction of actants to the design program) and *de-scription* (work of an analyst to explain negotiations during deployment of the design program). Employing the de-scripting strategy to understand how technologies are deployed, we would be required to "go back and forth continually between the designer and the user, between the designer's projected user and the real user[s], between *the world inscribed in the object and the world described by its displacement*" (Akrich 1992, 209; emphasis added). But de-scribing such back-and-forth movement between the designer and the actants in society requires not just a plan but an actual intervention whereby infrastructures, technical objects, institutions, and nonhumans (and people) are brought into motion and grounded in particular locations by the process of (concrete) design. It is in describing the world in motion triggered by technology that the analyst can attend to a range of actants and their reactions to the emplacement of the technology. These back-and-forth performances between human designers and the sociomaterial constituents of a technology thus describe the mundane practice of technology development.

De-scripting such a (concrete) design process would then be contingent on the recognition of a temporal emergence, accompanied by the movement of actants, all located within the particularities of place. These three facets also lie at the heart of attending to rhythms and cadences of change in a place. In other words, attending to the rhythms of the design interventions in infrastructure, one can uncover or de-script the world displacement that design intervention creates. This is a departure from the instantaneous but diachronic emergence of material resistance in scientific practice that Pickering suggests (1995, 66). Instead, resistance to technological deployment emerges not instantaneously but with the intersection of multiple rhythms that suffuse a place, each operating to different temporal cadences. Some of these cadences become evident relatively quickly (in a matter of minutes or days) while others take longer (ranging from weeks to even years).

The study of rhythms as an analytical construct has emerged recently within time geography as a means to "contribute to the temporal understanding of place and space" (Edensor 2010, 1). A temporal dimension to the constitution of place arises from the conviction that the properties of particular places are emergent phenomena tied to multiple and heterogeneous social practices organized through varied durations, sequences, or rhythms. Thus, temporalities that course through a place are key to the emergence of the place. But the temporality of place needs to be understood through the coming together of multiple and heterogeneous (social, seasonal, geophysical, and infrastructural) times rather than a singular, linear, and all-encompassing time arrow. The multiplicity and heterogeneity of time signify the multiple durations and sequences of practices that suffuse through a place. Rhythmanalysis, Lefebvre suggests, is a particularly useful analytical tool to identify the multiple place-associated temporalities that are instantiated through a range of multiscalar rhythms, including the sidereal, seasonal, diurnal, social, individual, and corporeal.

According to Lefebvre, "everywhere where there is interaction between place, time, and an expenditure of energy, there is *rhythm*" (Lefebvre 2004, 15). The definition of rhythm draws our attention to the components of place, time, and energy. It is their simultaneous mixing together that, Lefebvre suggests, produces rhythms. Thus, a rhythm is indicated in particular places when there is movement or action (and therefore expenditure of energy) and when there is a process of temporal change indicated through phases of growth, development, and decline. However, temporal change (or mobility/action) is characterized through the plural rather than the singular. Thus, there exist multiple temporalities and mobilities and their associated rhythms that energize and resonate within particular places. Indeed, Crang (2001) has suggested that a place is "not necessarily of singular time but a particular constellation of temporalities" (190). Far from being a modern (or Western) phenomenon, he notes that the "lived city has for a long time been a polyrhythmic ensemble" (190). The multiplicity of rhythms resounding in particular places grants these locations their distinctive timespace signatures. Borrowing from Tim Edensor's classification, I suggest in this chapter some distinctive constellations of rhythms that are identifiable within urban places: people, somatic, technomaterial, and socionatural (Edensor 2010). Of these four rhythm ensembles, it is the technomaterial and socionatural rhythms that are of particular interest in understanding the rhythms of flows coursing through sites where infrastructure development happen.

The rhythmic pulse of technomaterial and socionatural flows that courses through the various infrastructures of cities energizes their "body politic" (Harvey 2003) even as they imbue unique spatiotemporal characteristics to the places they interconnect. As in Lefebvre's view from a window of the Paris streetscape with its ebbs and flows of people and traffic, the variegated rhythms marking the diurnal flux in traffic, automobiles, water, waste, gas, electrons, and bytes braided together instill particular patterns to places in similar ways. But in inscribing these rhythms and cadences to places, infrastructures assemble together heterogeneous networks that string together a diverse array of human, social, nonhuman, inanimate, technical, institutional, professional, and political bodies. Considering places to be suffused by braiding flows together with the help of multiple infrastructures, a chaotic and potentially infinite network of heterogeneous connections strings together in particular locations. Consequently, identifying and tracing network connections in order to proclaim the particular spatiotemporal characteristics of a place can quickly become an unmanageable, if not unsurmountable, task for the analyst. In this context, paying attention to flows and analyzing their particular rhythms that resonate within places presents a far more concise and manageable task to achieve the same result.

When de-scripting the designs of infrastructures, one must account for instances when different rhythms are inserted into the movement. These rhythms mark differently ordered impulses of energy expenditure and time that spatiotemporally shape how the process of designing evolves. Thus, in the evolution of a design, there are instances when certain rhythms are inserted to favor the designer's inscription, while in other instances, counterinscriptions manifest themselves, which lead to rhythms that limit or block the design venture. I discuss here two rhythmic moments in the design process: *affordances* and *congestions*. Coming from the psychology of design, *affordance* refers to "a relationship between the properties of an object and the capabilities of an agent that determines just how the object could possibly be used" (Norman 2013, 11).[8] In recent times, the turn in research to mobilities has accentuated concrete or other materialities of infrastructural supports within the performative staging of movement (O. B. Jensen 2016; see also 2013 with regard to how the material emerges within situational mobilities). Affordance has acquired renewed significance as a handle for the articulation of "material pragmatism," or the inquiry into how concrete materialities convey mobile situations. Affordance in this light is the ability of materialities to enable particular mobile situations (O. B. Jensen, Lanng, and Wind 2016, 2017). In the deployment process, though, affordances are understood as actions that a device allows from actors—human and nonhuman (Akrich and Latour 1992). Affordance specifically facilitates actions or movements that further the objectives of the program of design. They release rhythms that smooth or hasten the design program.

Congestions, on the other hand, facilitate a counterprogram. These are the Pickeringesque resistances that are presented by the sociomaterial constituents displaced by the intervention. These sociomaterial resistances bubble forth from the deep wells of historical residues (we encountered some of them in chapter 2) of earlier efforts to reorder the city. The existence of these residues rooted in historical action manifests as congestions in the encounters with design efforts. In mobility studies, friction (Cresswell 2014) offers an analogous conceptualization of the manifestation of stickiness in real-world situations. But such stickiness, he notes, is particularly generative of a situational politics that does not possess an inherent orientation; it could be used to further the agenda of the powerful just as it could be a weapon of the weak (Cresswell 2014, 111; see also 2016). These congestions introduce alternative rhythms that slow down, redirect, or even halt the design and development of infrastructures, thereby spurring new expenditures of energy by designers to overcome congestive rhythms.

Case of the Vrishabhavathi River Elevated Road

As the locus of India's knowledge economy centered on information and biotechnology industries and business process outsourcing, the resulting demographic and economic shifts in Bengaluru have certainly played an important part in the prominence that personal transport use has acquired in the city. At the same time, the growing footprint of the new middle classes in public space, urban advocacy organizations, news and media, and urban governance has, as we saw in chapters 3 and 4, powerfully emphasized personal automobility. This preference for automobile travel is reflected through a shift in infrastructural priorities articulated by a range of actors: middle-class groups, advocacy organizations, and news outlets. A distinguishing feature of these changed infrastructure priorities is the attention lavished on eliminating friction and roughness in automobile flows.[9] Friction in these flows within this worldview indicate technical blocks that slow the speed of vehicular flows. Thus, excess vehicular flow, busy intersections, multiuse streets, nonmotorized transport, narrow conduits, and multiple intersections are some common settings for friction in vehicular flow. Within the context of changed infrastructure priorities, redesign of transportation infrastructures to establish flyovers, underpasses, signal-free corridors, and elevated expressways are some ways to facilitate the smooth flows of personal automobility. An example in southwestern Bengaluru was the project to construct an elevated road at Deepanjali Nagar over the Vrishabhavathi River.

Figure 6.3 presents a schematic plan of the Vrishabhavathi River elevated road (VRER). This proposed road would connect two arterial roads, Chord Road and Mysore Road, and in the process would divert flows at their intersection to create a signal-free intersection (KIMCO junction in figure 6.3). The VRER was conceived by the city government of Bengaluru (the BBMP) with funding from JNNURM, the national urban renewal program. According to the design

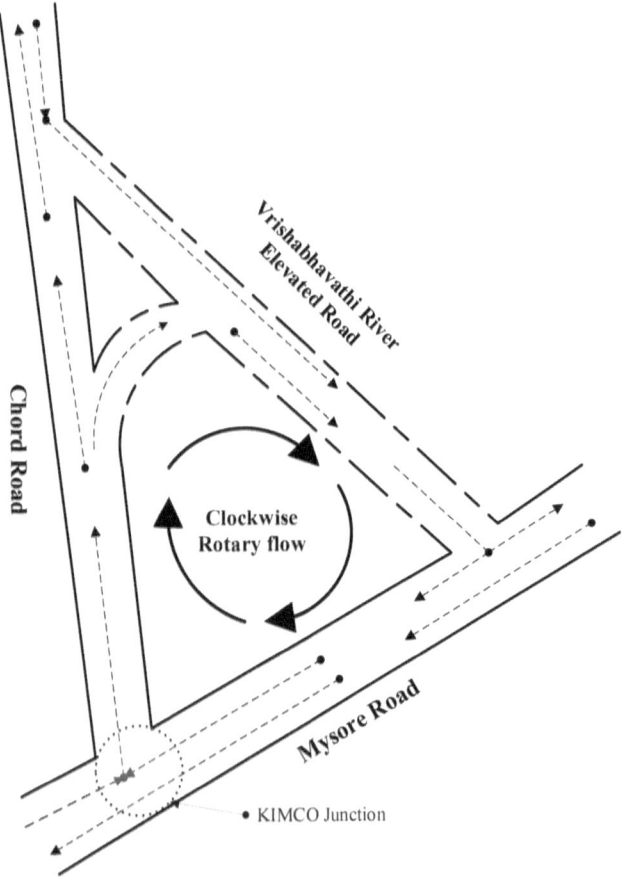

Figure 6.3
Plan for clockwise rotary flow of traffic.

plan, the VRER collects automobile flows through two up-ramps on Chord Road and distributes them at the other end through three down-ramps—one toward Bengaluru city, a second dedicated to buses toward the Mysore Road Bus Terminal (not shown in the figure), and a third toward Mysore.

The novelty of the VRER arises from the ability of the design to exploit a hitherto "vacant" geographical feature in the neighborhood, a loop in the Vrishabhavathi River, to create a pathway between the Chord Road and Mysore Road. Over a distance of 500 meters, the main stem of the elevated road is placed directly over the channel of the river. According to the plan, the elevated roadway would be supported on concrete columns lowered into the riverbed (figure 6.4). The Vrishabhavathi River, a minor tributary within the Cauvery River's watershed, originates north of the city and flows through the core of the heavily urbanized metropolitan region of Bengaluru. Prior to entering this neighborhood, it runs parallel to Mysore Road as it flows from the northeast to the southwest. Despite being classed as a river, the Vrishabhavathi is frequently referred to in newspapers as the "Vrishabhavathi drain" or even "stormwater drain," indicating that natural flows have long been subsumed within sewage, solid waste, and other

Figure 6.4
VRER constructed over the Vrishabhavathi River.

human and industrial effluent flows. The river itself announces its status as a waste carrier with a pervasive putrefying odor. At Mysore Road, the Vrishabhavathi meets yet another minor river (drain) and takes a sharp bend to create the channel over which the VRER has been erected.

To the south of the elevated road bordered by the river and Mysore Road is a government-run heavy electrical equipment factory. Beside the river and adjacent to this factory, at the point where the elevated road meets Mysore Road, is the Gali Anjaneya Temple, a popular, historic Hindu temple. Diagonally across Mysore Road from the temple is the Mysore Road Bus Terminal, operated by the government-run Karnataka State Road Transport Corporation (KSRTC), a major public corporation (entirely owned by the government of Karnataka) that operates intercity buses throughout the state. KSRTC's Mysore Road Bus Terminal is a satellite terminal for intercity buses that operate between Bengaluru and towns such as Mysore in southwest Karnataka. The construction of the VRER began in early 2006. The road was to be completed by February 2008, but even though more than 90 percent of the construction work was completed by this date, the VRER inched toward completion because multiple design complications challenged its execution. Examining the affordances and congestions in the design and implementation process will clarify the temporal development of the project and the multiple rhythms—social, seasonal, institutional and religious—that have collided with it.

Affordances Offered by the VRER

The primary design motivation of the VRER was to provide a conduit for smoother automobile flows at KIMCO Junction—the intersection of Chord Road with Mysore Road. By redesigning the junction as a signal-free zone, it would allow automobile flows to pass this intersection without waiting at the traffic light. The detailed report for the project notes that

> the provision of the flyover/bridge will result in a completely conflict-free stretch within the study area. All movements around the area will be one-way. The flyover/bridge will carry Chord road to Bangalore and Mysore to Bangalore traffic. The stretch of Mysore road from Bangalore to KIMCO junction will carry Bangalore–Mysore and Chord road–Mysore traffic and the stretch of Chord road from KIMCO junction to the entry ramp to the bridge will cater to Mysore–Bangalore and Bangalore–Chord road traffic. (STUP Consultants P. Ltd 2007, 57)

Such an intersection redesign would require eliminating cross-flows at this intersection by rerouting automobile flows appropriately. Two affordances in the design of VRER are necessary to achieve the objective of intersection redesign. First, the VRER needs to be designed to facilitate the task of collecting automobile flows from Chord Road and distributing these flows at the other end of the VRER on Mysore Road. In order to do so, in the original plan for the VRER was for two ramps on the up side (so-called up-ramps) and three ramps on the down side (so called down-ramps; figure 6.5 shows both sets of ramps in July 2013). The construction of the VRER reflects this design affordance. One up-ramp is designed to collect automobile flows coming south on Chord Road, while a second shorter up-ramp collects flows coming up Chord Road from KIMCO junction. At the Mysore Road end of the VRER, three down-ramps split and direct the collected automobile flows either toward the city (ramp 1), Mysore (ramp 2), or the KSRTC terminal across Mysore road (ramp 3). As we shall see, congestions in the execution ensured that ramp 3 was never constructed. The ramps were designed to facilitate the collection and distribution of automotive flows. But these affordances designed into the VRER serve their function if and only if they are integrated with a second affordance in the design of automobile flows. Automobile flows on Chord Road and Mysore Road between the VRER and KIMCO junction have to be redirected to allow for unidirectional flows of traffic in these stretches (as shown in figure 6.3). The design for collection and distribution in the VRER locks the pattern of automobile flows on Chord and Mysore Roads between VRER and the KIMCO junction in a particular unidirectional, clockwise rhythm. Altering the rhythms of traffic flow on these roads will adversely affect the design affordances that VRER creates for automobile flows. Therefore, in order for the VRER to succeed, BBMP's engineers had to ensure clockwise circulation of automotive traffic in this tri-legged rotary with each leg having unidirectional traffic flow.

One means of grasping the rhythms of affordances is to adopt an intimate Lefebvrian mode of rhythmanalysis. Lefebvre offers an uncomplicated means of grasping the rhythms of a place: park yourself on a balcony or stick your head out of a window and soak in the rhythms that animate the surrounding environment. The balcony, like the window in a house, provides a privileged position of neither being totally immersed in the flows and rhythms suffusing a place nor being entirely exterior to them. Lefebvre, thus, insists that

> in order to grasp and analyse rhythms, it is necessary to get outside them, but not completely... to situate oneself simultaneously inside and outside. A balcony does the job admirably, in relation to the street.... In the absence of which, you could content yourself with a window. (Lefebvre 2004, 28)

The liminal location of the balcony provides the analyst with a vantage point to observe and grasp the rhythms of a place. Employing the

Figure 6.5
VRER with its up-ramps (a) and down-ramps (b).

Lefebvrian strategy, I located myself on a first-floor balcony facing KIMCO junction (see figure 6.3), where Chord Road terminates at Mysore Road in a T- junction. I did so twice: in July 2012 and then in July 2017. In July 2012, the VRER project was not yet complete and the clockwise rotary flow had not been implemented. As a result, traffic circulation still followed the earlier pattern, with both Chord Road and Mysore Road having a divided carriageway for a two-way flow of traffic at KIMCO junction. In July 2017, the clockwise rotary had been implemented, with the result that both Chord Road and Mysore Road now possessed a unidirectional flow of traffic (for the most part) at the KIMCO junction. I sought to briefly portray rhythms of automotive flow circulating in this intersection at the two times in order to grasp the nature of changes in rhythms wrought by the completion of the VRER.

On the afternoon of July 25, 2012, I arrived at the KIMCO junction and found a deserted balcony on a second floor above some shops facing KIMCO junction. As I looked out from the balcony, I could see Chord Road coming downhill to meet Mysore Road in front of me. Facing me in the junction, there was a line of unfinished concrete pillars (with steel cables jutting out from their tops) that would carry the Metro overhead past KIMCO junction toward its terminus on Mysore Road farther east and away from the city center. Blocking my view up Chord Road was the incomplete structure of the Deepanjali Nagar Metro station. The station structure was constructed over Chord Road and was supported on three sets of pillars, rising on either side of the road and from the central median. Marching out from the station structure was a single line of concrete pillars (to support the Metro line) that formed the median separating the upstreams and downstreams of automotive traffic on Chord Road. At the point where Chord Road flared as it entered KIMCO junction, the single line of median pillars came to an abrupt end and was replaced by paired pillars, one on the sidewalk on either verge of the junction. After three sets of paired pillars, the single line of pillars resumed again along the left-hand side of the junction. The space between the pillars on the left and the far walls was occupied by piles of steel scaffoldings, pipelines, and other construction materials and debris. This and the steel-sheet fencing between the pillars on the left rendered the space between the roadway and the sidewalk behind the pillars unusable for uninterrupted movement of any kind. Instead, autorickshaws waiting for rides and people waiting for buses had parked themselves along the pillars, thereby transforming it into the de facto verge of the junction on the left-hand side.

Automotive traffic crawled along in both directions on Chord Road and Mysore Road. On Chord Road, traffic emerged from beneath the station structure and trundled downhill to the junction, where it faced a traffic light directly in front of my balcony. At the junction, traffic either waited for the green light to turn right and merge onto Mysore Road going west or made a free left to continue on Mysore Road toward the city. Vehicular traffic that came downhill on Chord Road was separated from the uphill stream by a line of concrete pillars and then by an irregular line of stone blocks that threaded into the junction. Within the junction were two crumbling traffic islands that served to guide traffic merging from one road to the other (figure 6.6a). The island on the left bore the high-mast light pole that illuminated the junction at night. A line of dust in the junction reached back and connected the island to the traffic divider on Mysore Road, thereby connoting (for pedestrians) a space in the junction that was largely unused by vehicles and therefore relatively safe to wait at before venturing to cross the remainder of the road. The side of the junction to the right offered a few dust trails or relatively safe zones where pedestrians or other nonmotorized travelers could navigate the uninterrupted streams of traffic on Mysore Road.

The defining rhythm of KIMCO junction was the timed cycle of traffic lights at the junction. Two poles carried the lights regulating traffic streams in the junction. One was located in front of my balcony and governed vehicles entering the junction from Chord Road as well as the vehicles heading out of the city on Mysore Road. The other, on the central median of Mysore Road to my right, directed vehicles on Mysore Road heading toward the city (figures 6.6a and 6.6b). Since I had arrived at the junction in the early afternoon before the start of peak evening traffic, the cycle of traffic lights was set at 120 seconds and included a brief rest phase of 5 seconds when all traffic in the junction was expected to come to a standstill and pedestrians could attempt to traverse it. The rest phase was indicated by the blaring of an electronic signal. Every two minutes, all lights turned red and traffic in the junction petered out. Heralded by the blaring signal, pedestrians scurried across traffic lanes aware that the rest phase was all too brief. The 5-second pause was usually only long enough for most to cross one stream of traffic and reach a safe space on the traffic median. There, they would wait for the next rest phase or, more commonly, attempt to continue crossing the road by exploiting gaps in traffic flow or using hand signals to communicate with drivers to allow them to get to the other side. After the pause, the cycle would commence again with a minute-long green signal for vehicles moving away from the city center along Mysore Road or making a right turn toward Chord Road. The next minute was almost equally divided between a green for traffic heading up Mysore Road toward the city

Shabby Automobility

Figure 6.6
Photographs taken at KIMCO Junction, July 2012.

center and a green for automobiles on Chord Road, followed again by a blast of the electronic signal and a red light for all vehicular flows.

Early in the afternoon on July 25, 2017, I located myself on the still deserted second-floor balcony facing KIMCO junction. From this vantage point, I could observe once again the cadence of automotive flows coursing through the junction. At that time, the structure of the junction was markedly different. The central median was missing on Chord Road and on Mysore Road coming from the city, and both roads were now one way (figures 6.7a and 6.7b). The junction possessed only one traffic island—the one on the left, which carried the high-mast light pole. A concrete barrier snaked from this island and connected with the median on Mysore Road, thereby passively discouraging vehicles that entered the junction from the Mysore side from performing a U-turn. Instead, all vehicles coming up Mysore Road were funneled toward Chord Road below the Deepanjali Nagar Metro station, where they could either take the tunnel on the right to get onto the VRER or the tunnel on the left to continue along Chord Road. Meanwhile, vehicles motoring down Mysore Road from the city side (which was now a one-way road) entered the junction without a break (figure 6.7b). While some vehicles continued along Mysore Road, others peeled off and climbed up Chord Road intent on taking either one of the gaping openings below the Metro station. Here they wove with the traffic entering Chord Road from the opposite direction (figure 6.7a).

The continuous braiding of these two streams of traffic on Chord Road (in front of my eyes), often accompanied by honking, the squealing of brakes, and slowing down, became a defining rhythm of the new traffic arrangement in the junction. This discordant rhythm of merging traffic was accompanied by the periodic but muffled clatter of a Metro train as it moved back and forth on the rails far above the junction. The key difference in the rhythm of automotive flows observed at the junction was in the ceaseless, almost unregulated flow of vehicles that coursed through the intersection in 2017. In comparison, in 2012, the timed cycle of traffic lights had introduced a regular cadence in automotive flows. In 2017, only one pole carried traffic lights, but the lights themselves did not work, and motorists paid scant attention to their presence. Instead, they hurtled through the junction with the single-minded purpose of traversing the intersection. The only effort to control traffic is the raised pedestrian crossing that spans all four lanes of Mysore Road on the city side just prior to entering the intersection. Although most vehicles slowed as they approach the crossing, pedestrians were daunted by the prospect of navigating four lanes of speeding vehicles without a median break and choose not to cross

Figure 6.7
Photographs taken at KIMCO Junction, July 2017.

the road here (figure 6.7b). Most instead attempt to walk over to the left side of the intersection to cross the road, where the median on the Mysore side of the intersection provided a safe space for pedestrians to pause before tackling the next stream of traffic.

The biggest difference that the construction of VRER and its affordance of a clockwise rotary motion have made is the uninterrupted stream of automobiles surging through the junction at any given instant. In the past, the regular cycle of traffic lights interrupted this flow, with all cross-flows being completely stanched, albeit briefly. But with the clockwise rotary and the explicit goal of providing a seamless flow for automobiles in this region, all such controls on automotive traffic have been relaxed. The speedier movement of automotive flows through the intersection has been accompanied by the discordant braiding of traffic on Chord Road and the hesitant and restricted rhythms of pedestrian and other nonautomotive flows at the intersection. Through a limited Lefebvrian rhythmanalysis, it becomes evident that the affordance of the project to provide the means for speedier and seamless automotive circulation has been achieved to an extent. But as we shall see next, this change was achieved by managing a range of social, hydrological, institutional, and religious rhythms that threatened the design program proposed by the promoters of the VRER.

Congestions in the Design of the VRER
The displacement of the VRER in the world has given rise to three blocks that have inserted alternate rhythms: the KSRTC, the Vrishabhavathi River (drain), and the Gali Anjaneya Temple beside the river. The VRER was designed with a down-ramp to provide dedicated access for KSRTC buses coming up Mysore Road to the bus terminal across the road. This ramp was designed as a flyover that would leap over Mysore Road directly to the terminal on the other side. However, even as the construction progressed on the VRER, in 2007, KSRTC refused to pay for the dedicated down-ramp to its terminal. Since the KSRTC as an organization is answerable only to the state government and is operationally and institutionally insulated from the BBMP (the city government), there was little the BBMP could do to influence the decision. The VRER was now redesigned with only two down-ramps (ramp 1 and ramp 2) instead of three. Now with two down-ramps, the key affordance offered by the flyover, the clockwise traffic movement, could be kept, so this redesign did not seriously threaten the integrity of the scheme. However, the excision of the KSRTC down-ramp prompted another design modification that was to have a major displacement effect. With the KSRTC pulling out and the VRER not required to cross Mysore Road, VRER

did not have to be constructed to its original height. Instead, the height of the roadway was lowered, changed from 5.5 meters above the river to about 2 meters. This design change was the source of further complications with the river and the temple congesting the design rhythm.

The main stem of the VRER is designed with concrete pillars erected into the channel of the Vrishabhavathi River. Given the design affordance of ensuring a smooth signal-free movement for the entire volume of traffic circulating in the Chord Road–VRER–Mysore Road rotary, the VRER is constructed with numerous large pillars that support the weight of the five-lane carriageway. Human and industrial wastes of all kinds, as previously noted, have overwhelmed the Vrishabhavathi River's flows. Erecting these pillars into the flow of the Vrishabhavathi had the effect of slowing the flow of the river, leading to massive siltation and precipitation of the waste flotsam the river carries with it (figure 6.8). Lowering the pillars into the river interrupted the riparian rhythm, thereby prompting sedimentation of some of its waste load. This sedimentation and clogging are particularly serious at Mysore Road, where the river winds (and slows) through a bend and joins the secondary river as it funnels under a bridge on Mysore Road. The sedimentation becomes particularly critical when monsoon rains collide with Vrishabhavathi's sedimented rhythms to spill over into a wider societal domain.[10] Since the construction of the pillars of the VRER in 2006, seasonal monsoon rains in the city have prompted the swollen Vrishabhavathi River to breach its banks at Mysore Road, threatening to overwhelm shops and other commercial establishments at the junction of the VRER and Mysore Road.[11] A combination of the low clearance of the bridges over these rivers and the silted riverbed has reduced the volume of water that can be channeled through rivers (that meet here) at any given time. In the dry season, with the flow being low in the rivers, the reduced channel volume does not present a barrier. But in monsoon season, during heavy rains, which is not unusual in the city between June and September, this junction becomes a choke point for the sheer volume of water barreling down both rivers.

With the rise in water level during episodes of heavy rain, the smelly, muck-filled water spilled over into the historic, and popular, Hindu Gali Anjaneya Temple that sits at the junction of the VRER and the Mysore Road (the temple is visible on the right side of figure 6.5b). According to popular history, the temple was established in the fifteenth century.[12] It is dedicated to Anjaneya (also known as Hanuman), a divine figure of enormous strength and wisdom for Hindus who worship Vishnu and his righteous warrior-prince incarnation, Rama. While the historicity of a Hindu temple

Figure 6.8
Sedimentation of waste around VRER's pillars.

is an important criterion, a temple's popularity among the faithful often depends on the deity's *shakti*, or its strength, that itself is related to the unique characteristics or visage of the deity, its legendary lineage, and/or its capacity to grant the wishes of devotees. On that count, the Gali Anjaneya temple possesses a particularly robust footprint.[13] As a result of the temple's stature in the religious landscape, one special quality the temple has acquired of late, according to some websites, is its popularity among many political leaders, who make a point of praying at this temple prior to launching their electoral campaigns. The temple's important socioreligious footprint and its connections with the political elites in the city set in motion yet another round of redesign to the bridge. With the foul-smelling, sewage-filled water entering the temple and with the circulation of images of priests, and even the deity Anjaneya, in the temple standing in the foul water circulating in newspapers (figure 6.9), the normal rhythms of religiosity of devotees were disrupted.

The years 2007 and 2008 were a period of political uncertainty in Karnataka and Bengaluru. In November 2006, the government of Karnataka initiated a process of metropolitan expansion in Bengaluru with the city expanding its area from 224 square kilometers to 741 square kilometers.[14] At the same time, on the pretext of redrawing ward boundaries for the newly expanded Bengaluru city, the state government suspended all elected governments in Bengaluru and the surrounding areas, ostensibly to facilitate the process of metropolitanization. All local governments remained suspended for three years until March 2010, when elections to the newly constituted greater Bengaluru were held for the first time. During that period, the state government oversaw all of the city's municipal affairs (see Gore and Gopakumar 2015 for more details). Furthermore, with state elections in May 2008 held after a year-long period of political uncertainty at the state level on account of coalition politics in a minority government, the executive authority over the state government came under the control of the BJP party—a party that in Karnataka tends to represent the interests of upper-caste Hindus. In this political context, images of despoilment of normal rhythms of religiosity in the Gali Anjaneya temple became an important opportunity for the political leadership of the state to be seen attending to the needs of the faithful. Repeated flooding in the temple and the despoilment of religiosity prompted several key politicians in the state—the chief minister and members of the legislative assembly (MLA)—to visit the temple and scrutinize the design of the VRER. In the municipal elections of March 2010 (held for the first time after metropolitan expansion), the BJP came to power in the city government. With it, a new cast of characters—the mayor,

Figure 6.9
Anjaneya and his priest in floodwaters (source: *Deccan Herald*).

deputy mayor, members of the municipal standing committee on works, and the concerned municipal councilor—began visiting the site to assess the progress in construction.

The flooding of the temple thus led to an intense scrutiny of the VRER design. The eventual recommendation for redesign was to reduce the number of columns supporting the elevated road and increase the height of the VRER at Mysore Road to provide more clearance for floodwaters. This midstream design change required some constructed work to be demolished before the design modifications could be incorporated.[15] Making these modifications to the VRER was not only time-consuming, because construction could proceed only after demolishing parts of the VRER; it also created yet another problem. The foot of both down-ramps now terminated a couple of meters above the road surface of Mysore Road. Connecting both down-ramps to Mysore Road would require two tasks. Connecting ramp 1 toward the city would require raising and strengthening a local bridge across the Vrishabhavathi River, and connecting ramp 2 would require raising and remodeling the bridge carrying the arterial Mysore Road across the secondary river.[16] The second task was a critical one because it would mean disrupting important traffic flow toward the city. In addition, since the state government was considering an elevated flyover on Mysore Road, BBMP decided not to proceed (for the time being) with reconstructing the bridge on Mysore Road and connecting it to ramp 2.[17]

In March 2013, after the completion of ramp 1, the VRER was formally opened for traffic and the Bengaluru Traffic Police instituted the clockwise flow of traffic on the rotary on the morning of March 4. Ramp 2 at that time ended in midair, unconnected to Mysore Road. It was even appropriated as a space for parking vehicles (figure 6.10). Implementing the clockwise rotary scheme for traffic in the absence of ramp 2 was very problematic. For one, construction of ramp 1 had reduced the width of Mysore Road and, so, constricted traffic flow. In addition, on account of the trailing gore of ramp 1, vehicles that came down VRER and sought to head outward in the direction of Mysore were forced to make a wide U-turn farther up Mysore Road in order to change the direction of their vehicles. This further contributed to congested traffic on the road. Realizing that it was futile to expect a smooth traffic flow with the existing configuration, on that very afternoon,

Figure 6.10
Incomplete ramp 2 of the VRER in July 2013 showing the difference in height between the ramp and the bridge on Mysore Road.

the traffic police reversed the decision to institute clockwise movement in this rotary.[18] Instead they reinstated the bidirectional traffic flow on Mysore Road and Chord Road. VRER was reduced to being a faster connection for vehicles coming down Chord Road that then needed to head up Mysore Road toward the city center. However, this traffic movement grossly underutilized the VRER and would not justify the investment made by the city government. In order to salvage the scheme's affordance, BBMP, thus, had to ensure that ramp 2 could be made to join Mysore Road. Given that the level of the VRER could not be lowered more, the only solution was to raise the level of the bridge carrying Mysore Road across the secondary river to the level of ramp 2. In April 2015, the BBMP began work on the bridge over the secondary river. In April 2016, more than ten years after work on the VRER began, the bridge was raised to allow ramp 2 to connect with Mysore Road (figure 6.11, taken in July 2017, shows a more seamless connection than in figure 6.10).[19] Once ramp 2 was opened to traffic, the Bengaluru Traffic Police reinstituted the clockwise-rotary movement that I observed on July 25, 2017, and is still in effect.

Figure 6.11
VRER ramp 2 connected to Mysore Road (in the background) with the Gali Anjaneya temple in the foreground.

The congestion released as a result of the displacement of numerous entities through the process of constructing and designing the VRER offers a means to grasp the complex rhythms that constitute automotive flows in the city. In the case of VRER's construction, we find that the displacement of social, institutional, material, and artifactual entities (which operate to different cadences and temporalities) have impinged on the rhythms of construction, thereby affecting the flow of automobiles in the city. BBMP, as the promoter of the project, had to contend with an arena studded with historically rooted entities such as KSRTC—an organizational product of state efforts in the 1960 and 1970s to introduce professionally planned governance; the Vrishabhavathi River, a waterway classified since the late nineteenth century as a conduit for carrying wastes; and Hindu religiosity and its interlinkages with contemporary political practices.

Although KSRTC was an initial participant and beneficiary of the VRER project (KSRTC buses would have gained a dedicated elevated corridor to enter the satellite bus terminus without having to cross Mysore Road), it reneged on its commitments to pay for the dedicated corridor. In chapter 2, we saw that one of the responses of the government of Karnataka in order to address the combined social, economic, and demographic challenges in Karnataka and Bengaluru was to institute professionally staffed, single-purpose parastatal bodies that would manage key infrastructures with greater technical efficiency than government departments. KSRTC was one product of this shift. In order to ensure that parastatal bodies had the necessary autonomy to operate without political interference from line departments, political leaders such as councilors and legislators, or city governments, parastatal bodies were incorporated with boards composed largely of high state bureaucrats to whom they are accountable. The flip side to this functional autonomy is financial autonomy, or the absence of additional budgetary support provided to parastatals by the state government. In the absence of government support, despite being nonprofit entities, operational efforts of parastatal organizations are closely tied to their financial bottom line and to the project financing they receive from several sources, including international financial institutions such as the World Bank (Goldman 2011). As a result, parastatal organizations are rarely swayed by calls made in the public interest if such actions could potentially harm their financial standing or their revenue. Given that the VRER project could have affected KSRTC's financial standing by diverting its revenues, its decision to back out of the project arose from its functional autonomy. In addition, given KSRTC's accountability solely to its board, BBMP possesses very little leverage to induce the parastatal to reconsider its decision. The imperviousness of parastatal organizations to the will of an elected city government is not an isolated instance; it is common enough in Bengaluru, where the task of managing infrastructure has been divvied up among a handful of special-purpose parastatal organizations. As a result, city governance has come to be dominated by what Sudhira terms "bureaucratic entrepreneurship" (Sudhira 2017, 57) in the hands of a small set of important and unelected officials.

The design changes in the VRER, prompted by the exit of KSRTC, set in motion a new congestion brought about by the waste load carried by the Vrishabhavathi River. In chapter 2, we noted (following Malini Ranganathan, 2015) the terminological and discursive shift in the city's hydrological infrastructure impelled in the late nineteenth century by the shift away from open-air channels and tanks to piped water supply and sewerage. Happening as part of the colonial project of improvement, stormwater channels were recast as sanitary water drains, rivers became conveyors of unhealthy refuse and filth, and tanks were transformed into cesspools that received human wastes. The Vrishabhavathi River was one victim of this discursive recasting. Although long-time residents remember the river as a place of greenery, wildlife, and clean water, by the early twenty-first century, the river's flows had become a soup of sewage and industrial and household wastes, while its banks were littered with the plastic, glass, rags, polythene bags, sanitary napkins, hospital wastes, and other discards of modern lifestyles. The overflow of this toxic soup into the wider domain outside the riverine channel and images of these smelly waters swirling at the feet of Anjaneya became the provocation for a new congestion.

This congestion explicitly foregrounded the links between Hindu religiosity and the practices of political leaders in Bengaluru and Karnataka. Mines and Gourishankar (1990) have pointed out how the construction of political leadership in India (especially in South India) as "the big man" is rooted in the ability of leaders to use a variety of institutions, such as charities, dispensaries, schools, and temples, to be recognized in public as trustworthy individuals who have the welfare of the public in mind. But leaders who seek to continue building their stature must capitalize on occasions of public controversies. Research has shown that while everyday arenas of leadership evoke a sense of captaincy—a quality that includes effective bureaucratic management, knowledge of legal and administrative channels, and skills in resource distribution (Price and Ruud 2012)—such captaining roles are necessary, but they lack the moral weight that can propel a leader into the stratospheric heights of "lordly leadership" (Price and Ruud 2012, xxv). A lordly leader rises above mere captaincy to adopt the role of the protector of the moral order. Controversies surrounding deities residing in powerful temples marshal the optics that could potentially provide a leader with the visibility of a captain and be seen as a lord maintaining the moral order in the world. Doing so could potentially establish a leader with a lineage harking back to the religio-political style of leadership (that we saw in chapter 2) of the enlightened and venerable *dewans* and kings of the Mysore kingdom.[20] The flooding of the Gali Anjaneya Temple with the toxic muck from the Vrishabhavathi River swirling at the feet of Anjaneya became an occasion for leaders of the state to rehearse their *rajadharma*— reformers who uphold the moral order.

Fiction of Infrastructure Development

These congestions, we have seen, pull together multiple historically rooted social, institutional, material, and artifactual entities. In so doing, they demonstrate considerable power to slow down and potentially derail projects of infrastructure building. Yet the deep-rootedness of the congestions we encountered in the VRER case is rarely acknowledged publicly. Instead, infrastructure development is presented as an unproblematic technical enterprise that is a superficial overlay unhindered by and unconnected to history, society, and politics. Project documents contribute to this by presenting a fiction of the process of infrastructure development.

The withdrawal of the KSRTC from the VRER project was the catalyst that initiated a course of major redesign that then perforated the time and material boundaries set around the project by design proponents. Once the VRER spilled out of its boundaries, it infiltrated and became entangled with multiple sociopolitical residues, setting in motion a series of events beginning with the siltation and blockages in the Vrishabhavathi River, the subsequent flooding of the Anjaneya Temple, and heightened political scrutiny of the project—something that proponents would no doubt like to have avoided at all costs. According to early estimates provided in the detailed project report (DPR), this was to be an economically feasible and clear-cut project of infrastructure development that could be completed in sixteen months (including the monsoon) by February 2008 (STUP Consultants 2007, 116).[21] Indeed in the project's DPR, proponents note that the duration of the execution of infrastructure works by the city government ranges from six to nine months and thus the time frame proposed in this case appears more than sufficient for the purpose (79). Yet the work involved in the project took at least seven years before formal inauguration in March 2013 and three more years before all major barriers to realize the project's key design affordance of the clockwise rotary could be ironed out.

As part of the process of accessing JNNURM funds from the national government to finance infrastructure projects, the city government had to follow a structured process of managing project implementation.[22] A DPR was a key technique to demonstrate the willingness of the local government to mobilize processes at the national and state levels to access funds needed to support infrastructure projects—an infrastructural obligatory passage point (Callon 1984). The DPR explicitly assesses potential risks associated with the project. It notes that road projects such as this one face a range of risks related to land acquisition, shifting utilities, internal organizational risks, and coordination across multiple stakeholders, which it notes are particularly crucial to Bengaluru. According to the DPR, "stakeholders involved in Bangalore road projects are—BMP [the city government], utility companies, traffic police, public works department, residents association, shop owners association, Pollution Control Board" (STUP Consultants 2007, 81). According to the report, each of these entities can pose challenges to the completion of road projects. However, in the case of the VRER, the DPR has a restricted list of stakeholders who play a role in managing the risk for this project. The table determines a high to medium level of risk (unascertained, however) associated with the successful execution of the road project (see table 6.1). What is notable is that the risks mentioned in the report involve social entities alone. The risks posed by the flotsam, the Vrishabhavathi River, interrupted hydrological flows, monsoonal cloudbursts, temples, popular religiosity, and political *rajadharma* find no place in the DPR. In its stead is the recognition of the vital agency that social actors exercise in shaping project outcomes. Disregarding social actors can certainly seriously jeopardize project efforts, but the same could be said of the nonhuman entities in the VRER case.

Table 6.1
Managing Various Risks Involved with the VRER Project

Risk	Stakeholders	Severity of Risk
Acquisition of land	BBMP, government of Karnataka	Medium
Removal of encroachments	BBMP, BDA, government of Karnataka	Medium
Traffic management	BBMP, contractors, traffic police	High
Accidents	BBMP, contractors, traffic police	Medium
Construction debris	BBMP, contractors	Medium

Source: STUP Consultants (2007, 81).

By disregarding nonhuman entities and paying attention solely to the social and human entities that possess the agency to affect the project, the DPR is, in a Latourian sense, a thoroughly modern document. Bruno Latour in his excellent *We Have Never Been Modern* (1993), which examines the paradoxes of our modern existence, notes:

> The word modern designates two sets of different practices which must remain distinct if they are to remain effective, but have recently begun to be confused. The first set of practices, by "translation", creates mixtures between new types of beings, hybrids of nature and culture. The second, by "purification" creates two entirely distinct ontological zones: that of human beings on the one hand, and that of non-human beings on the other.... The second [corresponds] to what I call the modern critical stance. (Latour 1993, 10)

Purification, according to Latour, is an essential practice of modernity by which our lives are categorized into distinct, hermetically separated categories of nature and society. Mixing between the worlds of nature and society is untenable if one is to remain modern or produce a modern document. Thus, the world of nature and science is animated entirely by nonhumans, while at the same time, the world of society with its politics and risks is animated entirely by humans and social actors alone. Only human stakeholders exert agency in modern society. In this modern world, there is no place for monsoonal rhythms or interrupted hydrological flows, let alone Anjaneya or waste flotsam. In a modern cosmology, there is no scope for mixing between the worlds of nature and society.

The DPR treads this path of purification studiously. In fact, it is exceptionally careful in drawing in its circle of actors. With the exception of unnamed contractors, the only actors who have a voice in managing the risk associated with the project are those connected with the state—the government of Karnataka, BMP, BDA, or the traffic police. Straying out of this safe realm, it would seem, is like opening a can of worms—all manner of actors, linkages, and mixtures await acknowledgment and release into the wider world. Acknowledging their existence in the DPR is rather like recognizing the contingency of constructing infrastructure in a complicated world where all kinds of residues and hybridities proliferate. Instead, the DPR paints a comfortable portrait of an unproblematic construction process. According to the DPR, "The whole of the construction period is expected to last 16 months including the monsoon period from the date of handing over the site to the contractor" (STUP Consultants 2007, 116). The fact that the VRER project took ten years to complete instead of the stated sixteen months is testament to the unacknowledged complexities of developing infrastructures in Bengaluru. The DPR presents a purified fiction of infrastructure development in the city. The de-scription of the VRER project reveals the enduring complexities that pervade the process of automotive infrastructure development in contemporary Bengaluru.

Conclusion

What does this case of the VRER tell us about the automobility coursing through Bengaluru? As a political constellation, automobility endures in Bengaluru through the accumulation of various elements that possess a marked technopolitical quality. It has been constituted through the deployment of technologies and artifacts to construct a regime that orders space in the city to lock in particular political goals; assembles an infrastructure landscape that inscribes elite privilege; and composes the belonging of auto-mobile citizens on the streets of the city. These elements of automobility do not operate in isolation but instead interact to develop a composite experience of how residents of Bengaluru move from one place to another. However, the experience of moving around the city is not uniform for all residents. Depending on their mode of travel, the experience of the cityscape, their sense of belonging on the street, and the space on the street all change markedly. Thus, for automotive users, cityscape and street space are assembled to enable their movement, while for pedestrians, cyclists, and the pushcart vendors, these same aspects become disenablers for their circulation and movement.

Despite this, it would be incorrect to assume that the political phenomenon of automobility in the city is an unchanging juggernaut that is obdurately stamping its imprint on Bengaluru. Instead, the enterprise of automobility faces a constant, ongoing, and dynamic challenge that grinds down its achievements. The ongoing contestation of automobility arises from diverse historically rooted congestions. These congestions whittle away at engineers' and designers' conception of a smooth, seamless automobility that allows motorized travelers to zip from anywhere in the city to anywhere else with minimal disruption. The contestations slow down and on occasion disrupt efforts for seamless automobile flows. The engineers and designers have to inject considerable energy and time to ensure that the enterprise of automobility is conserved. What emerges instead is a shabby and untidy process that ensures that automobile flows are smoother, but excess energy and time to achieve this goal. The shabby automobility proliferating in Bengaluru recalls Tsing's characterization of global encounters as friction—"friction refuses the lie that global power operates as a well-oiled machine" (Tsing 2011, 6). Similarly, the juggernaut of automobility is conserved, but its machinery continues to be jammed.

However, it would also be incorrect to assume that the jamming of automobility is a sign that the constellation is not secure in Bengaluru and that it can be displaced with ease if we choose to move in the direction of an equitable and low-carbon mobility paradigm in Bengaluru. In concluding this book, the next chapter expands on how to displace the technopolitical constellation of automobility in the city. Elaborating on the empirical material, the conclusion makes three suggestions for displacing automobility: unlocking the regime of congestion, mobilizing pro-poor infrastructurescapes, and performing acts of taking back the streets and thereby franchising pedestrians, vendors, and bicyclists on the streets.

7 Displacing Automobility

We began chapter 3 by discussing the contestation surrounding the case of the construction of the steel flyover, a 7-kilometer elevated structure that was planned to provide a seamless connection for vehicles between central and north Bengaluru. It is particularly instructive to revisit the campaign against the steel flyover because it offers important insight into the struggle to displace the constellation of automobility in the city. Doing so allows us to locate a cosmopolitan "politics of hope" (Coutard and Guy 2007) that will shift the constellation to concede more space to underprivileged uses of road space even as it whittles down the overwhelming preponderance of imaginaries of an unjust and privileged automobility that currently circulates in Bengaluru.

Despite the vitality of the protests against the steel flyover, the perception that the organizations and leaders spearheading the protest spoke in a middle-class voice was quite prevalent. Leaders of Citizens for Bengaluru (CfB) belonged to the educated middle class and were predominantly professionals. Furthermore, group leaders had little history in community organization or in popular mobilization. The mobilization for the protest effort itself was conducted predominantly in English on social media and in broadcast media. In addition, given the history of middle-class activism in urban governance in Bengaluru (chapters 2 and 4 offer insight into their operation), it was expected that the campaign against the steel flyover would be yet another instance of a middle-class assertion on public space. Indeed, in the initial days, groups such as the Bengaluru Bus Commuter Forum that had struggled for more pro-poor and inclusive urban claims, explicitly distanced themselves from the campaign and its leaders in CfB whose interests were seen as selective and steeped in self-interest (Nagarajan 2017). However, by January 2017, the citizen campaign against the steel flyover had become successful in attracting a wider cross-class coalition of supporters.

Campaigners against the flyover increasingly gave their voice to wider urban mobility questions in the city. They explicitly championed the cause of developing an affordable commuter rail system for the city, which would benefit not just the middle class but also other members of the traveling public. Yet another venture that went beyond the predominant middle-class orientation was the launch of a common campaign, in alliance with the Bengaluru Bus Commuter Forum, to initiate a rollback of bus fares and introduce more buses in the city. Given the perceived middle-class orientation of CfB, the launch of a common campaign that would potentially benefit poorer sections was, I believe, a key moment in citizen mobilization against the politics of automobility in the city. It indicated a real prospect for forging cross-class social alliances that could effectively mobilize against automobility. In a city as polarized as Bengaluru, this was a landmark achievement. Possibly recognizing that the campaign was poised to grow, in early March 2017, the government abandoned the steel flyover project and decided not to proceed with constructing it.[1] The decision of the government not to construct the steel flyover is, to my mind, a landmark instance of mobilization to displace the grip that automobility has come to exercise on the city. This instance of protest against the ordering of mobility marks an instance of a "politics of hope" that can transform the constellation into what Chatterjee refers to as a "less malevolent hybrid" (Chatterjee 2004).[2]

The case of the campaign against the steel flyover is illustrative of a growing dissatisfaction among Bengaluru residents about how mobility and streets are organized in the city. The installation of the constellation of automobility in the city has made streets increasingly captive to automotive modes of travel. In previous chapters, I delineated the contours of Bengaluru's constellation of automobility. In this final chapter, I address the question "So, what can we learn from the incumbent constellation of automobility in Bengaluru?"

In the next section, I first summarize key points about the nature of automobility in the city. Based on the summary, I then focus on the contribution the empirical material in the book will make to scholarship, especially by locating the importance of the Bengaluru case described in this book for studies in mobility and urban environment. In other words, I explore why the Bengaluru case is significant for our efforts to conceive of equitable and sustainable urban places. In the final section, I conclude the book with a call to displace automobility around the world by reordering the mobility regime, relandscaping the city and its infrastructures, and reclaiming streets as spaces of diverse inhabitation. I argue that it is through conjoined efforts on these three fronts that we can develop an alternate constellation of mobility that will prize cities from the grip of automobility.

Installing Automobility in Bengaluru

Automobiles and associated modes of inhabiting and moving are deeply embedded in the cities of Europe and North America, but what is significant in the present moment is their rapidly growing presence in megacities of the global South. Large, urban agglomerations in India such as Bengaluru are not exceptions to this phenomenon. Scenes of streets choked with vehicles, especially private automobiles, are now a daily occurrence in Bengaluru. I have argued in this book that the rise of the automobile presence on Bengaluru's roads is a symptom, not a driver, of the installation of the constellation of automobility in the city. Beginning with Featherstone, Thrift, and Urry's (2004) pioneering volume that established it as a key topic for theory and research, automobility enjoins a wide-ranging examination of the car and its location within the cultural and ideological matrix of contemporary Western lives. In order to recognize the ramifications of automobility in Bengaluru, we have to look beyond automobile growth on its streets and investigate how decisions to intervene in urban mobility have resulted in imprinting automobiles profoundly on the spatial, political, and technological landscape of the city. Attending to this is vital because it directs us to the political constituent of automobility.

In this book, automobility is understood to have been installed in Bengaluru as a technopolitical constellation. Drawing on both Hecht's (2009) notion of technopolitics and Gandy's (2011) conception of constellation, a technopolitical constellation is understood here as a complex, multidimensional sociomaterial entity situated in a historical context and whose material designs have come to embody specific political goals. Thus, automobility cannot be explained solely through political or technological and material dimensions but is instead an amalgamation of the technological and political. As a constellation possessing such an amalgamated existence and immersed within a sociohistorical context, automobility in Bengaluru requires analytical unraveling that allows us to understand the different strands that have contributed to its installation. This process of teasing apart the threads that weave together automobility is an important task for two reasons. First, it is only through teasing apart these strands that it is possible to appreciate how automobility has become rooted within Bengaluru. The second, and related, reason is that the interweaving of its multiple dimensions signals the extraordinary persistence that automobility has acquired in Bengaluru. By enrolling an assortment of social, technological, and artifactual entities that together enact particular attitudinal, behavioral, and political responses, automobility has lodged itself deep within Bengaluru. In chapters 2 to 6, I embarked on the task of describing different dimensions of the city's automobility constellation.

Relying on a *longue dureé* historical imagination in chapter 2, I piece together the twists and turns in the evolution of a discourse on congestion in Bengaluru over the past two hundred years enunciated through a unique entourage of actors, and their chosen interventions have left behind residues that remain encrusted in the city's landscape and continue to shape the contemporary construction of automobility. Between 1799 and 1881, congestion in the city was interpreted as a product of the disorderliness that pervaded the indigenous arrangements of managing urban space in the precolonial settlement, or *peté*. The creation of a rival urban pole in the cantonment and the municipalization of urban administration materialized in distinct offices were interventions that sought to address disorderly congestion in this city. This period signals a profound start to a long history of decontextualized instrumental approaches to intervene and control congestion.

From 1881 to 1949, the discourse could be characterized as one of unhealthy congestion. This discourse was a composite created from a technoscientized development regime in the colonial kingdom of Mysore, a portrayal of native modes of urban management in planning, water supply, and sanitation as inferior and unhealthy and the reliance on new forms of scientific interventions in urban space that nevertheless complied with the norms associated with prevailing social hierarchies and inequalities. One of the residues from this period is a lasting predilection in statecraft toward technological instruments over any political or social means.

In the next period, from 1949 to 1991, congestion came to signify the absence of formal scientific planning to address urban growth. The consensus among the governing elites of this period was that unplanned efforts would result in an urban space suffused with congestion not just throughout the city but also at the level of individual sites and locations. Specific techniques and mechanisms of planning were deployed to rectify the congestion caused by unplanned growth with a view to promoting a dispersed, and therefore wholesome, settlement pattern. New actors such as a planning bureaucracy led by a statutory parastatal organization composed of technically qualified experts were instituted to plan for urban decongestion. The combination of a professionally qualified bureaucracy and technical strategies of planning was expected to eliminate congestion in Bengaluru. Instead, it has engendered a well-oiled and pervasive system of illegality in the use of land and the construction of buildings.

From 1991, the characterization of the discourse of congestion has shifted once again to one marked by congestion in infrastructure flows coursing through the city. Coinciding with the rise of Bengaluru as a node for technology enterprises, this shift has brought a new cast of actors, including special-purpose vehicles and public-private partnerships that seek to manage the process of developing infrastructures to streamline flow blockages. The rush for seamless infrastructure conduits in an age of global connectivity has deposited yet another layer of residues. Designs for seamless infrastructures are indexed against norms and aesthetics increasingly dictated by middle-class preferences, as well as an enormous desire to mobilize land for private accumulation. This historical denouement allows me to posit two aspects that are vital to the story of automobility in Bengaluru. First, instrumentality in addressing congestion in different time periods in Bengaluru's history appears as an almost default option. It makes its appearance through reliance on technologies, techniques, and technical institutions to achieve objectives of sociospatial change. One consequence of the instrumental approach has been the germination of residues as unintended products that continue to exert a powerful influence on the urban experience in Bengaluru. Second, the current narrative of traffic congestion in Bengaluru has similarly been narrowly interpreted as one arising directly from the recent but enormous growth in automobiles. Such a narrow interpretation is not unique to Bengaluru. Cities in the Western Hemisphere in the early to mid-twentieth century similarly demonstrated an instrumental approach to traffic congestion. But such an overtly instrumental approach is not without political ramifications. Indeed, instrumental approaches have become the conduit to weave political objectives into seemingly technical means to reduce congestion. Since 1991, political valences of approaches to address congestion in Bengaluru have been increasingly shaped by a middle-class articulation of norms and aesthetics for urban space and a state machinery that enables private accumulation in the pursuit of economic growth.

Chapters 3, 4, and 5 reveal the particular modes through which political valences have been inserted into Bengaluru's automobility constellation. Recent interventions for smoothing automobile flows in the city, I argue in chapter 3, assemble a power-filled structure that orders how people move around the city. It is helpful to identify the structure as a technopolitical regime because it spotlights how technological infrastructures and artifacts of mobility are enrolled to realize purposes that are profoundly political in their outcome. I demonstrate how discourses of infrastructure inadequacy and vehicular congestion have wrought a regime of congestion that unambiguously articulates a politics of takeover of the streets for the sole purpose of motorization. Through the efforts of the regime, streets are refashioned as conduits that facilitate the smooth transit of motor vehicles while marginalizing other uses. Thus, nonmotorized forms of moving and inhabiting streets associated with vending, walking, and cycling are increasingly being erased altogether from some streets and relegated to the margins of others. But recasting city streets as arteries for motorization has been accompanied in recent years by making the experience of moving around the city inequitable. The growing inequality in urban mobility in Bengaluru is illustrated in the case of public transit. The prevalence of greater automotive congestion on roads has become the motivation for the introduction and rapid spread of air-conditioned bus services and park-and-ride facilities that target the automobile-owning middle class. At the same time, less mobile and poorer urban groups, such as women, daily wage earners, and students, have had to contend with less affordable and more crowded bus services. This inhospitable environment in buses has led many more to abandon public transit in favor of private vehicles, contributing further to the vehicular congestion on the streets. This self-perpetuating dynamic has locked in the regime of congestion in the city streets.

Bengaluru's congestion is compounded by the powerful salience that road infrastructures have acquired in the city's landscape to shape the experience of urban commuters. In chapter 4, I argue that through their enduring presence, road infrastructures on the city landscape have activated particular circuits of actors, inscribed certain technopolitical sensibilities, and reinforced particular practices and experiences of motorization in the city. By proposing the visual analytical concept of infrastructurescape, I suggest that the recent uptake in motorization has been accompanied by the design of an infrastructurescape of privilege in Bengaluru studded with humongous overhead tollways and flyovers, elite partnership efforts such as ABIDe, road redesign and traffic management efforts that to some extent have been contested by grassroots infrastructurescapes composed of citizen groups, people's manifestos, protests, and localized neighborhood efforts to refashion cityscapes. Paying attention to the infrastructure landscape, we can attend to how actors, organizations, artifacts, technologies, and plans come together to enunciate a particular visual dimension to urban change. More important, this understanding demonstrates that landscapes are not inert backdrops but are instead laden with power and purpose. Chapter 4 reveals how the prevalent embedding of privileged normative orientations and the organizing motivations associated with the infrastructures of mobility in Bengaluru incorporate purposes that are often far removed from moving people sustainably or equitably. Instead, as we have seen, political elites see in big-ticket infrastructure the opportunity to gain popular legitimacy to advance their personal political interests. Or corporate elites propose exemplars such as the Tender SURE road redesign as models for new and world-class practices and designs. Together, these have attenuated landscapes of more inclusive mobility and inhabitation.

Chapter 5 articulated yet another facet of Bengaluru's incipient constellation of automobility: how belonging on and inhabiting streets is shaped to facilitate the occupation of the city by automobiles. In this chapter, I characterize these modes of belonging as automotive citizenship and show that this form of enfranchising of the automotive public is crafted on the streets of Bengaluru through the accumulation of a range of claims exerted by road and infrastructure designs and practices of driving. Thus, when mega-infrastructure projects such as the Nayandahalli interchange in southwestern Bengaluru was constructed, much of the designer's attention was lavished on the needs of automobiles zipping through the interchange. The needs of pedestrians, pushcart vendors, and bicyclists, however, have been utterly neglected. Similarly, social media allow traffic enforcement actors and the automotive public to collectively articulate a connotation of roads as spaces reserved primarily for uncongested automobile travel. Through this sociomaterial ensemble, automotive citizenship is understood as a durable phenomenon constituted through the performance of navigating and traversing urban space in the city.

Despite the deep political valences that are imbued within the constellation of automobility in Bengaluru, it would be a misreading to characterize it as an obdurate, totalizing force that will flatten the city unchallenged. Chapter 6 portrays instead the continuous, ongoing, and dynamic challenge that grinds down the achievements of the enterprise of automobility. The ongoing contestation of automobility arises from diverse historically rooted congestions. These congestions whittle away at engineers' and designers' conception of a smooth, seamless automobility that allows motorized travelers to zip from any given point in the city to anywhere else with minimal disruption. The case of the Vrishabhavathi River elevated road illustrates the diverse contestations that were sparked when the construction of the road was initiated to ensure signal-free automotive travel at an important road junction in the city. The contestations slow down, and on occasion, disrupt, efforts for seamless automobile flows. In response to these diverse sociomaterial contestations, engineers and designers have to inject considerable energy and time to ensure that the enterprise of automobility is conserved. What emerges instead is a shabby and untidy process that might still ensure that automobile flows are smoothened, but only after an expenditure of time and energy.

Implications

Automobility in Bengaluru has acquired an extraordinary degree of persistence on account of its situatedness in the city's history, society, and politics. So what can we learn from the emplacement of automobility in Bengaluru? I believe that the significance of Bengaluru stems from surmising two implications: one related to our understanding of automobility and another to the challenges facing equitable and sustainable cities.

First, a key implication that springs from this work is how the twists and trials of Bengaluru's case advance our understanding of automobility. As recent research has revealed, automobility is a sociotechnical condition inseparable from our contemporary modern existence. It is marked by an intense entanglement of the automobile in several facets of our contemporary lives: behavior and emotions, national identity, popular culture, work, travel, and even constitutional liberalism. These are just a few of the domains where the automobile leaves its footprint (see the special issue in 2004 of *Theory, Culture and Society* and in 2006 of *Sociological Review* for a detailed exposition). As a consequence, researchers have characterized automobility as a system (Urry 2004) or a regime (Böhm et al. 2006)—a powerful structuring force. It is the power embedded within automobility that has released a multifarious hydra-like entity that continues to exert an imprint on our lives. However, given the predominance in this literature of the Western Euro-American experience, automobility has been conceptualized as a preexisting phenomenon that continues to shape the lives of many. But the question of how the hydra-headed and power-infused phenomenon of automobility has come to be constituted and established has not been answered fully.

This, despite the fact that much of the recent historical research on the dawn of the automobile age in Western contexts describes eloquently how the varied political, fiscal, technological, regulatory, and cultural components have woven together the fabric of automobility. Christopher W. Wells's *Car Country: An Environmental History*, for instance, does a remarkable job in excavating how, over the first half of the twentieth century, through the collective operation of shifting priorities in government investment, technological breakthroughs in road design, and planning for car-centered landscapes, the United States has been molded into the eponymous Car

Country, thereby establishing the automobile at the center of public life. Although Wells portrays this profound transformation in exquisite detail, the work is notably thin on theorization on how automobility has come to be established in the United States. In the absence of conceptualization, the sheer volume of Wells's empirical material paints a powerful picture, but it offers few guides for painting similar pictures in other locations. Thus, while the book's readers become aware that manufacturing a car-centric society has multiple components, with few conceptual guides, they are unable to capitalize on their recently acquired awareness to analyze, let alone intervene, in an incipient automobility elsewhere.

Clearly there is a yawning gap in the literature. On the one hand, the historical literature illustrates a detailed picture of the installation of automobility in the West, which is notably atheoretical, while on the other hand, contemporary studies of automobility in the West are conceptually rigorous but have not focused on the processes of installation and instead regard automobility as a preexisting condition. The case of Bengaluru elaborated in this work fits squarely within this gap. This work seeks to illustrate a detailed picture of how automobility has become installed in Bengaluru, but it does so by adopting a conceptual vocabulary to index the processes involved. While the picture elaborates how involuted the processes of automobilization are, the conceptual vocabulary offers analytical pathways for interpreting the material. Through these pathways, one can attempt to grasp similar processes underway in other places (Western and non-Western). For example, the concept of automotive citizenship (introduced in chapter 5) is a powerful device for grasping processes of enfranchisement of automobiles that are proliferating on streets around the world. This work offers six analytical concepts that are, I believe, critical for understanding the installation and entrenchment of automobility: automobility as anthropocenic fluid; automobility as a technopolitical constellation; the regime of congestion; the infrastructurescape; automotive citizenship; and affordances and congestions in automobility. This analytical vocabulary provides concepts to assess the nature of automobility constituted in the context of choice and to assess the politics of streets and mobilities in locations around the world. The portability of the conceptual vocabulary is a major contribution of this work.

Second, how can the particularities of Bengaluru's predicament offer a guiding light for cities around the world as they aspire to break free from the clutch of automobility and move toward a more sustainable and equitable pathway? In a world that increasingly recognizes the pernicious environmental and social consequences of widespread autocentricity, recent scholarship has attempted to understand the stability of automobility's enterprise. Scholars reason that by understanding the sources of automobility's stability, we could suggest pathways that will lead us away from our current situation of an all-encompassing lock-in. Scholars of sustainability transitions who understand automobility as a sociotechnical regime have proposed one way to do this. While the concept of a sociotechnical regime is complex, it can be quickly defined as an entrenched structural element encompassing a range of actors (industrial firms, regulators, policymakers, users), established practices (of, say, planners and engineers), cultural norms, and discourses. Given its multidimensionality, sociotechnical regimes could be conceived as an interlinkage or alignment that binds together several constitutive regimes, such as a policy regime, a sociocultural regime, or a technological regime (Geels and Kemp 2012). Following this logic, automobility as a sociotechnical regime is characterized by a diversity of constituent regimes. The sources for the persistence of automobility can then be located within these component regimes: the sociocultural regime (Sheller 2012), the policy regime (Dudley and Chatterjee 2012), or the automobile industry regime (P. Wells, Nieuwenhuis, and Orsato 2012). Such a strategy emphasizes the translocality of automobility. The constituent regimes of automobility operate regardless of location. For instance, a policy regime is usually tied to political jurisdictions, and therefore all places within the political boundary are said to subscribe to this policy regime. In like fashion, a sociocultural regime operates through the norms and values prevalent within a community that could once again be spread over multiple places in a country.

In this book, I have adopted a different tack by seeking to inquire instead into the installation and operation of automobility that is intensely localized and situated. This allows us to examine empirically the constitution of automobility as a force for change within a specific localized setting. I make the claim that the localized flowering of automobility is a product of incredible power and agency rooted in the specific urban histories of society and politics. Thus, automobility is not understood here as a metaregime constituted from multiple interlocked regimes but is instead a political force—a constellation—that manifests the historically rooted operation of power and purpose. In such a construction, power and politics become central to the organization of automobility. In chapter 3, the assembling of the regime of congestion in Bengaluru has created a power-filled dynamic whose politics maximizes the occupation of streets in the city by automobiles while at the same time marginalizing the mobility needs of the urban poor and women. Similarly in chapter 5, we noticed that the interplay of power and politics reinforces the belonging of the automotive public on city streets while at the same time alienating nonmotorized society from these very streets. Through a combination of the power embedded within infrastructure projects, street designs, and social media to shape on-street behavior and the power of the practices of the automobilized urban society to create community on social media or appropriate sidewalks for cars, the politics of automotive citizenship is articulated daily. It is by means of these everyday acts of alienation that automobility as a power-filled constellation is established in Bengaluru. Such a localized characterization is not only profoundly distinct from the predominantly functionalist account extended by sustainable transitions, it also opens the pathway to dislocate automobility. If automobility is mobilized around a powerful political constellation, dislocating it would require mobilizing alternative (more sustainable and equitable) political constellations of multiple coexisting mobility systems in Bengaluru and elsewhere.[3] This is a valuable lesson that the case of Bengaluru offers for other cities struggling with automobility constellations. Addressing and dislocating automobility requires a technopolitical strategy. The next section expands on this vitally important implication.

Mobilizing an Alternative Constellation

If automobility is understood as a political constellation that deploys its politics on the streets of the city where it is emplaced, then displacing it will require emplacing an alternative politics of mobility in the city. A key move required to displace automobility would be to mobilize alternative constellations of mobility. Such constellations would not only promote new modes of travel in the city but would also recalibrate the relations between mobility and street infrastructures that act as conduits for channeling urban travel. Within the scope of an alternative mobility, such relations would be rooted in a social and political context that privileges the mobility needs of the nonmotorized. In this book, based on the analytical concepts of the regime of congestion, the infrastructurescape, and automotive citizenship, I demonstrate that automobility located in the city is constituted through three moments: the self-perpetuating ordering of mobility, the fashioning of an automotive landscape of privilege, and the enfranchising of automobiles on the streets. Displacing automobility would consequently require at least three corresponding moments that mobilize alternative constellations: reordering the mobility regime to empower nonautomotive modes of travel, relandscaping the city and its infrastructures to reinforce value commitments of inclusive mobility, and reclaiming streets as spaces for diverse inhabitation.

Reordering the mobility regime is easier said than done given the pervasiveness of a self-perpetuating lock-in in the current ordering of mobility in cities around the world. As we saw in Bengaluru, a locked-in regime of congestion forces more and more people to abandon public transport in favor of automotive modes, thereby reinforcing its predominance. Reordering mobility would require constituting an alternative regime of mobility. Techno-political regimes, we were reminded in chapter 3, arise through the enrolling of technology to achieve political ends in society. Alternative regimes of mobility would thus require assembling a cast of technological artifacts, infrastructures, discourses, plans, and social actors to promote explicitly political goals. Such a cast of entities would subscribe to an inclusive orientation that shelters the mobility needs of those who are marginal within the current calculus: urban poor, street vendors, women, and cyclists.[4]

The popular struggle against the steel flyover offers some important insights into reordering the mobility regime and thereby displacing automobility in the city. One insight is the possibility of fashioning a cross-class social alliance between urban poor groups and the middle classes to counter growing automobilization and the attendant marginalization of the mobility needs of the poorer sections. A second insight is the possibility of developing more sustainable and equitable intraurban mobility solutions, such as affordable buses and commuter trains as alternatives to expensive mega-transportation projects such as the Metro or overhead expressways. A final insight is the radical discourse of ending the reliance on megaprojects that beats at the heart of the struggle against the steel flyover. The three insights offered by the struggle, when brought together, could become the embryo for incipient regimes that will counter the reigning regime of congestion in Bengaluru. The question is, How does one initiate regime shift with the embryonic becoming the incumbent not just in Bengaluru but also in cities elsewhere? I believe that power lies at the crux of a regime shift. Regimes are power-infused entities with the sources of power dispersed throughout. Shifting regimes requires mobilizations that will infuse power into the embryonic regime. Grassroots mobilization is key for this to happen. Wide rainbow coalitions that span class, education, culture, and gender and mobilize a range of people to push governments for change, or influence media and public opinion, or shift the culture of mobility, can, I believe, engender regime change.

Infrastructurescapes in Bengaluru have specific normative orientations, organizational principles, and technological sensibilities. Together, these endow the visual landscape of the city with enormous power and purpose to shape the travel behavior of city residents. In diagnosing the three infrastructurescapes in the city, I proposed that the grassroots infrastructurescape appeared limited by the predominantly ideational element in its technological sensibility. As a result, the governmental and corporate infrastructurescapes have been able not only to marshal their purpose more effectively but also to be perceived as intervening to effect change in the city. In the absence of a purposeful technological dimension, interventions are predominantly educational, which seek to enhance awareness. Figure 7.1 is an example of a civil society intervention that attempts to counter the prevalence of the privileged corporate infrastructurescape by publicizing the costs associated with such elite involvement.

Yet another strategy that has received far less attention is the effort that seeks to secure urban spaces from intrusion. In chapter 4, I indicated an instance of residents inserting hand-cut stone bollards into the ground to block off particular street sections to through traffic in their neighborhoods (see figure 4.14). Such actions create spaces that are sheltered from through traffic that might have otherwise changed the rhythms of neighborhood living. Unfortunately, such acts of sheltering have been largely isolated in Bengaluru and have not spread to numerous areas (both rich and poor) as part of a plan to redesignate larger sections of the city as scapes of inclusivity and conviviality. In that context, when we call for relandscaping cities

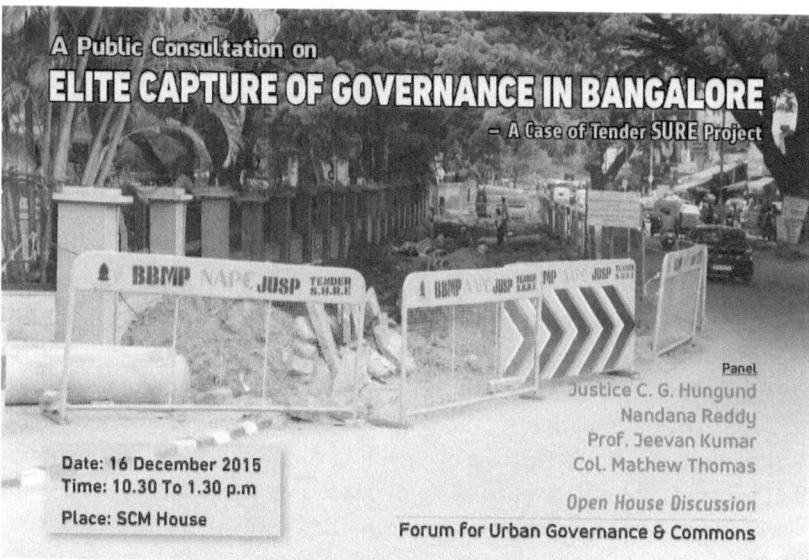

Figure 7.1
Invitation to a public consultation on Tender SURE (source: Forum for Urban Governance and Commons, Kshithij Urs, and Eshwarappa Madiwali).

and infrastructures to install alternative constellations of mobility, I am thinking of how scapes of inclusivity and conviviality can be sheltered and expanded. This would not only require articulating the composition of convivial scapes in terms of infrastructures, artifacts, and social groups but also shaping the perceptions of viewers to conform to the value commitments underlying such scapes. The key question would be how such spaces can be gradually expanded even as they are shielded from being overrun by other more privileged scapes with their elite-centric political commitments. Hard infrastructures such as hand-cut stone bollards are particularly effective in controlling how people can enter and exit sheltered scapes. Designing and conceiving such hard infrastructures in collaboration with scape actors could be a solution to fostering more such spaces. But hard infrastructures are not adequate if the value commitments behind such actions remain underspecified. What is needed is a clear articulation of the value commitments of inclusivity within such protected spaces. Will such spaces facilitate access for children, the aged, women, and street vendors and other pedestrian-scale activities? And how will scape actors intervene to ensure that access is sheltered from intrusions? An explicit articulation of value commitments will enable the grassroots infrastructurescape to compete on an equal footing with the more privileged scapes.

The third call for displacing automobility will ride on our ability to reclaim streets as spaces of diverse inhabitations. In chapter 5, we witnessed the unfolding of automotive citizenship from a range of sociomaterial interventions and practices on the streets of Bengaluru. Through these efforts, automobiles and drivers have enforced their claim of belonging on the streets. In order to displace automobility, it would be essential to counter the claim that streets primarily exist to serve the needs of automobiles and their drivers. Instead, we seek to redesignate streets as spaces that are put to a diversity of uses not limited to mobility alone but also involving socialization, exchange, shelter, providing green urban canopies for nonhumans, and so on. In their critique of the thrust in planning toward complete streets, Zavestoski and Agyeman (2015) call for "seeing streets not as fixed but constantly evolving physical, social, and symbolic spaces of creativity and contestation" (11–12). It is by enabling fluidity in use and perception that streets acquire an adaptable significance that promotes inclusion and serves social justice objectives of securing the rights of all residents, irrespective of social category, to streets and ultimately to the city. But how could one claim such a right to the streets and the city? In answering this question, it is important to remember that citizenship is understood as a sociomaterial performance that is exercised and wrested through a variety of acts ranging from the spontaneous and quotidian to the planned and deliberated. The central objective of acts of citizenship would be to orchestrate taking back the road from the clutch of automobility.

In chapter 5, I mentioned the group Hasiru Usiru's initiative Come Cross the Road. This is one planned data-driven effort that tried to gather information to understand the range of challenges that pedestrians face while navigating Bengaluru's roads. This venture made several recommendations to the government, which urges it to not only incorporate pedestrian views within transport policies but also to address the issue of pedestrian participation in the policymaking process. Similarly, as the Come Cross the Road report acknowledges, a progressive judicial reading of the law that links the right to walk on the street with justiciable human rights to livelihood, to the environment or to life, could bolster its cause in the policy discourse on transportation and street planning. The effectiveness of policy and judicial interventions cannot be underestimated. Such efforts do indeed carry the potential to unseal the policy discourse for marginalized voices of pedestrians and other nonmotorized claimants, thereby promoting greater participation. However, such deliberate acts also spur the need for more spontaneous mobilizations that take back the streets from automobiles and transform street-side practices. Here, such mobilizations can follow feminist and queer groups who have been pioneers in reclaiming spaces for the subjugated. Spontaneous mobilizations such as Reclaim the Night or Take Back the Night have spread across several cities in the world and offer a repertoire of bold acts that not only transgress socially constructed spatial exclusions but also promote behavioral change in wider society. But it is not only through political mobilization that streets can be reclaimed; it is by recognizing that the material, infrastructural, and technological participation in furthering a politics of belonging requires a strategy to enroll the materiality of roads, designs, infrastructures, and social media to push the political agenda of the right to streets.

Three calls could contribute to dislocating and displacing the political constellation of automobility that has installed itself as a succubus in many cities around the world. These calls herald a transformational shift in the location of streets and mobilities in cities. In considering these calls, the critical point is to acknowledge their technopolitical nature that enrolls technologies and artifacts to further political goals to transform urban streets and mobilities. In this understanding, transformational change away from automobility is not achieved through technological change that is divorced from political objectives; it requires making manifest the right to streets and mobilities to historically disenfranchised communities within technological and infrastructure designs. Agyeman (2013), in his manifesto for introducing just sustainabilities, proposes that achieving this goal requires an unequivocal attention to recognizing the rights of the other and making privilege visible. According to him, acknowledging the privilege underlying dominant narratives of shaping place requires giving space to counternarratives that arise from excluded cultures and groups. Thus, in order to introduce just sustainabilities in streets and mobilities in the case of Bengaluru, it is essential to make visible the privileged scapes, technologies, and infrastructures of political, social, and corporate elites underlying the constellation of automobility and at the same time to forefront alternative scapes, technologies, and infrastructures of mobility arising from urban subaltern groups: street vendors, pedestrians, daily wage laborers, working women, the aged, and the urban poor.

Notes

Preface

1. I follow Latour (2014, 2017) in the use of the term *Earthbound* to decenter the implicit anthropocentrism and reanimate the agency of the planet and the diversity of its residents—human, nonhuman, and inhuman.

2. With the term *terrane* I am indicating a post-anthropocenic condition whereby the earthbound abide by narratives of attachment, dependency, and responsibility (see Dibley 2012).

Acknowledgments

1. Some figures are reprinted from *New Indian Express* with permission from the copyright holders, Express Publications, India. One photograph is reprinted from the Deccan Herald with permission from proprietors, The Printers (Mysore) Private Limited, Bengaluru.

Chapter 1

1. The film is freely available for viewing on Youtube: https://youtu.be/hYxwSWfL3bI.

2. *Bangalore* was the former, but still popular, name of the city of Bengaluru. In this book, I uniformly use *Bengaluru* to refer to the contemporary metropolis. The use of *Bengaluru* or *Bangalore* is a politically charged one with a long history. *Bengaluru* is the English transliteration of the name in the native Kannada language, while *Bangalore* is the name that the English colonials used when referring to this region. *Bengaluru* has precolonial origins, while *Bangalore* is of colonial vintage. This difference was reinforced in colonial times with spatial separation and demarcation. *Bengaluru* referred to the native precolonial town, while *Bangalore* indicated the colonial settlement (a few miles away from the native town) for the civil and military elite. In recent times, the use of *Bengaluru* or *Bangalore* has acquired a different political cadence. *Bengaluru* has come to be associated with a native, rooted, son-of-the-soil

identification with the city, while *Bangalore* has become a brand that the globally mobile, English-speaking, middle classes associate with.

3. Being a large metropolitan city, fresh produce, including fruits, flowers, vegetables, fish, and meat from the surrounding hinterland, arrives in bulk very early in the morning each day at K. R. Market. It is then bought by shops and other commercial establishment, as well as households, for sale and consumption throughout the city.

4. In the Anglo-American context, Lewis Mumford in *The City in History* (1961) demonstrates how the sprawling industrial metropolis of the modern age is emblematic of the reliance on advanced technical means to further what he calls "a socially retarded civilization" that accomplishes little other than "become the means to increase congestion" (544). He identifies mechanical forces such as the motorcar and the road as key drivers behind the universalization of a placeless nonentity—the conurbation. Although predominantly located in the early twentieth-century urban contexts of Anglo-America, Mumford's dystopian imaginary of the industrial metropolis, despite its incapacity to trace contemporary forms of domination and inequality, is still relevant as cities around the world are contending with a host of crises involving burgeoning informal settlements, spiraling growth in motorization, and resource-consumptive lifestyles, as well as episodes of urban violence and fortification (Davis 2006; Graham 2011). In recent times, scholars have spoken about the damage to the socioecological fabric of cities from a patchwork of disjointed spaces interlinked by infrastructures of fear, suspicion, and exclusion, producing what Gyan Prakash (2010) refers to as "noir urbanism." Thus, while gated communities, enclaves, edge cities, and the suburban fringe, with their infrastructures of expressways and flyovers, have become desirable spaces, other spaces are characterized as slum cities, dead zones, or network holes that drop out of mainstream reckoning (MacLeod and Ward 2002; Pow 2015). The spatial disintegration marking capitalist accumulation points toward what Featherstone, following the philosopher Zygmunt Bauman, refers to as the "utopic-dystopic event horizon" (Featherstone 2010, 57)—a fearful urban world conditioned by violent collisions, disruptions, and collapse. This spatial disintegration is keenly evident in K. R. Market—the congested market on the ground and the placeless flyover suspended above. But K. R. Market also exemplifies the close juxtaposition of the contradictory utopia-dystopia event horizon in Bengaluru. On one side is the congested marketplace with multiple intersecting mobility modalities, while suspended above on the flyover is the space for fast, linear, motorized transits across spaces of congestion and slowness.

5. "Seven and a Half Million Cars Trigger Parking Wars in Delhi," *New York Times*, July 1, 2013; "Delhi's Traffic Chaos Has a Character of Its Own," *Guardian*, October 10, 2011.

6. "Why Mumbai Should Get Over Its Obsession with Cars," *Guardian*, November 27, 2014.

7. "Controlling Mumbai's Traffic," BBC News: https://www.bbc.com/news/business-21804350.

8. Although Chellan Rajan (1996), Kay (1997), and Newman and Kenworthy (1999) were early pioneers.

9. At the same time, Ladd (2011) suggests that despite the heavy presence of the automobile, Western cities nevertheless retain the potential for a more sustainable and less autocentric urban form.

10. Although see Zavestoski and Agyeman (2015) for a critique of the prevalent policy and planning practice of complete streets.

11. This is not to discount the value of recent research that attempts to historicize the rise of automobiles and the automotive industry in the early postcolonial period. See Tetzlaff (2016), for instance.

12. Although in terms of urban agglomeration, Bengaluru is considered the fifth largest in India after New Delhi, Mumbai, Kolkata, and Chennai.

13. "Bengaluru Is India's No 2 Petrol-Guzzler," *Deccan Herald*, April 17, 2017.

14. Thus, one sees articles such as "Is Bangalore a Garden City or a Concrete Jungle?" *DNA*, October 2, 2009; "Bangalore Has 1 Car for Every 2 People," *DNA*, July 20, 2011; "Bangalore Reduced to One Big Traffic Jam," *Hindu*, November 1, 2012; "Bangalore, a City of Two-Wheelers," *Hindu*, September 26, 2013; "Over 50 L Vehicles and Nowhere to Go," *Bangalore Mirror*, November 3, 2014; "Just Too Many Vehicles in Bengaluru," *Hindu*, October 30, 2015; "Over 60 Lakh Vehicles on Bengaluru Roads and Counting," *Hindu*, May 9, 2016.

15. "Google Maps Introduces Live Traffic Updates," *Hindu Business Line*, September 5, 2012.

16. Brahmins have traditionally occupied the pinnacle of the hierarchical caste structure in Indian society. Although primarily categorized as priests and religious preceptors, Brahmins were successful over time in cornering roles that required learning, education, and mastery over fields of codified knowledge, thus positioning the community as intellectual and professional elites in the country.

Chapter 2

1. According to IBM, "In 2011, the number of vehicles on the world's transport networks surpassed 1.1 billion. That number is expected to grow to 2.5 billion by 2050.... Most of this growth is now in emerging nations.... As the current transportation network will not be sufficient to handle the increase, many cities face increasing problems with transportation—congested freeways, city gridlock, pollution and parking problems, along with over-capacity and difficult-to-use public transport" (Huitema 2014, 2).

2. In the press release for the survey, Vinodh Swaminathan, IBM's director of intelligent transportation systems, noted that "we can't simply build our way out of congestion no matter which city," and emphasized what was required: "In order to improve traffic flow and congestion, cities need to move beyond knowing and reacting; they have to find ways to anticipate and avoid situations that cause congestion that could turn the world into one giant parking lot" (IBM 2011).

3. "Sanchara novu naraka: Bengalurige prashasti," *OneIndia Kannada*, September 10, 2011, Available: http://kannada.oneindia.com/news/2011/09/10/bangalore-6th-most-painful-city-for-commuters-globally-aid0038.html; "Bangalore 6th and Delhi 7th Most Painful City for Commuters in the World," *Economic Times*, September 10, 2011; "Bangalore '6th Most Painful' in the World for Traffic Congestion," *National*, June 28, 2012.

4. "Bangalore Is the 6th Worst City in the World for Commuting," *Times of India*, October 4, 2011.

5. "Causes of Traffic Congestion—Poor Roads No. 1 Cause of Traffic Congestion: TOI Survey," *Times of India*, March 19, 2008.

6. "Bangalore to Get 100 More CCTV Cameras," *Hindu*, November 29, 2012.

7. "Comprehensive Plan for Traffic Control Ready," *Hindu*, January 12, 2006.

8. "Network of Five Elevated Corridors Proposed to Fix Traffic Woes," *Hindu*, February 23, 2015; "Why Do We Find Ourselves in Such a Jam Today?" *Hindu*, February 28, 2012; "Setting the Wheels in Motion," *Hindu*, June 27, 2011; "Autorickshaw Lane: Boon or Bane?" *Hindu*, July 13 2007.

9. "Mr CM, Here's Why Bangalore Traffic Is a Nightmare," *New Indian Express*, December 17, 2015; "Multiple Agencies Make Bangalore Traffic Lose Its Way," *Hindu*, December 10, 2008.

10. "Jayanagar Cycle Track Inaugurated," *DNA*, September 23, 2012.

11. "The Vanishing Bicycle Tracks," *Hindu*, March 16, 2014; "Cycles-for-Hire Plan May Not Be a Smooth Ride," *New Indian Express*, March 20, 2017.

12. More often than not a result of the sociohydrological shifts resulting from the inability of urban land policies to curb speculative encroachment into the vestiges into Bengaluru's dense network of precolonial tank and canal irrigation systems (Ranganathan 2015; Nagendra 2010).

13. "Traffic Thrown out of Gear as KRRS, DSS, SUCI Take Out Rally," *Hindu*, June 24, 2014; "DSS Rally Causes Traffic Chaos," *Hindu*, July 23, 2009.

14. "Garment Workers' Stir Continues in Bengaluru, Traffic Hit for Second Day," *Hindu*, April 16, 2016.

15. Traffic on the streets of ancient Rome, crammed as it was with mule trains, wagons, porters, and elites on their sedan chairs, has received some attention in

Notes

scholarship. In these accounts, historians note how congestion was the outcome of a particular social, political, and spatial order. Thus, congestion was accompanied by numerous responses, such as regulations that restricted certain kinds of traffic to specific times of the day (van Tilburg 2007; Laurence 2013).

16. This argument was premised on the understanding that since congestion was the result of unpredictable and unmanageable horses, the shift to new mechanical, and therefore predictable, automobiles would ease congestion (McShane 1994).

17. Norton (2008) presents a compelling account of how streets in major metropolises in the United States in the first decades of the twentieth century were remade in the interests of improving safety and reducing automotive and pedestrian congestion.

18. A similar case of the unproblematic emergence of a scientific field is associated with congestion pricing or the cost of the effect of congestion on the roads for road users (Lay 2011).

19. Urban critics such as Jane Jacobs notably flagged the consequences that this preoccupation with motoring would have on the life of American cities. She notes, "The simple needs of automobiles are more easily understood and satisfied than the complex needs of cities, and a growing number of planners and designers have come to believe that if they can only solve the problem of traffic, they will thereby have solved the major problem of cities. Cities have much more intricate concerns, economic and social concerns than automobile traffic" (Jacobs 1961, 7).

20. This ambivalent relation to the centrality of the automobile in transport planning is also borne out in the report's historical legacy that juxtaposes its overt concern with conserving urban environmental areas with its acquiescence for urban highways and such projects of reconstruction that facilitate automotive travel (Gunn 2011).

21. The installation of the automobile as a powerful agent that shapes the trajectory of urban change is only now being examined carefully. Scholars have discerned that automobiles are enmeshed within a "system of automobility" that binds together a range of disparate spheres, such as land use, transportation engineering, public policy, consumer choice, and lifestyle (Urry 2004; Dennis and Urry 2009; C. W. Wells 2012). Others identify in (American) automobility a shared cultural covenant that is mobilized through a range of subjective and affective experiences arising from driving (Seiler 2008).

22. Most historians of the city agree that while Bengaluru's existence as a village or dispersed settlement can be traced back as early as the ninth century (a temple inscription from that time specifically mentions Bengaluru), thickening of this settlement into an urban node can be dated back to Kempegowda's efforts (Government of Karnataka 1990).

23. The idea that history matters arises from the appreciation that historical context is necessary for gaining systematic knowledge about sociopolitical processes (Tilly and Goodin 2006).

24. By focusing on the relevance of history for the present rather than doing history for history's sake, a reader could ascribe two shortcomings to this work. First, the charge that one encounters an instrumentalized applied historiography in these pages is justified. But at the same time, I would add that I resort to an applied orientation not to reduce history to an instrument but instead to realize it as a pedagogy that can better inform contemporary issues. I am guided by Robert Kelley's foundational work in public history where he exhorts fellow historians to delve into the "practical value of history" (Kelley 1978, 17). A second charge that could be leveled against the periodization presented here is the analytical neatness of this historicization, which is largely indifferent to the contingencies and messiness that accompany human actions when examined up close. Despite being guided by Collingwood's (1994) notion of the "historical imagination," the narrative presented in this chapter is arguably too immaculate and appears to be overly determined. A reason for this could be the broad stroke of periodization attempted here. With periods of multiple decades in length that often span entire human lifetimes, I am inspired by Guldi and Armitage's (2014) recent call for an "alternate history" manifesto where they argue for taking seriously the call for a public future of the past that *"longue-durée* history allows us to...ask about the rise of long-term complexes over many decades....Only by scaling of inquiries over such durations, can we explain and understand the genesis of contemporary global discontents" (Armitage and Guldi 2015, 222). The reengagement of history with the *longue durée*, they posit, is an ethical imperative in the face of the existential crisis prompted by the dawn of the Anthropocene.

25. In the process, I confine in one sweep all the richness and effects of about four hundred years of Bengaluru's history to little more than a minor note in the history of congestion.

26. *Congestion* is a complicated word with differing connotations depending on whether it is used in everyday parlance or in specialized fields of learning. In everyday parlance, congestion is associated with the phenomenon of overcrowding any given space by humans or by their vehicles. In medicine, it is commonly understood as a blockage (sometimes caused by excess mucus) that prevents normal function (say, of the nose in the example of nasal congestion). In engineering, *congestion* refers to the suboptimal functioning of a network, road, or pipe on account of excess material or data flow. In economics, congestion in public goods arises from the excess demand for a commodity, reducing its utility for all users. For early urban historians such as Lewis Mumford, as I have mentioned in the book's Introduction, congestion was not only symptomatic of overcrowding by humans and vehicles; it also unambiguously evoked a dystopic existence.

27. One of the earliest records of major irrigation works using tanks in South India reaches back to the seventh century. This period coincides with the "wider utilization and management of hydraulic technology" (Gurukkal 1986, 155).

28. Marshaled as a conquest state, the monarch of the Vijayanagara empire exercised ritual suzerainty over a vast region in southern India through a hierarchy of regional kingdoms (*nayakas*) and local chieftains (*palegars*). By accepting the overlordship of the Vijayanagara monarch, the local chieftains were able to retain a nominal degree of control in their region (Stein 1987, 72).

29. Even now one encounters the residues of precolonial spatial organization in the names of localities in the *peté* region of the city. Thus, one finds names such as *Arlepet* or the cotton market, *Akkipet*, or the rice market, and *Ganigarpet* or the oilers' market, even though land use in these locations does not necessarily correspond to their names.

30. Pani and others mention that such isolation was reinforced by a deliberate policy to economically isolate the *peté* from the cantonment and restrict traders and merchants of the *peté* from trading in the cantonment (Pani, Anand, and Vyasulu 1985).

31. *Bungalow*, as a term and as a building style that refers to a single-storey independent house, has its origins in the British colonial experience in India. Britishers, according to King (1984), appropriated native Bengali styles of house construction for housing their administrative and military elite in the newly developed cantonments. As King describes eloquently, the particular form that the bungalow took as a single-storey house with surrounding verandahs was closely related to the social and political context of European contact with the native Indians.

32. The East India Company managed British interests in India until the Indians rebelled against the yoke of company rule in 1857. Following this, the British crown assumed direct control over its Indian possessions.

33. Hettne mentions that the transition to direct colonial rule by the British after 1831 was motivated by their desire to forge a Western-oriented administrative society in Mysore: "Behind this political action was another change in British imperial policy. In the 1820s a liberal colonial school was gaining ground...and the new policy implied the westernization of Indian society" (Hettne 1978, 33). Similarly, M. Rao (1936, 43) notes that by 1881, "the whole population [of Mysore] has become accustomed to be governed under principles that were universally admitted to be essential....Justice was dispensed by regular courts, the assessment and collection of revenue were made under permanent rules, and generally the administration was carried on upon the same method...which prevailed throughout the British territory."

34. Hasan has pointed out that one of the first acts of C. M. Lushington, junior commissioner of the newly established British Commission in Bengaluru, was to relocate the office establishment to Tipu Sultan's palace in the fort because it was the only building available in the city providing sufficient accommodation (Hasan 1970, 139).

35. Hasan observes perspicaciously that "with this move [of administrative office buildings from the fort] began a long history of searching for more and more

accommodation for the ever-increasing Public Offices of the Mysore Government" (Hasan 1970, 139).

36. The *peté* became known as the Bangalore City municipality or just the city, while the cantonment became known as the Bangalore civil and military station municipality after 1881 (Government of Karnataka 1990, 646). The early constitution of these municipal entities was governed by Act 26 of 1850 and then subsequently by the Municipal Regulations Act of 1871, which brought their functioning directly under the colonial government's supervision. Each of these entities was governed by their respective municipal committees. Although Indians dominated the city committee, Europeans dominated the civil and military station committee (Srinivas 2010, 5).

37. The transfer was governed by a one-sided instrument of transfer (which placed a series of conditions for Mysore to retain percent of the kingdom's revenue) the kingdom of Mysore had to pay the colonial government of India (Hettne 1978, 56). The sense of insecurity created by these inequitable relations, although intense in the early years, gradually eased after the 1920s as a host of political circumstances, not least the rise of pan-Indian national movement, altered the balance of relations between the colonial government and Mysore. From the 1920s, therefore, one finds a new stridency in the tenor of Mysore's communication with the colonial government as it sought on multiple occasions to renegotiate the conditions of transfer in its favor (Hettne 1978, 64). Moreover, by then, Mysore's position as a "model state" that was addressing the task of "improving" its native population had received widespread recognition from the colonial government (C. Gowda 2007). This had not only further consolidated the position of Mysore's elites and their autonomy of agency but also the development machine in the province had acquired a critical momentum.

38. H. Shama Rao, an early historian of modern Mysore, states that "the first condition was that the body of laws and rules made for the transaction of public affairs approved by the Government of India up to the time of transfer were to remain in force.... Any material deviation from the administrative system thus settled required the concurrence of the Government of India" (M. S. Rao 1936, 45).

39. In 1891, Bengaluru's population was 180,366: 100,081 lived in the civil and military station and 80,285 in the city (Rice 1897, 41).

40. In 1905, Bengaluru became the first city in India to receive electric power for municipal purposes (Heitzman 2004, 33).

41. Despite its proactive policy initiatives and the presence of some private investment, the degree of success achieved by the government in catalyzing industrial take-off was rather sporadic (Baldwin 1959, 47).

42. College education in the arts and sciences experienced a parallel evolution and began in Bengaluru with Central College in 1875. With the founding of the University of Mysore in 1917, affiliated colleges were established in quick succession:

Intermediate College in 1927 and Maharani's College for Women in 1938 run by the government and Vijaya College in 1942 National College in 1945, SJR College in 1945, and Mount Carmel College in 1948 run by private educational trusts (Government of Karnataka 1990, 710).

43. So much so, that by the 1950s many referred to this region as the administrative center of the city (Venkatarayappa 1957, 84).

44. Although initiated as a chamber with a restricted membership open to landholders and merchants, where the *dewan* highlighted current achievements and future objectives of governance (C. H. Rao 1930, 2980), with the lowering of the property criterion for membership over time, the inclusion of women, and the introduction of communal representation through the Representative Assembly regulation of 1923, the assembly became more representative. These changes were accompanied by the gradual expansion in its role with regard to intervening in all taxation, budget, and legislative measures (Rao 1930, 3056). The legislative council, was similarly strengthened to be able to direct, to an extent, legislative and budget initiatives (Rao 1930, 3056). As a result of these initiatives, these chambers became sites for the articulation of a rational discourse on the kingdom's affairs.

45. The conference provided a venue for reflection on subjects intimately related to advancing the economic standing of Mysore and its citizenry: education, industry, and agriculture.

46. Gandy, in his seminal paper, "Bacteriological City and Its Discontents, "argues that "the term 'bacteriological city' is deployed to denote...a distinctive set of developments from science and technology to new forms of municipal administration" (Gandy 2006, 15). Speaking about nineteenth-century Europe, the bacteriological city, Gandy suggests, is an urban epoch arising from the alignment of scientifically testable notions of disease epidemiology (such as contagion theory) with innovative models of municipal financing, policy instruments, and new technical and managerial expertise (see also Gandy 2004).

47. This was certainly true of the typhoid epidemic of 1869, which was said to have originated in the native village of Ulsoor adjoining the Civil and Military Station (Secretary of State for India in Council 1870, 30): *Report on Measures Adopted for Sanitary Improvements in India from June 1869 to June 1870*. The Indian cholera epidemic of 1867–1868 and the epidemic of 1875 were particularly severe in the *peté* (Government of Karnataka 1990).

48. See Srinivas (2013b) for details about Bengaluru's early sanitary condition.

49. Arnold proposes that the successive cholera epidemics Bengaluru endured was one reason for the colonial government to institute the system of sanitary commissioners in each of the three presidencies (Arnold 1986, 145). Describing the history of public health in colonial South India, Gayathri (2010, 135) traces the origin of

commissioners of public health to 1863. She suggests that the colonial government, under the rubric of sanitation, sought to administer a number of competing things—epidemiology and disease control, as well as sanitary engineering. While a medical practitioner usually managed the former, an engineer administered the latter. Ronald Ross, the discoverer of the role mosquitos play in the transmission of malaria, was deputed in 1895 to the Bangalore Civil and Military Station and wrote a report that attempted to redress both aspects of sanitation: sanitary work and cholera preparedness (Ross 1923, 179–186).

50. Given the caste-based transgressions involved in granting entry to the municipal sweeper (predominantly from a Dalit caste) into the home to clean latrines on a daily basis, residents of the municipality protested against this law. Srinivas informs us that bearing these prejudices in mind, the municipality requested "the head of families…not to obstruct the work of overseers who may visit their premises" (Srinivas 2013b). So great were these prejudices that Ross records his heartfelt indignation at not being allowed to disinfect wells during an incidence of cholera outbreak in 1895 in the native Blackpally locality of the civil and military station, largely because the native rules would not allow a European near the well (Ross 1923, 183).

51. In chapter 6, we shall confront the residues of this shift in the case of flooding along the Vrishabhavathy River (commonly referred to as a sanitary water drain) and how it impinges on the rhythms of automobile flows in the city.

52. A second bout of plague occurred between 1902 and 1903, followed by an influenza epidemic in 1914.

53. Thriveni documents a string of curative measures Mysore organized in response to the epidemic, including the establishment of a special bureaucracy led by the plague commissioner, the creation of special plague hospitals, the trapping of rats and other rodents, and the founding of a vaccine institute and a biomedical laboratory (Thriveni 2013, 2–3).

54. See also Subramanian (1985) for the constitution and spread of piped water supply from a protected water source that parallels the sanitizing of Bengaluru in this period.

55. Although the first extensions to the city, such as Chamarajpet and Sheshadripuram in 1892, and to the civil and military station, such as Cleveland Town and Benson Town in 1883, predate the plague, the multiple overlapping social, spatial, and biomedical motivations to decongest urban habitation, improve sanitation, and offer well-ventilated and well-drained locations are a legacy of the plague infestation.

56. Shobha (2012), however, presents a history suggesting that the interest to plan Malleshwaram (and Basavangudi) predate the epidemic.

57. Stephens was speaking in the context of Fraser Town, the extension planned by the civil and military station in 1906 in response to multiple waves of plague

infestation. But it applies in equal measure to extensions such as Basavangudi and Malleshwaram.

58. Jawaharlal Nehru (1882–1964) was the first prime minister of independent India. His contributions to the institutionalization of science, democratic socialism, and industrial planning, in addition to several spheres of domestic and foreign policy, were so profound that they provided a doctrinal foundation for the nation (Parekh 1991; see also Sharma 2014 for facets of Nehruvian ideology and Arnold 2013).

59. After 1947, the kingdom of Mysore became the state of Mysore with an elected chief minister serving as the executive head. On November 1, 1956, Mysore and other Kannada-speaking districts in neighboring states were reorganized into Mysore state and then renamed (on November 1, 1973) into the present state of Karnataka. Through all these changes, Bengaluru has retained its position as the administrative capital and largest city.

60. One of BCIT's most lasting contributions was the inauguration of Rajajinagar as an industrial suburb spread over 377 acres to house industries and provide housing for industrial workers (Singh 1964, 112).

61. The reason Bengaluru emerged as a choice hub for an industrial agglomeration has been a subject of some interest. Most ascribe this choice to a long tradition of state support for industrial development (by pioneering potentially unviable manufacturing enterprises, providing avenues for joint ventures with private investors, and extending financial and technical assistance to enterprises) and the easy availability of various factors of production—capital extended by private financiers, labor given the extensive hinterland spanning multiple southern Indian states, electricity, and educational establishments (Venkatarayappa 1957, 56, 64).

62. Despite the importance of mega-PSU, formal manufacturing in the textile sector remained the largest source of employment in this period (Heitzman 1999, 2001). Nevertheless, employment in the informal sector—a range of productive work done in household or street-side settings through legal or semilegal arrangements—overwhelmingly overshadowed formal industrial employment. Reflecting a trend toward growing informalization of labor throughout this period, employment in the informal sector, according to Heitzman, rose from 50 percent in 1971 to almost 75 percent by 1991 (Heitzman 2001).

63. Between 1941 and 1991, Bengaluru city's population was increasing at a steady pace showing a decadal increase of between 30 and 40 percent. But two spurts are especially noticeable—between 1941 and 1951, the population of the city nearly doubled, from 406,760 to 778, 977, and between 1971 and 1981, the population rose by 60 percent, from 1.5 million to 2.47 million (Government of Karnataka 1990, 137).

64. Given the largely ad hoc arrangements for land development and urban expansion in the 1940s, some earlier efforts were made to regulate growth through a coordinated planning process. The 1952 master plan proposed by BMP's Bangalore

Development Committee was an early response but lacked sufficient legal standing to accomplish its aims (R. K. S. Gowda 1972, 102).

65. In the period after independence, the objective of administering and planning the city gifted it with multiple overlapping jurisdictions. For example, in 1981, BMP had jurisdiction over 151 square kilometers. The urban agglomeration (defined by the 1981 Census of India), which included seventeen towns and seventy-nine outgrowths, had a footprint of 365.65 square kilometers. The metropolitan planning area covered an area of 1,279 square kilometers (Ravindra 1996, 57). In 1985, the creation of the Bangalore Regional Metropolitan Area provided an even bigger jurisdictional whorl of 8,000 square kilometers. Service and infrastructure providers for water supply, public transport, and electricity operate through their own jurisdictional areas that often only imperfectly overlap. The thicket of administrative agencies and their overlapping jurisdictional domains inserts, as we shall see, a pervasive element of congestion in the city.

66. The ODP is a preliminary step that culminates in the preparation of the CDP. The ODP "affords general guidance in regulating the development of land" (Gowda 1972, 103). The CDP, as the name suggests, is an extensive document that "formulates in detail the long-term needs and potentialities of the area" (Ravindra 1996, 93). The KTCP mandates Bengaluru's planning authority to produce a revised CDP every ten years. Accordingly, revised CDPs were produced in 1995 and 2005 (Bangalore Development Authority n.d., 2).

67. A World Bank team that examined the Cauvery water supply scheme also suggested that the Mysore government institute an autonomous board for implementing and operating the project. In response, the state government constituted the Bangalore Water Supply and Sewerage Board under an act of the state legislature (BWSSB 2014).

68. Professionalization of public management and the founding of what came to be called "new public management" (Dunleavy and Hood 1994) was deeply influenced by the parentage of "business-type managerialism" and new institutional economics–inspired doctrines (Hood 1991, 5).

69. A green belt, as a growth boundary for the city, has been a pervasive presence in generations of planning documents beginning with the master plan of 1952. It finds mention as the "rural tract"—a 235 square kilometer girdle in the ODP of 1972, or the considerably expanded 839 square kilometer green belt in the CDP of 1985 (Ravindra 1996, 94). Similarly, the idea of satellite cities or growth poles has a long history in Bengaluru's planning practice, going as far back as the master plan of 1952 that speaks of industrial townships on the peripheries adjacent to existing public sector units (Singh 1964, 116). The structure plans of 1995 and 2005 for the metropolitan region, prepared by the Bangalore Metropolitan Region Development Authority (BMRDA), also similarly speak of seeking to balance decentralization and containment through push and pull factors (Government of Karnataka 2006, 26).

70. Acknowledging the pervasive illegality, in 2010, Karnataka state introduced the *Akrama Sakrama* scheme *(which translates into illegal-legal)* to regularize an expected 700,000 instances of land use and construction activity in violation of planning laws (Nair 2013, 46). This coupled dynamic of illegality and regularization is a defining facet of master-planned land use in the city.

71. Although some vital events that color the manifestation of flow congestion may have preceded 1991, the year itself has acquired enormous significance in fields of inquiry into the reform of contemporary Indian political economy (Bardhan 1998; Jenkins 1999). Many scholars see a deliberate shift in India's political economy in 1991 away from the earlier paradigm of dirigiste (state-permitted and state-regulated) industrialization to an economically liberalized one grounded on largely unfettered private accumulation.

72. These same policy frameworks that were key to promoting the growth of the software-driven IT industry in India acted to disincentivize and suppress growth in computer hardware manufacturing (Mascarenhas 2010, 100; see also C. R. Subramanian 1992).

73. Dijk (2003) presents a detailed analysis of factors that have promoted the clustering of ICT enterprises in Bengaluru. The comparison with Silicon Valley, though, may not be quite as founded as projected on at least two counts. First, the internal dynamics of the ecosystem of the IT industry in Bengaluru are qualitatively different from those in Silicon Valley (Parthasarathy 2004, 674). Second, Bengaluru is not quite the undisputed hub of the software industry in India (Heitzman 2004, 198).

74. Heitzman proposes a different explanation. He suggests that the presence of the IT industry in public spheres such as urban governance and infrastructure development stems from an existential angst to ensure that Bengaluru remains a competitive location (Heitzman 1999, PE-10).

75. While the liberalization of India's economy in 1991 brought with it significant social, economic, and political shifts, a notable shift has been away from the original developmentalist imaginary of the nation toward a consumerist one. Implicated centrally within this consumerist vision are India's "new middle classes" (Fernandes 2006), who, although highly differentiated internally, are united in the consumptive basis underlying their lifestyles, their urban aesthetics, and even their environmentalism (Baviskar 2002).

76. Empirical investigation into the cultural preferences of the new middle classes, however, paints a more nuanced picture with lifestyle choices persistently informed by old middle-class values rooted in culture and context (Upadhya 2008).

77. The BATF owes its existence to S. M. Krishna, chief minister of the state from 1999 to 2004, and was co-terminus with Krishna's tenure. Although often characterized as an icon of reform, Krishna's reform strategy largely centered around iconic projects, personalities, and BATF-like initiatives (Pani 2006).

78. The focus on visibility was significant on three counts. First, it furthered the IT industry's preoccupation with a global or international image for the city. Second, this focus allowed the industry to address infrastructures in a superficial fashion because the bulk of infrastructures (pipes, cables and conduits) are underground and invisible to passersby. Third, and most important, visible infrastructure redesign was key because they could contribute to creating legitimacy for their efforts to transform infrastructure (Gopakumar 2009).

79. "Karnataka to Put Bangalore Infrastructure on Fast Track—IT.in Boycott Decision to Be Reconsidered," *Hindu Business Line*, September 9, 2005.

80. Ramesh Ramanathan and his domestic partner, Swati Ramanathan, founded Janaagraha the Centre for Citizenship and Democracy (Janaagraha for short) in 2001 to "work with citizens to catalyse active citizenship in city neighborhoods" (Janaagraha 2018). Prior to this, Ramesh was a financial manager with Citibank in New York. Ramesh and Janaagraha have been particularly successful in mobilizing people (predominantly from the new middle classes, businesses, and the IT industry) around the cause of reforming urban governance in order to run Bengaluru efficiently like a corporate entity. Ramesh was a member of both BATF and ABIDe. Janaagraha has been the prime mover in numerous campaigns on the city's political and administrative landscape that seek to reinvent processes of local democracy and governance through a predominantly middle-class, issue-based prism. As an instance, Janaagraha's Jaagte Raho campaign organized a series of events in the run-up to the 2010 municipal elections, including a discussion on the party manifestos, know-your-candidate drive, and a pledge-to-vote campaign. A far more intrusive effort was the role Janaagraha adopted to mobilize and monitor financial participation in infrastructure projects (Coelho, Kamath, and Vijayabaskar 2011; Dasgupta 2012).

81. Chapter 4 describes the evolution of Tender SURE in some detail.

82. Among other things, BMP implemented the Mysore Road and Double Road flyovers, as well as the Mekhri grade separator, through this scheme. The BDA used funds from this scheme to construct several grade separators on the outer ring road (KUIDFC 2006, 3–4). The two flyovers became iconic representations of the world-class image of the city.

83. The development plan for each city comprises an overarching vision statement with more specific mission statements for different urban infrastructure, economic, and social sectors. In addition, the plan contains strategies for transforming different sectors with specific interventions to achieve this end.

84. This shift is evident in the efforts to experiment with multiple institutional innovations, such as borrowing from capital markets, public-private partnerships, privatization, and community participation (Kundu 2002), that seek to enhance financial accountability for infrastructure projects.

85. Three examples of special-purpose vehicles for elevated tollways radiating out from Bengaluru on national highways are the Bangalore Elevated Tollway Limited operational since 2010, the Navayuga Bengalooru Tollway Limited operational since 2010, and the Navayuga Devanahalli Tollway Limited operational since 2012.

86. Land use planning and development within these dedicated infrastructure corridors have been tasked to specialized parastatal bodies, such as the Bangalore International Airport Planning Authority (governing a humongous 792 square kilometers), the Bangalore-Mysore Infrastructure Corridor Planning Authority (governing 702 square kilometers), and the IT Corridor Planning Authority.

Chapter 3

1. Other actors too were active in protesting the government's decision. The Citizen Action Forum mounted a legal challenge against the flyover by filing a case in the National Green Tribunal against its implementation. Another of the initial opponents of the flyover was the Namma Bengaluru Foundation, an organization founded by Rajeev Chandrashekhar, member of Parliament and leader of the ABIDe task force (Nagarajan 2017).

2. "Bengaluru Celebs Throw Their Weight against Steel Flyover," *New Indian Express*, October 16, 2016; "Steel Flyover—#beda #beku Trends in Online Media," *Bangalore Mirror*, October 26, 2016; "From Beda to Beku: Anti-Steel Flyover Activists Want Commuter Rail," *Hindu*, December 10, 2016.

3. I do not imply intentionality when I suggest that the regime's politics are unambiguous. If anything, a regime disperses agency across the entities constituting the regime, thereby preventing a clear assignment of responsibility or intentionality for its actions to any one actor.

4. This colonially derived distinction in the nineteenth century regarding how and for what purpose urban interventions were constructed marks a notably different point of departure for comprehending the historicity of urban infrastructure provision in Indian cities. Thus, while contemporaneous Western cities and associated regimes of infrastructure provision were imprinted with the universal infrastructural ideal (Graham and Marvin 2001) and the creation of the networked city (Tarr and Dupuy 1988), Indian cities in the colonial city were fragmented along racial and class lines (Balbo 1993).

5. As Goldman and Longhofer (2009) have noted, world cities are imagined to be key sites of ingenuity and energy in a globalizing world economy. However, making world-class cities requires, in their words, that "the local city must be upended...lead[ing] to mass displacement [of people who live in places where new world-class projects are located] and mounting inequality" 33).

6. Joerges (1999) has pointed out that Winner's story of Robert Moses is most likely apocryphal. A closer look at the facts surrounding this story of parkway design, he suggests, does not reveal clear discriminatory intention on Moses's part. Be that as it is, this story does serve the purpose of illustrating the role that technological design plays in structuring societal outcomes.

7. For Hommels (2005), the question of change in sociotechnical orders, especially in the urban context, is particularly vexatious because once inserted into places, urban structures become resistant to change, thus continuing to shape urban processes. She demonstrates that urban obduracy manifests itself in the interaction between mental models of different social actors, the endurance of cultural traditions, or (most relevant to this work) the embeddedness of technologies within a heterogeneous ensemble.

8. For instance, in some Indian languages, the word for defecating is "going outside," indicating that until recently, norms of ritual purity prevented Indians from even conceiving the possibility of expelling wastes within the confines of the home.

9. Anjaria, in his study of street hawkers in Mumbai, has observed that when the state apparatus has repeatedly preyed on and extorted from hawkers in the absence of a defined regulatory process, they have suffered financial, mental, and physical hardship (Anjaria 2006).

10. See also Anand (2006) for how pedestrian fencing and impenetrable traffic dividers have become an inseparable component of road improvement projects and have thus impeded the free circulation of pedestrians on the road.

11. These phases are offered here for analytical distinction and convenience. Through these phases, I suggest that the predominant articulation of the regime of congestion underwent a shift in 2010. This distinction does not indicate that there was absolutely no overlap in strategies across the phases. Although efforts such as flyovers have been designed and constructed even after 2010, I believe the overarching thrust of these phases still holds.

12. "Causes of Traffic Congestion—Poor Roads No. 1 Cause of Traffic Congestion: ToI Survey," *Times of India*, March 19, 2008.

13. "Infrastructure Gets a Raw Deal," *New Indian Express*, December 24, 2006. See also "Lost in Transit," *New Indian Express*, June 20, 2009; "No Bang for the Buck," *India Today*, December 13, 2004; and "Narayana Murthy's Appeals to Leaders," *Hindu*, October 16, 2005.

14. Private financing of infrastructure projects was a major plank for reforming urban development in India, more often than not initiated by multilateral or bilateral international institutions. One major example was the USAID-supported Financial Institutions Reform and Expansion–Debt Market Component or FIRE(D) project.

15. ₹ is the international symbol for Indian rupees. In the Indian numbering system, 1 crore is equivalent to 100 million.

16. "Focus on Infrastructure," *New Indian Express*, May 1, 2006.

17. The total population of vehicles registered in the city increased from 1.45 million in 2000 to 2.47 million (2005), 3.69 million (2010), and 5.95 million (2015) (RITES 2011, KRTO 2015).

18. "More Vehicles Bring More Woes," *New Indian Express*, November 1, 2008; "City Has One Vehicle for Every Two People," *Hindu*, February 24, 2013; "'Alarming' Shift towards Private Vehicles," *Hindu*, July 14, 2015.

19. "Government Keen on Monorail for the City: Minister," *Hindu*, January 22, 2014; "Leaders Fret over Congestion," *Hindu*, February 4, 2016.

20. Details of subsidized bus routes are available at https://www.mybmtc.com/en/service/timings/spl/Special percent20Services/ats (accessed September 12, 2017).

Chapter 4

1. The notion that films carry powerful social messages was widely realized in (South) Indian cinema to the extent that films have acquired significance in the practice of democratic politics. Indeed, careers in film have paved the way for popular film stars to play an active role in regional politics (Prasad 1999; Dickey 1993). In Kannada cinema too, an iconic figure like Dr. Rajkumar acquired significant political stature with his public support for the cause of Kannada-language primacy during the Gokak agitation of the early 1980s (Prasad 2004).

2. "Flyover Fails to Resolve Traffic Woes," *New Indian Express*, May 16, 2011.

3. ₹ is the international symbol for Indian rupees. In the Indian numbering system, 1 crore is equivalent to 100 million.

4. Sadoway et al. (2018) describe consultants as one of JNNURM's most vital legacies.

5. See Gore and Gopakumar (2015) for more details regarding the political consequences of the metropolitan expansion of Bengaluru.

6. Janaagraha is a citizen group based in Bengaluru that actively seeks to catalyze change in the quality of citizenship and urban services in the city (see note 80, chapter 2).

7. Indeed, *landscape* refers to the "various components that make up the visual appearance of a place, including natural geomorphology, elements of cultivation, such as trees, flowers, crops, gardens, and parks, and the built environment of buildings, roads, paths, monuments and so on" (Jones et al. 2004, 116).

8. As a sociotechnical assemblage, an infrastructurescape has important parallels with Actor-Network Theory (ANT; Latour 2005). These parallels are evident in the heterogeneity of construction materials that are employed and the heterogeneous engineering (Law 1987) used to assemble both actor networks and

infrastructurescapes. Where they diverge is in the explicit perspectival and spatial orientation of infrastructurescapes. Such an orientation in infrastructurescapes makes it an invaluable concept to understand fluid phenomena such as congestion and decongestion.

9. The use of the Kannada language in referring to the scape is a deliberate move. This use is not only an index of the rootedness of the scape in social and political organizations arising from local particularities but also reflects the high degree of introspection of the gaze that focuses on Bengaluru and Karnataka to the exclusion of other considerations. Thus, although Sarkarada Bengaluru literally means "official Bengaluru," it could also mean the government (of Karnataka's) Bengaluru where the root word *sarkar* refers to the government, specifically the government of Karnataka. Here, the implication is that the Sarkarada Bengaluru scape manifests the authorship and political calculus of the government of Karnataka in reimagining the city. Similarly, Namma Bengaluru literally means "our Bengaluru," but the use of the Kannada word *namma* implies the rootedness of the scape in the terrain of grassroots organizations that seek to imagine a city hospitable to the urban subaltern—poor and marginalized sections of society who rarely figure in official reports or actions.

10. It is worth noting that the infrastructurescape is mobilized by the Karnataka *Sarkar* (government of Karnataka) rather than the city government of Bengaluru (the Bruhath Bengaluru Mahanagara Palike, BBMP). Customarily, city governments across India have been subsidiary political formations, constituted with a limited role in policy production or infrastructure development. Consistent with this trend, key directions regarding infrastructure are proposed by the *Sarkar* rather than BBMP.

11. As described in chapter 2, parastatal bodies are state-owned corporations instituted after the 1960s to bring technical expertise into public management. Parastatal bodies, such as the Bangalore Development Authority (BDA), Bangalore Water Supply and Sewerage Board (BWSSB), Bangalore Metropolitan Transport Corporation (BMTC), and Bangalore Metropolitan Land Transport Authority (BMLTA), manage most major infrastructure domains in the city.

12. In a city where infrastructure projects tend to drag on for years, this was a massive development. "Infrastructure Leap—Wow! Three Days, Seven Underpasses," *New Indian Express*, November 30, 2007. Although the underpasses took several days longer than planned, the construction of these underpasses became controversial, with media reporting on both procedural violations and inadequate study prior to the start of construction: "Palike Bungles on Underpass Projects," *New Indian Express*, January 19, 2008; "BBMP Buried All Rules under Cauvery Underpass," *New Indian Express*, November 26, 2008.

13. "Expressway Ready, Fly to KIA in 20 Minutes," *Times of India*, January 3, 2014.

14. NICE projects along the Bangalore Mysore Infrastructure Corridor, of which the peripheral ring road is only one component, have been embroiled in numerous

Notes

controversies that relate to the enormous area of environmentally sensitive and agriculturally productive land that has been transferred by the Karnataka government to NICE (Ranganathan 2006; Goldman 2011).

15. The task force consisted of senior bureaucrats (including principal secretaries of finance, public works department, urban development, and infrastructure in the state government), commissioners of city government and Bengaluru police, executive officers of city parastatal bodies, Bengaluru International airport, and representatives of industry associations ("Infrastructure Leap—Wow!").

16. "Bangalore Needs a Vision Reboot," *Economic Times*, May 10, 2011.

17. BCCF is an experimental collaborative platform between the Confederation of Indian Industry (CII, an industry association) and Janaagraha. Since then, the idea of creating a collaborative platform catalyzed by business interests with civil society and governments has spread to a generalized venture, City Connect (City Connect 2011), which has established chapters in five cities, including Bengaluru.

18. See Sami (2014) for a comparison between the BATF and ABIDe task forces. Despite their important differences in objectives and interventions, similarities stem from the core group in both cases where the similarities are seen to be drawn almost solely from an elite segment of society who possess vast technomanagerial and corporate governance connections, and from the opportunities this platform provides for this group to direct their knowledge into policy and planning processes.

19. India Urban Space Foundation was launched in 2007 and has since been renamed Jana Urban Space Foundation (JUSP). A constituent of the Jana group—"a clutch of social enterprises aimed at urban transformation in India" (Jana Urban Space Foundation 2018a)—JUSP, along with its sister concern, Janaagraha, was cofounded by Swati Ramanathan, an urban design professional and Ramesh Ramanathan's domestic partner. According to its website, JUSP's goal is to "catalyze a more thoughtful transition for a rapidly urbanizing India through three streams of activities that involve practice and policy: Urban Planning, Urban Design, and Policies for Planning and Design" (Jana Urban Space Foundation 2018b).

20. "Will It Be Third Time Lucky for Tender SURE Roads?" *Deccan Herald*, July 13, 2013.

21. ABIDe was established in October 2008 by the chief minister of Karnataka, B. Yediyurappa, as a predominantly planning- and governance-oriented task force. The task force sought to intervene in four key areas in Bengaluru: governance, road traffic management and transportation, the urban poor, and public security (Sami 2014, 133).

22. The Big10 arterial roads are the ten major arterial roads radiating from the city center—Mysore Road, Kanakapura Road, Bannerghatta Road, Hosur Road, Sarjapur Road, Old Airport Road, Old Madras Road, Bellary Road, Tumkur Road, and Magadi Road. These roads, named after the town (or city) the roads travel toward, carry a major share of vehicular traffic flowing into and out of the city.

23. "Traffic Cure Finds Direction," *New Indian Express*, February 20, 2009.

24. Bengaluru Bus Prayankira Vedike (Bengaluru Bus Commuters Forum) is a platform for several community-based organizations and nonprofit organizations that strive for an affordable, accessible, and just bus service in Bengaluru.

25. The presence of multiple groups with their own limited agendas of action, compounded by the inability of these groups to articulate an inclusive ideological platform to bring multiple groups together, is a weakness common to recent new social movements in Karnataka (Assadi 2004).

26. The regressive evolution of the Kannada language movement is a much-lamented phenomenon among social observers (Srinivasaraju 2008; Murthy 2006). However, others, like Janaki Nair, an astute observer of politics and culture in Bengaluru, notes that despite the undemocratic (and increasingly exclusionary) resolutions of (often) legitimate linguistic anxieties of Kannada nationalism, the process of change in the Kannada language movement and emerging strategies and modes of mobilization need to be linked to particular sociospatial and political-economic structures that Bengaluru and Karnataka are embroiled within (Nair 2000).

27. Although the function held on March 15, 2010, to release the People's Manifesto was supported by several well-established voluntary organizations in the city, it was not well attended, which prompted questions regarding the representative nature of these efforts. "Power to the People Runs into Apathy," *DNA*, March 16, 2010. This highlights challenges of popular legitimacy that groups in the NB scape face.

28. Although Rao (2013) notes that HU's core group consists of eight members, an email in the HU Yahoo group (no. 15862, May 18, 2012, HU email archive) lists a larger core group of twenty-five members who meet regularly and have specialized roles in member recruitment and mobilization.

29. This expansion in HU's spheres of emphasis has been ongoing. While in 2008 and 2009, an overarching effort was the Campaign to Reclaim Bangalore's Commons (A. Rao 2014), by 2012, the HU's core group was self-identifying as addressing the areas of streets, mobility, and commons (no. 15862, May 18, 2012, HU email archive).

30. A good example is the *Pedestrians in Bangalore—Walking a Tightrope* report that came out of HU's Come, Cross the Road campaign in July 2011. Part of the reason for this shift in organizational focus has been, according to Rao (2014, 139), the onset of protest fatigue due to the nonachievement of goals.

31. Misgivings about Praja and its activities become clear in some email conversations (archived by HU's Yahoo group account) between key members of the HU and Praja networks (no. 6871, May 15, 2009; no. 15797, May 1, 2012; and no. 19446, November 12, 2014).

Notes

Chapter 5

1. In the face of the enormous global circulation of people, money, information and goods, formal regimes of citizenship have begun mutating, prompting scholars to theorize emerging architectures of membership as emphasizing a "weak citizenship" composed of "plural, layered, and mercurial conception(s) of belonging" (Aneesh 2016, 196).

2. Actor-Network Theory lies at the core of an intellectual project asserting that the impregnation of the material and /artifactual within the collective human experience or the "missing masses" is something that has been consistently ignored by the social sciences, with the result that "the society they [sociologists] try to recompose with bodies and norms constantly crumbles" (Latour 1992, 152). Latour proposes instead an alternate "sociology of associations" that is "limited to the tracing of new associations and the designing of assemblages" (Latour 2005, 7) composed of heterogeneous (material, nonhuman, and artifactual) ties. Indeed, terming it "relational materiality," Law and Mol have suggested that it is the heterogeneity of material relations that actually makes the social (or for that matter, any material entity) stable (Law and Mol 1995).

3. Although recent developments in environmental law demonstrate a paradigmatic shift toward posthumanistic ecocentrism. Indeed, legal scholars have noted the shift away from anthropocentric utilitarian legal instruments toward instruments linked with the intrinsic values of nature separate from any human use value (Emmenegger and Tschentscher 1994; see also Bruckerhoff 2008 on how the intrinsic value of nature could be incorporated within legal jurisprudence by expanding notions of environmental health and environmental rights). These legal developments parallel critiques of anthropocentrism emanating from fields as diverse as political theory, environmental ethics, and cultural studies (Dobson 2012; Rae 2016).

4. Indeed, some have suggested that the material backdrop is not just passively constitutive of political engagement but that devices and technologies have been invested with specific political and moral capacities to actively shape our existence in preferable directions (Marres and Lezaun 2011). A good example is everyday carbon accounting tools such as the "Augmented Teapot" and associated Tea Light. The Augmented Teapot visually informs the consumer through the Tea Light when it is a good (less energy intensive) time to prepare tea (for more, see Marres 2016). Through the visual intimation, the teapot is nudging humans to behave as responsible energy consumers. Thus, the teapot in this example is delegated with a specific moral agency.

5. Often characterized as the deficit model of science communication, the existing nature of the relation between scientific experts and lay citizens was rooted in the enlightenment project of science and modernity, which cast citizens as essentially technologically illiterate and the role of experts was to continually enhance the public understanding of science.

6. Indeed some have argued that the close identification of technoscience with the modern Indian state arises from its role as the epistemological engine of national development (Raina 1997).

7. Following Sheller and Urry (2003), I use the term *auto-mobility* to refer to the mobility achieved by relying on automobiles and to differentiate it from the technopolitical constellation of automobility.

8. Translated from the Kannada original by the author. "Signal free" refers to roads that employ grade separators to ensure that traffic flow along the corridor is junction free and thus not regulated by traffic lights.

9. The interchange includes two sets of flyovers. One along outer ring road that spans Mysore Road was inaugurated in October 2012; the second flyover (inaugurated in March 2015) along Mysore Road leaps over the outer ring road flyover. "Nayandahalli Flyover to Finally Open This Month," *Times of India*, February 12, 2015.

10. In order to make room for the flyover, Bangalore Development Authority (the builder) acquired and demolished several houses in the immediate neighborhood. "25 Houses Razed in Nayandahalli for Flyover," *Deccan Herald*, July 1, 2014.

11. "Twitter Traffic," *Hindu*, December 8, 2015. While several road intersections now possess dedicated Twitter handles, only a few, such as @Silk_Board, @Sony WorldJn, and @Jayadeva_Flyover, have attracted a steady following. Twitter handles for intersections or flyovers become sites for spontaneous humor to lighten the tortuous experience of driving through these traffic-choked junctions. Handles such as @WFRising employed by neighborhood groups such as Whitefield Rising purport to represent specific neighborhoods but more often than not represent specific agendas of transportation and congestion.

12. For instance, in May 2017, the official Twitter handles of the deputy commissioner of traffic police for east Bengaluru had about 83,500 followers, the additional commissioner of traffic police for Bengaluru had more than 50,000 followers, and the Bengaluru city traffic police had 345,000 followers. In comparison, the official handle for the chief minister for the entire state of Karnataka only had about 120,000 followers.

13. Bengaluru city traffic police sees social media platforms as a vital piece of their public accountability and complaint redressal mechanism. In pursuing this, the organization has been a pioneer in setting up a Twitter dashboard that not only allows public complaints to be automatically redirected to appropriate jurisdictions but also allows monitoring of response to complaints. "Bengaluru Police Get a Twitter Dashboard for Real-Time Monitoring of Complaints," *Economic Times*, March 23, 2016.

14. The "I Change my City" initiative has developed its own app that allows Bengaluru's residents to record, transmit, and follow up on any instance of everyday governance problems—for example, uncollected garbage or malfunctioning streetlights.

Notes 243

I Change my City is described as "Janaagraha's path-breaking initiative to cultivate and nurture the spirit of active citizenship" (ichangemycity 2019).

15. "With Just 1 Percent Usage, Skywalks a Dismal Failure," *Deccan Herald*, May 6, 2017.

16. "Skywalks Push Pedestrians onto the Road," *Hindu*, April 29, 2017.

17. "Parking in Bangalore: It Is Hell Out There on Weekends," *Times of India*, August 13, 2014;

18. "The Parking Nightmare," *Deccan Herald*, July 6, 2013.

19. According to the CCTR report, India's Supreme Court expanded the constitutionally guaranteed right to life to include the right to movement and the right to livelihood through two landmark cases—*Frank Coralie v. Union Territory of Delhi and Others* ([1981] 1 SCC 608), as well as *Olga Tellis v. Bombay Municipal Corporation* (AIR 1986 SC 180) (Hasiru Usiru 2013, 36–37).

Chapter 6

1. Project documents prepared by the Indian Urban Space Foundation (IUSF) suggest that the roads were chosen for redesign based on "the need to demonstrate the impact of intelligent design on rejuvenating/enhancing central areas and to show the long-term financial benefit with lower life-cycle costs" (Indian Urban Space Foundation 2012, ii).

2. "New Year Will See Bangalore's 7 Central Business District Roads Upgraded," *DNA*, January 3, 2013.

3. "What Tender SURE? St Marks Road Dug Up Four Times in Two Years," *Deccan Herald*, March 24, 2017; "Tender SURE Road Dug Up to Keep Vidhan Soudha Aglow," *Times of India*, March 23, 2017; "No Digging for 20 Years, Tender SURE? BWSSB Digs Up St Marks," *Deccan Chronicle*, May 26, 2015.

4. "Residents Want a Say in the Redesign of Madivala Market," *Hindu*, March 24, 2017.

5. Hilgartner's (2000) *Science on the Stage* is yet another work that has employed an explicit performative metaphor. It seeks to understand the role that scientific advisers play in the presentation and reception of science on the public stage of the American politico-institutional landscape.

6. Indeed, Pickering announces that "the performative idiom that I seek to develop subverts the black and white distinctions of humanism/antihumanism and moves into a posthumanist space, a space in which human actors are still there but are now inextricably entangled with the nonhuman" (Pickering 1995, 26).

7. Elaborating on this, Orlikowski (2007), speaking to organizational studies, diagnoses that the widespread disregard for materiality has resulted in an inability to

fathom how organizational practices are incredibly entangled within the sociomaterialities of the workplace.

8. The relational element at the core of the concept of affordance is a novel conceptualization because it marks the attention in the design process not just to the capabilities of the agent (the social dimension) or the properties of the object (the material dimension) but to sociomaterial ties. Such a conceptualization marks the point of departure for a renewed interest in design as a generative arena where nascent entanglements of the material with the social are forged (Yaneva 2009; Storni 2012).

9. Indeed, according to Badami, the vital essence that animates the field of transport planning has been to overcome the problem of the "friction of distance" (Badami 2009, 50). The notion of friction of distance hinges on the idea that traversing distance requires an expenditure of time that could be put to more productive use in other domains if it is avoided. Thus, minimizing the friction of distance, and therefore the time of travel, has emerged as the holy grail of the field. Motorized movement, with its potential to maximize time savings, is particularly attractive.

10. The problem of localized flooding of the Vrishabhavathi River has also been exacerbated by major infrastructural works, such as flyovers and underpasses that block natural hydrological channels that drain the stormwater in many parts of the city. See "Flyover Blamed for Temple Flooding," *Bangalore Mirror*, August 17, 2011.

11. "They've Had It Up to Their Ears," *Hindu*, August 17, 2011.

12. "Gali Anjaneya Temple," *Hindu*, March 8, 2012. Some other accounts place the origins of the temple in the twelfth century—for example, "A Temple Surrounded by Serenity," *Deccan Herald*, May 3, 2004.

13. Blogs written by the faithful mention that this temple was one of the Anjaneya temples founded by Vyasaraja Tirtha, an important fifteenth-century prelate of the Madhva school of Hinduism. Accounts also mention that Anjaneya's unique visage and posture in this temple make him a *shantha-swaroopi* (a peaceful form ready to grant the wishes of those who seek him (see http://vayusutha.in/vs4/temple41.html).

14. Metropolitan expansion in Bengaluru was engineered by incorporating seven city municipal councils (Rajarajeshwarinagar, Dasarahalli, Bommanahalli, Mahadevapura, Krishnarajapuram, Byatrayanapura, and Yelahanka), the Kengeri town municipal council, and 111 villages.

15. The contractor or the third-party quality monitor had not foreseen that already-completed work would have to be demolished because of social and political complications. With the project running almost three years late, in an effort to cut costs, the demolition was carried out informally or "unscientifically," as newspapers reported. BBMP sought to initiate legal action against the contractor and the third-party quality monitor: "BBMP to Issue Notices to Consultant over Shoddy Construction," *Hindu*, November 16, 2010; "A Clogged Drain and a Shaky Flyover along Mysore Road," *DNA*, November 16, 2010.

Notes 245

16. Independent review and monitoring of the project, as mandated by JNNURM, in its review of the progress in construction, made a note of this in its report (NCPE Infrastructures India 2013, 20).

17. "Gali Anjaneya Road over Drain Thrown Open to Traffic," *Hindu*, March 5, 2013.

18. "Tough Day for Motorists as Stretch of Mysore Road Is Made One-Way," *Hindu*, March 5, 2013.

19. "Mysore Road to Become Motorable by May 31," *DNA*, May 23, 2016.

20. The kingship of the kings of the Mysore kingdom was deployed through the hybrid concept of *rajadharma* that combined the European concept of improvement with *dharma*—the Hindu concept of maintaining the cosmic order (Ikegame 2007). It is the moral might of *rajadharma* that political leaders of postcolonial Karnataka have sought to embrace.

21. The auditor of the national government, the comptroller and auditor general, notes in his report that there were several irregularities in the initial stages of the construction process with regard to land acquisition, tendering, and utility shifting (Comptroller and Auditor General 2013), and he attributes project delays to these irregularities. The narrative presented here does not deny these controversies, but these serve to highlight the messy and contentious process inherent in buoying up automobility in the city.

22. JNNURM was conceived as a reform-driven exercise (self-identified as a mission) that attempts to fashion a uniform basis for how (major) cities in India are governed and how they conduct their project execution. With this aim in mind, JNNURM marshaled an array of strategies, techniques, and processes as technologies of governance (Gopakumar 2015), as well as organizational signatures (Sadoway et al. 2018), such as reliance on legal reforms and management consultants. The proliferation of consultants scripting compliance with a range of strategies and techniques is a defining attribute of JNNURM. For the VRER, the project's project management consultant, STUP, authored its DPR.

Chapter 7

1. "Karnataka Drops Bengaluru Steel Flyover Project," *Hindu*, March 2, 2017.

2. The very recent proposal of the government of Karnataka to revive and execute a plan for a network of elevated corridors criss-crossing Bengaluru without even a shred of public consultation would appear to foreclose as premature any notion that a transformative juncture in how the city moves is at hand. See "More #Beku Than #Beda," *Hindu*, March 17, 2019; "Elevated Corridor: CM Promises 'Detailed Discussions' Soon after Elections," *Hindu*, March 19, 2019.

3. Here it bears paying attention to what Kathryn Furlong (2014) specifies as the need to move beyond the Western "modern infrastructure ideal" of single,

standardized, and universal infrastructure systems and instead incorporate the dynamics of coexistence with multiple modalities of infrastructure systems.

4. Such an inclusive orientation is contingent on articulating a composite pedestrianism that comprises pedestrianism as embodied practice (Lee and Ingold 2006); as politics (Middleton 2011) but also as a form of rationality (Patton 2007); and as a method of inquiry into the urban (Srinivas 2015).

References

ABIDe. 2010. *Plan Bengaluru 2020—Bringing Back a Bengaluru of Kempe Gowda's Dreams*. Bengaluru: Agenda for Bengaluru Infrastructure and Development (ABIDe).

Abraham, Itty, and Ashish Rajadhyaksha. 2015. "State Power and Technological Citizenship in India: From the Postcolonial to the Digital Age." *East Asian Science, Technology and Society* 9 (1): 65–85.

Adas, Michael. 1990. *Machines as the Measure of Men: Science, Technology, and Ideologies of Western Dominance*. Ithaca, NY: Cornell University Press.

Agyeman, Julian. 2013. *Introducing Just Sustainabilities: Policy, Planning and Practice*. London: Zed Books.

Akrich, Madeleine. 1992. "The De-Scription of Technical Objects." In *Shaping Technology/Building Society—Studies in Sociotechnical Change*, edited by Wiebe E. Bijker and John Law, 205–224. Cambridge, MA: MIT Press.

Akrich, Madeleine, and Bruno Latour. 1992. "A Summary of a Convenient Vocabulary for the Semiotics of Human and Nonhuman Assemblies." In *Shaping Technology/Building Society Studies in Sociotechnical Change*, edited by Wiebe E. Bijker and John Law, 259–264. Cambridge, MA: MIT Press.

Aldred, Rachel. 2010. "'On the Outside': Constructing Cycling Citizenship." *Social and Cultural Geography* 11 (1): 35–52.

Anand, Nikhil. 2006. "Disconnecting Experience: Making World-Class Roads in Mumbai." *Economic and Political Weekly* 41 (31): 3422–3429.

Anand, Nikhil. 2011. "Pressure: The PoliTechnics of Water Supply in Mumbai." *Cultural Anthropology* 26 (4): 542–564.

Aneesh, Aneesh. 2016. "Differentiating Citizenship." In *After Capitalism: Horizons of Finance, Culture, and Citizenship*, edited by Kennan Ferguson and Patrice Petro, 196–214. New Brunswick, NJ: Rutgers University Press.

Anjaria, Jonathan S. 2006. "Street Hawkers and Public Space in Mumbai." *Economic and Political Weekly* 41 (21): 2140–2146.

Anjaria, Jonathan S. 2012. "Is There a Culture of the Indian Street?" *Seminar* 636.

Appadurai, Arjun. 1987. "Street Culture." *India Magazine* 8 (1): 12–22.

Appadurai, Arjun. 1996. *Modernity at Large: Cultural Dimensions of Globalization*. Minneapolis: University of Minnesota Press.

Armitage, David, and Jo Guldi. 2015. "The Return of the Longue Durée: An Anglo-American Perspective." *Annales. Histoire, Sciences Sociales: English Edition* 70 (2): 219–247.

Arnold, David. 1986. "Cholera and Colonialism in British India." *Past and Present* 113:118–151.

Arnold, David. 2000. *Science, Technology and Medicine in Colonial India*. Cambridge: Cambridge University Press.

Arnold, David. 2012. "The Problem of Traffic: The Street-Life of Modernity in Late-Colonial India." *Modern Asian Studies* 46 (1): 119–141.

Arnold, David. 2013. "Nehruvian Science and Postcolonial India." *Isis* 104 (2): 360–370.

Assadi, Muzaffar. 2004. "New Social Movements in Karnataka: History, Strategies and Discourses." *Karnataka Journal of Politics* 4 (32): 72–88.

Aziz, Abdul. 1993. *Decentralised Planning: The Karnataka Experiment*. New Delhi: Sage.

Badami, Madhav G. 2009. "Urban Transport Policy as if People and the Environment Mattered: Pedestrian Accessibility the First Step." *Economic and Political Weekly* 44 (33): 43–51.

Baindur, Vinay. 2017. "The Politics of Entrepreneurial Vision Group Plans and Their Impact at the Local (Government) Level, Bengaluru." In *Entrepreneurial Urbanism in India: The Politics of Spatial Restructuring and Local Contestation*, edited by Kanekanti Chandrashekar Smitha, 113–133. Singapore: Springer Singapore.

Bakker, Karen. 2003. "Archipelagos and Networks: Urbanization and Water Privatization in the South." *Geographical Journal* 169 (4): 328–341.

Balbo, Marcello. 1993. "Urban Planning and the Fragmented Cities of Developing Countries." *Third World Planning Review* 15 (1): 23–35.

Baldwin, George B. 1959. *Industrial Growth in South India: Case Studies in Economic Development*. Glencoe, IL: Free Press.

Bangalore Development Authority. *Draft Master Plan—2015*. Bangalore, n.d.

#bangaloretraffic. 2019. https://twitter.com/hashtag/bangaloretraffic?lang=en.

Barad, Karen. 2003. "Posthumanist Performativity: Toward an Understanding of How Matter Comes to Matter." *Signs: Journal of Women in Culture and Society* 28 (3): 801–831.

References

Bardhan, Pranab. 1998. *The Political Economy of Development in India.* New Delhi: Oxford University Press.

BATF. 2001. *The Second Bangalore Summit Status Report.* Bangalore: Bangalore Agenda Task Force.

Bauman, Zygmunt. 2000. *Liquid Modernity.* Cambridge: Polity Press.

Baviskar, Amita. 2002. "The Politics of the City." *Seminar: A Symposium of the Changing Contours of Indian Environmentalism* 516:41–47.

Baviskar, Amita. 2008. "Between Violence and Desire: Space, Power and Identity in the Making of Metropolitan Delhi." *International Social Science Journal* 55: 89–98.

BBMP. 2009. *Proposed Capital Investment Plan for Bangalore City (2009–12).* Bangalore: Office of the Commissioner.

Beckmann, Jorg. 2004. "Mobility and Safety." *Theory, Culture and Society* 21 (4–5): 81–100.

Bender, Barbara. 2006. "Place and Landscape." In *Handbook of Material Culture*, edited by Christopher Y. Tilley, Webb Keane, Susanne Kuchler, Mike Rowlands, and Patricia Spyer, 303–314. Thousand Oaks, CA: Sage.

Bengaluru Bus Prayaanikara Vedike. 2013. *Bengaluru Bus Prayaanikara Vedike.* https://blorebusvedike.wordpress.com/.

Bengaluru Janara Vedike. 2010. *Janara Pranalike People's Manifesto.* Bangalore, India: Bengaluru Janara Vedike.

Benjamin, Solomon. 2010. "Manufacturing Neoliberalism: Lifestyling Indian Urbanity." In *Accumulation by Dispossession: Transformative Cities in the New Global Order*, edited by Swapna Banerjee-Guha, 92–124. New Delhi: Sage India.

Benjamin, Solomon, and R. Bhuvaneshwari. 2006. "Urban Futures of Poor Groups in Chennai and Bangalore: How These Are Shaped by the Relationships between Parastatals and Local Bodies." In *Local Governance in India—Decentralization and Beyond*, edited by N. G. Jayal, A. Prakash, and P. K. Sharma, 221–267. Delhi: Oxford University Press.

Bijker, Wiebe E. 2006. "Why and How Technology Matters." In *The Oxford Handbook of Contextual Political Analysis*, edited by Robert E. Goodin and Charles Tilly, 681–706. Oxford: Oxford University Press.

Bijker, Wiebe E. 2007. "Dams and Dikes, Thick with Politics." *Isis* 98 (1): 109–123.

Bijker, Wiebe E. 2010. "How Is Technology Made? That Is the Question!" *Cambridge Journal of Economics* 34 (1): 63–76.

BMRCL. 2016. Bengaluru: Bangalore Metro Rail Corporation Limited.

Böhm, Steffen, Campbell Jones, Chris Land, and Mat Paterson. 2006. "Introduction: Impossibilities of Automobility." *Sociological Review* 54 (s1): 1–16.

Bonham, Jennifer. 2006. "Transport: Disciplining the Body That Travels." In *Against Automobility*, edited by Steffen Böhm, Campbell Jones, Chris Land, and Matthew Paterson, 57–74. Malden, MA: Blackwell.

BPAC. 2013. *Agenda for Bangalore (AfB)*. http://demo.bpac.in/agenda-for-bangalore/.

Braun, Bruce, and Sarah J. Whatmore. 2010. "The Stuff of Politics: An Introduction." In *Political Matter: Technoscience, Democracy, and Public Life*, edited by Bruce Braun and Sarah J. Whatmore, ix–xl. Minneapolis: University of Minnesota Press.

Bruckerhoff, Joshua J. 2008. "Giving Nature Constitutional Protection: A Less Anthropocentric Interpretation of Environmental Rights." *Texas Law Review* 86 (3): 615–646.

Buchanan, Colin. 1983. "Traffic in Towns: An Assessment after Twenty Years." *Built Environment* 9 (2): 93–98.

Buscher, Monika, John Urry, and Katian Witchger. 2011. "Introduction: Mobile Methods." In *Mobile Methods*, edited by Monika Buscher, John Urry, and Katian Witchger, 1–19. London: Routledge.

BWSSB. 2014. *Meeting the Vital Need for Water: A Golden Journey*. Bengaluru: BWSSB

Callon, Michel. 1984. "Some Elements of a Sociology of Translation: Domestication of the Scallops and the Fishermen of St Brieuc Bay." *Sociological Review* 32 (1 Suppl.): 196–233.

Chakrabarty, Bidyut. 1992. "Jawaharlal Nehru and Planning, 1938–41: India at the Crossroads." *Modern Asian Studies* 26 (2): 275–287.

Chakrabarty, Dipesh. 1992. "Of Garbage, Modernity and the Citizen's Gaze." *Economic and Political Weekly* 27 (10 and 11): 541–547.

Chakravartty, Paula. 2001. "Flexible Citizens and the Internet: The Global Politics of Local High-Tech Development in India." *Emergences: Journal for the Study of Media and Composite Cultures* 11 (1): 69–88.

Chandrashekhar, Lalita. 2011. *Undermining Local Democracy: Parallel Governance in Contemporary South India*. New Delhi: Routledge.

Chatterjee, Partha. 2004. *The Politics of the Governed*. New Delhi: Permanent Black.

Chella Rajan, Sudhir. 1996. *The Enigma of Automobility: Democratic Politics and Pollution Control*. Pittsburgh: University of Pittsburgh Press.

Chella Rajan, Sudhir. 2006. "Automobility and the Liberal Disposition." In *Against Automobility*, edited by Steffen Böhm, Campbell Jones, Chris Land, and Matthew Paterson, 113–130. Malden, MA: Blackwell.

References

Citizens for Bengaluru. 2018. "About Us—Citizens for Bengaluru." http://citizensforbengaluru.in/index.php/about-us/.

City Connect. 2011. "Welcome to City Connect." https://www.cityconnect.in/.

Coelho, Karen, Lalitha Kamath, and M. Vijayabaskar. 2011. "Infrastructures of Consent: Interrogating Citizen Participation Mandates in Indian Urban Governance." IDS working paper 362. Sussex, UK: IDS.

Coelho, Karen, and Nithya Raman. 2010. "Salvaging and Scapegoating: Slum Evictions on Chennai's Waterways." *Economic and Political Weekly* 45 (21): 19–23.

Collingwood, R. G. 1994. *The Idea of History*. Oxford: Oxford University Press.

Collins, H. M., and Steven Yearley. 1992. "Epistemological Chickens." In *Science as Practice and Culture*, edited by Andrew Pickering, 301–326. Chicago: University of Chicago Press.

Comptroller and Auditor General. 2013. *Report of the Comptroller and Auditor General of India on Local Bodies*. Report 6. Bengaluru: Government of Karnataka.

Coutard, Olivier, and Simon Guy. 2007. "STS and the City: Politics and Practices of Hope." *Science, Technology and Human Values* 32 (6): 713–734.

Crang, Michael. 2001. "Rhythms of the City: Temporalised Space and Motion. TimeSpace." In *Timespace: Geographies of Temporality*, edited by Jon May and Nigel Thrift, 187–207. London: Routledge.

Cresswell, Tim. 2013. "Citizenship in Worlds of Mobility." In *Critical Mobilities*, edited by Ola Soderstrom, Didier Ruedin, Shalini Randeria, Gianni D'Amato, and Francesco Panese, 81–100. Lausanne: EPFL Press.

Cresswell, Tim. 2014. "Friction." In *The Routledge Handbook of Mobilities*, edited by Peter Adey, David Bissell, Kevin Hannam, Peter Merriman, and Mimi Sheller. London: Routledge.

Cresswell, Tim. 2016. "Afterword—Asian Mobilities/Asian Frictions?" *Environment and Planning A: Economy and Space* 48 (6): 1082–1086.

Crook, Robert, and James Manor. 1998. *Democracy and Decentralisation in South Asia and West Africa: Participation, Accountability and Performance*. Cambridge: Cambridge University Press.

D'Andrea, Anthony, Luigina Ciolfi, and Breda Gray. 2011. "Methodological Challenges and Innovations in Mobilities Research." *Mobilities* 6 (2): 149–160.

Dant, Tim. 2004. "The Driver-Car." *Theory, Culture and Society* 21 (4–5): 61–79.

Dasgupta, Simanti. 2012. "Rethinking Participation: Water, Development and Democracy in Neo-Liberal Bangalore." *South Asia: Journal of South Asian Studies* 35 (3): 520–545.

Davis, Mike. 2006. *City of Quartz: Excavating the Future in Los Angeles (New Edition)*. London: Verso Books.

Dennis, Kingsley, and John Urry. 2009. *After the Car*. Cambridge: Polity Press.

Desforges, Luke, Rhys Jones, and Mike Woods. 2005. "New Geographies of Citizenship." *Citizenship Studies* 9 (5): 439–451.

Dibley, Ben. 2012. "The Shape of Things to Come: Seven Theses on the Anthropocene and Attachment." *Australian Humanities Review* 52:139–153.

Dickey, Sara. 1993. "The Politics of Adulation: Cinema and the Production of Politicians in South India." *Journal of Asian Studies* 52 (2): 340–372.

Dikshit, Giri S., G. R. Kuppuswamy, and S. K. Mohan. 1993. *Tank Irrigation in Karnataka: A Historical Survey*. Bangalore: Gandhi Sahitya Sangha.

Directorate of Census Operations Karnataka. 2011. *District Census Handbook—Bangalore. Series 30 Part XII-A. Village and Town Directory*. New Delhi: Office of the Registrar General and Census Commissioner of India.

Divall, Colin. 2010. "Mobilizing the History of Technology." *Technology and Culture* 51 (4): 938–960.

Dobson, Andrew. 2012. *Green Political Thought*. New York: Routledge.

Doron, Assa, and Ira Raja. 2015. "The Cultural Politics of Shit: Class, Gender and Public Space in India." *Postcolonial Studies* 18 (2): 189–207.

Dudley, Geoff, and Kiron Chatterjee. 2012. "The Dynamics of Regime Strength and Instability: Policy Challenges to the Dominance of the Private Car in the United Kingdom." In *Automobility in Transition? A Socio-Technical Analysis of Sustainable Transport*, edited by Frank W. Geels, Rene Kemp, Geoff Dudley, and Glenn Lyons, 83–103. New York: Routledge.

Dunleavy, Patrick, and Christopher Hood. 1994. "From Old Public Administration to New Public Management." *Public Money and Management* 14:9–16.

Edensor, Tim. 1998. "The Culture of the Indian Street." In *Images of the Street: Planning, Identity and Control in Public Sphere*, edited by Nicholas R. Fyfe, 205–221. London: Routledge.

Edensor, Tim. 2004. "Automobility and National Identity: Representation, Geography and Driving Practice." *Theory, Culture and Society* 21 (4–5): 101–120.

Edensor, Tim. 2010. "Introduction: Thinking about Rhythm and Space." In *Geographies of Rhythm: Nature, Place, Mobilities and Bodies*, edited by Tim Edensor, 1–20. Farnham, UK: Ashgate.

Elam, Mark, and Margareta Bertilsson. 2003. "Consuming, Engaging and Confronting Science: The Emerging Dimensions of Scientific Citizenship." *European Journal of Social Theory* 6 (2): 233–251.

Eliasson, Jonas. 2008. "Lessons from the Stockholm Congestion Charging Trial." *Transport Policy* 15 (6): 395–404.

Emmenegger, Susan, and Axel Tschentscher. 1994. "Taking Nature's Rights Seriously: The Long Way to Biocentrism in Environmental Law." *Georgetown International Environmental Law Review* 6 (3): 545–592.

Enqvist, Johan, Maria Tengo, and Bodin Orjan. 2014. "Citizen Networks in the Garden City: Protecting Urban Ecosystems in Rapid Urbanization." *Landscape and Urban Planning* 130:24–35.

Environment Support Group. 2012. "Bangalore Road Widening and Other Urban Transport Projects Impacted Communities Unite." Bangalore: Environment Support Group.

Evans, Peter. 1995. *Embedded Autonomy: States and Industrial Transformation*. Princeton, NJ: Princeton University Press.

Facebook. 2019. "Bangalore Citizen Traffic Control." https://www.facebook.com/groups/127531223960412/about/.

Falcocchio, John C., and Herbert S. Levinson. 2015. *Road Traffic Congestion: A Concise Guide*. New York: Springer International.

Featherstone, Mark. 2010. "Event Horizon: Utopia–Dystopia in Bauman's Thought." In *Bauman's Challenge: Sociological Issues for the 21st Century*, edited by Mark Davis and Keith Tester, 127–147. New York: Springer.

Feenberg, Andrew. 1999. *Questioning Technology*. London: Routledge.

Felt, Ulrike, and Maximilian Fochler. 2010. "Machineries for Making Publics: Inscribing and De-Scribing Publics in Public Engagement." *Minerva* 48 (3): 219–238.

Fernandes, Leela. 2006. *India's New Middle Class: Democratic Politics in an Era of Economic Reform*. Minneapolis: University of Minnesota Press.

Flyvbjerg, Bent. 2014. "What You Should Know about Megaprojects and Why: An Overview." *Project Management Journal* 45 (2): 6–19.

Furlong, Kathryn. 2014. "STS beyond the 'Modern Infrastructure Ideal': Extending Theory by Engaging with Infrastructure Challenges in the South." *Technology in Society* 38:139–147.

Gaete-Reyes, Mariela. 2015. "Citizenship and the Embodied Practice of Wheelchair Use." *Geoforum* 64:351–361.

Gandhi, Ajay. 2015. "The Postcolonial Street: Patterns, Modes and Forms." In *Cities in South Asia*, edited by Crispin Bates and Minoru Mio, 265–286. New York: Routledge.

Gandy, Matthew. 2004. "Rethinking Urban Metabolism: Water, Space and the Modern City." *City* 8 (3): 363–379.

Gandy, Matthew. 2006. "The Bacteriological City and Its Discontents." *Historical Geography* 34 (1): 14–25.

Gandy, Matthew. 2011. "Introduction." In *Urban Constellations*, edited by Matthew Gandy, 4–9. Berlin: Jovis Verlag.

Gandy, Matthew. 2014. *The Fabric of Space: Water, Modernity, and the Urban Imagination*. Cambridge, MA: MIT Press.

Gartman, David. 2004. "Three Ages of the Automobile: The Cultural Logics of the Car." *Theory, Culture and Society* 21 (4–5): 169–195.

Gayathri, V. 2010. "Coping with Diseases: Public Health and Medicine in Colonial South India, 1883–1925." PhD diss., Pondicherry University.

Geels, Frank W., and Rene Kemp. 2012. "The Multi-Level Perspective as a New Perspective for Studying Socio-Technical Transitions." In *Automobility in Transition? A Socio-Technical Analysis of Sustainable Transport*, edited by Frank W. Geels, Rene Kemp, Geoff Dudley, and Glenn Lyons, 49–81. New York: Routledge.

Geels, Frank W., Rene Kemp, Geoff Dudley, and Glenn Lyons, eds. 2012. *Automobility in Transition? A Socio-Technical Analysis of Sustainable Transport*. London: Routledge.

Ghertner, Asher D. 2015. *Rule by Aesthetics: World Class City Making in India*. New York: Oxford University Press.

Ghosh, Asha. 2005. "Public-Private or a Private Public? Promised Partnership of the Bangalore Agenda Task Force." *Economic and Political Weekly* 40 (47): 4914–4921.

Ghosh, Asha. 2006. "Banking on the Bangalore Dream." *Economic and Political Weekly* 41 (8): 689–692.

Gieryn, Thomas F. 2006. "City as Truth-Spot: Laboratories and Field-Sites in Urban Studies." *Social Studies of Science* 36 (1): 5–38.

Goldman, Michael. 2011. "Speculative Urbanism and the Making of the Next World City." *International Journal of Urban and Regional Research* 35 (3): 555–581.

Goldman, Michael, and Wesley Longhofer. 2009. "Making World Cities." *Contexts* 8 (1): 32–36.

Google. 2019. "BTP—Bangalore Traffic Police—Apps on Google Play." https://play.google.com/store/apps/details?id=com.kabhos.android.apps.fb.btp.

Gopakumar, Govind. 2009. "Developing Durable Infrastructures: Politics, Social Skill and Sanitation Partnerships in Urban India." *Review of Policy Research* 26 (5): 571–587.

Gopakumar, Govind. 2012. *Transforming Urban Water Supplies in India: The Role of Reform and Partnerships in Globalization*. New York: Routledge.

Gopakumar, Govind. 2014. "Experiments and Counter-Experiments in the Laboratory of Water Supply Partnerships in Bengaluru, India." *International Journal of Urban and Regional Research* 38 (2): 393–412.

Gopakumar, Govind. 2015a. "Intrusiveness of Urban Renewal in India: JNNURM as a Development Fix." *Canadian Journal of Development Studies* 36 (1): 89–106.

Gopakumar, Govind. 2015b. "Who Will Decongest Bengaluru? Politics, Infrastructures and Scapes." *Mobilities* 10 (2): 304–325.

Gopakumar, Govind. 2016. "Social Life of a Bus." *Journal of Video Ethnography* 3 (1).

Gordin, Michael D., Helen Tilley, and Gyan Prakash. 2011. "Introduction: Utopia and Dystopia beyond Space and Time." In *Utopia/Dystopia: Conditions of Historical Possibility*, edited by Michael D. Gordin, Helen Tilley, and Gyan Prakash, 1–17. Princeton, NJ: Princeton University Press.

Gore, Christopher, and Govind Gopakumar. 2015. "Infrastructure and Metropolitan Reorganization: An Exploration of the Relationship in Africa and India." *Journal of Urban Affairs* 37 (5): 548–567.

Government of India. 2005. *Jawaharlal Nehru National Urban Renewal Mission: Toward Better Cities...Government of India*.

Government of India. 2017. *Road Transport Year Book: 2013–14 and 2014–15*. 2017. https://data.gov.in/catalog/road-transport-year-book-2013-14-and-2014-15.

Government of Karnataka. 1963. "The Karnataka Town and Country Planning Act, 1961." No. 11 of 1963. Bangalore: Karnataka Gazette.

Government of Karnataka. 1976. "The Bangalore Development Authority." No. 12 of 1976. Bangalore: Karnataka Gazette Extraordinary.

Government of Karnataka. 1990. *Karnataka State Gazetteer—Bangalore District*. Bangalore: Karnataka Gazetteer.

Government of Karnataka. 2006. *Bangalore Metropolitan Region (BMR) Structure Plan*. Bangalore: Bangalore Metropolitan Region Development Authority.

Gowda, Chandan. 2007. "Development, Elite Agency and the Politics of Recognition in Mysore State, 1881–1947." PhD diss., University of Michigan.

Gowda, Chandan. 2010. "'Advance Mysore!' The Cultural Logic of a Developmental State." *Economic and Political Weekly* 45 (29): 88–95.

Gowda, Rajeev, Ashwin Mahesh, and Sridhar Pabbisetty. 2014. "Centre for Public Policy (CPP): Indian Institute of Management Bangalore." In *How Think Tanks Shape Social Development Policies*, edited by James G. McGann, Anna Viden, and Jillian Rafferty, 97–108. Philadelphia: University of Pennsylvania Press.

Gowda, Rame K. S. 1972. *Urban and Regional Planning*. Mysore: Prasaranga.

Graham, Stephen. 2011. *Cities under Siege: The New Military Urbanism*. London: Verso Books.

Graham, Stephen, and Simon Marvin. 2001. *Splintering Urbanism: Networked Infrastructures, Technological Mobilities, and the Urban Condition*. London: Routledge.

Guffin, Bascom. 2015. "Concrete Politics and Subversive Drivers on the Roads of Hyderabad, India." In *Transport, Mobility, and the Production of Urban Space*, edited by Julie Cidell and David Prytherch, 64–80. New York: Routledge.

Guldi, Jo, and David Armitage. 2014. *The History Manifesto*. Cambridge: Cambridge University Press.

Gullberg, Anders, and Arne Kaijser. 2004. "City-Building Regimes in Post-War Stockholm." *Journal of Urban Technology* 11 (2): 13–39.

Gunn, Simon. 2011. "The Buchanan Report, Environment and the Problem of Traffic in 1960s Britain." *Twentieth Century British History* 22 (4): 521–542.

Gupta, Narayani. 1991. "Urbanism in South India: Eighteenth and Nineteenth Century." In *The City in Indian History: Urban Demography, Society, and Politics*, edited by Indu Banga, 121–147. New Delhi, India: Manohar Publications.

Gurukkal, Rajan. 1986. "Aspects of the Reservoir System of Irrigation in the Early Pandya State." *Studies in History* 2 (2): 155–162.

Hannam, Kevin, Mimi Sheller, and John Urry. 2006. "Editorial: Mobilities, Immobilities and Moorings." *Mobilities* 1 (1): 1–22.

Haraway, Donna. 2015. "Anthropocene, Capitalocene, Plantationocene, Chthulucene: Making Kin." *Environmental Humanities* 6 (1): 159–165.

Hardie, James Keir. 1909. *India: Impressions and Suggestions*. New York: B. W. Heubsch.

Harris, Andrew. 2013. "Concrete Geographies: Assembling Global Mumbai through Transport Infrastructure." *City* 17 (3): 343–360.

Harvey, David. 2003. "The City as a Body Politic." In *Wounded Cities: Destruction and Reconstruction in a Globalized World*, edited by Jane Schneider and Ida Susser, 25–46. Oxford: Berg.

Hasan, M. Fazlul. 1970. *Bangalore through the Centuries*. Bangalore: Historical Publications.

Hasiru Usiru. 2013. *Pedestrians in Bangalore—Walking a Tightrope: A Report on Bangalore's Pedestrian Issues from a Rights Perspective*. Bengaluru: Hasiru Usiru.

Hawken, Paul. 2017. *Drawdown: The Most Comprehensive Plan Ever Proposed to Reverse Global Warming*. New York: Penguin.

Hazareesingh, Sandip. 2007. *The Colonial City and the Challenge of Modernity: Urban Hegemonies and Civic Contestations in Bombay City, 1900–1925*. Hyderabad: Orient Longman.

Hecht, Gabrielle. 2009. *The Radiance of France: Nuclear Power and National Identity after World War II*. Cambridge, MA: MIT Press.

Heitzman, James. 1999. "Corporate Strategy and Planning in the Science City: Bangalore as 'Silicon Valley.'" *Economic and Political Weekly* 34 (5): PE2–11.

Heitzman, James. 2001. "Becoming Silicon Valley." *Seminar* 503.

Heitzman, James. 2004. *Network City: Planning the Information Society in Bangalore*. New Delhi: Oxford University Press.

Held, David. 1995. *Democracy and the Global Order—From the Modern State to Cosmopolitan Governance*. Stanford, CA: Stanford University Press.

Henderson, Jason. 2006. "Secessionist Automobility: Racism, Anti-Urbanism, and the Politics of Automobility in Atlanta, Georgia." *International Journal of Urban and Regional Research* 30 (2): 293–307.

Hensher, David A., and Sean M. Puckett. 2005. "Road User Charging: The Global Relevance of Recent Developments in the United Kingdom." *Transport Policy* 12 (5): 377–383.

Hettne, Bjorn. 1978. *The Political Economy of Indirect Rule: Mysore 1881–1947*. London: Curzon Press.

Hilgartner, Stephen. 2000. *Science on Stage: Expert Advice as Public Drama*. Stanford. CA: Stanford University Press.

Hillman, Mayer. 1983. "The Wrong Turning: Twenty Years On from Buchanan." *Built Environment* 9 (2): 104–112.

Hodson, Mike, and Simon Marvin. 2010. "Can Cities Shape Socio-Technical Transitions and How Would We Know If They Were?" *Research Policy* 39 (4): 477–485.

Hommels, Anique. 2005. "Studying Obduracy in the City: Toward a Productive Fusion between Technology Studies and Urban Studies." *Science, Technology and Human Values* 30 (3): 323–351.

Hood, Christopher. 1991. "A Public Management for All Seasons?" *Public Administration* 69:3–19.

Hughes, Thomas. 1987. "The Evolution of Large Technological Systems." In *Social Construction of Technological Systems: New Directions in the Sociology and History of Technology*, edited by W. Bijker, T. Hughes, and T. Pinch. Cambridge, MA: MIT Press.

Hughes, Thomas P. 1983. *Networks of Power—Electrification in Western Society, 1880–1930*. Baltimore: Johns Hopkins University Press.

Huitema, Eric-Mark. 2014. *Building a Smarter Transportation Management Network*. Thought Leadership White Paper. Somers, NY: IBM Corporation.

IBM Corporation. 2011. *IBM Global Commuter Pain Survey: Traffic Congestion Down, Pain Way Up*. CTB10. https://www-03.ibm.com/press/us/en/pressrelease/35359.wss.

ichangemycity. 2019. "About I Change My City." https://www.ichangemycity.com/about-us.

ICRA. 2017. "Bangalore Metropolitan Transport Corporation (BMTC)." ICRA.

iDeCK. 2006. *Revised City Development Plan for Bangalore*. Bangalore: KUIDFC.

Ikegame, Aya. 2007. "The Capital of Rajadharma: Modern Space and Religion in Colonial Mysore." *International Journal of Asian Studies* 4 (1): 15–44.

Indian Urban Space Foundation. 2012. *Project Tender S.U.R.E. Report*. Bengaluru: Indian Urban Space Foundation.

Irani, Lilly. 2015. "Hackathons and the Making of Entrepreneurial Citizenship." *Science, Technology, and Human Values* 40 (5): 799–824.

Irwin, Alan. 1995. *Citizen Science: A Study of People, Expertise and Sustainable Development*. London: Routledge.

Irwin, Alan. 2001. "Constructing the Scientific Citizen: Science and Democracy in the Biosciences." *Public Understanding of Science* 10 (1): 1–18.

Irwin, Alan, and Mike Michael. 2003. *Science, Social Theory and Public Knowledge*. Maidenhead: Open University Press.

Isin, Engin F. 2008. "Theorizing Acts of Citizenship." In *Acts of Citizenship*, edited by Engin F. Isin and Greg M. Nielsen, 15–43. New York: Zed Books.

Isin, Engin F. 2009. "Citizenship in Flux: The Figure of the Activist Citizen." *Subjectivity* 29 (1): 367–388.

Jacobs, Jane. 1961. *The Death and Life of Great American Cities*. New York: Random House.

Jain, Angela, and Massimo Moraglio. 2014. "Struggling for the Use of Urban Streets: Preliminary (Historical) Comparison between European and Indian Cities." *International Journal of the Commons* 8 (2): 513–530.

Jain, Sarah. 2005. "Violent Submission: Gendered Automobility." *Cultural Critique* 61: 186–214.

Jana Urban Space Foundation. 2018a. "About Us." http://www.janausp.org/aboutus.php.

Jana Urban Space Foundation. 2018b. "Our Founder." http://www.janausp.org/founder.php.

References

Janaagraha. 2018. "About Us." *Janaagraha* (blog). Accessed April 10, 2019. http://www.janaagraha.org/about-us/.

Jasanoff, Sheila. 2006. "Technology as a Site and Object of Politics." In *The Oxford Handbook of Contextual Political Analysis*, edited by Robert E. Goodin and Charles Tilly, 745–765. Oxford: Oxford University Press.

Jasanoff, Sheila, and Sang-Hyun Kim. 2009. "Containing the Atom: Sociotechnical Imaginaries and Nuclear Power in the United States and South Korea." *Minerva* 47 (2): 119–146.

Jenkins, Rob. 1999. *Democratic Politics and Economic Reforms in India*. Cambridge: Cambridge University Press.

Jensen, Anne. 2011. "Mobility, Space and Power: On the Multiplicities of Seeing Mobility." *Mobilities* 6 (2): 255–271.

Jensen, Ole B. 2009. "Flows of Meaning, Cultures of Movement—Urban Mobility as Meaningful Everyday Practice." *Mobilities* 4 (1): 139–158.

Jensen, Ole B. 2013. *Staging Mobilities*. London: Routledge.

Jensen, Ole B. 2016. "Of 'Other' Materialities: Why (Mobilities) Design Is Central to the Future of Mobilities Research." *Mobilities* 11 (4): 587–597.

Jensen, Ole B., Ditte Bendix Lanng, and Simon Wind. 2016. "Mobilities Design—Toward a Research Agenda for Applied Mobilities Research." *Applied Mobilities* 1 (1): 26–42.

Jensen, Ole B., Ditte Bendix Lanng, and Simon Wind. 2017. "Artefacts, Affordances and the Design of Mobilities." In *Mobilising Design*, edited by Justin Spinney, Suzanne Reimer, and Philip Pinch, 143–154. London: Routledge.

Joerges, Bernward. 1999. "Do Politics Have Artefacts?" *Social Studies of Science* 29 (3): 411–431.

Jones, Martin, Rhys Jones, and Michael Woods. 2004. *An Introduction to Political Geography: Space, Place and Politics*. New York: Routledge.

Joshi, Rutul, and Yogi Joseph. 2015. "Invisible Cyclist and Disappearing Cycles: The Challenges of Cycling Policies in Indian Cities." *Transfers* 5 (3): 23–40.

Joshi, Rutul, Yogi Joseph, and Y. V. Chandran. 2016. "The Structures of Mobility and Challenges of Low Carbon Transitions in India." In *Low Carbon Mobility Transitions*, edited by D. Hopkins and J. Higham, 119–136. Oxford: Goodfellow.

Kamath, Lalitha. 2013. "Achieving Global Competitiveness and Local Poverty Reduction? The Tale of a Public-Private Partnership for Urban Regeneration in Bangalore, India." In *The Routledge Companion to Urban Regeneration*, edited by Michael E. Leary and John McCarthy, 273–283. New York: Routledge.

Kamath, Lalitha, and M. Vijayabaskar. 2009. "Limits and Possibilities of Middle Class Associations as Urban Collective Actors." *Economic and Political Weekly* 44 (26 and 27): 368–376.

Karvonen, Andrew, and Bas van Heur. 2014. "Urban Laboratories: Experiments in Reworking Cities." *International Journal of Urban and Regional Research* 38 (2): 379–392.

Kaufmann, Vincent. 2002. *Re-thinking Mobility: Contemporary Sociology*. Aldershot: Ashgate.

Kaviraj, Sudipta. 1997. "Filth and the Public Sphere: Concepts and Practices about Space in Calcutta." *Public Culture* 10 (1): 83–113.

Kay, Jane Holtz. 1997. *Asphalt Nation: How the Automobile Took Over America and How We Can Take It Back*. Berkeley: University of California Press.

Keil, Roger, ed. 2013. *Suburban Constellations: Governance, Land and Infrastructure in the 21st Century*. Berlin: Jovis Verlag.

Kelley, Robert. 1978. "Public History: Its Origins, Nature, and Prospects." *Public Historian* 1 (1): 16–28.

Kharola, P. S. 2013. "Analysing the Urban Public Transport Policy Regime in India." *Economic and Political Weekly* 48 (48): 95–102.

King, Anthony D. 1976. *Colonial Urban Development: Culture, Social Power, and Environment*. London: Routledge.

King, Anthony D. 1980. "Colonialism and the Development of the Modern Asian City: Some Theoretical Considerations." In *The City in South Asia: Pre-Modern and Modern*, edited by Kenneth Ballhatchet and John Harrison. London: Curzon Press.

King, Anthony D. 1984. "The Bungalow: An Indian Contribution to the West." *History Today* 32 (11): 38–44.

King, Anthony D. 1990. *Urbanism, Colonialism, and the World Economy—Cultural and Spatial Foundations of the World Urban System*. London: Routledge.

Kirk, Jason A. 2005. "Banking on India's States: The Politics of World Bank Reform Programs in Andhra Pradesh and Karnataka." *India Review* 4 (3): 287–325.

Kitchin, Rob, Tracey P. Lauriault, and Gavin McArdle. 2015. "Knowing and Governing Cities through Urban Indicators, City Benchmarking and Real-Time Dashboards." *Regional Studies, Regional Science* 2 (1): 6–28.

KRTO. 2015. "Total Vehicles Registered and Kept for Use in Bengaluru Metropolitan City as on December 2015." KRTO.

KUIDFC. 2006. *Infrastructure Development and Investment Plan (IDIP) 2006–30*. Bangalore: KUIDFC.

KUIDFC. 2017. "KUIDFC—Who We Are." http://www.kuidfc.com/ENG/about.htm.

Kundu, Amitabh. 2002. "Institutional Innovation for Urban Infrastructural Development: The Indian Scenario." In *Development and Cities—Essays from Development in Practice*, edited by David Westendorff and D. Eade, 174–189. Oxford: Oxfam GB.

Ladd, Brian. 2011. "Cities on Wheels: Cars and Public Space." In *Blackwell Companion to the City*, 265–274. Malden, MA: Blackwell.

Latimer, Joanna, and Rolland Munro. 2006. "Driving the Social." In *Against Automobility*, edited by Steffen Böhm, Campbell Jones, Chris Land, and Matthew Paterson, 32–54. Malden, MA: Blackwell.

Latour, Bruno. 1992. "Where Are the Missing Masses? The Sociology of a Few Mundane Artifacts." In *Shaping Technology/Building Society: Studies in Sociotechnical Change*, edited by W. Bijker and John Law. Cambridge, MA: MIT Press.

Latour, Bruno. 1993. *We Have Never Been Modern*. Cambridge, MA: Harvard University Press.

Latour, Bruno. 2005. *Reassembling the Social: An Introduction to Actor-Network-Theory*. New York: Oxford University Press.

Latour, Bruno. 2014. "Agency at the Time of the Anthropocene." *New Literary History* 45:1–18.

Latour, Bruno. 2017. *Facing Gaia: Eight Lectures on the New Climatic Regime*. Hoboken, NJ: Wiley.

Laurence, Ray. 2013. "Traffic and Land Transportation in and near Rome." In *The Cambridge Companion to Ancient Rome*, edited by Paul Erdkamp, 246–261. Cambridge: Cambridge University Press.

Law, John. 1987. "Technology and Heterogeneous Engineering: The Case of Portuguese Expansion." In *The Social Construction of Technological Systems—New Directions in the Sociology and History of Technology*, edited by Wiebe E. Bijker, Thomas P. Hughes, and Trevor Pinch. Cambridge, MA: MIT Press.

Law, John. 2009. "Actor Network Theory and Material Semiotics." In *The New Blackwell Companion to Social Theory*, edited by Bryan S. Turner, 141–158. Chichester: Wiley.

Law, John, and Annemarie Mol. 1995. "Notes on Materiality and Sociality." *Sociological Review* 43 (2): 274–294.

Lay, Maxwell G. 2011. "An Historical Review of the Assessment and Management of Congestion." *Road and Transport Research* 21 (2): 32–45.

Lee, Jo, and Tim Ingold. 2006. "Fieldwork on Foot: Perceiving, Routing, Socializing." In *Locating the Field: Space, Place, and Context in Anthropology*, edited by Simon Coleman and Peter Collins, 67–85. Oxford: Berg.

Lefebvre, Henri. 2004. *Rhythmanalysis: Space, Time, and Everyday Life*. New York: Continuum.

Lewis, Simon L., and Mark A. Maslin. 2015. "Defining the Anthropocene." *Nature* 519 (7542): 171–180.

Ludden, David. 2005. "Development Regimes in South Asia: History and the Governance Conundrum." *Economic and Political Weekly* 40 (37): 4042–4051.

MacLeod, Gordon, and Kevin Ward. 2002. "Spaces of Utopia and Dystopia: Landscaping the Contemporary City." *Geografiska Annaler: Series B, Human Geography* 84 (3–4): 153–170.

Mahadevia, Darshini. 2011. "Branded and Renewed? Policies, Politics and Processes of Urban Development in the Reform Era." *Economic and Political Weekly* 46 (31): 56–64.

Manimala, Mathew J. 2008. "Evolution of the Bangalore ICT Cluster: A Stage Theory Based on the Crystal Growth Model." In *Knowledge Matters: Technology, Innovation and Entrepreneurship in Innovation Networks and Knowledge Clusters*, edited by Elias G. Carayannis and Piero Formica. New York: Palgrave Macmillan.

Manor, James. 1977. "Political Change in an Indian State: Mysore 1917–1955." New Delhi: Manohar Publications.

Manor, James. 2007. "Successful Governance Reforms in Two Indian States: Karnataka and Andhra Pradesh." *Commonwealth and Comparative Politics* 45 (4): 425–451.

Marres, Noortje. 2016. *Material Participation: Technology, the Environment and Everyday Publics*. Basingstoke: Palgrave Macmillan.

Marres, Noortje, and Javier Lezaun. 2011. "Materials and Devices of the Public: An Introduction." *Economy and Society* 40 (4): 489–509.

Mascarenhas, R. C. 2010. *India's Silicon Plateau: Development of Information and Communication Technology in Bangalore*. Hyderabad, India: Orient Black Swan.

McCann, Eugene, and Kevin Ward. 2011. *Mobile Urbanism: Cities and Policymaking in the Global Age*. Minneapolis: University of Minnesota Press.

McFarlane, Colin, and Jonathan Rutherford. 2008. "Political Infrastructures: Governing and Experiencing the Fabric of the City." *International Journal of Urban and Regional Research* 32 (2): 363–374.

McShane, Clay. 1994. *Down the Asphalt Path: The Automobile and the American City*. New York: Columbia University Press.

McShane, Clay, and Joel A. Tarr. 1997. "The Centrality of the Horse in the Nineteenth-Century American City." In *The Making of Urban America*, edited by Raymond A. Mohl, 105–130. Wilmington, DE: Scholarly Resources Inc.

McShane, Clay, and Joel Tarr. 2007. *The Horse in the City: Living Machines in the Nineteenth Century*. Baltimore: Johns Hopkins University Press.

Mehta, Vikas. 2015. "The Street as Ecology." In *Incomplete Streets: Processes, Practices, and Possibilities*, edited by Stephen Zavestoski and Julian Agyeman. New York: Routledge.

Merriman, Peter. 2006. "'Mirror, Signal, Manoeuvre': Assembling and Governing the Motorway Driver in Late 1950s Britain." In *Against Automobility*, edited by Steffen Böhm, Campbell Jones, Chris Land, and Matthew Paterson, 75–92. Malden, MA: Blackwell.

Meyer, William S., Richard Burn, James S. Cotton, and Herbert H. Risley. 1908. *The Imperial Gazetteer of India*, vol. 6. Oxford: Clarendon Press.

Michael, Mike. 2006. *Technoscience and Everyday Life: The Complex Simplicities of the Mundane*. Maidenhead: Open University Press.

Michael, Mike. 2009. "Publics Performing Publics: Of PiGs, PiPs and Politics." *Public Understanding of Science* 18 (5): 617–631.

Middleton, Jennie. 2011. "Walking in the City: The Geographies of Everyday Pedestrian Practices." *Geography Compass* 5 (2): 90–105.

Mines, Mattison, and Vijayalakshmi Gourishankar. 1990. "Leadership and Individuality in South Asia: The Case of the South Indian Big-Man." *Journal of Asian Studies* 49 (4): 761–786. https://doi.org/10.2307/2058235.

Ministry of Finance. 1996. *The India Infrastructure Report: Policy Imperatives for Growth and Welfare*. New Delhi: National Council of Applied Economic Research.

Ministry of Transport. 1964. *Traffic in Towns: A Study of the Long Term Problems of Traffic in Urban Areas. Reports of the Steering Group and Working Group Appointed by the Minister of Transport*. London: H. M. Stationery Office.

Ministry of Urban Affairs and Employment. 1996. *Urban Development Plans Formulation and Implementation (UDPFI) Guidelines—Volume 1*. New Delhi: Government of India.

Mohan, Dinesh. 2013. "Moving around in Indian Cities." *Economic and Political Weekly* 48 (48): 40–48.

Monstadt, Jochen. 2009. "Conceptualizing the Political Ecology of Urban Infrastructures: Insights from Technology and Urban Studies." *Environment and Planning A* 41 (8): 1924–1942.

Monstadt, Jochen, and Sophie Schramm. 2013. "Beyond the Networked City? Suburban Constellations in Water Supply and Sanitation." In *Suburban Constellations: Governance, Land and Infrastructure in the 21st Century*, edited by Roger Keil, 85–94. Berlin: Jovis Verlag.

Moore, Jason W., ed. 2016. *Anthropocene or Capitalocene? Nature, History, and the Crisis of Capitalism*. Oakland, CA: PM Press.

Moorhouse, Geoffrey. 1971. *Calcutta*. New York: Harcourt.

Moorhouse, H. F. 1991. *Driving Ambitions: An Analysis of the American Hot Rod Enthusiasm*. Manchester: Manchester University Press.

Mumford, Lewis. 1961. *The City in History*. New York: Harcourt.

Murthy, K. S. Dakshina. 2006. "Rajkumar and Kannada Nationalism." *Economic and Political Weekly* 41 (19): 1834–1835.

Nagarajan, Kedar. 2017. "The Case Until Now: NGT to Hear the Bengaluru Steel Flyover Next on 30 January." *Caravan*. https://caravanmagazine.in/vantage/bengaluru-steel-flyover-ngt.

Nagendra, Harini. 2010. "Maps, Lakes and Citizens." *Seminar* 613:19–23.

Nair, Janaki. 1996. "'Memories of Underdevelopment': Language and Its Identities in Contemporary Karnataka." *Economic and Political Weekly* 31 (41–42): 2809–2816.

Nair, Janaki. 2000. "Language and the Right to the City." *Economic and Political Weekly* 35 (47): 41–46.

Nair, Janaki. 2002. "Past Perfect: Architecture and Public Life in Bangalore." *Journal of Asian Studies* 61 (4): 1205–1236.

Nair, Janaki. 2005. *The Promise of the Metropolis: Bangalore's Twentieth Century*. New Delhi: Oxford University Press.

Nair, Janaki. 2013. "Is There an 'Indian' Urbanism?" In *Ecologies of Urbanism in India: Metropolitan Civility and Sustainability*, edited by Anne Rademacher and K. Sivaramakrishnan, 43–70. Hong Kong: Hong Kong University Press.

Nair, Janaki. 2015. "Indian Urbanism and the Terrain of the Law." *Economic and Political Weekly* 50 (36): 54–63.

Nandy, Ashis. 1998. "Introduction—Indian Popular Cinema as a Slum's Eye View of Politics." In *The Secret Politics of Our Desires: Innocence, Culpabilitiy, and Indian Popular Cinema*, edited by Ashis Nandy. New Delhi: Oxford University Press.

Narayan, R. K. 1944. *Mysore*. Mysore: Indian Thought Publications.

National Police Mission. 2016. "Draft Project Proposal on BTRAC—Technology Driven Traffic Management. Micro Mission: 03 (Communication and Technology)." New Delhi: Government of India.

NCPE Infrastructures India. 2013. "JNNURM Project for Construction of Grade Separator at Gali Anjaneya Junction." Bengaluru: BBMP.

References

Newman, Peter, and Jeffrey Kenworthy. 1999. *Sustainability and Cities: Overcoming Automobile Dependence*. Washington DC: Island Press.

Nielsen, Kenneth Bo, and Harold Wilhite. 2016. "The Rise and Fall of the 'People's Car': Middle-Class Aspirations, Status and Mobile Symbolism in 'New India.'" In *Cars, Automobility and Development in Asia*, edited by Arve Hansen and Kenneth Bo Nielsen, 171–190. New York: Routledge.

Norman, Don. 2013. *The Design of Everyday Things*. New York: Basic Books.

Norton, Peter D. 2008. *Fighting Traffic: The Dawn of the Motor Age in the American City*. Cambridge, MA: MIT Press.

Orlikowski, Wanda J. 2007. "Sociomaterial Practices: Exploring Technology at Work." *Organization Studies* 28 (9): 1435–1448.

Pani, Narendar. 2006. "Icons and Reform Politics in India: The Case of S. M. Krishna." *Asian Survey* 46 (2): 238–256.

Pani, Narendar. 2009. "Resource Cities across Phases of Globalization: Evidence from Bangalore." *Habitat International* 33 (1): 114–119.

Pani, Narendar. 2010. "Imaginations of Bengaluru." In *Bengaluru, Bangalore, Bengaluru*, edited by Narendar Pani, Sindhu Radhakrishna, and Kishor G. Bhat, 1–26. New Delhi: Sage.

Pani, Narendar, Tara Anand, and Vinod Vyasulu. 1985. "Impact of Colonialism on the Economic Structure of Indian Cities: Bangalore 1800–1900." In *Essays on Bangalore*, vol. 1, edited by Vinod Vyasulu and Amulya Kumar N. Reddy. Bangalore: Karnataka State Council for Science and Technology.

Parekh, Bhikhu. 1991. "Nehru and the National Philosophy of India." *Economic and Political Weekly* 26 (1–2): 35–39, 41–43, 45–48.

Parthasarathy, Balaji. 2004. "India's Silicon Valley or Silicon Valley's India? Socially Embedding the Computer Software Industry in Bangalore." *International Journal of Urban and Regional Research* 28 (3): 664–685.

Parthasarathy, Balaji. 2010. "The Computer Software Industry as a Vehicle of Late Industrialization: Lessons from the Indian Case." *Journal of the Asia Pacific Economy* 15 (3): 247–270.

Patton, Jason W. 2007. "A Pedestrian World: Competing Rationalities and the Calculation of Transportation Change." *Environment and Planning A: Economy and Space* 39 (4): 928–944.

Pfaffenberger. 1992. "Technological Dramas." *Science, Technology and Human Values* 17 (3): 282–312.

Philip, Kavita. 2016. "Telling Histories of the Future: The Imaginaries of Indian Technoscience." *Identities* 23 (3): 276–293.

Pickering, Andrew. 1995. *The Mangle of Practice: Time, Agency, and Science*. Chicago: University of Chicago Press.

Pow, C. P. 2015. "Urban Dystopia and Epistemologies of Hope." *Progress in Human Geography* 39 (4): 464–485.

Prakash, Gyan. 2002. "The Urban Turn." In *Sarai Reader 2002: The Cities of Everyday Life*, edited by Ravi S. Vasudevan, Jeebesh Bagchi, Ravi Sundaram, Monica Narula, Geert Lovink, and Shuddhabrata Sengupta, 2–7. New Delhi: New Media Initiative.

Prakash, Gyan. 2010. *Noir Urbanisms: Dystopic Images of the Modern City*. Princeton, NJ: Princeton University Press.

Prasad, M. Madhava. 1999. "Cine-Politics: On the Political Significance of Cinema in South India." *Journal of the Moving Image* 1 (Autumn): 37–52.

Prasad, M. Madhava. 2004. "Reigning Stars: The Political Career of South Indian Cinema." In *Stars: The Film Reader*, edited by Lucy Fischer and Marcia Landy, 97–114. New York: Routledge.

Price, Pamela and Arild Engelsen Ruud. 2012. *Power and Influence in India: Bosses, Lords and Captains*. New Delhi: Routledge India.

Rae, Gavin. 2016. "Anthropocentrism." In *Encyclopedia of Global Bioethics*, edited by Henk ten Have, 146–156. Cham: Springer International.

Raina, Dhruv. 1997. "Evolving Perspectives on Science and History: A Chronicle of Modern India's Scientific Enchantment and Disenchantment (1850–1980)." *Social Epistemology* 11 (1): 3–24.

Ramachandran, M. 2009. *Urban Renewal: Policy and Response*. New Delhi: Academic Foundation.

Ramanayya, T. V., and K. M. Anantharamaiah. 2008. *Bangalore Traffic Improvement Program BTRAC 2010—Strategic Improvement Plan*. Bangalore: Indian Institute of Management.

Ranganathan, Malini. 2015. "Storm Drains as Assemblages: The Political Ecology of Flood Risk in Post-Colonial Bangalore." *Antipode* 47 (5): 1300–1320.

Rao, Anuradha. 2013. "Re-Examining the Relationship between Civil Society and the Internet: Pessimistic Visions in India's 'IT City.'" *Journal of Creative Communications* 8 (2–3): 157–175.

Rao, Anuradha. 2014. "Information and Communication Technologies (ICTs) and Civil Society in an 'IT City': Experiences of Civic and Political Engagement in Bangalore." PhD diss., National University of Singapore.

Rao, C. Hayavadana, ed. 1929a. *Mysore Gazetteer*. Vol. 3: *Economic*. Bangalore: Government Press.

Rao, C. Hayavadana, ed. 1929b. *Mysore Gazetteer*. Vol. 4: *Administrative*. Bangalore: Government Press.

Rao, C. Hayavadana, ed. 1930. *Mysore Gazetteer*. Vol. 2: *Modern Part IV*. Bangalore: Government Press.

Rao, M. Shama. 1936. *Modern Mysore*. Bangalore: Higginbothams.

Ravindra, A. 1996. *Urban Land Policy—A Metropolitan Perspective*. New Delhi: Concept Publishing Company.

Raygorodetsky, Gleb. 2018. *The Archipelago of Hope: Wisdom and Resilience from the Edge of Climate Change*. New York: Pegasus Books.

Rice, B. Lewis. 1897. *Mysore: A Gazetteer Compiled for Government*. Vol. 2: *I Mysore, by Districts*. London: Archibald Constable.

RITES. 2011. *Comprehensive Traffic and Transportation Plan for Bengaluru*. Bengaluru: Karnataka Urban Infrastructure Development Finance Corporation.

Rosario, Clifton, and Lawrence Liang. 2006. *Of Master Plans and Illegalities in an Era of Transition*. Bangalore: Alternative Law Forum.

Ross, Ronald. 1923. *Memoirs with a Full Account of the Great Malaria Problem and Its Solution*. London: John Murray.

Roy, Ananya, and Aihwa Ong. 2011. *Worlding Cities: Asian Experiments and the Art of Being Global*. Malden, MA: Wiley Blackwell.

Roy Chowdhury, Supriya. 2003. "Old Classes and New Spaces: Urban Poverty, Unorganised Labour and New Unions." *Economic and Political Weekly* 38 (50): 5277–5284.

Sadoway, David, and Govind Gopakumar. 2017. "(Un)Bundling Bangalore: Infrastructure Bundling 'Best Practices' and Assembling Novel Scapes." *Geoforum* 79: 46–57.

Sadoway, David, Govind Gopakumar, Vinay Baindur, and Madhav G. Badami. 2018. "JNNURM as a Window on Urban Governance—Its Institutional Footprints, Antecedents, and Legacy." *Economic and Political Weekly* 53 (2): 71–81.

Sami, Neha. 2014. "Power to the People? A Study of Bangalore's Urban Task Forces." In *Contesting the Indian City: Global Visions and the Politics of the Local*, edited by Gavin Shatkin. Oxford: Wiley-Blackwell.

Sardar, Ziauddin. 2002. "The Ambassador from India." In *Autopia: Cars and Culture*, edited by Peter Wollen and Joe Kerr. London: Reaktion Books.

Saxenian, Annalee. 2002. "Bangalore: The Silicon Valley of Asia?" In *Economic Policy Reforms and the Indian Economy*, edited by Anne O. Krueger, 169–193. Chicago: University of Chicago Press.

Secretary of State for India in Council. 1870. *Report on Measures Adopted for Sanitary Improvements in India from June 1869 to June 1870*. London: George Edward Eyre and William Spottiswoode.

Seiler, Cotten. 2008. *Republic of Drivers: A Cultural History of Automobility in America*. Chicago: University of Chicago Press.

Sharma, Chanchal Kumar. 2014. "Rise and Demise of Nehruvian Consensus: A Historical Review." *South Asian Journal of Socio-Political Studies* 15 (1): 16–23.

Sheller, Mimi. 2012. "The Emergence of New Cultures of Mobility: Stability, Openings, and Prospects." In *Automobility in Transition? A Socio-Technical Analysis of Sustainable Transport*, edited by Frank W. Geels, Rene Kemp, Geoff Dudley, and Glenn Lyons, 180–202. London: Routledge.

Sheller, Mimi. 2018. *Mobility Justice: The Politics of Movement in an Age of Extremes*. Brooklyn: Verso.

Sheller, Mimi, and John Urry. 2000. "City and the Car." *International Journal of Urban and Regional Research* 24 (4): 737–757.

Sheller, Mimi, and John Urry. 2003. "Mobile Transformations of 'Public' and 'Private Life.'" *Theory, Culture and Society* 20 (3): 107–125.

Sheller, Mimi, and John Urry. 2006a. "Introduction: Mobile Cities, Urban Mobilities." In *Mobile Technologies of the City*, edited by Mimi Sheller and John Urry. New York: Routledge.

Sheller, Mimi, and John Urry. 2006b. "The New Mobilities Paradigm." *Environment and Planning A* 38 (2): 207–226.

Shobha. 2012. "Bengalurunalli plague mattu Malleswaram badavaneya rachane (1889–1902)." *Itihasa Darshana* 27:262–267.

Singh, R. L. 1964. *Bangalore: An Urban Survey*. Varanasi, India: Tara Publications.

Sivaramakrishnan, K. C. 2011. *Re-Visioning Indian Cities: The Urban Renewal Mission*. New Delhi: Sage.

Sperling, Daniel, and Deborah Gordon. 2009. *Two Billion Cars: Driving Toward Sustainability*. Oxford: Oxford University Press.

Spinney, Justin, Rachel Aldred, and Katrina Brown. 2015. "Geographies of Citizenship and Everyday (Im)mobility." *Geoforum* 64:325–332.

Srinivas, S. 2010. "Landmarks in the Annals of Bangalore's Municipal Administration." *March of Karnataka* 45 (5): 4–9.

Srinivas, S. 2013a. "Dharmambudhi Tank Once Quenched Bangalore's Thirst." *March of Karnataka* 50 (6): 10–11.

Srinivas, S. 2013b. "Sanitary Condition in 19th Century Bangalore." http://karna takahistory.blogspot.ca/2013/08/sanitary-condition-in-19th-century.html?view =magazine.

Srinivas, Smriti. 2015. *A Place for Utopia: Urban Designs from South Asia*. Seattle: University of Washington Press.

Srinivasaraju, Sugata. 2008. *Keeping Faith with the Mother Tongue: The Anxieties of a Local Culture*. Bangalore: Navakarnatak Publications.

Stallmeyer, John Charles. 2006. "Architecture and Urban Form in India's Silicon Valley: A Case Study of Bangalore." PhD diss., University of California, Berkeley.

Star, Susan L. 1999. "The Ethnography of Infrastructure." *American Behavioral Scientist* 43 (3): 377–391.

Stein, Burton. 1987. *The New Cambridge History of India I. 2—Vijayanagara*. New York: Cambridge University Press.

Stengers, Isabelle. 2015. *In Catastrophic Times: Resisting the Coming Barbarism*. London: Open Humanities Press.

Stephens, J. H. 1922. "Fraser Town—A Plague-Proof Town in India." *American City* 26 (3): 235–238.

Stone, Clarence N. 1989. *Regime Politics: Governing Atlanta, 1946–88*. Lawrence: Kansas University Press.

Stopher, Peter R. 2004. "Reducing Road Congestion: A Reality Check." *Transport Policy* 11 (2): 117–131.

Storni, Cristiano. 2012. "Unpacking Design Practices: The Notion of Thing in the Making of Artifacts." *Science, Technology, and Human Values* 37 (1): 88–123.

STUP Consultants P. Ltd. 2007. *Detailed Project Report as per JNNURM Guidelines for Construction of Bridge at Gali Anjaneya Junction*. Bengaluru: BBMP.

Subramanian, C. R. 1992. *India and the Computer: A Study of Planned Development*. New Delhi: Oxford University Press.

Subramanian, D. K. 1985. "Bangalore City's Water Supply—A Study and Analysis." In *Essays on Bangalore*, vol. 4, edited by Vinod Vyasulu and Amulya Kumar N. Reddy. Bangalore: Karnataka State Council of Science and Technology.

Sudhira, H. S. 2017. "Entrepreneurial Governance in a Resilient City: Bengaluru, India." In *Entrepreneurial Urbanism in India: The Politics of Spatial Restructuring and Local Contestation*, edited by Kanekanti Chandrashekar Smitha, 57–69. Singapore: Springer Singapore.

Sundaresan, Jayaraj. 2013. "Urban Planning in Vernacular Governance: Land Use Planning and Violations in Bangalore." PhD diss., London School of Economics and Political Science.

Tarr, Joel A., and Gabriel Dupuy. 1988. *Technology and the Rise of the Networked City in Europe and America*. Philadelphia: Temple University Press.

Tetzlaff, Stefan. 2016. "Revolution or Evolution? The Making of the Automobile Sector as a Key Industry in Mid-Twentieth Century India." In *Cars, Automobility and Development in Asia*, edited by Arve Hansen and Kenneth Bo Nielsen, 62–79. New York: Routledge.

Thatchenkery, Tojo, Don Kash, and Roger Stough. 2004. "Information Technology Services and Economic Development: The Indian Experience." *Technological Forecasting and Social Change* 71 (5): 771–776.

Thrift, Nigel. 2004. "Driving in the City." *Theory, Culture and Society* 21 (4–5): 41–59.

Thriveni. 2013. "Plague Outbreak Eradication Campaign under Colonial Mysore." *International Journal of Scientific and Research Publications* 3 (5): 1–3.

Tilburg, Cornelis van. 2007. *Traffic and Congestion in the Roman Empire*. London: Routledge.

Tilly, Charles, and Robert E. Goodin. 2006. "It Depends." In *The Oxford Handbook of Contextual Political Analysis*, edited by Robert E. Goodin and Charles Tilly, 3–32. Oxford: Oxford University Press.

Tsing, Anna Lowenhaupt. 2011. *Friction: An Ethnography of Global Connection*. Princeton University Press.

Upadhya, Carol. 2004. "A New Transnational Capitalist Class? Capital Flows, Business Networks and Entrepreneurs in the Indian Software Industry." *Economic and Political Weekly* 39 (48): 5141–5143, 5145–5151.

Upadhya, Carol. 2008. "Rewriting the Code: Software Professionals and the Reconstitution of Indian Middle Class Identity." In *Patterns of Middle Class Consumption in India and China*, edited by Christophe Jaffrelot and Peter van der Veer, 55–87. London: Sage.

Upadhya, Carol. 2009. "Imagining India: Software and the Ideology of Liberalisation." *South African Review of Sociology* 40 (1): 76–93.

Upadhya, Carol. 2010. "Taking the High Road? Labour in the Indian Software Outsourcing Industry." In *Labour in Global Production Networks in India*, edited by Anne Posthuma and Dev Nathan, 300–320. New Delhi: Oxford University Press.

Urban Development Department. 2009. *Urban Development Policy for Karnataka*. Bengaluru: Government of Karnataka.

Urry, John. 2000. "Mobile Sociology." *British Journal of Sociology* 51 (1): 185–203.

Urry, John. 2004. "The 'System' of Automobility." *Theory, Culture and Society* 21 (4–5): 25–39.

Urry, John. 2005. "The Complexities of the Global." *Theory, Culture and Society* 22 (5): 235–254.

Urs, Kshithij, and Richard Whittell. 2009. *Resisting Reform? Water Profits and Democracy.* New Delhi: Sage.

Van Dijk, Meine Pieter. 2003. "Government Policies with Respect to an Information Technology Cluster in Bangalore, India." *European Journal of Development Research* 15 (2): 93–108.

Venkatarayappa, K. N. 1957. *Bangalore (A Socio-Ecological Study).* Bombay: University of Bombay.

Visvesaraya, M. 1917. *Speeches by Dewan of Mysore 1910–11 to 1916–17.* Bangalore: Government Press.

Wadiyar Bahadur, Sri Krishnaraja. 1921. *Speeches by His Highness Maharaja of Mysore 1902–20.* Bangalore: Government Press.

Walks, Alan. 2015. "Driving Cities: Automobility, Neoliberalism, and Urban Transformation. In *The Urban Political Economy and Ecology of Automobility: Driving Cities, Driving Inequality, Driving Politics*, edited by Alan Walks, 3–20. New York: Routledge.

Wells, Christopher W. 2012. *Car Country: An Environmental History.* Seattle: University of Washington Press.

Wells, Peter, Paul Nieuwenhuis, and Renato J. Orsato. 2012. "The Nature and Causes of Inertia in the Automotive Industry: Regime Stability and Non-Change." In *Automobility in Transition? A Socio-Technical Analysis of Sustainable Transport*, edited by Frank W. Geels, Rene Kemp, Geoff Dudley, and Glenn Lyons, 123–139. New York: Routledge.

Williams, Arthur Rev. 2010. "A Wesleyan View. In *Bengaluru, Bangalore, Bengaluru*, edited by Narendar Pani, Sindhu Radhakrishna, and Kishor G. Bhat, 82–89. New Delhi: Sage.

Winner, Langdon. 1977. *Autonomous Technology: Technics-out-of-Control as a Theme in Political Thought.* Cambridge, MA: MIT Press.

———. 1986. *Whale and the Reactor.* Chicago: University of Chicago Press.

Wissink, Bart. 2013. "Enclave Urbanism in Mumbai: An Actor-Network-Theory Analysis of Urban (Dis)Connection. *Geoforum* 47: 1–11.

World Bank. 2009. *Project Appraisal Document on a Proposed Grant from the Global Environment Facility Trust Fund in the Amount of US$20,330,000 to India for a Sustainable Urban Transport Project (GEF-SUTP).* Report No. 51144-IN. Washington, DC: World Bank.

Yaneva, Albena. 2009. "Making the Social Hold: Toward an Actor-Network Theory of Design." *Design and Culture* 1 (3): 273–288.

Zavestoski, Stephen, and Julian Agyeman. 2015. "Complete Streets: What's Missing?" In *Incomplete Streets: Processes, Practices and Possibilities*, edited by Stephen Zavestoski and Julian Agyeman, 1–14. New York: Routledge.

Index

Page numbers followed by an "f" or "t" indicate a figure or table, respectively.

Actant, 176
Actor Network Theory (ANT), 141, 175, 237n8, 241n2, 261, 271
Advertisement, 19f, 58, 80, 88f, 109, 111, 116, 117f, 135, 147, 148, 148f
Advisor on urban affairs, 89
Affordances, 22, 151, 178, 179, 182, 183, 213, 259
Agency, 26, 61–63, 69, 75–77, 84, 86, 96, 116, 135, 141, 155, 171, 174, 175, 200, 214, 221, 228n37, 235n3, 241n4, 255, 261, 266
Agenda for Bangalore (AfB), 61, 106, 247, 250
Agenda for Bengaluru Infrastructure Development (ABIDe), 20, 60, 89, 90, 106, 118, 120, 122–124, 210, 234n80, 235n1, 239n18, 247
Akrama Sakrama, 233n70
Alternative Law Forum, 267. *See also* Bengaluru *Janara Vedike*
Ambassador, 14, 267
American, 30, 68, 75, 212, 222n4, 225n19, 225n21, 243n5, 248, 258, 262, 264, 265, 269, 274, 275
Anjaneya, 182, 190, 191, 193, 194, 196, 198, 199, 201, 244n12, 245n17, 264, 269

Anthropocentrism, 221, 241n3, 266
App, 159, 160, 242n14, 254. *See also* Janaagraha
Architect, architecture, architectural, x, xiii, 52, 59, 63, 79, 89, 109, 141, 146, 241n1, 264, 269
Artifact, artifactual, 11, 22, 71, 73, 75, 76, 107, 109, 110, 113, 130, 132, 133, 135, 139, 141–143, 174, 175, 197, 199, 202, 208–210, 216, 218, 219, 241n2, 261, 269
Ashok, R, 115, 116. *See also* Bengaluru: minister-in-charge
Asian Development Bank, 62, 86
Assemblage, x, 109, 168, 237n8, 241n2, 266
Attara Katcheri, 39, 44
Autocentric, 12, 213, 223n9
Auto-mobile, 160, 161, 162
 citizen, 161, 202
 public, 138, 139, 168
Automobile, 2, 3, 5, 8, 10–12, 14, 15, 17, 18, 20–23, 26, 29–31, 64, 65, 68, 75, 80, 81, 89, 91, 95, 133, 134, 137–139, 144, 147, 148, 151, 155, 156, 159, 160, 166, 173, 178, 179, 181–183, 188, 190, 197, 202, 207, 209–213, 215, 218, 219, 223n9, 223n11,

Automobile (*continued*)
  225n16, 225nn19–21, 230n51, 242n7, 254, 260, 262, 265
  constitutional liberalism, 212
  culture, 15
  domination, 12, 13, 15, 80
  industry regime, 214
  national identity, 212
  personhood, 12
  popular culture, 212
  middle-class aspirations, 14, 15, 265
  status symbol, 14, 265
Automobility, ix, x, xi, xii, 1, 4, 11–14, 28, 30, 81, 96, 143, 144, 146–148, 161, 166, 167, 168, 174, 179, 180, 202, 203–209, 211–216, 218–220, 225n21, 245n21, 250, 252, 254, 257, 258, 263, 265, 268, 270, 271, 276
  constellation, 15, 16, 18, 20–23, 65, 171, 173, 202, 203, 205–209, 213–215, 219, 220, 242n7
  culture of, 80, 268
  political constellation, 15, 16, 18, 20, 22, 23, 171, 173, 202, 207, 209, 213–215, 219, 220, 242n7
  tipping points, 13
Automobilization, xv, 80, 81, 137, 216
Automotive
  age, 21
  citizenship, vii, 22, 135, 137, 139, 141, 143–149, 151, 153, 155, 157, 159, 161, 163, 165–168, 211, 213, 215, 218,
  congestion (*see under* Congestion)
  domination, 12, 13
  industry, 223n11, 271
  landscape, 20–22, 68, 97, 101, 135, 161, 168, 202, 211, 215
  presence, 12, 14, 17, 18, 20,
  public, 22, 158, 211, 215
  regime, 13, 271
  traffic, 29–31, 62, 183, 185, 190

Automotive/automobile flows, 68, 183, 188, 190, 197, 202, 211
Autonomy, autonomous, 11, 35, 40, 41, 42, 52, 144, 197, 228n37, 232n67, 253, 271

Bacteriological city, 45, 229n46, 254
Bangalore Agenda Task Force (BATF), 20, 59, 60, 84, 89, 105, 106, 118, 123, 124, 171, 172f, 233n77, 234n80, 239, 249, 254
Bangalore Blueprint Action Group (BBAG), 106
Bangalore Chamber of Commerce and Industry, 61, 118
Bangalore City Connect Foundation (BCCF), 61, 106, 118, 119, 239n17. *See also* Tender SURE
Bangalore City Corporation, 50. *See also* Bruhath Bengaluru Mahanagara Palike (BBMP)
Bangalore City Improvement Trust (BCIT), 50, 53
Bangalore City Municipality, 39, 45, 47, 228n36
Bangalore civil and military station municipality, 228n36
Bangalore Development Authority (BDA), 27, 53, 54, 55, 59, 62, 84, 85–88, 116, 118, 200t, 201, 232n66, 234n82, 238n11, 242n10, 248, 255
Bangalore Development Committee, 232n64
Bangalore Electronic City Tollway, 113
Bangalore Elevated Tollway Limited, 235n85
Bangalore International Airport Planning Authority, 235n86
Bangalore Local Planning Authority, 51, 53
Bangalore Metropolitan Land Transport Authority (BMLTA), 119, 238n11

Index

Bangalore Metropolitan Region Development Authority (BMRDA), 232n69, 255
Bangalore Metropolitan Transport Corporation (BMTC), 90, 238n11, 258
Bangalore Metro Rail Corporation Limited (BMRCL), 90, 249
Bangalore People's Forum, 124, 125. *See also* Bengaluru *Janara Vedike*
Bangalore Political Action Committee (BPAC), 106
Bangalore Regional Metropolitan Area, 232n65
Bangalore road widening and Transport Projects Impacted Communities (BATPIC), 125, 127, 253
Bangalore Summit, 84, 249
Bangalore Town Improvement Committee, 49, 50
Bangalore Traffic and Transport Initiative (BTTI), 61, 106, 119, 120, 122
Bangalore Traffic Improvement Project (B-TRAC), 26, 160
Bangalore/Bengaluru Traffic Police (BTP), 89, 155, 158, 160, 195, 196, 200, 242nn12–13, 254
Bangalore Transport Service, 53
Bangalore Water Supply and Sewerage Board (BWSSB), 53, 232n67, 238n11
Bangalore-Mysore Infrastructure Corridor, 63, 238n14
Bangalore-Mysore Infrastructure Corridor Planning Authority, 235n86
Basavangudi, 48, 230n56, 231n57
Bengaluru, xii, xiii, xiv, xv, 1, 16, 17f, 18, 18t, 19–23, 25–29, 31–33, 33t, 34–36, 38–40, 42–65, 67–70, 73, 81–86, 88, 88f, 89–90, 93–96, 99–103, 103f, 104–107, 110–113, 114f, 115, 116, 116f, 118, 119f, 120, 122f, 123–130, 132f, 133t, 134, 135, 137–139, 146–148, 148f, 151, 155, 157f, 158, 160–162, 165–171, 173, 179–182, 193, 197, 198, 200, 202, 203, 205–235, 237–240, 242, 244, 245, 247–251, 255, 256, 258, 260, 264, 265, 267–269, 271
garden city, 223n14
International Airport, 239n15
minister in charge, 104, 111, 115
Bengaluru Bus Commuter Forum, 1, 85, 113, 125, 205, 206, 240n24
Bengaluru Bus Manifesto, 128
Bengaluru Bus Prayanikara Vedike (BBPV), xiv, 1, 124, 125, 127, 240n24, 249. *See also* Bengaluru Bus Commuter Forum
Bengaluru for Kannada and Kannadiga Kannada Sene, 124
Karnataka Rakshana Vedike (KRV), 124
Bengaluru *Janara Vedike*, 125, 126f, 129, 249. *See also Janara Pranalike*
Binny Mills. *See under* Textile
Body politic, 57, 178, 256
Bollards. *See* Stone bollards
Bowring, Lewin, 38
Brahmin, 19, 49, 123, 145, 223n16
Brand Bangalore, 88, 110, 116, 118, 130, 133t
British, 6–8, 16, 20, 33, 36, 38–40, 44, 69, 227nn31–34, 248, 256, 270
British Commission, 38, 227n34
British municipalization, 33t
Bruhath Bengaluru Mahanagara Palike (BBMP), 117f, 169, 200t, 238
Buchanan report, 31, 250, 256, 257
Building bylaw, 55, 56
Bureaucratic entrepreneurship, 198
Bus, 2f, 1–3, 7–9, 19f, 27–29, 55, 56, 60, 72, 75, 80, 82, 85, 90, 91–93, 93f, 94–96, 101, 103, 113, 118, 119f, 120, 122, 122f, 123–125, 127–129, 133, 137, 139, 147, 149, 151, 156, 171, 181, 182, 185, 190, 197, 205, 206, 210, 216, 223n7, 237n20, 240n24, 249, 255

Bus (*continued*)
  Big10, 118, 119f, 120, 122, 123, 133, 239n22
  Bus Day, 129 (*see also* Bangalore Metropolitan Transport Corporation)
  conductors (ticket collectors), 94
  low-floor, 82, 91, 93
  mini buses, 92, 93
  ordinary buses, 91, 92, 94, 95
  subsidized bus routes, 237n20
  Volvo, 91–93, 93f

Calcutta, 6, 7, 260, 264
Canal irrigation, 224n12
Cantonment, 36–40, 69, 208, 227n30, 228n36
Capitalism, 13, 247, 264, 274
Car-centered, car-centric, car-centricity, 65, 212, 213
Cars, xi, 1–3, 6–9, 12–15, 26, 28–31, 55, 65, 81, 89, 95, 104, 113, 137, 139, 143, 147, 161, 164, 207, 212, 215, 222n4, 223n14, 225n21, 251, 252, 254, 261, 265, 267–271
Caste, 19, 34, 35, 38, 39, 46, 47, 49, 145, 193, 223n16, 230n50
  Dalit, 230n50
Cauvery River, 52, 181
Cauvery Water Supply Scheme, 232n67
Census, 16, 18, 232n65, 252
Chamarajpet, 230n55
Chief Minister, 19, 60, 84, 86, 104, 111, 115, 116, 119, 147, 158, 171, 193, 231n59, 233n77, 239n21, 242n12
Cholas, 34
Cholera epidemic, 229n47, 229n49, 230nn49–50, 230nn52–53
Citizen, citizenry, 27, 43, 44, 55, 59, 62, 67, 70, 71, 72, 77, 91, 94, 105, 106, 125, 127, 129, 139–141, 143, 145–147, 155, 156, 157–161, 166, 167, 202, 205, 206, 210, 229n45, 234n80, 237n6, 241n5, 250, 251, 253, 258, 264, 268, 273
Citizens Against Steel Flyover, 67. *See also* Steel Flyover
Citizens for Bengaluru (CfB), 67, 205. *See also* Steel Flyover
Citizenship, vii, 22, 61, 72, 128, 129, 132, 133t, 135, 137, 139, 140, 141, 142, 143, 144, 145, 146, 147, 149, 151, 153, 155, 157, 159, 161, 163, 165–168, 211, 213, 215, 218, 219, 234n80, 237n6, 241n1, 243n14, 247, 251, 252, 253, 258
  automotive, vii, 22, 135, 137, 139, 141, 143–147, 149, 151, 153, 155, 157, 159, 161, 163, 165–168, 211, 213, 215, 218
  entrepreneurial, 146, 258
  liberal disposition, 144
  mobile, 22, 143, 144
  studies, 144, 168, 252
  technological, 144–146, 247,
Citizen subject, 140, 145, 147, 166
City. *See also* Urban; Mobility
  council, 84, 104, 105, 244n14
  edge cities, 13, 222n4
  enclaves, 33t, 53, 222n4
  engines of economic growth, 102
  gated communities, 222n4
  Indian, iii, xi, 6, 7, 9–11, 15, 16, 20, 68–71, 73, 77–80, 85, 96, 102, 235n4, 258, 259, 263, 265, 267, 268, 276
  modern, 16, 33, 38, 45, 70, 253, 260, 266
  roads, 5, 17, 25, 28, 31, 82, 101, 137, 155, 158
  socioecological fabric, 222
  streetscape design, 13
  transport system, 7, 62
  Western, 12, 21, 29–31, 64, 65, 68, 96, 107, 223n9, 235n4 (*see also under* Automotive)

world-class, 61, 62, 64, 72, 73, 77, 84, 88, 89, 96, 97, 130, 235n5, 254
unintended, 70
City-building. *See under* Regime; Street; Urban
City Challenge Fund, 62
City Development Plan (CDP), 83, 87, 102, 258
City Improvement Trust, 50, 53
Cityscape, 2, 82, 88, 127, 135, 202, 210
CIVIC Bangalore, 84, 124
Civil and Military station, 45–50, 228n36, 229n47, 230n50
Civil society, 20, 59, 72, 77, 143, 217, 239n17, 266
Colonial, colonialism, colonialists, 1, 4, 6, 7, 14, 16, 18, 20, 33, 33t, 36, 38, 40–42, 45, 47, 69, 77, 198, 208, 221, 227n31, 227n33, 228nn36–37, 229n49, 230n49, 235n4, 248, 254, 257, 258, 260, 265, 270
  India, 20, 40, 42, 228n37, 229n49, 248, 254
  Mysore kingdom, 18, 20, 41, 208, 258, 270
Commuter, 26, 83, 89, 90, 91, 94, 95, 101, 114, 120, 127, 149, 156, 157, 159, 206, 210, 216
Comprehensive development plan (CDP), 51
Concrete boxes, 113
Confederation of Indian Industry (CII), 123, 169, 239n17
Congestion, vii, 3–11, 16, 21–23, 25–33, 33t, 34, 35, 37–41, 43–57, 59, 61, 62–65, 67–69, 71, 73, 75, 77, 79, 81, 83, 84, 85, 87, 89–91, 93, 95–97, 101, 105, 108, 110, 113–117, 120, 124, 129, 134, 135, 137–139, 147, 148, 155–158, 165, 178, 179, 182, 183, 190, 197–199, 202, 203, 208–211, 213–216, 222n4, 224n2, 224n3, 224n5, 225nn15–18, 226nn25–26, 232n65, 233n71, 236nn11–12, 237n19, 238n8, 242n11, 253, 258, 261, 269, 270. *See also* Regime: of congestion
  automobile, 8, 10, 22, 29, 31, 89, 95, 134, 137, 139, 155
  automotive, 30, 138, 139, 225n17
  charges, 10
  discourse on, 7, 25, 26, 49, 75, 87, 89, 95, 96, 208, 209
  flow, 33, 56, 57, 62, 233n71
  historical periodization, 21, 32, 33, 65
  Indian roads, 4, 10, 224n5
  native, 33, 33t, 38, 208
  qualitative, 4–6
  quantitative, 4, 5, 8–10
  regime of, vii, 21, 23, 67, 68, 69, 71, 73, 75, 77, 79, 81, 83–85, 87, 89–91, 93, 95–97, 148, 203, 210, 213–216, 236n11
  technocratic, 21 (*see also* Traffic: congestion)
  as a technopolitical regime, 21, 65, 68, 73, 75–77, 95, 96, 209
  traffic, 4, 5, 8–10, 21, 25–31, 62, 64, 89, 90, 101, 137, 147, 155–158, 209, 224nn2–3, 224n5, 253, 258, 270
  unhealthy, 33t, 40, 45, 49, 54, 208
  unplanned, 33, 33t, 50, 53, 54, 56, 208 (*see also* Infrastructure)
Conservancy lanes, 48
Conservancy tax (kachara terige), 46
Constellation, xii, 15, 16, 18, 20–23, 65, 89, 171, 173, 177, 202, 203, 205–209, 213–215, 218–220, 242n7, 254, 260, 263
  automobility, 15, 16, 18, 20, 22, 23, 65, 171, 173, 202, 203, 205–209, 213–215, 219, 220, 242n7
  political (*see under* Political)
  technopolitical, 23, 65, 202, 207, 213, 219

Contagion theory, 229
Contestation, 20, 72, 73, 79, 109, 139, 140, 146, 173, 176, 202, 205, 211, 218, 248, 257
  sociomaterial, 211
Corporate elite, 56, 84, 101, 134, 135, 211, 220
Corporate-outsourced NGOs (CONGOs), 59
Corporate task forces, 87, 89. *See* Megaprojects
Councillors, 104, 197
Counterstatement, 174–176
CRS water works, 52
Cubbon, Mark Sir, 38
Cubbon Park, 44, 147
Curb, 142, 151, 162, 165
Cutcheri, 38, 39

Deccan plateau, 32, 34
Decentralization, 20, 232n69, 249
Deconcentrate, 55
Decongest, decongesting, decongestion, xvi, 8, 9f, 10, 26, 34, 40, 48, 49, 56, 97, 101, 107, 108, 110–113, 116, 120, 124, 125, 128, 129, 134, 135, 173, 208, 230n55, 238n8, 255
Dehistoricization, dehistoricizing, 29–31
Delhi, 7, 8, 9f, 70, 79, 222n5, 223n12, 224n3, 243n19, 248–250, 252, 256, 257, 262–271
Democracy, democratic, undemocratic, 52, 61, 63, 104, 146, 167, 231, 234n80, 237n1, 240n26, 250, 251, 253, 257, 258, 259, 273, 276
Democratic socialism, 231
De-script, de-scripting, de-scription, 176, 178, 202, 247
Designer, 153, 162, 171, 176, 178, 179, 202, 211, 225n19
Detailed project report (DPR), 199, 245n22

Development, developmental, developer, developmentalist, 8, 9, 15, 16, 20, 27, 29, 31, 38, 40, 41–44, 49, 49–55, 57, 58–64, 67, 69, 70, 74, 80, 82–89, 99, 101, 102, 105–109, 111–113, 115, 120, 124, 129, 130, 133–135, 144, 146–148, 174, 176, 177, 179, 182, 199, 202, 208, 228n37, 231n61, 232n64, 232n66, 232n69, 233n75, 234n83, 235n86, 236n14, 238nn10–12, 239n15, 241n3, 242n6, 247–251, 255
  machine, 228n37 (*see also* Mysore)
  plan, 51, 62, 234n83, 263
  regime, 41, 42, 208, 262
Dewan, 19, 40, 41, 43, 44, 199, 229, 271. *See also* Mysore
Directorate of Urban Land Transport, 27, 129
Dirigiste, 233n71
Disorderly congestion, 33t, 34, 38, 208. *See also* Congestion
Displacement, 22, 56, 125, 127, 171, 176, 190, 197, 235n5, 276
Double Road flyover, 99, 234n82
Down-ramp, 181, 183, 184, 190, 194
Drain, drainage, xiii, 33, 46–48, 120, 151, 152, 169, 173, 181, 182, 190, 198
Dystopia, 5–7, 23, 222n4, 253, 255, 262, 266

East India Company, 227n32
Economy, x, 1, 36, 50, 51, 58, 70, 73, 105, 118, 144, 179, 233n71, 233n75, 235n5, 249, 251, 257, 260, 262, 265, 267, 271, 274, 275
Education, educational, 7, 16, 19, 41–44, 61, 69, 91, 93, 127, 129, 145, 155, 216, 217, 223n16, 228n42, 229n42, 231n61, 275
Electric, electrical, electricity, 6, 42, 44, 52, 59, 70, 169, 182, 228n40, 231n61, 232n65

Electronic City, 59, 114f
Elevated road, 87, 103, 111, 149, 151, 173, 179–182, 194, 197, 211
Elites, 10, 16, 35, 42, 43, 49, 69, 76, 84, 97, 101, 118, 130, 134, 135, 193, 208, 211, 220, 223n16, 224n15, 228n37
Encroachment, 27, 200t, 224n12
Energy, 47, 63, 69, 142, 144, 170, 177, 178–179, 202, 211, 212, 235n5, 241n4, 275. *See also* Rhythm
Engineering, 28, 30, 31, 42–44, 57, 65, 112, 118, 120, 225n21, 226n26, 230n49, 237n8, 261
Engineers, 41, 43, 46, 49, 71, 114, 183, 202, 211, 214
English, 36, 37, 41, 155, 156, 160, 205, 221n2, 222n2, 248
Environment Support Group, 117, 125, 127, 253. *See also* Bengaluru *Janara Vedike*
Epidemic, epidemiology, 46–48, 229nn46–47, 229n49, 230n49
  bubonic, 47
  cholera, 229n47, 230nn49–50, 248
  influenza, 230n52
  plague, 47–49, 230nn52–53, 230n55, 230n57
  typhoid, 229n47
Europe, European, 5, 29, 30, 37, 41, 139, 207, 227n31, 228n36, 229n46, 230n50, 245n20, 252, 258, 270, 271
Expressway, 5, 10, 33t, 87, 112–114, 117, 180, 216, 238

Facebook, 18, 67, 155, 156, 158, 253
Fencing, 153, 161, 162, 163f, 165, 185, 236n10
Fernandes, Leo, 117
Film, 1–3, 49, 99, 221n1, 237n1, 266
Flooding, 25, 28, 32, 47, 64, 70, 193, 194, 199, 230n51, 244n10
Floor Area Ratio (FAR), 55

Flows, xi, 8, 27, 28, 33t, 46, 48, 57, 64, 68, 77, 85, 101, 102, 105, 108, 109, 142, 143, 145, 158, 162, 178–183, 188, 190, 191, 197, 198, 200–202, 209, 211, 212, 230n51, 259, 270
  infrastructure, 209
  metabolic, 46, 48, 57
  traffic, 8, 28, 178, 183
Flyover, 2–4, 10, 11, 27, 33t, 67, 82, 84, 85, 87, 88f, 90, 99, 100, 100f, 101, 113, 115, 115f, 117, 137, 173, 174, 180, 182, 190, 195, 205, 206, 210, 216, 222n4, 234n82, 235nn1–2, 236n11, 237n2, 242nn9–11, 244n10, 244n15, 245n1, 264. *See also* Megaprojects
  segmented arch, 67, 112, 112f, 132
FM radio stations, 18
Friction, 179, 202, 244n9, 251, 270

Garment workers, 28, 125, 224n14
Global, xi, 11, 16, 20, 22, 25, 33, 58, 59, 63, 64, 73, 81, 84, 86, 88, 105, 108, 109, 116, 118, 123, 124, 133t, 134, 135, 145, 202, 207, 209, 222n2, 224n3, 226n24, 234n78, 235n5, 241n1, 248–250, 254, 256–259, 262, 265–267, 270, 271, 273–275
Globalization, globalized, 33, 58, 63, 73, 81, 105, 118, 235n5, 248, 254, 256, 265, 273–275
Global South, 16, 20, 22, 109, 207
Google Maps, 18, 19f, 223
Government–civil society partnerships, 20
Government of India, 9f, 40, 80t, 90, 106, 228nn37–38, 255, 263, 264
Government of Karnataka, 18, 44, 47, 48, 53, 64, 67, 85, 88, 90, 104, 111, 120, 124, 182, 193, 197, 200t, 201, 225n22, 228n36, 229n42, 231n63, 232n69, 238nn9–10, 239n14, 245n2, 251, 255, 270

Grade separator, 30, 62, 84, 87, 99, 101, 111–113, 115f, 147, 148, 234n82, 242n8
Green belts, 33t, 54
Growth boundaries, 54, 232n69
Growth poles, 54, 232n69

Hampi, 35
Hasiru Usiru (HU), xiv, 124, 125, 127, 128f, 129, 167, 219, 243n19, 256. See Bengaluru *Janara Vedike*
High-mobility corridors, 90. *See also* Agenda for Bengaluru Infrastructure Development; Mobility: urban; Technomanagerial
Highway, xi, 30, 31, 64, 74, 82, 87, 144, 225n20, 235n85
Hindu, Hinduism, 45, 182, 191, 193, 197, 198, 244n13, 245n20
Hindustan Aircraft Ltd., 51
Hindustan Machine Tools, 51
Historicization, 226n24
History Manifesto, 226n24, 256
Horse, 6, 29, 225n16, 262, 263
Hoysalas, 34
Human agency, 141, 175
Human-nonhuman symmetry, 175
Hydrological infrastructure, 47
Hygiene, 47, 53

Illegal, illegality, 28, 33 t, 52, 55, 56, 71, 99, 125, 138, 209, 233n70, 267
Immobilities, immobility, immobilization, immobilize, 22, 107, 139, 143, 155, 156, 165
Indian, iii, xi, xii, 4–7, 9–11, 14–16, 20, 23, 41, 43, 49, 51, 57, 58, 61, 68–71, 73, 77–81, 85, 88, 96, 99, 102, 107, 115f, 116f, 117f, 123, 145, 146, 167, 169, 221, 223n16, 224n9, 224n11, 227nn31–33, 228nn36–37, 229n47, 231n61, 233n71, 235n2, 235n4, 236n8, 236n13, 236n15, 237n16, 237n18, 237nn1–3, 238n12, 239n17, 240n23, 242n6, 243n1, 248, 249, 251, 252, 255, 256, 258, 259, 260, 261–268, 270, 276
  modernity, 14
  roads, 4, 6, 10, 14, 23, 78, 96
  society, 14, 69, 223n16, 227n33
  (*see also* City)
Indian Institute of Research, 43
Indian Telephone Industries, 51
Industrial, Industrialization, industrializing, xi, 11, 19, 33 t, 41–44, 47, 50–55, 70, 81, 105, 182, 191, 198, 214, 222n4, 228n41, 231n58, 231nn60–62, 232n69, 233n71, 248, 253, 265, 273, 274
Industry, industries, 1, 17, 42, 43, 50, 51, 57–61, 63, 69, 72, 83, 84, 87, 88, 106, 114, 118, 119, 123, 169, 179, 214, 223n11, 229n45, 231n60, 233nn72–74, 234n78, 239n15, 239n17, 265, 270, 271, 273, 274, 275
  biotechnology, 17, 179
  information technology, 17, 179
Information and communication technology (ICT), 57
Infrastructure, x, xvi, 5, 10, 15, 16, 20–22, 25, 27, 31, 33t, 34, 47, 50, 53, 57–73, 75, 76, 81–91, 96, 99–116, 116f, 117, 117f, 118, 120, 123, 124, 127, 128, 130, 132, 133, 133 t, 134, 135, 142, 143, 146–148, 153, 166–171, 174, 176, 178–180, 197–202, 206, 209–211, 215, 216, 218–220, 222n4, 233n74, 234n78, 235n86, 235n4, 236nn13–14, 237n16, 238nn10–12, 238n14, 239n15, 245n16, 245n3, 246n3, 247, 251, 253–256, 260, 262–264, 267, 269. *See also* Congestion: discourse on
  artifacts, 71, 110, 113, 146, 210
  of automobility, 21, 22, 167 (*see also* City; Political society; Regime: sociotechnical; Urban)

bimodal system, 71
decongesting, 101, 110, 128
inadequacy, 82, 83, 86–88, 209
landscape of automobility, 21, 202
material, 10, 14, 109, 117, 219
mega-infrastructure investments, 68, 87
supply-oriented, 10
Infrastructure Development Corporation of Karnataka (iDeCK), 63
Infrastructurescape, vii, 21, 23, 97, 99, 100, 101, 103, 105, 107–111, 113–115, 117–119, 121, 123–125, 127–132, 132f, 133, 133t, 134, 135, 210, 213, 215–218, 237n8, 238n8, 238n10. *See also* Infrastructure
decongestion, 97, 108, 110, 238n8
governmental scape, 122
grassroots, 210, 216, 218
normative orientation, 133t, 134, 216
organizational principle, 129, 130, 133t, 216
perspectival approach, 107, 108
technological sensibility, 109, 110, 113, 122, 129, 130, 132, 133, 133t, 135, 217
Instrumentalization, instrumentalized, 29, 226n24
International Tech Park Limited (ITPL), 92
Intersection, 1–3, 13, 30, 32, 62, 80, 83, 85, 109, 111, 133, 148, 149, 151–153, 156, 158, 160, 162, 165, 173, 176, 179, 180, 182, 185, 188, 190, 242n11
IT corridor, 59, 63
IT Corridor Planning Authority, 235n86
IT industry, 57, 60, 61, 63, 83, 87, 88, 233nn72–74, 234n78. *See also* Bengaluru; Silicon Valley of India; Software

Janaagraha, 61, 105, 106, 118, 119, 160, 234n80, 237n6, 239n17, 239n19, 243n14, 259. *See also* Ramanathan, Ramesh
Jana Urban Space Foundation (JUSF), 120, 239n19, 258
Janara Pranalike, 125, 126f, 129, 249. *See also* People's Manifesto
Jawaharlal Nehru National Urban Renewal Mission (JNNURM), 61, 101, 103f, 255
Jayanagar, 138f, 224n10
Junction, 7, 8, 82, 120, 148, 165, 170, 171, 180, 182, 183, 185–191, 211, 242n11, 264, 269

Kannada, 36, 49, 50, 99, 124, 125, 171, 221n2, 224n3, 231n59, 237n1, 238n9, 240n26, 242n8, 264
Karanjis, 46
Karnataka, 16, 17f, 18, 20, 27, 28, 34, 44, 47, 48, 51–53, 61–64, 67, 70, 82, 84–86, 90, 99, 104, 111, 115, 120, 124, 147, 158, 182, 193, 197, 198, 200t, 201, 225n22, 228n36, 229n42, 231n59, 232n69, 233n70, 234n79, 238n9, 239n14, 240n25, 242n12, 245n20, 245n1, 245n2, 248, 251, 252, 255, 260, 264, 265, 267–270
Karnataka Housing Board, 53
Karnataka Industrial Area Development Board, 53
Karnataka Industrial Investment and Development Corporation, 53
Karnataka Slum Clearance Board, 53
Karnataka State Road Transport Corporation, 53
Karnataka Town and Country Planning Act (KTCP), 51, 255
Karnataka Urban Infrastructure Development and Finance Corporation (KUIDFC), 27, 61, 63, 99, 267
Kempegowda, 32, 35, 225n22

KIMCO junction, 180, 182, 183, 185, 186, 187f, 188, 189f
Krishna, SM, 60, 84, 171, 233n77, 265. *See also* Chief Minister

Land categorization, 52, 54, 55
Landscape(s), 15, 16, 20, 21, 22, 36, 57, 58, 60, 68, 71, 72, 76, 97, 99, 101, 104, 107–109, 134, 135, 160, 161, 168, 193, 202, 207, 208, 210, 211, 212, 215, 216, 234n80, 237n7, 243n5, 249, 253, 274
Land use, 5, 27, 28, 34, 51, 53–56, 63, 70, 209, 225n21, 227n29, 233n70, 235n86, 269
Leader, leadership, 20, 58–60, 62, 81, 106, 111, 114, 115, 117, 118, 133, 135, 144, 145, 158, 193, 198, 199, 205, 235n1, 236n13, 237n19, 245n20, 258, 263
Lefebvrian rhythm analysis, 183, 190. *See also* Rhythmanalysis
Legal, legally, ix, 51, 53, 55, 64, 70, 71, 139, 140, 141, 163, 167, 175, 198, 231n62, 232n64, 233n70, 235n1, 241n3, 244n15, 245n22, 267
Lock-in, 214, 216
Longue-durée, 208, 226n24

Mahesh, Ashwin, 19, 118, 120, 123, 255
Majestic, 28
Malleshwaram, 48, 49, 127, 230n56, 231n57
Manifesto(s), 16, 102, 109, 110, 111, 125, 126f, 128, 129, 130, 133, 210, 226n24, 234n80, 240n27, 249, 256. *See also* Bengaluru *Janara Vedike*; *Janara Pranalike*; People's Manifesto
Man-made lakes, 27. *See also* Tanks
Market, 1, 2f, 3–5, 11, 15, 23, 26, 29, 32, 34, 57, 58, 92f, 120, 145, 170, 173, 222n3, 227n29, 234n84, 236n14, 243n4

Master Plan, master planning, 27, 33 t, 51, 70, 231n64, 232n69, 248
Material agency, 174, 175
Materialization, materialized, 38, 39, 40, 143, 208
Material participation, 142, 143, 262
Material publics, 22
Media, 3, 17, 18, 20, 22, 26, 41, 49, 58, 61, 64, 67, 83, 84, 87–89, 110, 111, 117, 119, 135, 137, 139, 145, 146, 147, 155–160, 162, 179, 205, 211, 215, 216, 219, 235n2, 238n12, 242n13, 250, 266. *See also* Social: media
Median, 100, 153, 156, 158, 159f, 161, 162, 170, 171, 185, 186, 188, 190
Mega cities, 61, 62, 85, 207
Mega Cities scheme, 61, 62, 84, 85, 86, 99
Mega-infrastructure, 67, 68, 84, 85, 86, 87, 96, 132, 148, 153, 211
Megaprojects, 82, 84, 86, 90, 113, 216, 253
 infrastructure projects, 61–64, 67, 85–87, 96, 102, 132, 148, 153, 200, 211, 215, 234n84, 236n14, 238n12
Mega City Scheme, 84, 85, 86
Mysore Road flyover, 85
 private financing, 236n14
 super bureaucrats, 86, 87, 96
Mekhri grade separator, 234n82
Metabolic flow, 46, 48, 57
Metro, 87, 90, 91, 113, 118, 120, 147, 148, 149, 151, 153, 154f, 185, 188, 216, 249. *See also* Megaprojects; Traffic and transit management centers
Metropolitan, metropolitanization, xi, 7, 8, 15, 51, 54, 68, 70, 90, 119, 122, 181, 193, 232n65, 232n69, 237n5, 238n11, 244n14, 249, 255, 258
 city, cities, xi, 1, 9, 16, 18, 54, 222n3, 260

Index

India, 1, 8, 15, 18
region structure plan, 54, 232n69, 255
MG Road, 169, 171. *See also* Road
Middle class, 14, 15, 28, 50, 55, 56, 58, 64, 72, 73, 78, 84, 88, 94, 95, 105, 106, 107, 118, 134, 135, 145, 146, 147, 155, 160, 179, 205, 206, 209, 210, 216, 222n2, 233nn75–76, 234n80, 253, 260, 265, 270
See also Automobiles: middle-class aspirations; Congestion
activists, 105 (*see* Janaagraha; Ramanathan, Ramesh)
aesthetics, 33t, 58, 78, 209, 233n75
newly renovated citizens, 105
Military, 34, 35, 36, 38, 45, 46, 47, 48, 49, 50, 221n2, 227n31, 228n36, 228n39, 229n47, 230nn49–50, 256
Ministry of Urban Development, 8, 9f
Mobilities, x, xvi, 12, 91, 101, 107, 109, 110, 142, 143, 177, 178, 213, 219, 220, 251, 252, 255, 256, 259, 268, 275
mobilities turn, 109, 142
Mobility, iii, x, xi, xv, 1, 3, 5, 11–13, 15, 20–22, 28, 29, 31, 32, 62, 68, 69, 81, 82, 87, 89–91, 93, 95, 96, 99–102, 107–109, 114, 125, 129, 130, 132, 134, 135, 138, 142–144, 148, 151, 153, 177, 179, 203, 206, 209–211, 214–216, 218, 220, 222n4, 240n29, 242n7, 249, 251, 256, 259, 260, 268, 276
equitable constellation, 21
low-carbon, 21, 22, 203, 259
marginalization, 216
personal, 93
public sphere, 12
regime, xi, 13, 21, 215, 216
social, 15, 93, 155
urban, 1, 15, 21, 22, 29, 31, 68, 89, 95, 206, 207, 210, 216, 259 (*see also* Agenda for Bengaluru Infrastructure Development; High-mobility corridors; Technomanagerial)
Mobility studies, 108, 134, 144, 179
Mobilization, mobilized, mobilizers, 4, 67, 70, 72, 75, 105, 110, 113, 124, 127–129, 134, 174, 205, 206, 215, 216, 219, 225n21, 238n10, 240n26, 240n28
Model State, 228n37. *See also under* Mysore
Modernity, modernist, 7, 14, 64, 78, 79, 143, 201, 241n5, 248, 249, 250, 254, 257
Monsoon, 28, 191, 199–201
Moral, 42, 47, 72, 141, 145, 175, 198, 199, 241, 245
Moses, Robert, 31, 236n6
Wantagh Parkway (Long Island), 74
Motorization, 6, 11, 22, 29, 80, 80t, 96, 97, 101, 143, 210, 222n4
Motor vehicles, 3, 4, 6, 8–11, 15, 27, 80, 80t, 89, 90, 130, 137, 153, 210
Mumbai, 8, 222n6, 223n7, 223n12, 247, 256, 271
Municipal, municipalities, municipality, 20, 39, 44–48, 77, 84, 102–106, 193, 194, 228n36, 228n40, 229n46, 230n50, 234n80, 243n19, 244n14, 268
elections, 104, 193, 234n80
scavenger, 46
sweeper, 230n50
Municipalization, 33t, 39, 40, 47, 69, 208
Murthy, N R Narayana, 58, 60, 106, 236n13
Mysore, 33t, 36, 37f, 39, 41–52, 63, 70, 181–183, 190, 195, 227n33, 228n35, 228nn37–38, 229n45, 230n53, 231n59, 232n67, 235n86, 238n14, 255, 256, 257, 258, 262, 264, 267, 270, 271
Economic Conference, 44, 229n45

Mysore (*continued*)
  Industrial and Testing Laboratory, 44
  Legislative Council, 229n44
  model state, 228n37
  Representative Assembly, 44, 229n44
  University of Mysore, 41, 43, 228n42
  (*See also* Dewan; British; Wodeyar, Chamarajendra, X; Wadiyar, Krishnaraja)
Mysore kingdom, 18–20, 36, 38, 40–43, 46, 199, 208, 228n37, 229n44, 231n59, 245n20
Mysore road. *See under* Road
Mysore road bus terminal, 181, 182
Mysore road flyover, 1–2, 84, 85, 99, 195, 234n82, 242n9

Namma Bengaluru (NB), 110, 124, 130, 133t. *See also* Infrastructurescape
Nandi Infrastructure Corridor Enterprise (NICE), 113
National identity, 14, 212, 252, 257
Native, 33, 33t, 35–39, 45–47, 49, 69, 208, 221n2, 227n31, 228n37, 229n47, 230n50
Nayandahalli interchange, 148, 149f, 150f, 152f, 211, 242n10
Nehru, Jawaharlal, 61, 101, 231n58, 250, 255
Neoliberalism, 13, 249, 271
New Public Management, 232n68, 252
Nilekani, Nandan, 19, 58
Nonhumans, 141, 175, 176, 178, 179, 200, 201, 218, 221, 241n2, 243n6, 247
Nonmotorized, 22, 23, 29, 62, 68, 81, 101, 151, 153, 162, 164–166, 186
Non-Western, 96, 213

Ontology, x, 109, 141
Outer Ring Road. *See under* Road
Outline development plan (ODP), 51
Overcrowded, overcrowding, 7, 33, 45, 48, 94, 95, 226n26

Palayam, 35
Palegars, 227n28
Parastatal, 33t, 52, 53, 63, 104, 105, 111, 114, 115, 116, 118, 123, 197, 198, 208, 235n86, 238n11, 239n15, 249
Parking, 7, 26, 27, 55, 104, 125, 153, 160, 162–165, 195, 222n5, 223n1, 224n2, 243nn17–18
Partnership, 1, 20, 33 t, 61, 63, 76, 105, 106, 118, 122–124, 128, 129, 132, 133t, 209, 210, 234n84, 254, 255, 259
Pavement, 78, 118, 120, 147, 152, 153, 161, 162, 164, 165
  tiles, 161, 165
Pedestrian, pedestrianism, 2, 3, 6, 7, 12, 15, 23, 29, 30, 35, 45, 81, 90, 96, 120, 139, 147, 151, 153, 159, 160, 162, 164–169, 186, 188, 190, 202, 203, 211, 218, 219, 220, 225n17, 236n10, 240n30, 243n16, 246n4, 248, 256, 265
People's Manifesto, 125, 126f, 129, 133, 210, 240n27, 249. *See also Janara Pranalike*
Performative, 22, 78, 143, 146, 174, 175, 176, 178, 243nn5–6
Periodize, periodization, 21, 32, 33, 33t, 34, 65, 226n24
Peté (petteh), 1, 32–36, 38–40, 45, 208, 227nn29–30, 228n36, 229n47
Pillar, 147–149, 151, 185, 186, 191, 192f
Plague, 47–49, 230n52, 230n53, 230n55, 230n57, 268–270
Plan Bengaluru, 2020, 60, 89, 118, 120, 247
Planned, planning, 13, 15, 20, 27, 30, 31, 33, 33t, 35, 47, 48, 49, 50–56, 59–61, 63, 67, 69, 70, 71, 80, 81, 82, 84, 89, 102, 115, 118, 120, 123, 134, 197, 205, 208, 212, 218, 219, 223n10, 225n20, 230n57, 231n58,

232nn65–66, 232n69, 233n70, 235n86, 238n12, 239nn18–19, 239n21, 244n9, 247, 248, 250–253, 255–257, 263, 265, 268, 269, 273, 274
"car windshield view," 81
pedestrian fencing, 153, 162, 165, 236n10
planning framework, 54, 80
Urban Development Policy (Karnataka state), 82, 270
Plot, 55
Policy circuit, 59, 101, 104, 105
Policy regime, 214, 260
Political, xi, 1, 4, 10–13, 15, 16, 19–23, 28, 30–34, 38, 40–42, 49, 52, 58, 59, 63, 65, 68–77, 82, 84, 95–97, 101, 104, 106, 108, 109, 111, 114, 115, 117, 118, 124, 128–130, 132, 133, 133t, 134, 135, 139, 140–146, 148, 155–158, 167, 168, 171, 173–175, 178, 193, 197–200, 202, 207–209, 211, 212, 214–216, 218–220, 221n2, 225n15, 227n31, 228n37, 233n71, 234n80, 237n1, 238nn9–10, 240n26, 241nn3–4, 244n15, 245n20, 247–252, 254, 255, 257, 259, 260, 262–271
autonomy, 40, 41
community, 139, 140, 141, 168
constellation, 15, 16, 18, 20, 22, 171, 202, 215, 219, 220
participation, 140–143
society, 70–72, 77, 96, 104, 124 (*see also* Infrastructure: bimodal system; Sociotechnical: footprints)
theory, 141, 241n3
valences, 73, 209, 211
Politics, iii, x, xi, xvi, 12–14, 20, 40, 47, 68, 72–74, 76, 77, 95, 104, 107, 109, 141, 142, 146, 179, 193, 199, 201, 210, 212–215, 235n3, 237n1, 240n26, 246n4, 248–257, 259, 260, 262–269, 271, 273–276

of automobility, 206
of belonging, 219
of hope, 205, 206
Postcolonial, 14, 50, 68, 144, 223n11, 245n20, 247, 248, 252, 253
Posthumanist, posthumanistic, 22, 174, 175, 241n3, 243n6, 248
Postindependence, 16, 96
Post-liberalization, post-liberalized, 57, 145
Praja, 125, 128, 129, 240n31. *See also* Citizen
Precolonial, 1, 16, 39, 208, 221n2, 224n12, 227n29
Premji, Azim, 58, 60
Privatization, 234n84, 275
Privilege, privileged, vii, 19, 21, 31, 50, 68, 75, 78, 91, 99, 101, 105, 107, 109, 111, 113, 115, 117, 118, 119, 121, 124, 125, 127, 128, 129, 131, 133, 134, 135, 139, 145, 146, 147, 155, 183, 202, 205, 210, 215, 217, 218, 220
ecosystem, 19
networks of, 19, 20, 123
structure, 19, 123
Proselytize, proselytization, 133t, 134, 135
Public, 1, 5, 8, 12, 19, 25, 26, 39, 42, 44, 50, 53, 56–61, 64, 67, 68, 70, 72, 74, 77, 78, 82–86, 88, 91, 100, 104, 110, 113, 118, 125, 127, 128, 133–135, 138, 139, 141–143, 145–147, 149, 158, 165, 168, 173, 179, 182, 197, 198, 205, 206, 210, 211, 213, 215, 216, 217f, 226n24, 226n26, 228n35, 233n74, 237n1, 239n21, 241n5, 242n13, 243n5, 245n2, 247, 250, 252–254, 257, 258, 260–264, 268, 274
administration/administrative, 38, 39, 52, 53, 252
eye, 160, 161
health, 46, 61, 91, 229n49, 230n49, 254

Public (*continued*)
  history, 226n24, 260
  management, 40, 54, 145, 232n68, 238n11, 252, 257
  policy, 10, 28, 225n21, 255
  public–private partnership, 33t, 59, 63, 76, 209, 234n84, 254, 259
  public works department (PWD), 44, 46, 200, 239n15
  sector enterprises, 16, 50, 51, 57, 232n69
  transport/transportation, 27, 31, 59, 62, 70, 80, 84, 94, 95, 125, 130, 216, 223n1, 232n65, 260
Publics, 22, 135, 139, 142, 144, 253, 262, 263
Purification, 201
Push-cart/pushcart vendor, 151, 162, 202, 211

Rajadharma, 199, 200, 245n20, 258
Rajajinagar, 127, 231n60
Ramanathan, Ramesh, 19, 105, 106, 118, 234n80, 239n19. *See also* Janaagraha
Ramp, 164, 181, 182, 183, 184f, 190, 194, 195, 195f, 196, 196f
Raya, Achyuta, 32
Regime, xi, 13, 41, 42, 43, 47, 68, 69, 76, 77, 79, 80, 81, 82, 84, 89, 95, 96, 97, 168, 202, 208, 210, 212, 214, 216, 235nn3–4, 241n1, 252, 256, 260, 261, 262, 269, 271
  of congestion, vii, 21, 23, 67–69, 71, 73, 75, 77, 79, 81, 83–85, 87, 89, 90, 91, 93, 95–97, 148, 203, 210, 213, 214, 215, 216, 236n11 (*see also* Congestion; Automobilization; Silicon Valley of India)
  Euro-American history, 68
  hybrid entity, 79, 96
  of mobility, 215, 216

sociotechnical, 76, 214
  technopolitical, 65, 68, 73, 75, 76, 77, 95, 96, 209 (*see also* Technopolitical regimes; *see also under* Congestion)
Relational materiality, 241n2
Religiosity, 173, 193, 197, 200
Research, 11, 14, 15, 22, 26, 41, 42, 43, 106, 107, 125, 134, 142, 174, 178, 198, 207, 212, 223n11, 251, 254, 255, 257, 259–263, 265, 268, 270, 271
Residency road. *See* Road
Resident, 36
Residential associations, 127
Residues, 21, 33, 33 t, 34, 47, 49, 65, 173, 179, 199, 201, 208, 209, 227n29, 230n51
Rhythm, rhythmic, 6, 78, 85, 174, 176, 177–179, 182, 183, 185, 186, 188, 190, 191, 193, 197, 201, 217, 230n51, 251, 252
  hydrological, 190
  institutional, 182, 190
  religious, religiosity, 193
  riparian, 191
  social, 182, 190
Rhythmanalysis, 22, 177, 183, 190, 262
Right to walk, 167, 219
River. *See* Cauvery River; Vrishabhavathi River
Road, ix, 1–10, 12–15, 17, 18, 22, 25–31, 35, 45, 48, 49, 53, 60–62, 64, 65, 67, 68, 72, 75, 77, 79, 81–83, 85, 87–90, 93, 96, 99–101, 103, 104, 106–108, 113, 114f, 118, 120, 122–125, 127, 129, 130, 133–135, 137, 138, 143, 146–148, 148f, 149, 151, 153, 155–167, 169, 170, 170f, 171–173, 180, 182, 183, 185, 186, 188, 190, 194, 195, 200, 207, 210–212, 219, 222n4, 223n14, 224n5, 225n18, 226n26, 236n10, 236n12, 237n7,

238n14, 239n22, 240n30, 242n8, 242n11, 243n16, 243nn1–3, 245n17, 247, 250, 253, 255, 256, 257, 261, 269, 270
Bellary, 112, 112f, 113, 239n22
Chord, 181–183, 185, 186, 188, 190, 191, 196
Commercial street, 37
Design, designer, redesign, 5, 30, 31, 60, 101, 118, 120, 123, 133, 162, 164, 169, 190, 191, 194, 197, 210, 211, 212, 219, 243n1
elevated, 87, 103, 111, 149, 151, 173, 179, 180, 181, 182, 194, 211
Hosur, 156, 162, 170, 171, 239n22
Indian, 4, 6, 10, 14, 23, 78, 96
infrastructure development, 15
MG road, 169, 171
Mysore, 1–2, 84, 85, 99, 148, 151, 180–183, 185, 186, 188, 190, 191, 194, 195, 195f, 196, 196f, 197, 234n82, 239n22, 242n9, 244n15, 245n19
Nayandahalli interchange (*see* Nayandahalli interchange)
orbital ring roads, 111, 113
Outer Ring road (ORR), 84, 104, 112, 113, 120, 148, 151, 158, 163, 164, 234n82, 242n9 (*see also* Expressway; Nayandahalli interchange)
Residency, 169
signs, 14
space, 3, 4, 5, 9, 29, 30, 68, 83, 89, 120, 146–149, 151, 153, 155, 158, 160, 161, 163, 165, 166, 168, 205
spatial partitioning, 5
Vittal Mallya (VM), 118, 120, 121f, 122
widening, 10, 85, 87, 104, 107, 125, 127, 253 (*see also* T-junction)
Roadway, 4, 67, 151, 153, 162, 165, 166, 181, 185, 191
Rotary, 180f, 183, 185, 190, 191, 195, 196, 199

Sanitary, 49, 198, 229n48, 268, 269
  commissioners, 229n49
  department, 46
  engineers/engineering, 46, 230n49
  water drains, 33t, 47, 198, 230n51
Sanitation, 16, 47–49, 70, 230n49, 254, 263
Sarkarada Bengaluru (SB), 110, 111, 130, 133, 133t. *See also* Infrastructurescape
Satellite cities/townships, 33t, 54, 232n69
Scape, xvi, 14, 71, 108–111, 113, 114–116, 118–120, 122, 124, 125, 128–130, 132–135, 162, 217, 218, 220, 238n9, 240n27, 251, 255, 267
Science and technology, 42, 43, 142, 229n46, 247, 248, 251, 257, 258, 265, 269
Science and Technology Studies (STS), 21, 68, 73, 144, 168, 174, 251, 253,
Scientific, scientifically, ix, 29, 41–44, 50, 71, 144, 176, 208, 225n18, 229n46, 241n5, 243n5, 252, 258, 266, 270
Sedimentation, 191, 192f
Selfie, 160
Settlement, 1, 32, 35, 36, 37, 39, 46, 53, 54, 56, 69, 70, 71, 92, 93, 208, 221n2, 222n4, 225n22, 273
Sewage, 47, 169, 181, 193, 198, 274
Sewerage network, 45
Siddharamaiah, S, 115, 147
Sidewalk, 3, 56, 70, 138, 139, 142, 147, 151, 154f, 160, 162, 164–166, 166f, 169, 170, 185, 215, 274
Signal-free, 10, 90, 112, 147, 148, 180, 182, 191, 211, 242n8
Signal-free corridor, 27, 67, 85, 87, 112, 113, 125, 180. *See also* Steel Flyover
Signalized, 30
Signboard, 171, 172f, 173

Silicon Valley of India (India's Silicon Valley), 57, 61, 64, 81, 82, 233n73, 265, 267, 269. *See also* Regime: of congestion
Siltation, 191, 199. *See also* Vrishabhavathi River
Social, socialized, 1, 2f, 5, 6, 7, 11–20, 22, 29, 31, 32, 34, 39, 40, 42–45, 47, 49, 52–55, 58, 60, 65, 67, 71, 74, 75, 78, 80, 85, 93, 94, 97, 101, 102, 104, 107–110, 114, 118, 122–124, 129–130, 132–135, 139–143, 145, 146, 155, 156, 161, 174, 177, 178, 182, 190, 197, 199, 200, 201, 206, 208, 213, 215, 216, 218, 219, 220, 222n4, 225n15, 225n19, 227n31, 230n55, 233n75, 234n83, 236n7, 237n1, 238n9, 239n19, 240nn25–26, 241n2, 244n8, 247–249, 252, 254, 255, 257–261, 265, 266, 270, 271
justice, 129, 134, 218, 274, 275
media, 18, 20, 22, 67, 137, 139, 147, 155–160, 205, 211, 215, 219, 242
Socialism, socialist, 50, 128, 231n58
Socioeconomic, 16, 41, 44, 63, 69, 142
Sociomaterial, sociomateriality, 108, 142, 176, 179, 207, 211, 218, 244n8, 265. *See also* Contestation
Sociospatial, socio-spatial, 32, 33 t, 48, 71, 76, 139, 209, 240n26
Sociotechnical, socio-technical, 1, 16, 71, 76, 109, 110, 130, 132f, 135, 143, 146, 212, 214, 237n8, 247, 252, 254, 257, 259, 261, 268, 271
ensemble, 75, 139
footprints, 71
orders, 96, 236n7
Software, 26, 57, 58, 106, 233n72, 265, 270
Software glass, 58
South India, xii, 16, 32, 36, 198, 226n27, 227n28, 229n49, 231n61,
237n1, 248, 250, 252, 254, 256, 263, 266
Spatio-temporal, 178
Special-purpose vehicles, 33t, 63, 209, 235n85
Sreenivasa, Vinay, 91, 92, 94, 113. *See also* Bengaluru Bus Commuter Forum
Stakeholder, 59, 60, 84, 106, 118, 200
Steel Flyover, 67, 205, 206, 216, 235, 245, 264
Steward, stewarding, 115, 116, 117, 118
Stewardship, 115, 128, 130, 133t
Stone bollards, 120, 130, 131f, 133, 135, 217, 218
Storm water, 27, 47, 198, 244n10
Stormwater drainage/drains, 47, 120, 151, 152, 169, 181
Street, iii, 1–9, 11–13, 17, 21, 23, 26, 28–31, 35, 37, 38, 45, 46, 58, 60, 64, 65, 67, 68, 70, 71, 77–81, 85, 93, 95, 96, 118, 120, 130, 131f, 132, 134, 135, 137, 138, 147, 149f, 156, 159, 161, 166, 167, 170, 171, 173, 179, 183, 202, 203, 206, 207, 210, 211, 213–220, 223n10, 224n15, 225n17, 231n62, 236n9, 240n29, 242n14, 247, 248, 252, 253, 258, 263, 271, 273, 276
Indian, 4, 5, 7, 15, 77–79, 81, 248, 252, 276
space, 5, 6, 21, 68, 77, 80, 81, 202, 206, 215, 218
street-side artifacts, 22, 139
street-side fencing, 161, 162
Western, 7, 78
Streetscape, 3, 13, 79, 129, 130, 171, 178
autonormative design, 13
democratized design, 13
Structure Plan, 54, 232n69, 255
Sultan, Tipu, 227n34
Super–bureaucrats, 86, 87, 88, 89, 96, 114
Sustainable/sustainability transitions, 214, 215

Index

Tamils, 36, 171
Tanks, xiii, 27, 28, 34, 44, 46, 47, 56, 198, 224n12, 226n27, 252, 268.
  See also Stormwater drainage/drains
  Dharmambudhi, 46, 268
  Sampangi, 46
Task force, 59, 60, 84, 87, 89, 106, 114, 118, 120, 122, 171, 235n1, 239n15, 239n18, 239n21, 249, 254, 267
Technocratic, 18, 21, 63, 94, 104, 105, 111, 115, 135, 159
Technogenesis, 141
Technological, 12, 15, 16, 18, 22, 26, 28, 33, 41–43, 45, 47, 58, 65, 68, 73–76, 84, 101, 107, 109, 110, 113, 119, 122, 123, 129, 130, 132, 133, 133t, 135, 139, 142, 144–146, 160, 167, 174–176, 207–209, 212, 214, 216, 217, 219, 220, 236, 241, 247, 256, 257, 261, 270
Technological drama, 173, 175, 265
Technology, technologies, 17, 18, 21, 33, 41–43, 57, 60, 68, 72–74, 81, 112, 113, 114, 118, 123, 124, 142, 144–146, 155, 158, 161, 167, 168, 174, 176, 179, 216, 226n27, 229n46, 247, 248, 249, 251, 252, 253, 256–259, 261–265, 269–271, 274, 275
  Segmented Element, 112
  as legislation, 74, 167
  design, 73, 74, 176
Technomanagerial, 59, 239n18, 89
Technomaterial, 177, 178
Technopolitical, techno-political, xi, 16, 23, 65, 68, 73, 75–77, 87, 95, 96, 101, 202, 207, 209, 210, 213, 215, 219
Technopolitical regime, 65, 68, 73, 75, 76, 95, 96, 209
  constitution of infrastructures, 87
  diffused political agency, 76, 77
  public-private coalitions, 76
Temple, Gali Anjaneya, 182, 190, 191, 193, 194f, 196f, 199, 244nn12–13

Tender Specifications for Urban Road Execution (Tender SURE), 106, 120
Tender SURE, 106, 120, 122–124, 138, 169–171, 211, 217f, 234n81, 239n20, 243n3. *See also* Bangalore City Connect Foundation
Textile
  Bangalore Woolen, Cotton, and Silk (Binny) Mills, 42
  Maharaja of Mysore Spinning and Manufacturing Mills, 42
T-junction, 170, 171
Traffic, 1, 3–8, 9f, 10, 14, 15, 18, 19f, 21, 25, 27–31, 35, 60, 62, 64, 87, 89, 90, 99, 100, 101, 111–113, 119, 120, 130, 137, 148, 149, 151, 153, 155–157, 157f, 158–163, 165, 166, 169, 171, 173, 178, 180f, 182, 185, 186, 188, 190, 195, 196, 211, 217, 222n5, 223n7, 223n15, 224nn7–9, 224nn13–15, 225n15, 225n19, 236n10, 237n2, 239n22, 240n23, 242n11, 245n17, 248, 250, 253, 261, 263, 264, 265, 267, 270
  automotive, 29–31, 183, 185, 190
  Bangalore/Bengaluru, 18, 26, 61, 83, 106, 137, 155, 157f, 158, 209, 224, 242nn12–13, 248, 267
  blockage, 27, 28
  congestion, 5, 8, 9, 25–31, 64, 89, 90, 101, 137, 147, 155–157, 209, 224n3, 224n5, 236n12, 253, 258, 270
  control center, 8
  dystopian, 6
  enforcement, 155, 158, 160, 161, 211
  engineering, 30, 65, 120
  flow, 8, 149, 159, 178, 180f, 183, 185, 186, 195, 196, 224n2, 239n22, 242n8
  island, 186, 188
  jam, 18, 113, 156, 159, 223n14
  lights, 142, 186, 188, 190, 242n8

Traffic (*continued*)
  management, 22, 26, 29, 31, 65, 82, 91, 92, 110, 113, 139, 160, 200t, 210, 239n21, 264
  media and technology, 27, 155, 158, 161
  police, 83, 89, 137, 138f, 155, 158, 160, 161, 195, 196, 200t, 201, 242, 254
  regulations, 29
  signal, 26, 85, 100, 159
  studies, 31
  tags, 18 (*see also* Bangalore Traffic Police)
Traffic and transit management centres (TTMC), 82, 91, 92f, 113
Traffic in Towns, 31, 250, 263
Transit-Oriented Development (TOD), 80
Transport, transportation, x, 10, 25, 26, 28, 54, 55, 60, 62, 80, 82, 84, 87, 90, 91, 102, 122, 127, 130, 133, 180, 216, 219, 223n1, 224n2, 239, 242n11, 258, 261, 265, 267
Transport, transportation engineering, 31, 225n21
Transport, transportation network, 25, 223n1, 258
Transport planning, 15, 31, 80, 81, 120, 225n20, 244n9
Tweet, 138, 138f, 158, 159f
Twitter, 18, 67, 137, 138f, 155–157, 157f, 158, 159, 159f, 242, 248
Two-wheelers, 9, 165, 223n14

Underpass, underpasses, 30, 62, 67, 82, 85, 87, 88, 99, 101, 103, 103f, 107, 110, 111f, 113, 117, 130, 137, 147, 180, 238n12, 244n10
  magic-box, 111, 111f, 112, 114
United States, 29, 30, 212, 213, 225n17, 259, 274, 275
Unplanned congestion, 33, 33t, 50
Unplanned growth, 26, 33 t, 53, 54, 56, 208

Unsanitary, 46, 47
Urban, urbanism, urbanization, x, xi, xii, 1, 2, 5, 8, 9f, 10, 12, 14, 15, 18–22, 27–31, 33–35, 38–40, 43–45, 47–51, 54–56, 58–65, 67–73, 76, 77, 79, 80, 82–86, 89, 91, 96, 101–107, 110, 111, 115, 118, 119, 120, 123, 124, 127, 129, 132, 134, 135, 139, 155, 158, 159, 173, 174, 177, 179–181, 205–210, 214, 215, 217f, 218–220, 222n4, 223n9, 223n12, 224n12, 225nn19–22, 226n26, 229n46, 230n55, 231n64, 232n65, 233nn74–75, 234n80, 248, 253
  aesthetics, 233n75, 235n4, 236n7, 237n6, 238n9, 239n15, 239n19, 246n4, 248, 249, 251, 253–260, 262–271, 273–276
  agglomeration, 207, 223n12
  autocentric form, 223n9
  commuter, 101, 210
  contestations, 73 (*see* Contestation)
  highways, 225n20(chap.2)
  horse, 29
  infrastructure, x, 25, 53, 58, 76, 85, 86, 99, 104, 107, 134, 234n83, 235n4, 267
  landscape, 21, 36, 60, 71, 72, 76, 101, 104
  mobility, 1, 15, 21, 22, 29, 31, 68, 89, 95, 210, 216, 259 (*see also* Mobility; Technomanagerial)
  modernity, 7, 78
  modernization, 33
  morphology, 34
  noir urbanism, 222n4, 266
  nucleus, 36
  planning, 15, 30, 50, 239n19, 248, 253, 269, 274
  poor, 56, 61, 70, 71, 77, 91–94, 96, 124, 214, 216, 220, 239n21, 249
  settlement, 36, 39, 53, 54, 56

space, 3, 4, 34, 35, 39, 40, 47, 48, 50, 65, 70, 73, 105, 109, 120, 124, 139, 169, 208, 209, 211, 217, 239n19, 243n1, 256, 258, 275
violence, 222n4, 249
Urban Reform Incentive Fund, 62
Usable past, 32
Utopic-dystopic event horizon, 222n4

Vehicles, vehicular, 2–6, 8–11, 14, 15, 17, 18t, 27–29, 33t, 45, 63, 64, 76, 80, 82, 83, 87–91, 95, 130, 137, 138, 147, 149, 151, 153, 154f, 155, 161–164, 164f, 165, 186, 188, 195, 196, 205, 207, 209, 210, 223n14, 223n1, 226n26, 235n85, 237nn17–18, 260
Vending, vendors, 2, 3, 23, 85, 109, 139, 151, 162, 165, 167, 170, 202, 203, 210, 211, 216, 218, 220
Vijayanagara empire, 32, 34, 35, 227n28
Visvesvaraya, M, Sir, 41, 43
Vrishabhavathi/Vrishabhavathy River, 149, 153, 173, 180, 181, 181f, 182, 190, 191, 194, 197, 198, 199, 200, 230n51, 244n10
Vrishabhavathi River elevated road (VRER), 179, 180, 181, 181f, 182, 183, 184f, 185, 188, 190, 191, 192f, 193–195, 195f, 196, 196f, 197–200, 200t, 201, 202, 211, 245n22

Wadiyar, Krishnaraja, 41, 271
Waste, 22, 46, 47, 48, 49, 63, 77, 173, 178, 181, 182, 191, 192f, 197, 198, 236n8, 275
Waste   flotsam, 191, 201
Water supply, 46, 47, 52, 53, 60, 71, 72, 84, 198, 208, 230n54, 232n65, 232n67, 238n11, 247, 255, 263, 269
Western, x, 5–7, 11, 12, 14, 21, 29–31, 51, 64, 65, 68, 69, 78, 96, 107, 139, 144, 177, 207, 209, 212, 213, 223n9, 227n33, 235n4, 245n3, 247, 257

Wodeyar, Chamarajendra, X, 40
World-class city, 61, 62, 64, 68, 72, 77, 84, 88, 89, 96, 97, 130, 235n5
Worlding, 68, 267

Yediyurappa, B.S., 60, 115, 115f, 116f, 117f, 239n21. *See also* Chief Minister

Zoning, 5, 52, 55, 56. *See also* Green belts; Illegal, illegality

Urban and Industrial Environments

Series editor: Robert Gottlieb, Henry R. Luce Professor of Urban and Environmental Policy, Occidental College

Maureen Smith, *The U.S. Paper Industry and Sustainable Production: An Argument for Restructuring*

Keith Pezzoli, *Human Settlements and Planning for Ecological Sustainability: The Case of Mexico City*

Sarah Hammond Creighton, *Greening the Ivory Tower: Improving the Environmental Track Record of Universities, Colleges, and Other Institutions*

Jan Mazurek, *Making Microchips: Policy, Globalization, and Economic Restructuring in the Semiconductor Industry*

William A. Shutkin, *The Land That Could Be: Environmentalism and Democracy in the Twenty-First Century*

Richard Hofrichter, ed., *Reclaiming the Environmental Debate: The Politics of Health in a Toxic Culture*

Robert Gottlieb, *Environmentalism Unbound: Exploring New Pathways for Change*

Kenneth Geiser, *Materials Matter: Toward a Sustainable Materials Policy*

Thomas D. Beamish, *Silent Spill: The Organization of an Industrial Crisis*

Matthew Gandy, *Concrete and Clay: Reworking Nature in New York City*

David Naguib Pellow, *Garbage Wars: The Struggle for Environmental Justice in Chicago*

Julian Agyeman, Robert D. Bullard, and Bob Evans, eds., *Just Sustainabilities: Development in an Unequal World*

Barbara L. Allen, *Uneasy Alchemy: Citizens and Experts in Louisiana's Chemical Corridor Disputes*

Dara O'Rourke, *Community-Driven Regulation: Balancing Development and the Environment in Vietnam*

Brian K. Obach, *Labor and the Environmental Movement: The Quest for Common Ground*

Peggy F. Barlett and Geoffrey W. Chase, eds., *Sustainability on Campus: Stories and Strategies for Change*

Steve Lerner, *Diamond: A Struggle for Environmental Justice in Louisiana's Chemical Corridor*

Jason Corburn, *Street Science: Community Knowledge and Environmental Health Justice*

Peggy F. Barlett, ed., *Urban Place: Reconnecting with the Natural World*

David Naguib Pellow and Robert J. Brulle, eds., *Power, Justice, and the Environment: A Critical Appraisal of the Environmental Justice Movement*

Eran Ben-Joseph, *The Code of the City: Standards and the Hidden Language of Place Making*

Nancy J. Myers and Carolyn Raffensperger, eds., *Precautionary Tools for Reshaping Environmental Policy*

Kelly Sims Gallagher, *China Shifts Gears: Automakers, Oil, Pollution, and Development*

Kerry H. Whiteside, *Precautionary Politics: Principle and Practice in Confronting Environmental Risk*

Ronald Sandler and Phaedra C. Pezzullo, eds., *Environmental Justice and Environmentalism: The Social Justice Challenge to the Environmental Movement*

Julie Sze, *Noxious New York: The Racial Politics of Urban Health and Environmental Justice*

Robert D. Bullard, ed., *Growing Smarter: Achieving Livable Communities, Environmental Justice, and Regional Equity*

Ann Rappaport and Sarah Hammond Creighton, *Degrees That Matter: Climate Change and the University*

Michael Egan, *Barry Commoner and the Science of Survival: The Remaking of American Environmentalism*

David J. Hess, *Alternative Pathways in Science and Industry: Activism, Innovation, and the Environment in an Era of Globalization*

Peter F. Cannavò, *The Working Landscape: Founding, Preservation, and the Politics of Place*

Paul Stanton Kibel, ed., *Rivertown: Rethinking Urban Rivers*

Kevin P. Gallagher and Lyuba Zarsky, *The Enclave Economy: Foreign Investment and Sustainable Development in Mexico's Silicon Valley*

David N. Pellow, *Resisting Global Toxics: Transnational Movements for Environmental Justice*

Robert Gottlieb, *Reinventing Los Angeles: Nature and Community in the Global City*

David V. Carruthers, ed., *Environmental Justice in Latin America: Problems, Promise, and Practice*

Tom Angotti, *New York for Sale: Community Planning Confronts Global Real Estate*

Paloma Pavel, ed., *Breakthrough Communities: Sustainability and Justice in the Next American Metropolis*

Anastasia Loukaitou-Sideris and Renia Ehrenfeucht, *Sidewalks: Conflict and Negotiation over Public Space*

David J. Hess, *Localist Movements in a Global Economy: Sustainability, Justice, and Urban Development in the United States*

Julian Agyeman and Yelena Ogneva-Himmelberger, eds., *Environmental Justice and Sustainability in the Former Soviet Union*

Jason Corburn, *Toward the Healthy City: People, Places, and the Politics of Urban Planning*

JoAnn Carmin and Julian Agyeman, eds., *Environmental Inequalities Beyond Borders: Local Perspectives on Global Injustices*

Louise Mozingo, *Pastoral Capitalism: A History of Suburban Corporate Landscapes*

Gwen Ottinger and Benjamin Cohen, eds., *Technoscience and Environmental Justice: Expert Cultures in a Grassroots Movement*

Samantha MacBride, *Recycling Reconsidered: The Present Failure and Future Promise of Environmental Action in the United States*

Andrew Karvonen, *Politics of Urban Runoff: Nature, Technology, and the Sustainable City*

Daniel Schneider, *Hybrid Nature: Sewage Treatment and the Contradictions of the Industrial Ecosystem*

Catherine Tumber, *Small, Gritty, and Green: The Promise of America's Smaller Industrial Cities in a Low-Carbon World*

Sam Bass Warner and Andrew H. Whittemore, *American Urban Form: A Representative History*

John Pucher and Ralph Buehler, eds., *City Cycling*

Stephanie Foote and Elizabeth Mazzolini, eds., *Histories of the Dustheap: Waste, Material Cultures, Social Justice*

David J. Hess, *Good Green Jobs in a Global Economy: Making and Keeping New Industries in the United States*

Joseph F. C. DiMento and Clifford Ellis, *Changing Lanes: Visions and Histories of Urban Freeways*

Joanna Robinson, *Contested Water: The Struggle Against Water Privatization in the United States and Canada*

William B. Meyer, *The Environmental Advantages of Cities: Countering Commonsense Antiurbanism*

Rebecca L. Henn and Andrew J. Hoffman, eds., *Constructing Green: The Social Structures of Sustainability*

Peggy F. Barlett and Geoffrey W. Chase, eds., *Sustainability in Higher Education: Stories and Strategies for Transformation*

Isabelle Anguelovski, *Neighborhood as Refuge: Community Reconstruction, Place Remaking, and Environmental Justice in the City*

Kelly Sims Gallagher, *The Globalization of Clean Energy Technology: Lessons from China*

Vinit Mukhija and Anastasia Loukaitou-Sideris, eds., *The Informal American City: Beyond Taco Trucks and Day Labor*

Roxanne Warren, *Rail and the City: Shrinking Our Carbon Footprint While Reimagining Urban Space*

Marianne E. Krasny and Keith G. Tidball, *Civic Ecology: Adaptation and Transformation from the Ground Up*

Erik Swyngedouw, *Liquid Power: Contested Hydro-Modernities in Twentieth-Century Spain*

Ken Geiser, *Chemicals without Harm: Policies for a Sustainable World*

Duncan McLaren and Julian Agyeman, *Sharing Cities: A Case for Truly Smart and Sustainable Cities*

Jessica Smartt Gullion, *Fracking the Neighborhood: Reluctant Activists and Natural Gas Drilling*

Nicholas A. Phelps, *Sequel to Suburbia: Glimpses of America's Post-Suburban Future*

Shannon Elizabeth Bell, *Fighting King Coal: The Challenges to Micromobilization in Central Appalachia*

Theresa Enright, *The Making of Grand Paris: Metropolitan Urbanism in the Twenty-first Century*

Robert Gottlieb and Simon Ng, *Global Cities: Urban Environments in Los Angeles, Hong Kong, and China*

Anna Lora-Wainwright, *Resigned Activism: Living with Pollution in Rural China*

Scott L. Cummings, *Blue and Green: The Drive for Justice at America's Port*

David Bissell, *Transit Life: Cities, Commuting, and the Politics of Everyday Mobilities*

Javiera Barandiarán, *From Empire to Umpire: Science and Environmental Conflict in Neoliberal Chile*

Benjamin Pauli, *Flint Fights Back: Environmental Justice and Democracy in the Flint Water Crisis*

Karen Chapple and Anastasia Loukaitou-Sideris, *Transit-Oriented Displacement or Community Dividends? Understanding the Effects of Smarter Growth on Communities*

Henrik Ernstson and Sverker Sörlin, eds., *Grounding Urban Natures: Histories and Futures of Urban Ecologies*

Katrina Smith Korfmacher, *Bridging the Silos: Collaborating for Environment, Health, and Justice in Urban Communities*

Jill Lindsey Harrison, *From the Inside Out: The Fight for Environmental Justice within Government Agencies*

Anastasia Loukaitou-Sideris, Dana Cuff, Todd Presner, Jonathan Crisman, and Maite Zubiaurre, *Urban Humanities: New Practices for Reimagining the City*

Govind Gopakumar, *Installing Automobility: Emerging Politics of Mobility and Streets in Indian Cities*

www.ingramcontent.com/pod-product-compliance
Lightning Source LLC
Chambersburg PA
CBHW021346300426
44114CB00012B/1102